THE WINTER QUEEN
Elizabeth of Bohemia

THE
WINTER QUEEN
Elizabeth of Bohemia

Carola Oman

PHOENIX
PRESS

5 UPPER SAINT MARTIN'S LANE
LONDON
WC2H 9EA

A PHOENIX PRESS PAPERBACK

First published in Great Britain
by Hodder & Stoughton Ltd in 1938
This paperback revised edition published in 2000
by Phoenix Press,
a division of The Orion Publishing Group Ltd,
Orion House, 5 Upper St Martin's Lane,
London WC2H 9EA

A CIP catalogue record for this book
is available from the British Library.

Printed and bound in Great Britain by
Clays Ltd, St Ives plc

ISBN 1 84212 057 3

CONTENTS

ILLUSTRATIONS

BIBLIOGRAPHY

ABELIN, J., *Theatrum Europaeum*. Frankfurt, 1643–62.

AIKIN, L., *Memoirs of the Court of King James I*. London, 1822.

AMOS, A., *Great Oyer of Poisoning*. London, 1846.

Ansbach, Memoirs of the Margravine of, Ed. A. Broadley and L. Melville. London, 1914.

ARBER, E., *Stuart Tracts 1603–93*, Ed. C. Firth. London, 1903.

Archaeologia, Vols. 12, 15, 16, 21, 35, 37, 39, 62. London, 1796–1857.

ARETIN, J. VON, *Beyträge zur Geschichte und Literatur*, Vol. vii. Parts 8 & 9. Munich, 1806.

BECKER, A., *Die Pfalz und die Pfälzer*. Neustadt an der Haardt, 1924.

BENGER, E., *Memoirs of Elizabeth Stuart, Queen of Bohemia*. London, 1825. ✕

BESANT, SIR W., *London in the Time of the Stuarts*. London, 1903.

Beschreibung der Reiss, Empfahrung des Herrn Frederick des V mit der Hochgebornen Fürstin und Königlichen Princessin Elizabethen, Jacob des Ersten Königs in Gross Britannien Einigen Tochter. Heidelberg, 1613.

BIRCH, T., *Court and Times of James I and Charles I*. London, 1848.
   Life of Henry, Prince of Wales. London, 1760.

BODEMANN, E., *Correspondance de la Duchesse Sophie de Hanovre avec son frère, etc.* Leipzig, 1886.

BODERIE, A. LE FÈVRE DE LA. *Ambassades*. Paris, 1750.

BRADLEY, E., *Life of the Lady Arabella Stuart*. London, 1889. ✕

BREVAL, J., *History of the House of Nassau*. Dublin, 1758.

BRIENNE-LOMÉNIE, H., COMTE DE, *Mémoires*, ed. M. Petitot. Paris, 1824.

BROMLEY, SIR G., *Collection of Original Royal Letters*. London, 1837.

BUNNETT, F., *Louise Juliane, Electress Palatine*. London, 1862.

BURY, BARONESS BLAZE DE, *Memoirs of the Princess Palatine*. London, 1853.

Cabala. London, 1691.

Cambridge Modern History, vol. iv., " The Thirty Years' War". Cambridge. 1900.

CALDERWOOD, D., *History of the Kirk of Scotland*, Ed. T. Thomson. Edinburgh, 1845.

CARLETON, SIR D., *Letters from and to*. London, 1757.

CARTE, T., *History of England*. Oxford, 1851.
  Ormonde Papers. Oxford, 1851.
CARY, R., Earl of Monmouth, *Memoirs of*, Ed. G. Powell. London, 1905.
CAUS, S. DE, *Hortus Palatinus*. Frankfurt, 1620.
CHARVÉRIAT, E., *Histoire de la Guerre de Trente Ans*. Paris, 1878.
CLARENDON, *Life of Edward Hyde, Earl of*, by himself. Oxford, 1827.
  State Papers. Oxford, 1767–86.
  History of the Rebellion. Oxford, 1888.
CLARK, G. N., *The Seventeenth Century*. Oxford, 1929.
CLIFFORD, LADY A., *Diary of*, with intro. by V. Sackville West. London,
  1923.
COBBETT, W., *State Trials*, ii. London, 1809.
COKE, R., *Detection of the Court and State of England*. London, 1719.
COOPER, E., *Life and Letters of Lady Arabella Stuart*. London, 1866.
CORNWALLIS, J., LADY. *Private Correspondence of*, 1613–44. London, 1842.

Debrett, Coronation Edition, 1938. Ed. C. Hankinson.
D'EWES, SIR S., *Autobiography and Correspondence of*, Ed. J. Halliwell.
  London, 1845.
DEVON, F., *Issues of the Exchequer, during the Reign of James I*. London, 1836.
DOUGLAS-IRVINE, H., *Royal Palaces of Scotland*, Ed. R. Rait. London, 1911.
DOUGLAS, R., *The Scots Peerage*, Ed. Sir J. B. Paul. Edinburgh, 1909–11.

ELLIS, H., *Original Letters*, Series II, Vol. III. Series III, Vol. IV. London, 1827.
ESTRADES, G. COMTE D', *Ambassades*. Amsterdam, 1718.
EVELYN, J., *Memoirs of*, Ed. W. Bray. London, 1827.
EVERETT GREEN, M., *Elizabeth, Electress Palatine and Queen of Bohemia*.
  London, 1909.
  Lives of the Princesses of England, Vols. V and VI. London, 1854–5.

FISHER, H. A. L., *History of Europe*, Vol. II. London, 1935.
FITZ-SIMON, FATHER H., *Diary of the Bohemian War of 1620*. Dublin, 1881.
FORESTER, H., *Memoirs of Sophie, Electress of Hanover*. London, 1888.
Fortescue MS. Ed. S. R. Gardiner. Camden Society. London, 1871.

GALLUS, G. VON, *Geschichte der Mark Brandenburg*, iv. Zullichau, 1799.
GARDINER, S. R., *The Thirty Years' War*. London, 1874. *Letters and other
  documents illustrating the relations between England and Germany at the
  commencement of the Thirty Years' War*. Camden Society. London,
  1865–8.
GINDELY, A., *History of the Thirty Years' War*, Trans. A. Brook. New York,
  1884.

GODFREY, A., *A Sister of Prince Rupert.* London, 1909.
GOODMAN, G., *Court and Times of James I.* London, 1839.
GRANGER, J., *Biographical History of England.* London, 1824.
GROTIUS, H., *Epistolae.* Amsterdam, 1687.
GUALDO PRIORATO, G., *Historia delle Guerre 1630-39.* Venice, 1640.

Haghe Jaarboek, Die. 'S-Gravenhage, 1921.
HALLIDAY, A., *History of the House of Guelph.* London, 1821.
HAMILTON, *Duke of, M.S.S., Supplementary Vol. to Eleventh Report, App.*
   (6) [21], *Hist. M.S.S. Comm.* London, 1932.
HARINGTON, SIR J., *Nugae Antiquae.* London, 1804.
HARINGTON OF EXTON, J. LORD, *Accounts of. Exchequer of Receipt Miscell-*
   anea. Public Record Office.
HARRIS, M., *Coventry.* London, 1911.
HARRISON, J., *Short relation of the Departure of . . . Frederick, King-Elect of*
   Bohemia . . . towards Prague. Dort. 1619.
HAUCK, K., *Briefe der Kinder des Winterkönigs.* Heidelberger Jahrbücher, 15.
   Heidelberg, 1908.
   Elisabeth, Königin von Böhmen. Heidelberg, 1905.
   Pfalzgraf Rupprecht, der Kavalier. Heidelberg, 1906.
   Karl Ludwig, Kurfürst von der Pfalz. Heidelberg, 1898.
HÄUSSER, L., *Geschichte der Rheinischen Pfalz.* Heidelberg, 1845.
HAVARD, H., *Michiel van Mierevelt.* Paris, 1894.
HEINSIUS, N., *Sylloge Epistolarum,* iii. Leyden, 1727.
HECK, R. *Die Regentschaft der Gräfin Sophia Hedwig.* Dietz, 1923.
HERVEY, M., *Life of Thomas Howard, Earl of Arundel.* Cambridge, 1921.
Historical MSS. Commission, Second, Tenth and Fifteenth Reports.
HOWELL, J., *Epistolae Ho-Elianae.* London, 1754.
HURTER, F., *Geschichte Kaiser Ferdinands II.* Schaffhausen, 1850.
Hutchinson,Memoirs of the life of Col., by his widow, ed. H. Child. London,
   1904.

James I, Narrative History of, for the first Fourteen Years. London, 1651.
James I, Secret History of the Court of, ed. Sir W. Scott. Edinburgh, 1911.
James the Sext, Historie and Life of King, Bannatyne Club. Edinburgh, 1830.
James VI of Scotland, Correspondence of, with Sir R. Cecil. Ed. J. Bruce.
   Camden Society. London, 1861.
James VI, Letters to. Maitland Club. Edinburgh, 1835.

Kennet, W., *Complete History of England,* vol. ii. London, 1706.
KHEVENHÜLLER, F., *Annales Ferdinandei,* vol. ix. Regensburg, 1721.

KLOPP, O., *Tilly im Dreissigjährigen Kriege*. Stuttgart, 1861.

KOCHER, A., *Memoirs of Sophia, Electress of Hanover*.

LELAND, J., *Collectanea*, ed. T. Hearne. London, 1774.

LISTER, LADY T., *Lives of the Friends and Contemporaries of Lord Chancellor Clarendon*. London, 1852.

LLOYD, D., *Memoirs of the Lives and Actions of Eminent Persons*. London, 1668.

LUNDORP, M., *Acta Publica*. Frankfurt, 1625.

LUTZOW, F., COUNT, *Bohemia*. London, 1896.

Prague. London, 1907.

LYSONS, D., *Environs of London*, vol. i, part i. London, 1792.

Magna Britannia. London, 1806.

Manuscripts. Additional, Ashmole, Balfour, Bethune, Brienne, Colbert, Conrart, Cottonian, Cottrell, Craven, Dupuy, Fortescue, Français, Harleian, Lambeth, Lamarre, Landsdowne, Rawlinson, Stowe, Talbot, Tanner.

MANWARING, G., *Life and Works of Sir H. Mainwaring*. London, 1920.

Matthews, Sir T., Letters of, ed. J. Donne. London, 1660.

MAXWELL, J., *Laudable Life, etc. of Prince Henry*. London, 1612.

A Monument of Remembrance. London, 1613.

MELVILL, J., *Autobiography and Diary of*, ed. R. Pitcairn, Woodrow Society. Edinburgh, 1842.

MENZEL, W., *Briefe der Princessin Elisabeth Charlotte von Orleans an die Raugräfin Louise. Litterarische Verein*, vol. vi. Stuttgart, 1843.

Mercure François. Paris, 1619 et seq.

Mercurius Gallobelgicus. Cologne, 1596–1630.

MORYSON, FYNES. *An Itinerary containing his Ten years Travel*. Glasgow, 1907.

MOSER, F. VON, *Patriotisches Archiv*. Mannheim, 1787.

MOYSIE, D., *Memoirs of the Affairs of Scotland*. Bannatyne Club. Edinburgh, 1830.

NAPIER, M., *Memoirs of the Marquis of Montrose*. Edinburgh, 1856.

NICHOLS, J., *Progresses of James I*. London, 1828.

Nieuwe Tydinge uyt Oostenrijch, Bohem, etc. Antwerp, 1620.

Nyevelt, Baroness S. van Zuylen van, *Court Life in the Dutch Republic*. London, 1906.

OPEL, J., *Elisabeth Stuart*. Bonn, 1870.

Der niedersächsisch-dänische Krieg. Halle, 1872–94.

Palatinat, Correspondance politique. Archives des Affaires Etrangères. Bibl. Nat. Paris.

PEPYS, S., *Diary of*, ed. Richard, Lord Braybrooke. London, 1906.

PERCY, T., *Reliques of Ancient English Poetry.* London, 1869.

PUFENDORF, S., *Commentarium de rebus Suecicis.* Frankfurt, 1705.

RALEIGH, SIR W., *History of the World.* London, 1614.
   Works of. Oxford, 1829.

RICCIUS, J., *De Bellis Germanicus.* Venice, 1649.

RIEMER, J. DE, *Beschryving van's Graven Hage.* Delft, 1730.

ROE, SIR T., *Letters relating to the mission of,* ed. S. R. Gardiner. Camden
   Miscellany. Vol. vii. London, 1875.
   Negotiations in his Embassy to the Ottoman Porte, ed. S. Richardson. London,
   1740.

RUSDORF, J., *Mémoires et négociations secrètes de M. de.* Leipzig, 1789.

RYMER, T., *Foedera.* London, 1715.

RYE, W., *England as seen by Foreigners in the Days of Elizabeth and James I.*
   London, 1865.

SANDARS, L., *Old Kew, Chiswick and Kensington.* London, 1910.

SCHOTEL, G., *De Winterkoning.* Tiel, 1859.

SCOTT, E., *Rupert, Prince Palatine.* London, 1899.

SENKENBERG, R., *Continuation of F. Haberlin's "Neueste Deutsche Reichs-
   geschichte".* Halle, 1774.

SHARP, T., *Coventry Pageants.* Coventry, 1825.

SMITH, L. PEARSALL, *Life and Letters of Sir Henry Wotton.* London, 1907.

SOLTL, *Der Religionskrieg, etc.,* vol. i. *Elisabeth Stuart.* Hamburg, 1840.

SOMERS, J., LORD, *Collection of Scarce and Valuable Tracts,* vol. ii. London,
   1809.

SPANHEIM, F., *Mémoire sur la vie, etc. de Princesse Louise Julianc, Electrice
   Palatine.* Leyden, 1645.
   *Commentaire Historique de la vie, etc. de Messire Christolfe, Vicomte de
   Dhona.* Geneva, 1639.

State Papers, Domestic. James I (quoted as S.P. 14).
   Charles I (quoted as S.P. 16).
   Interregnum (quoted as S.P. 19-27).
   Charles II (quoted as S.P. 29).

State Papers, Foreign. German States (quoted as S.P. 81).
   Holland (quoted as S.P. 84).
   Flanders (quoted as S.P. 77).
   Venetian (quoted as S.P. 99).
   Foreign News-Letters (quoted as S.P. 101).

STEVENSON, G., *Letters of Madame*. London, 1925.

STOW, J., *Survey of London*. London, 1876.

STRICKLAND, A., *Queens of Scotland and English Princesses*, vol. viii. London, 1859.

Sydney State Papers, ed. A. Collins, London, 1746.

SYPESTEYN, C. VAN, *Het Hof van Boheme*. Amsterdam, 1886.

THURLOE, J., *State Papers*. London, 1742.

TIPPING, H., *English Homes*. Period iv. vol. i. London, 1920.

VARNHAGEN VON ENSE, K., *Königin Sophie Charlotte von Preussen*. Leipzig, 1872.

VERTUE, G., *Catalogue of King Charles I's Collection*. London, 1757.

WARBURTON, E., *Memoirs of Prince Rupert*. London, 1849.

WARD, A., *The Electress Sophia and the Hanoverian Succession*. London, 1903.

WENDLAND, A., *Briefe der Elisabeth Stuart*, Litterarische Verein Stuttgart, vol. 228. Tübingen, 1902.

Die Heirath der Prinzessin Henriette Marie von der Pfalz, Neue Heidelberger Jahrbucher, vol. 14.

Elizabeth Stuart. Ibid., 13.

WEISS, J. G., *Lord Craven und die Familie des Winterkönigs*. Badischen Historischen Commission. Karlsruhe, 1924.

Neues zur Geschichte des Hauses Pfalz in 17 Jahrhundert. Karlsruhe, 1934.

Neuentdeckte Briefe der Herzogin Sophie von Braunschweig. Leipzig, 1934.

WHEATLEY, H., *London, Past and Present*. London, 1891.

WHITELOCKE, B., *Memorials of English Affairs*. London, 1732.

WICKHAM LEGG, J., *Coronation Order of King James I*. London, 1902.

WICQUEFORT, A. DE, *L'Ambassadeur et ses fonctions*. Hague, 1682.

Wills from Doctors' Commons, ed. J. Nichols and J. Bruce. Camden Society. London, 1862.

WINWOOD, SIR R., *State Papers* iii. London, 1725.

WOTTON, SIR H., *Reliquae*. London, 1850. 1685.

The Queen's signature, reproduced on the cover, comes from a letter written by her from the Hague to Sir Balthazar Gerbier, painter, architect, and courtier. The original is in the collection of Mr. A. T. Loyd of Lockinge House, Berkshire.

CHAPTER I

"THE FIRST DOCHTOUR OF SCOTLAND"

I

THE birth of a daughter to James VI of Scotland and his consort Anne of Denmark, in August 1596, did not arouse much interest even in their own country. The very date and place of the princess's birth were variously reported.[1] Her baptism was unanimously recorded as having taken place on the twenty-eighth of the following November, "without solemnitie" and "without inviting of any strangeris". The scene was the Chapel Royal of Holyroodhouse, where her grandmother Mary Stuart had been married both to Darnley and Bothwell. The English gentleman who named the child had spent many months of an arduous life vainly trying to gain possession of the Casket Letters.

"Little or no triumphe wes maid but in guid fare and cheir because that it wes in wynter season and ill weather", wrote a discreet chronicler in the office of the king's secretary. Other reasons were that the penurious king was just approaching another violent collision with the clerical zealots of his realm: a prince, Henry Frederick, had been baptized with expensive pomp, two years earlier; the queen was not yet one and twenty.

[1] *Life of James the Sext*, p. 373, gives August 15th, and Falkland Palace; Calderwood, v. 438, August 19th at Dunfermline; Harleian MS. 1368, i, says August 19th. James himself once declared that he and three of his children, Henry, Elizabeth and Charles, had been born on the 19th day of a month, and a poem by J. Maxwell, "Princesse Elizabeth's happie Entrie into the World," published on her marriage, makes a point of the fact that her natal day was "the festivall of that holy Matron and Martyr St. Thecla" and "next unto St. Helen's Day" August 18th.

Use this about the marriage

There were likely to be more royal christenings in the chapel of Holyroodhouse. However, "violers and taborers to make music", "wyld meit and veniesoun", and sixty-three ells of scarlet "London cloth", to clothe pages and lacqueys, were ordered "to the baptisme of the Princess", and the king had new socks, of crimson velvet laced with gold. The Queen of England, for whom Mr Robert Bowes of Aske, Treasurer of Berwick, stood proxy, was "sole godmother", and "the whole Honour in the Solemnity and of all the Ceremonies, was given alone to Her Majesty, with good observance of all due Compliments". The fact that his mistress had sent no christening gift was passed over by her disturbed deputy "in the fairest and most indifferent terms" that he could muster. "The Bailiff and Chiefs of Edinburgh being called to the Feast", brought with them "in name of the whole town" a present which sounded magnificent, but actually put them to little immediate expense. A golden casket, containing a document inscribed in golden letters, was offered by them to the infant's mother. They had hit upon the brilliant idea of granting the princess 1000 Scots marks—"to be paid at her Marriage".[1] The terrible old lady in London must be placated whenever possible, so her ambassador was invited to "hold up" the infant, and gave her the name of his mistress, after which she was "cryed and called by the Lyon Herald, Lady Elizabeth, first dochtour of Scotland".[2]

Alexander, seventh Lord Livingstone, and his wife, Helen, or Helenor, only daughter of Andrew Hay, eighth Earl of Erroll, were chosen by the king to superintend the education and upbringing of his daughter. Both guardians came of families well known to him, and as far as birth and character went, his choice was unexceptionable. Lord Livingstone was a

[1] Rymer's *Foedera*, 16. 304.
[2] Moysie's *Memoirs*, p. 127. Treasurer's Accounts, Register House, Edin., Nov.–Dec. 1596, published in *Letters to James VI*, Maitland Club, p. lxxii.

nephew of Mary Livingstone, one of Queen Mary's famous "four Maries". He was Keeper of the royal palace of Linlithgow and father of a growing family. Unfortunately, in the opinion of the authorities of the Kirk of Scotland, Lady Livingstone was a Catholic. A Jesuit member of her family, Father Edmund Hay, had achieved several converts in it, including her brother, the ninth Earl of Erroll. Hays predominated in positions of trust around the princess. Two sisters, Alison and Elizabeth Hay, were "Mistress-nurse" and "Keeper of the Coffers" in her household. The Kirk raised loud cries of alarm and complaint, and the king made explanations. He said that he had delivered his daughter—now three months old—not to Lady Livingstone, but to her husband, "a man known of good religion". Unless Lady Livingstone satisfied the Kirk, she should not be allowed to come near the princess. Lord Livingstone was formally exempted from "all raids, wars, gatherings, assizes and inquests" in consideration of his new duties, and Lady Livingstone continued at her post, "an obstinate Papist". Five years later the Kirk was still complaining of her. Before this another princess had been consigned to her care. But the Lady Margaret, born in December 1598, lived only two years. Anne of Denmark had ceased to bear healthy children.[1]

Linlithgow Palace, in which most of the Princess Elizabeth's infancy was spent, was a source of pride in Scotland. When her great-grandmother had first set eyes upon it, she had announced that never had she beheld a more princely palace; and Mary of Guise had beheld the royal palaces of France. It stood in rich pastoral country, midway between Stirling and Edinburgh, within a day's ride of either, and, as might have been expected from its situation, had seen much Scottish history in the making. The calm sheet of water beneath its "pleasand loch" was "swoming full of fine perches and other notable fish".

[1] Calderwood's *History of the Kirk of Scotland*, v. 452 and vi. 169. *Treasurer's Accounts*, p. lxxxiv.

It had a park, and folds enclosed by hedges of brilliant broom, a garden and a "little garden", a Great Hall, a hundred feet long and thirty feet wide, provided with a minstrels' gallery and a dais, a long gallery, a chapel with deep pointed windows and canopied niches, many fine withdrawing rooms and bed-rooms, large and small, a courtyard with a fountain,[1] and a principal entrance over which presided the figures, brightly painted, of a pope, a knight and a labouring man. When James VI presented the lordship of Linlithgow to his bride as a "morrowing gift", "coal-heuchs" were mentioned amongst its appurtenances. The ground on the west and north sloped down to the loch, across which was the noblest view of the queen's dower-palace, rising against a background of light-coloured hills.

The climate of Scotland suited the Lady Elizabeth. "Heate is always more troublesome to me than colde", she declared in her forty-second year, writing to the Archbishop of Canterbury from the panting hot flats of the Low Countries on a May day.[2]

When the child was five, Elizabeth Hay sent to the Treasurer's office, bills for a brush, "ane birse to straik her hair", and a quarter of an ell of satin to make a diminutive mask, so that a fair complexion should not be damaged by wind or sun. Gowns were supplied, of materials and colours that do not suggest much taste in whoever made the choice—of yellow satin, of figured velvet, black upon red, of white satin upon carnation, of Spanish taffetas, trimmed with plush, of orange and popinjay crepe, with metal fringe round the neck—"gold and silver freingeis therto, to be put about hir craig". In winter the princess was clothed in warm purple serge and brown Spanish frieze, and had hose of "skarlot Frenche staming", a coarse linsey woolsey, generally dyed red. But she also got

[1] Of which that in front of Holyroodhouse is a copy.
[2] S.P. 16, 356. 152.

little luxuries—dolls, "babies", and two pairs of embroidered gloves, and two pairs of "silk shanks".[1]

Another royal infant—Charles, Duke of Albany—had been born at Dunfermline, but he had been so delicate that he had been baptized hurriedly the same day. At his public baptism, his sister's guardian, Lord Livingstone, was created Earl of Linlithgow.[2]

The exact style of costume worn by the children of James I and VI and Anne of Denmark in their nurseries may be studied in the Innocents' Corner of Westminster Abbey. The Princess Mary, "a most beautiful infant", who died at the age of seventeen months, is represented reclining on a square tomb. She is quaintly attired in a womanly dress. Such a stiff stay bodice, quilled ruff, fashionable head-dress and long-sleeved hoop-skirted gown was worn by her sister Elizabeth in her Linlithgow days. The youngest princess, Sophia, "a royal rose-bud, plucked by premature fate that . . . she might flower again in the rosary of Christ", lived only twenty-four hours, and is depicted asleep in her cradle. The princesses, like all children of their day, were promoted directly from swaddling-bands and baby-caps to miniature adult costume. The fine woollen lace-trimmed baby-caps of the first daughter of Scotland are described as "lane mutchis" with "pearling to them".[3]

At New Year, the great season for holiday and merry-making, the king's gifts to Prince Henry and the Lady Elizabeth were despatched from Holyroodhouse to Stirling and Linlithgow, where the children were being reared. The prince, at the age of six, received bows and arrows, "golf clubbis" and racquets. His sister, at the same age, got "a fair case" covered with velvet, containing combs, and two more

[1] *Treasurer's Accounts*, pp. lxxiv–lxxxiii.
[2] Douglas's *Peerage of Scotland*, ii. 127.   Moysie, 377.
[3] *Treasurer's Accounts*, p. lxxiv.

dolls, "twa babeis, to be playeis". Duke Charles, aged three, was also the recipient of "babeis".[1] He was still distressingly delicate and could neither walk nor talk. "Duke Robert", a younger brother, born in January 1602, had died four months later.

At Linlithgow the only surviving Daughter of Scotland passed her seventh winter peacefully. One Johne Fairny guarded her chamber door. On the first floor was the great withdrawing-room in which her grandmother Queen Mary had been born, and on the ground floor was the gaunt Guard-room in which her great-uncle, the Regent Moray, had died of his wounds after being shot in the High Street outside. Beyond came a vast, echoing kitchen, redolent of barrelled salt fish, and beeves and hams stored on stands, the bakery, the cellars, and the stables in which her ponies were kept. Queen Margaret's Bower, the most perfect little room in the palace, square within, hexagonal without, was attained by a spiral staircase. From its windows, according to tradition, Margaret Tudor had gazed south in vain for the return of "the Flowers of the Forest", slain by the English on Flodden Field. The north side of the palace, which was the oldest, had been propped up over half a century ago, but looked as if it needed attention again.

II

When Sir Robert Cary knocked at the gate of Holyrood-house on the night of Saturday, March 26th, 1603, he was told that the king was abed. But the arrival of a messenger from England, "be-blooded with great falls and bruises", roused sleeping courtiers.

Eager gentlemen hurried reeling Sir Robert down the chill passages of a dark and bodeful palace, where windows looked out on hills, craggy and lion-shaped, and the air struck more

[1] *Treasurer's Accounts*, pp. lxxvi, lxxvii, lxxxiv, lxxxvi.

nimbly on the senses than at Richmond on Thames. They brought him to a great chamber where a man of six and thirty, with light, rolling eyes, a straggling, reddish-brown beard and moustache, and hair already thinning on the temples, lay in a canopied bed. Sir Robert Cary dropped on his knees and saluted James, King of England, Scotland, France and Ireland.

The happiest moment in James Stuart's life had come, but he had learnt from infancy to dissemble. He extended a soft hand for his new subject's kiss, and, in broad Scots, gravely bade him welcome. Then, as he should, he asked to hear at length the history of the last hours of his cousin of England. He was greedy for reassuring details. When opening her last Parliament seventeen months ago on a cold autumn day, she had staggered beneath the weight of her royal robes, and required assistance to mount her throne. Yet she had rallied to open a ball with a French duke, to hunt, to go a-Maying, to snatch the miniature of Mr Secretary Cecil from his niece and dance away with it like a skittish schoolgirl. Since he had heard of her "wery near approaches to her everlasting rest", her "neerest kinsman and most apparant aire", had been haunted by a new fear—that she might live on for years, semi-imbecile. Cecil seemed confident, and had sent him a draft of the proclamation of the King of Scotland's accession to the throne of England, which had sounded in his ears like sweetest music. But the seventy-year-old queen could not be persuaded to name her successor. She had no intention that her subjects should turn from the waning moon to worship the rising-sun. And there was always King Henry VIII's will, a terrible bogey. It was said to have been lost, and in any case had never borne the king's signature, "in his own most gracious hand". But it had quite clearly declared that in the event of all his children dying without issue, the descendants of his younger sister, the Duchess of Suffolk, were to inherit. Even if Henry VIII's will were not duly executed, another legal difficulty remained.

James VI of Scotland was of alien birth, and therefore "devoid of inheritable blood". When Sir Robert Cary's famous story of the passing of Elizabeth Tudor [1] was ended, her successor was not yet satisfied.

"He asked me what letters I had from the Council. I told him, none."

Indeed, the Council had done their best to detain Sir Robert from his dramatic journey. But he brought with him a sure token that Elizabeth of England had "surrendered her mortall kingdom for an immortall". "I had brought him a blue ring from a fair lady". King James took the sapphire ring which Lady Scroope, Sir Robert Cary's sister, had drawn from the dead queen's finger.[2] He said composedly, "It is enough: I know by this you are a true messenger". He delivered the wounded and weary knight to Lord Hume, with orders that his own surgeons should attend him, adding graciously: "I know you have lost a near kinswoman [3] and a loving mistress; but take here my hand. I will be as good a master to you, and will requite this service with honour and reward".

In his memoirs, Sir Robert Cary complains that shortly after his arrival in his new capital, King James "deceived my expectation, and adhered to those that sought my ruin". What gorgeous hopes of preferment may have filled his fevered brain as he flung from a royal bed-chamber at Richmond on Thames to one in Holyroodhouse, he does not say. Apparently he never discovered that the king himself had warned Sir Robert Cecil

[1] *Memoirs of Robert Cary*, p. 70 et seq.

[2] According to another version, James had sent the ring to Lady Scroope "with positive orders to return it to him by a special messenger as soon as the Queen was actually expired. Lady Scroope had no opportunity of delivering it to her brother, Sir Robert, whilst he was in the Palace of Richmond, but waiting at the window till she saw him at the outside of the gate, she threw it out to him, and he well knew to what purpose he received it." Brydge's *Peers of King James*, p. 413.

[3] Mary Boleyn, Sir Robert's grandmother, and Anne Boleyn, Queen Elizabeth's mother, were sisters.

of Sir Robert Cary's intention to be the herald of Queen Elizabeth's death, a project denounced by the council as "contrary to such commandments as we had power to lay upon him, and to all decency, good manners and respect".

Yet, in the eyes of the world, Sir Robert Cary did not do so badly, for he was immediately appointed a gentleman of the king's bedchamber, and although he soon lost this post, he was presently given charge of the king's younger son, Prince Charles, and he died Baron Leppington and Earl of Monmouth. His wife became "Mistress of the sweet coffers" to the new queen, and his daughter Philadelphia, aged eight, was appointed lady-in-waiting to a princess aged six and a half—the king's elder daughter, the Lady Elizabeth.

In the last days of May, the queen and Prince Henry arrived at Linlithgow, and the Lady Elizabeth departed with them for Holyroodhouse.

III

Anne of Denmark prepared to set off for London, with her two eldest children, in a condition of mingled excitement and exasperation which had long been habitual to her.

On her arrival in Scotland, as a bride of fifteen, she had been a cheerful, brightly coloured, masterful young Scandinavian. A good complexion, a tall, slight figure, and a very pleasant manner, had distracted attention from the facts that her features were rather sharp and she was entirely ungraceful. Thirteen years as consort of a king, who though obviously her inferior in physique and apparently indolent, never for a moment allowed her to assume superiority over him, had not suited her. At the date of their arrival in England the new king and queen were united by three emotions only; all however were powerful—love of their children, sense of humour and worldly interest. James had no sentimental attachment to

Scotland, a country in which he had been thwarted and bullied, long after he had passed the age for public tears, by a nobility many of whom behaved like criminal lunatics, and a clergy who were impatient of his royal authority and impertinently critical of his private life. His passionate love of beautiful things had found what vents it could during a career in which a more straightforward man would probably have perished. The son of Mary Stuart was notably lacking in physical charm. To hide his perpetual unease he had cultivated traits of pawkiness and buffoonery, so that few about him could tell when his majesty was consciously and when unconsciously ridiculous. At six and thirty, he, who had never been young, knew himself ageing. He panted for England, a land flowing with milk and honey, where he would be free at last from hourly dread of personal violence. For "Alas!" as he wrote secretly to Sir Robert Cecil, "it is a farre more barbarouse and stiffe nekkit people that I rule over. Saint George surelie rydes upon a towardlie rydding horse, quhaire I ame daylie burstin in daunting a wylde unreulie coalte." [1]

His wife was equally eager to enjoy riches and civilization. Unlike her children, she had known neither peace nor comfort in Scotland. This might have reconciled her to the loss of their company. But she was beyond reason on that subject. Her maternal instincts had been outraged when her first-born, Prince Henry, had been reft from her as a babe of weeks, to be handed over to the Earl of Mar, hereditary guardian of the heir of Scotland. James, who had no intention that his son should be used, as he had been used, to depose a parent from the throne, had been adamant, and Anne had emerged the loser from their first serious conflict. During the years that had followed there had been the inevitable whispers that an unhappy queen inclined to entertain more stirring gallants than her king. If there was any truth in such rumours, Caesar had

[1] Hatfield MS., cxxxv. 76.

seen to it that no open scandal ever attached itself to the name of
his consort. Anne's looks, which had been dependent on youth
and health, faded. She came to bear children that did not
survive, and to use ill-health as an excuse to avoid unpleasant
duties. Privately she sought consolation in the Church of
Rome. Openly she pursued every prospect of amusement
with a vigour that had in it something gallant.

James, King of England, Scotland, France and Ireland, was
proclaimed at the Mercat Cross in Edinburgh, "with greate
solemnities and pompe", "fires of joy shyned from the Basse",
and on Tuesday, the 5th of April, his Majesty set out for his
promised land, "accompanied with multitudes of his Nobility,
Lords, Barons and gentlemen of Scotland", and the French
Ambassador, whose lady "was carried between Edenburgh
and London by eight porters . . . in a chare with slings".
The queen, who was expecting another child, bade her husband
"God-speed" in the High Street, and a royal couple who had
been through many trials together were observed to shed tears
at parting. A large number of the beholding crowd, deeply
touched, followed their example, and lifting up their voices,
loudly mourned the departure of their sovereign for the dark
and dangerous South.[1]

Sir Robert Cecil, however, had as he claimed "steered King
James's ship into the right harbour without cross of wave or
tide that could have overturned a cock-boat". In England
the voice of the nation had fully ratified the council's proclamation of James I. The will of Henry VIII had been quietly
set aside, together with all questions respecting inheritable
blood. Not a voice was raised on behalf of the Lady Arbella
Stuart, or Lord Beauchamp, or Lord Derby, or Lord Hunting-
don, whose claim dated back to George, Duke of Clarence, or
eight other candidates descended from Edward III, including
those arch-Papists the King of Spain and his sister, the

[1] Nichols's *Progresses of King James I*, i. 60.

Infanta Isabella, wife of the Archduke Albert, Governor of Flanders. England was prepared to accept the King of Scotland, and to accept him with enthusiasm. Reassuring reports quickly reached Edinburgh from Berwick. Thereafter the king's progress was a triumph, but not uninterrupted, for the hospitality offered to him on his route was so agreeable that he spent over a month getting south. Great noblemen vied with one another in detaining him in country houses whose appointments surpassed his most optimistic expectations. English keepers, attired in smart new green suits, and attended by well-liking merry men, appeared in appropriate landscapes with ingratiating offers to show his Majesty some sport.

In London, except that a visitation of the plague was taking place, everything appeared to be going well; from Scotland, however, arrived news that sent John Erskine, Earl of Mar, hurrying back north. The queen, despite her condition, had seized upon the absence of his father and his guardian to make one more attempt to gain possession of Prince Henry. At Stirling Castle, old Lady Mar had firmly refused to allow Anne and a large party of armed partisans to remove the heir. Anne, overcome by grief and wrath, had been brought to bed prematurely of a still-born child—a fourth son. Everyone concerned sent messengers bearing explanatory letters, galloping south to the king in London, and from his palace of Greenwich, Solomon delivered a judgment which, while preserving the dignity of his consort, upheld the authority of a dutiful subject. He ordered Mar to entrust the prince to the Duke of Lennox and rejoin him in London as soon as possible. Anne, highly dissatisfied, consented to accept her son from the hands of Lennox, collected her daughter from Linlithgow, and proceeded to Edinburgh. Here she was soothed by the discovery that "divers Ladies of honour come voluntarily into Scotland to attend her Majestie in her journey into England", were awaiting her. Two of them, a mother and daughter, exactly fulfilled her long-cherished dreams of southern refinement and elegance. Lady Harington, wife of Sir John Harington of Exton, was the heiress of Sir Robert Kelway, late surveyor of the Courts of Wards and Liveries to Queen Elizabeth. Her husband was of an old Rutlandshire family, descended in the female line from the Bruce. Sir John Harington's mother had been a Sidney, aunt to Sir Philip Sidney. The eldest Harington daughter, Lucy, who had come to Scotland with her mother, was about one and twenty, and had for nine years been the wife of William Russell, Earl of Bedford. Both the English court ladies were pleasant-looking in a well-bred, unemphatic way, with fair hair, beautiful hands and fashionably oval faces of slightly pinched features. Their manners were exquisite. Anne appointed Lady Bedford a lady of her Privy Chamber, recovered her health and spirits, and drove in a coach to St. Giles's, with her son by her side. She was followed by an imposing train of English and Scottish ladies and gentlemen, and was enthusiastically cheered. Orders for new clothing for the queen, her children and their pages and lacqueys "at thair removing heirfra towardis Ingland" were issued, and preparations began in a hurry. Anne's own requirements were not many. She was aware that at the end of her journey the wardrobe of a lady reputed to have possessed no less than two thousand sumptuous *toilettes* was awaiting her. She ordered one new gown and mantle, of figured taffetas, white satin and purple velvet. A white satin dress already in existence was hastily "all oppinit up and maid of ane uther new fashoun". For the use of the Lady Elizabeth, a fair child of less than seven, on a journey through midsummer England in a heat-wave, a costume of red Spanish taffetas to wear "neerest her sark", and "rouge broun satin" was mercilessly prepared. The untravelled princess was also provided with an exciting novelty in the shape of a nightdress-case, "ane pook, to put hir nichtgeir in".[1]

Thursday, June 2nd, was the date appointed for the great flitting from Holyroodhouse. At Berwick a bevy of "noble personages" sent from London "by especiall direction from the Lords of the Counsell . . . to attend the Queen in her journey" had been waiting for three weeks. On the night of June 1st the Lady Elizabeth was reported sick. Her illness was evidently some mere childish disorder, probably occasioned by over-excitement, for the queen's departure took place as arranged, and on the next day the Princess was considered well enough to "follow her mother softlie".[2] The first chapter in her life ended when she crossed the Tweed.

[1] *Treasurer's Accounts*, p. lxxxvii.   [2] Calderwood, vi. 232.

CHAPTER II

"THE PEARL OF BRITAIN"

I

IN England the weather was "of a burning heat". The Princess
Royal passed from a landscape of green hills, dotted by
swarthy peel-towers, across a broad river into a grey-walled
town, overlooking the North Sea, and packed with fine folk
speaking finicking English. Her new governess, the Countess
of Kildare, was presented to her. The Keeper of Linlithgow
Castle and his lady would not be able to stay with her in the
South.

The progress of a new queen, and a prince and princess with
Stuart faces and Tudor Christian names, was as enthusiastically
applauded as that of a new king had been two months before.
At York "the King's daughter" was presented with a "purse of
twenty angells of gold", and at Leicester, where she arrived
before her mother and brother, Mr Mayor brought solemnly
to her lodgings in the house of a Mr Pilkington a gift of wine
and sugar.[1] "In regard she was not able to undertake so
great journies as her majesty", the princess often travelled on at
a gentle pace throughout the day, while her mother, who
halted to attend entertainments, caught her up at agreed
"stopping-places all the way from Berwick to Windsor".
Most of these "stopping-places" were country houses renowned
for their antiquity and beauty. Thomas Durie, the queen's
Scots fool, in his new coat of green cloth, the queen herself in

[1] Nichols, i. 170, 172.

her new Edinburgh-built coach and six, Prince Henry, on his
French nag, attended by his pages of honour, the young Laird
of Mellerstain and Dik Doddiswode, and the Lady Elizabeth
in a litter with her mistress-nurse, Alison Hay, arrived in dusk
of many an evening that month to find their beds made in
scenes of unfamiliar opulence. The road to Windsor Castle
appeared to lead through a succession of nobly timbered parks,
in which arose a series of houses of myriad glinting windows,
rich in heavily carved oak staircases, ornamental plaster ceilings,
and furniture and hangings whose embroidery was a testimony
to the peaceful lives led by their daughters. The gentry of
every neighbourhood, and many from further afield, were
pompously assembled to greet royalty. The Lady Anne
Clifford, a high-born damsel of thirteen, calmly wrote in her
diary, that her mother and she killed three horses in one day
"with extremity of heat", in their anxiety to get from Tytten-
hanger, near St Albans, to Wrest, Bedfordshire, on their
pilgrimage towards Dingley near Warwick, to meet the queen.
They were rewarded by being kissed by the queen, and seeing
Prince Henry. They had to go on to another house next day to
see "where the Lady Elizabeth, her Grace, lay which was the
first tyme ever I saw hir, my Lady Kildare and ye Lady Harington being hir governesses". The princess was making a short
stay at Combe Abbey, a residence of Sir John Harington, while
her mother and brother inspected the glories of Holmby
House. On June 27th the king met his wife and son at Easton
Neston. The princess was the first of the family to arrive at
Windsor three days later, "accompanied with her governess,
the Lady Kildare, in a litter with her, and attended with thirty
horse. She had her trumpeters and other formalities as well as
the best."

On the 2nd of July she was present at a brilliant ceremony,
a Chapter of the Order of the Garter at which her brother was
installed knight. Little Lady Anne Clifford, who had been

much upset by the decision that she was "not high enough" to figure in the funeral procession of the late queen, had a day after her own heart on this occasion. "I stood with my Lady Elizabeth's Grace in the shrine of the great hall at Windsor, to see the King and all the knights set at dinner. Thither came the Archduke's Ambassador, who was received by the King and Queen in the great hall, where there was such an infinite company of lords and ladies and so great a Court as I think I shall never see the like again."[1] The Archduke Albert's Ambassador was Charles, Prince d'Aremberg, a nobleman so gouty and so hesitant of speech that the king confided to the genial Duc de Sully, "The Archduke has sent me an Ambassador who can neither walk nor talk. He hath demanded an audience of me in a garden, because he cannot come upstairs into a room."[2] To the French Ambassador, M. de Beaumont, he said, even more confidentially, "Look at this little knight, your master's son-in-law. What do you think of him? Is he not very lively?" A project for a double marriage between the two eldest children of France and England was being suggested. James assured de Beaumont that his daughter was already enamoured of the Dauphin's portrait. Later, on the same crowded day, the Ambassador was formally presented to the princess. He wrote to Paris that she was very well bred and handsome, rather tall for her years, and seemed to be of a gentle disposition, "rather pensive than gay".[3]

From Windsor the royal family removed to Hampton Court. The plague was on the increase, a distressing circumstance, since the Coronation was fixed for July 25th. There is no evidence that Elizabeth was present at a ceremony at which her mother caused astonishment by refusing to partake of the Sacrament, and her father by his levity during the payment of homage. Amongst those raised to the peerage by the king

[1] *Diary of Lady Anne Clifford*, pp. 7, 8, 9.
[2] Nichols, i. 161.   [3] Brienne MS. Bibl. Nat. Paris, 32, 158.

C

during his coronation festivities was the husband of his daughter's governess, Lady Harington. Sir John was created Baron Harington of Exton.

On July 20th an establishment including seventy servants, of whom twenty-two were to fulfil duties above-stairs and forty-eight below, was formed for Prince Henry and his sister at Oatlands.[1] [2] But neither child remained long at the handsome red-brick palace near Weybridge. Before Michaelmas the prince had set up house at Hampton Court, and the dismissal of her State Governess had entailed a change of residence for the princess. Lady Kildare lost her appointment owing to her husband's implication in a plot.

Plots pursued James I with the persistent attachment of the domestic cat to those who regard it with physical repulsion. On August 5th of this year he announced a public thanksgiving in celebration of the anniversary of his escape from the Gowrie Conspirators. That dark tragedy had been enacted when his daughter was less than four years old. The two half-baked plots to which his attention was already being directed in his new country were of a pattern familiar to him in his Scottish days. One, engineered by a priest named Watson, went by the name of the "Bye" Plot, or the "Surprise". Its object was to seize the king's person and exact from him some concessions towards Catholics. "Cobham's" or "the Main" plot was more ambitious, and according to most unsatisfactory evidence, aimed at killing "the King and his cubs" and placing his cousin, the inoffensive Arbella Stuart, on the throne. Lord Cobham himself declared that Sir Walter Raleigh had instigated him to

[1] Nichols, i. 193.

[2] It was built by Henry VIII, and became a favourite residence of Anne of Denmark after 1607, when she obtained it from Robert Cecil in exchange for her dower palace of Hatfield. Theobalds forms the background of a full-length portrait of the queen, at Windsor Castle, and appears to have resembled Hampton Court in many respects. It was destroyed during the Civil Wars.

conspire with the Archduke Albert's Ambassador, the lethargic d'Aremberg, and as a reward for their services Spain had promised both of them handsome pensions. Lord Cobham, Lord Grey de Wilton, a young Puritan, and Sir Griffin Markham, a Catholic gentleman, were all actually led to the scaffold on a dark and rainy morning in the following December. After a nerve-racking delay, carefully planned by an acute royal psychologist, a merciful respite was announced, and they were consigned to the Tower of London, where Cobham, like the unfortunate and protesting Sir Walter, lingered a prisoner for fourteen years.

Lady Cobham, born Lady Frances Howard, and widow of Henry Fitzgerald, eighth Earl of Kildare, whose title she had continued to use after her second marriage to the eighth Lord Cobham, eventually dissociated herself from her conspirator husband. But on October 30th, 1603, she was still sufficiently enamoured of him to send him a letter vowing him eternal fidelity, whether he was guilty or merely unfortunate.[1] She had been discharged from attendance on the Lady Elizabeth six weeks before, and on October 19th a Privy Seal order had committed the keeping and education of the princess to those staunch Protestants, the Lord Harington of Exton and "the lady his wife". An allowance of £1,500 a year was made to them for the child's "diet", and Harington was instructed to send in accounts of further expenses incurred on her behalf, such as "her removal now to his house".

II

The princess's first removal was to Exton Hall, the Rutland-shire seat of the Harington family. She made a short stay there while some necessary alterations were made at another and more magnificent home where she was to spend the next five years.

[1] S.P. 14. 36. 12.

Combe Abbey, two and a half miles north of Coventry, had been a monastic foundation. A pious Norman landlord, in the days of King Stephen, had presented to Cistercian brethren a site "remote, low, woody and convenient for pasturage". After the Dissolution of the Monasteries the abbey had passed into the hands of John Dudley, Duke of Northumberland, but this nobleman, who perished on the scaffold in 1553, never took up residence at Combe. It was left to Sir Robert Kelway, and his son-in-law, the first Lord Harington, to convert a stately religious house into a splendid domestic habitation. This they accomplished at great expense, but with taste and restraint.

The home prepared for the seven-year-old princess in the autumn of 1603 was not entirely strange to her, for she had paid a flying visit there in the preceding June on her journey south. In appearance it presented clear evidence of four centuries of monastic occupation, and with their property something of the high-souled austerity and practical ability of the original inhabitants seemed to have passed to its third lay possessors. The Haringtons were renowned as "persons eminent for prudence and piety".

The destruction of the old conventual church at Combe had left the south side of the cloister garth open. This square had been transformed into a forecourt, and round it on three sides ran Gothic cloisters, which had been skilfully incorporated into a modern building. The cloisters contained a typical round-headed Norman doorway, flanked by deeply recessed, many-columned window apertures, and in the south and west walks fine late-Gothic windows. The Elizabethan upper storey jutted out on wooden corbels, surmounted by pediments. Great seven-light windows had been introduced into the centres of the east and west wings.

The house was as nobly planned within as without. Its rooms were panelled and hung with tapestries representing mythological deities, prophets, huntsmen and Roman emperors. Its large chimney-pieces of stone below and wood above, all painted to resemble oak, displayed the Harington coat of arms. The fireplaces of the Jacobean house were merely hearthstones, lying in recesses on which timber from the estate, kept together by ornamental andirons, spluttered and flared against ornamented iron firebacks. The ribbed plaster ceilings, like the heavily carved staircases and well-polished floors, reflected many a green shade from the "goodly woods" outside. The furniture was mostly ponderous and highly decorated. There were canopied oak bedsteads, and buffets and court cupboards, all rejoicing in bulbous, gadrooned columns. There were table desks and oaken joint stools, and box chairs and arm-chairs of uncompromising hardness, but there were also chairs, with footstools to match, covered with blushing velvets, filled with soft cushions and trimmed with fringed galon secured by a multitude of brass-headed nails. There were "farthingale" chairs, without arms, designed to display the decoration of a hoop petticoat to its fullest extent. Such chairs were covered with "Turkey-work" of knotted woollen pile, or embroidery of bright silks on canvas, or of many-coloured wools on twill. Their intricate patterns were of foliage and fruit and flowers and birds and beasts of the fields. Since the ladies who designed them gave little thought to proportion, the lively rabbit often appeared as large as the stately hart, and the butterfly the same size as the pomegranate. For tables there were long, well-waxed dining-tables, and draw-tables, and side-tables and gate-leg tables with hinged flaps. The princess's wardrobe was accommodated either "by the walls" hanging on pegs, shrouded by curtains, or in travelling trunks of wood, leather covered, and inlaid coffers of marquetry of holly and bog oak, in which were laid "sweet-bags" of musk and civet. For her jewellery, in the spring of 1605, she received from a foreign prince—the Duke of Würtemberg

—a silver casket of great beauty.[1] No possible object upon which the casual eye might rest in the Jacobean nobleman's house was left unembellished, and there is no reason to think that the dragons, gryphons, centaurs and mermaids of whose existence she was hourly informed, seemed to the little princess a whit less credible than her "ruffe dog" for whose shearing Lord Harington gravely entered twelve-pence in his accounts, her monkeys, whose beds of herbs and cotton cost three and threepence, or her parrots, whose cages were renewed by a joiner for three and tenpence. From Lord Harington's accounts [2] and letters,[3] and the Memoir of his heir, written by his cousin Sir John Harington,[4] it is possible to form a tolerably exact picture of the household at Combe. Early rising was followed by family prayers. The heir, who rose "every morning at four or five", was able to accomplish an hour's holy reading as well as three or four hours of study before indulging in "some honest and noble recreation" such as riding abroad or conversing with friends, until dinner-time. The princess, unlike her Tudor predecessors and her brothers, was not required to spend her mornings learning Latin and Greek. In her father's opinion "to make women learned and foxes tame had the same effect—to make them more cunning". She was taught Italian and French, and from her French tutor and her French tirewoman she acquired a proficiency in their language which was to prove invaluable to her.[5] Dinner at Combe was preceded by "a prayer, chapter and psalm", and the whole household met again for prayer after supper, before retiring for the night at a laudably early hour. At these frequent religious exercises solemn warnings against the Church of Rome

[1] Rye, p. lxxxvi.

[2] Those for the last six months of his guardianship are preserved at the Public Record Office, E. 407. 57. 2.

[3] S.P.D. 1603–10, 1611–18.   [4] Harington's *Nugae Antiquae*, ii. 308–17.

[5] When she first met her husband, French was their only common tongue, and throughout their married life he wrote to her in that language.

and an existence of idle pleasure were repeated with tireless fervour, and as far as the old faith was concerned, the impression made upon the mind of the infant Elizabeth was lifelong. The interval between dinner at noon and supper about seven was again dedicated by the heir of the Haringtons to "study", but as the princess had instructors in music [1] and dancing resident at Combe, it may be concluded that some of her afternoons were spent in acquiring these accomplishments. There is no record of the inevitable sewing that must have taken place, and she never became a friend of her needle. She soon learnt to write an excellent letter, but from her earliest days there is every indication that the Lady Elizabeth's favourite lesson was her riding lesson. A score of horses for her use were kept by Lord Harington in his stables, and if she learnt desirable Protestantism from him, she certainly also learnt to live beyond her income. Lord Harington's "princelike housekeeping" eventually ruined his family. More than once during his guardianship he petitioned successfully for an increased allowance,[2] but he never succeeded in emerging from debt. Like Lord Linlithgow before him, he obtained permission to absent himself from Parliament, so as to be able to devote all his energies to his royal charge, and his notions of the duty of a host of royalty were imposing. Since both of his daughters were married and his heir was about to set out on a foreign tour accompanied by a "Mr Tovey, a grave learned and religious man, and formerly the headmaster of the Free School at Coventry", he imported a niece [3] of a suitable age to be a companion to the princess. The Lady Elizabeth grew up with everything handsome about her. She had in daily

[1] She received some of her musical education from the celebrated Dr John Bull, organist of the Chapel Royal and first Professor of Music at Gresham College. The benediction sung as an anthem at her wedding was specially composed for the occasion by her old tutor.

[2] S.P. 14. 32. 76.

[3] Anne Dudley Sutton was the daughter of Theodosia, sister of Lord Harington, and Edward, ninth Baron Dudley.

attendance, besides her nurse, three chamberwomen, a French dresser and her tutors, a physician, two Scots footmen dressed in the royal livery, grooms of the presence-chamber and grooms of the bedchamber. Her household further included a sempstress, a laundress, grooms of the stable, yeomen of the horse, yeomen of the cellar and sumptermen. "With God's assistance", wrote her harassed but flattered host, "we hope to do the Lady Elizabeth such service as is due to her princely endowments and natural abilities, both which appear the sweet dawnings of future comfort to her royal father".[1]

James I liked to receive well-written letters, often in foreign tongues, from his promising children, and the first efforts of Elizabeth's pen which have been preserved are stiff little notes of dutiful compliments addressed to her father and to her elder brother. She never, unfortunately, learnt to date her correspondence satisfactorily, but it is possible from internal evidence to give approximate dates to some of her early letters. Soon after her arrival at Combe her handwriting, so rigidly erect as to be in occasional danger of falling backwards, did great credit to her seven years. "My dear and worthy brother", she wrote between lines ruled in red ink, "I most humbly salute you, desiring to hear of your health, from whom, though I am now removed far away, none can be nearer in affection than your most loving sister, Elizabeth." [2] As she grew older, and especially when she wrote in French or Italian, she adopted a slanting and more ornate handwriting. Some signatures of her carefree schoolroom days are accompanied by almost as many attendant flourishes as those of her famous namesake and godmother. Her father's letters confirm the evidence of contemporaries that James VI of Scotland spoke "the full dialect of his country". Anne of Denmark, who had learnt her English north of the Tweed, spelt refer "refarre", Oatlands "Ottelands", and wrote of "your maister"

---

[1] *Nugae Antiquae*, i. 371.   [2] Harl. MS. 6986. 84.

and "lugging the sowe's eare". No phraseology or spelling in the letters of Elizabeth Stuart suggest that she spoke anything but the English of the dramatist in whose native county she spent the important formative years from seven to thirteen, or that of the version of holy writ authorized by her father when she was eight, and first published when she was fifteen. Some of Elizabeth's early letters to her parent reached court in a romantic fashion, according to Sir John Harington, poet and courtier, cousin of Lord Harington. Sir John, in an epistle to Prince Henry, detailing the accomplishments of a favourite dog, Bungey by name, affirms that this sagacious beast was capable of delivering "such matters as were entrusted to his care" at Greenwich Palace, and bringing back to his master at Bath or Kelstone "goodlie returnes from such Nobilitie as were pleased to emploie him.   Nor was it ever told our Ladie Queene that this Messenger did ever blab aught concerninge his highe truste." "Although", boasts the wit, "I mean not to disparage the deedes of Alexander's Horse, I will match my Dogge against him for good carriage. For if he did not bear a great Prince on his backe, I am bold to saie he did often bear the sweet wordes of a greater Princesse on his neck." [1]

Combe, like most country houses of its size and date, was largely self-supporting and self-sufficing. To Lord Harington's pained surprise, his elevation to the peerage had not been greeted with generous applause by most of his neighbours, many of whom were Catholics.[2] However, during the first spring that she spent there, an invitation to a local entertainment arrived for Elizabeth. The Mayor and Corporation of Coventry had decided that it was their duty to invite their sovereign's daughter to visit them. Their decision was not entirely spontaneous. A poor gentleman named Massie, who

[1] *Nugae Antiquae*, i. 390. The letter is dated June 14th, 1608.
[2] *Nugae Antiquae*, i. 374.

made a precarious living by contracting for pageants, had come to them with the startling news that "the Lady Elizabeth's Grace was desirous to see Coventry". She was, moreover, coming within two days, expecting to witness a fascinating pageant which Massie had offered to the Corporation, but which had been refused on account of its exorbitant cost. The alarmed worthies sent a messenger galloping to Combe, and received a chilling reply that nothing was known there of such a project. They saved the situation by despatching a formal invitation to the princess to honour their town at an early date, and began to make their preparations. But the ingenious Massie's pageant was sternly excluded from a programme far more suited to their guest's rank than her years.

April 3rd, 1604, was finally chosen for the revelries, and on that morning the Mayor and Aldermen, in their scarlet gowns, rode out of Coventry as far as a local landmark known as Jabet's Ash, on Stoke Green. There they encountered Lord Harington riding bareheaded in front of a rich coach which contained his charge. The Mayor alighted from his horse to kiss the princess's hand; her procession, which included many ladies and gentlemen of distinction, in carriages or on horseback, mingled with his, and a solemn progress was made through streets lined by the different Companies of the City, standing in their gowns and hoods. The first halt was made outside a noble perpendicular church, facing a broad open space which was the hub of the town. The princess entered St Michael's and listened to a learned and lengthy sermon. She was next escorted from the south porch of the church to the building which was the centre of all municipal business—a distance of only a few steps—and enthroned on a dais, in a gilded medieval chair of state, she partook alone of a banquet in St Mary's Hall. "Having finished her repast, she adjourned to the Mayoress's parlour, which had been fitted up in a most sumptuous manner for her reception." While the Mayor, Lord Harington and the attendant aldermen, gentlemen and ladies dined, the princess conversed with the Mayoress. The visit concluded with the presentation to the princess of a silver-gilt cup "which cost the City £29 : 16 : 8d", and another slow peregrination through streets lined by loyal mercers, cappers, drapers and tailors, up to the Bishopgate in the north of the town, down to Spon-End on the west, and finally out of Gosford Gate on the east, back to Jabet's Ash. There the Mayor and citizens took respectful leave of their guest, whose guardian "reconveyed her to Combe".[1]

III

Elizabeth's next visit to Coventry took place under far more exciting circumstances.

Warwickshire, that stronghold of Catholicism, was alive during the early days of November 1605 with strange rumours. They penetrated even to peaceful Combe, causing its master grave disquiet. Wednesday, November 6th, was an unusual day at the Abbey. It opened with the arrival of a groom, bearing a letter to Lord Harington from a Protestant neighbour. After reading the news sent by Mr. Benock, the owner of Combe settled at his writing-desk, and servants were ordered to make ready for a journey to London. Lord Harington addressed himself to the omniscient Sir Robert Cecil, now Lord Salisbury. His neighbour's letter, which he enclosed, informed him that all Mr Benock's horses had been seized last night by papists. "It cannot be but some great rebellion is at hand." The Princess Elizabeth's guardian asked for instructions, "fearing she may be seized should a rebellion take place".[2] During the afternoon fresh reports of trouble

[1] Nichols, i. 429; Sharp's *Coventry Pageants*, pp. 75, 76; Poole's *Coventry*, p. 404; Reader's *New Coventry Guide*, p. 52.
[2] S.P.D., 1603–11, vol. xvi. *Gunpowder Plot Book*, pp. 21, 22.

came in, and quite shaken out of his usual equanimity, Lord
Harington determined not to wait for authority from London.
An instant packing of the princess's effects was ordered, and
she was hastily conveyed towards a place of more safety.
This place proved to be Coventry town, filled with excited
citizens, who had put themselves in arms. Elizabeth was lodged
in a new house with a fine quadrangle and elaborate exterior
leadwork. Mr Hopkins, of Earl Street, like many of his
wealthy brethren, lived in comfort. The decorated plaster
ceiling of his banqueting-parlour, and his carved stone chimney-
place pieces, were as good as many at Combe.[1] Having placed
his "great charge" in safety, and written again to Lord Salisbury, advising him of his action, Lord Harington rode off
with another hero, Sir Fulk Greville, to spend five days "in
peril of death". They roused the Protestant gentlemen of their
county, and attacked the desperate Catholic conspirators who,
on hearing that the best-known plot of James I's reign had
failed, had retired to Holbeach House on the borders of
Staffordshire. In London, the son of Henry Darnley had, very
naturally, thought of gunpowder as soon as he had read the
mysterious letter of warning sent by a well-wisher to Catholic
Lord Monteagle.[2] The cellars of the Parliament House,
whose inhabitants were to have received "a terrible blowe . . .
and yet not seie who hurts them", had been searched, and Guy
Fawkes, "a very bad and desperate fellow", had been discovered standing amongst abundance of explosive, ready with
dark lantern, watch, touchwood and slow match "to blow the
Scots back again into Scotland". But it took many days of
interrogation and torture to draw from him the names of his
confederates, and their intention, after the destruction of the
king and the Prince of Wales, to have surprised "the person of
the Lady Elizabeth, the King's daughter, in Warwickshire, and

[1] "Palace Yard", as it is now called, still stands, having survived employment as a coaching-inn and a young ladies' seminary.
[2] S.P., 14. 216. 2. Somers, ii. 103-4.

presently proclaim her Queen." When the full nefariousness of "the late divilish conspiracy" was divulged to Elizabeth by her guardian, her comment was exemplary "What a Queen should I have been by this means! I had rather have been with my Royal Father in the Parliament House, than wear his Crown on such condition."[1] It now transpired that great care had been expended on the Warwickshire branch of the plot. A hunting-match at Dunchurch on November 5th had been announced, with the object of drawing away from Combe the princess's guardian and all able-bodied men. Elizabeth was then to have been carried off to Ashby St Legers, the house of Lady Catesby, mother of one of the principal conspirators, and her proclamation as Elizabeth II—though without mention of the necessary change in her religion—had been all ready for publication. Even her marriage to an unnamed English Catholic had been discussed. Unfortunately for the Catholic gentlemen, who had arrived at Dunchurch wearing concealed armour, Lord Harington had failed to be attracted by the advertised hunting-match, and when they had made on to Combe next day, they had discovered that their bird was flown two hours before.[2]

Gunpowder Treason was more than a nine days' wonder in Warwickshire. In the following January, according to a letter of Lord Harington, everyone at Combe, including the princess, was still "very ill and troubled" after their "sad affright".[3] Prince Henry, in London, received letters of congratulation on his escape from two juvenile correspondents. His sister sent him a beautifully written little note, in French, full of pious sentiments.[4] From Sedan, where he was being educated under the eye of his maternal uncle, a young German prince, also writing in French, expressed his horror on having learnt of a "wicked conspiracy" which, he was convinced,

---

[1] *Nugae Antiquae*, i. 374.   [2] Birch, *Court and Times of James I*, i. 39.
[3] *Ibid.*   [4] Harl. MS. 6986. 131.

proceeded from "the direct agency of Antichrist".[1] "Frideric", as he signed himself in a large, flowing hand garnished with many tremulous loops, was the elder son of Frederick IV, Elector Palatine. He was four days older than Prince Henry's sister, and hopes of an English marriage for him were already being cherished by his Protestant relatives.

At length, on the last day of January 1606, Guy Fawkes, broken with torture, was assisted up the ladder to his execution on a scaffold appropriately erected opposite the Parliament House. At Combe, Lord Harington continued to voice fears of "some evil-minded Catholics in the West, whom the Prince of Darkness hath in alliance", but the next disturbance to his well-ordered household was of a pleasurable nature. He was commanded to bring the Lady Elizabeth to Court. Her uncle, the King of Denmark, was expected upon a visit of about forty days' duration. Christian IV had chosen an odd moment to visit a sister whom he had not seen for sixteen years, for throughout the month of June Greenwich Palace was enlivened by speculations whether the queen's brother or next baby would arrive first. Preparations for elaborate tournaments, to follow a christening at which the Danish king was to stand sponsor, went forward, but while contrary winds detained Christian, Anne gave birth to a daughter, who died next day. The funeral of the Princess Sophia, named after her grandmother, the late Queen-Mother of Denmark, took place on June 26th, and not until July 18th, "after many reports and long expecting", was Christian IV met upon the water-steps of Greenwich Palace by two charming children who gravely bade him welcome. He kissed his niece Elizabeth and his nephew Charles, and hurried to the bedside of his sister. His brother-in-law and his elder nephew had gone down to Gravesend to escort him up the river.[2] A second lovely niece

[1] Harl. MS. 7007. 76.
[2] Nichols, ii. 53; *Ambassades de M. de la Boderie*, i. 227

was awaiting his inspection in her nursery. Elizabeth's younger sister Mary, born in April of the previous year, was to survive another fourteen months.

The royal Dane, whom Elizabeth now saw for the first and last time, was pronounced by English observers to be remarkably like their queen, an unflattering comment, for portraits of Christian, which are extremely numerous, all represent him as decidedly coarse-looking. He showered presents during his visit, and to her dying day his niece's memories of her burly, good-humoured Danish uncle, who had to hold up two fingers and point to his watch to convey to the Lord High-Admiral of England that the hour was but two o'clock, were kept fresh by a full-length oil portrait, in which Christian's foppish love-lock contrasted strangely with his rubicund countenance of harsh features.

"My cousin, Lord Harington of Exton", wrote witty Sir John Harington from court, "doth much fatigue himself with the royal charge of the Princess Elizabeth; and, midst all the foolery of these times, has much labour to preserve his own wisdom and sobriety." The fooleries detailed by Sir John were indeed enough to cause the guardian of an observant child disquiet. "Now the gunpowder fright is got out of all our heads we are going on hereabouts as if the devil was contriving that every man should blow up himself with wild riot, excess, and devastation of time and temperance." [1] A contemporary poem [2] describes the "new courtier" of King James's day as being much inferior to his Elizabethan pre-decessor. The "old courtier" kept "20 old fellows in blue coats", a learned and pious chaplain and a hall hung with worn armour. He hunted his own hounds, and dispensed good cheer at Christmas-tide. His son keeps "a couple of painted madams" and drinks in taverns till he can't stand. His "new-fangled" lady-wife scorns knowledge of housekeeping and has a wardrobe

[1] *Nugae Antiquae*, i. 348–53.   [2] *Percy's Reliques*, ii. 318.

including "7 or 8 heads of other women's hair". His hall is full with pictures and his study of pamphlets and plays. His chaplain swears faster than he can pray. His kitchen is presided over by a French cook who sends up "kickshaws". At Christmas the new courtier arrives in London attended by gentlemen-ushers, footmen, pages and waiting-women. His father's flourishing manors are sold to keep him in such state and buy him a title.

A more severe critic, of the next generation, wrote of James I's court as "a nursery of lust and intemperance", and added that "the generallity of the gentry of the land soone learnt the court fashion and every greate house in the country became a sty of uncleannesse".[1] One "greate house" should have been excepted from this sweeping condemnation. After her convivial uncle's departure, Elizabeth Stuart was sent back to the virtuous shades of Combe, to long days of quiet and prayers, carefully supervised little acts of charity, and lessons. The chief visible changes in her world were the changes of the year, which brought midwinter breakfasts by candle-light, and spring floods, and haymaking, and games of battledore and shuttlecock in the garden, and frost again fading the tapestries of the rides in Warwickshire woods.[2]

[1] Hutchinson, 89–90.
[2] A duodecimo volume of 162 pages, privately printed, entitled *Memoirs of the Queen of Bohemia, by one of her ladies*, contains many attractive anecdotes of Elizabeth's life at Combe Abbey and has been quoted in biographies of the queen. On a fly-leaf of the copy in the Bodleian a manuscript note explains that the memoirs were written by the Lady Frances Erskine and begun about 1753. From internal evidence it appears that they were produced between 1759 and 1768 and that Lady Frances was actually the author, not merely the editress. There are several minor inaccuracies, but the fact that Arabella Stuart is represented as being introduced to Elizabeth in Nottinghamshire, at a date when she was certainly in Surrey, seems conclusive. See *Cecil Papers*, v. 100, 134; v. 134, 39; and v. 135, 176, also Ashmolean MS, v. 1729, 80–81.

IV

The friendship of Elizabeth and Henry Stuart has been too often and mawkishly panegyrized, but nobody who has studied the dozens of little notes that passed between this young brother and sister [1] can fail to receive a poignant impression of valour and innocence. Their phraseology is frequently tortuous and stilted, but through the formal sentences sounds the unmistakable note of a sincere affection, and it is a pathetic fact that a fear that they may, by some malignity of fate, be prevented from seeing as much of one another as they wish, even when they are master and mistress of their own actions, is repeatedly expressed by the young princess.

"I had rather be the messenger myself", she wistfully declares after humble apology for presenting "this ill penned object to your princely view". "I have changed my logings, but I do not change ever", "the immense Ocean of my affection", and "jusques au tombeau" are flamboyancies likely to have been popular with any youthful authoress in days when the figures of Viola and Sebastian were familiar upon the stage. The following is a typical example of her early style:

WORTHY PRINCE AND MY DEAREST BROTHER,

I received your most welcome letter and kynd token by Mr Hopkins, highly esteeming them as delightfull memeorialls of your brotherly love. In which assuredly (whatsoever else may fayle) I will ever endeavour to equall you, esteeming that time happiest when I enjoyed your company, and desiring nothing more than the fruition of it again: that as nature has made us neerest in our love together, so accident may not seperate us from living together. Neither do I account it the leste part of my present comfort that though I am deprived of

[1] Harl. MS. 6986. 7007.

D

your happy presence yet I can make these lines deliver this true message, that I will ever bee during my lyfe

your most kinde and loving sister

ELIZABETH.[1]

She secured her letters with strands of floss silk of many gay colours—gold, rose, carmine, royal blue, amethyst, lemon and grass-green—amongst which are twisted tinsel threads, now almost black. Her seals, with three exceptions, when apparently she borrowed a seal from a neighbour or visitor, bear the device of the Scots Lion rampant. Her handwriting varies according to her choice of pen, but is always good, and a letter to her brother's tutor, the Dean of Durham, on the occasion of his marriage, is a remarkable effort for a child of eight.[2] One of her signatures, of unusual beauty, is gorgeously achieved in gold ink.[3]

Prince Henry's "delightfull memeorialls of brotherly love" are written in a small and slightly over-driven hand, much inferior to that of his sister as far as legibility is concerned, but decidedly more adult. He uses long, narrow strips of paper, which he often fills to their utmost capacity, while his sister prefers—or was obliged to use—a large, oblong sheet, and leaves wide margins. The burden of Elizabeth's song is always the same. She longs to see her brother again. A few days seem an age when he is not present. Henry, or "Henrie" as he occasionally signs himself, is very much the elder brother in his replies. "There is nothing I wish more than that we might be in one companie. But I fear that there be other considerations which maketh the king's Majestie to think otherwyse." [4] Sir Charles Cornwallis's [5] assertion that the Prince sometimes enjoyed teasing his impetuous young sister [6] seems confirmed

---

[1] Harl. MS. 6986. 89.   [2] *Ibid.*, 82.
[3] *Ibid.*, 113.   [4] Harl. MS. 7007. 62.
[5] Sir Charles Cornwallis, courtier and diplomatist (d. 1629), was author of two tracts concerning Henry, Prince of Wales.   [6] Somers, ii. 223.

by Henry's reminder: "That you are displeased to be left in solitude, I can well believe, for you damsels and women are sociable creatures, but you know that those who love each other best cannot always be glued together." [1]

The brother whom Elizabeth Stuart idolized was declared by several sycophantic contemporaries to be startlingly like his royal namesake, the hero of Agincourt. Some points of likeness were obvious. Henry Stuart, like Henry Plantagenet, had tawny hair and a piercing, authoritative eye. "In body he was strong and erect, of middle height, his limbs gracefully put together, his gait kinglike, his face long and somewhat lean ... in countenance resembling his sister, as far as a man's face can be compared with that of a very beautiful girl. His forehead bore marks of severity, his mouth had a touch of pride." [2] His athletic prowess and *bons mots* were remarkable, and he seems to have possessed all Henry V's talent for inspiring boundless enthusiasm. His personal magnetism is described by Cornwallis as "a certaine kinde of extraordinary unspeakable excellency". But, like Henry Plantagenet, Henry Stuart was also arrogant, combative and a prig. Cornwallis's eulogistic mention of the collecting-boxes for charity, into which servants of a fourteen-year-old master were compelled to drop a coin every time "horrible oathes" escaped them, strike somewhat coldly on the ear, and this Henry's asceticism was not the reaction after an educative progress down the primrose path. Anyone, however, who feels inclined to condemn Henry Stuart as a narrow-minded young autocrat would do well to consider the descriptions of his father's court offered by Sir John Harington,[3] Francis Osborn, Sir Anthony Welldon and Sir Edward Peyton.[4]

When Elizabeth was eleven she was allowed to visit that court for Christmas and New-Year. M. le Fèvre de la Boderie,

[1] Harl. MS. 7007. 38.
[2] Somers, ii. 231.
[3] *Nugae Antiquae.*
[4] *Secret History of the Court of James I.*

French Ambassador, observed her carefully, and wrote home that the English princess was full of virtue and merit, beautiful, graceful, very well nourished, and spoke French fluently—much better than her elder brother. "I assure you that it will not be her fault if she is not dauphiness—and she might have worse fancies—for she is not at all vexed when it is mentioned to her." She was, in short, perfection, and in his opinion a better match could not be made for the Dauphin; but it was his duty to warn Henri IV that it would be useless for him to count upon securing her as a daughter-in-law unless he was prepared to give a daughter, in exchange, to the Prince of Wales. The heir of England had promised his sister not to consent to a French marriage for himself unless she became Dauphiness.[1] A Scottish writer was also recording his impressions of Elizabeth this season. "Although she has not yet passed her twelfth year, yet all behold in her lively proofs of most excellent and noble disposition. Her wit is acute, her memory tenacious, her judgment discerning beyond her tender years. In piety she equals Flavia, the daughter of Clementius, the Roman consul; in her knowledge of a variety of languages she is to be compared, or rather preferred, to Zenobia, the Palmyrian queen, to Aretis and Cornelia. She also diligently cultivates music,[2] and is a great proficient in the art: for this tranquil, liberal science most fittingly accords with the temper of the most placid and illustrious maiden."[3] Her Scottish admirer concludes his praises with adding that his

[1] Boderie, iii. 7.

[2] A virginal, traditionally the property of Elizabeth and exhibited at the Victoria and Albert Museum, is sufficiently beautiful to explain her docility in practising. It is of late sixteenth-century Venetian workmanship, and enclosed in a rich stamped and gilt leather case of sober hue. Internally it is brilliantly decorated with eighteen small pictures in coloured glass, and with plaques of silver foliage and enamel, on copper. Its keyboard of forty-five keys, and other parts, are enamelled in a similar manner. Life-size representations of two spirited birds are amongst its attractions, and in its colouring, which is still glowing, royal blue, peacock blue, scarlet, leaf-green, amethyst, amber and peach-pink are successfully combined.

[3] Rosa T. Idaea Jacobi. London, 1608.

paragon's manners are most gentle—"in fine, whatever was excellent or lofty in Queen Elizabeth, is all compressed in the tender age of this virgin princess, and, if God spare her to us, will be found there accumulated". A year later, an eminent Italian, transmitting to Rome a detailed description of the English royal family, confirmed the popular report that "the daughter", for whom a crafty sire was already entertaining offers of marriage from both Catholic and heretic princes, is "handsome and of a noble expression of countenance".[1]

Meantime, the indefatigable Lord Harington continued his warnings against the hollow pleasures of this world, and was reassured by the receipt of a copy of verses dedicated to him by his charge. Elizabeth's first and only recorded effort as a poetess is performed in an exacting metre, and the robe of Polymnia seems over-long for her. The following verses are chosen from amongst thirty-three, which, in spite of the over-whelming correctitude of the sentiments, preserve a touching early-morning freshness:

> " Earthly things do fade, decay.
> Constant to us not one day.
> Suddenly they pass away.
> And we cannot make them stay . . .
>
> O, my God, for Christ his sake
> Quite from me this dulness take;
> Cause me earth's love to forsake
> And of heaven my realm to make . . .
>
> This is only my desire,
> This doth set my hart on fire,
> That I may receave my hyre,
> With the saints' and angels' quire.
>
> O my soul of heavenly birth.
> Doe thou scorn this basest earth.
> Place not here thy joy and mirth,
> Where of bliss is greatest dearth . . .

---

[1] "Description of England", by Cardinal Bentivoglio, Nuncio at Brussels, 1609. Transcript from Tanner MS., printed by Aikin, *Court of James I*, i. 331–6.

O Lord, glorious and most kind,
Thou has these thoughts put in my mind.
Let me grace increasing find,
Me to thee more firmly bind . . .

To me grace, O Father send,
On thee wholly to depend,
That all may to thy glory tend:
Soe let me live, soe let me end." [1]

V

"My honourable good lord," wrote Lord Harington to
Lord Salisbury, on October 25th, 1609 "I must crave pardon
that I wait not on your lordship myself, with the book of
accounts for her Grace, for this last half year. My wife being
not yet thoroughly recovered of her sickness, and the Prince
calling often for her Grace to ride abroad with him, causeth
my more necessary attendance. I have sent the accounts by
this bearer, my servant." [2]

The princess and her brother were now meeting "at least
once in two days". Henry was at Hampton Court, and
Elizabeth established in a house belonging to Lord Harington,
at Kew. At thirteen she had her own barge upon the Thames.[3]
A suite of apartments, in that quarter of the palace known as the
Cock-pit, was set aside for her use when she visited her parents
at Whitehall. She went with them and her brothers, on an
April day, to inspect "a stately building, sodainely erected" by
the Lord Treasurer, in the Strand. "Many of the upper shoppes
were richly furnished with wares." The king christened the
new commercial edifice "Britain's Burse", an address that was
to appear on the title-pages of many popular publications
dealing with Elizabeth's marriage and later misfortunes.[4]

On the following Twelfth Night she was present at a

[1] Verses by the Princess Elizabeth given to Lord Harington of Exton,
her preceptor, 1609. *Nugae Antiquae*, ii. 411–16.
[2] S.P. 14. 47. 126.   [3] Nichols, ii. 248.   [4] Devon, p. 91.

gorgeous tournament organized by her favourite brother. Ben Jonson wrote the speeches uttered by the various maskers before Prince Henry's Barriers, and an actor representing Merlin voiced unhappily prophetic lines in praise of "that most Princely maid, whose form might call the world to war. She shall be Mother of Nations. . . ." Elizabeth presented the prizes to the heroes of the tilt-yard next day, after presiding opposite her elder brother at a supper given by him at St James's. The king went home after the supper, but his elder children proceeded to witness a comedy which lasted two hours. "A set banquet in the gallery" followed the comedy. According to the Dutch Ambassador, the dishes served at it were truly extraordinary, and so was the behaviour of the guests. The prince led his sister twice round the table, which was a hundred and twenty feet long, adorned with crystal bearing fountains of rose-water, and confectionery in the shapes of flower-gardens, windmills, dryads, cavaliers and the planetary system. As soon as the host and hostess had withdrawn, an orgy of souvenir-collecting took place. The long board was over-turned, and every vestige of food and even table-ware was shamelessly appropriated. This scene took place at 3 A.M.[1]

Two months later the first of Elizabeth's suitors to appear in person arrived to stay with her brother at St James's. Frederick Ulrich of Brunswick was her first cousin, the eldest of the eleven children of Henry Julius, Duke of Brunswick, and Elizabeth of Denmark. He had studied at Helmstadt and Tübingen; a polite fiction was kept up during his visit to England that he was merely completing his education by a tour of foreign countries. But James I still hoped to see his daughter Queen of France, and even Anne of Denmark did not encourage her nephew's suit. More than a year later the Duchess of Brunswick, who had in the meantime become a

[1] S.P. 81. 11. 107. Add. MS. 17677-ff. 747, 767. *Archaeologia*, xii. 258.

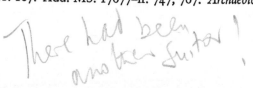

There had been another suitor!

widow, wrote on her son's behalf demanding outright whether
Elizabeth was free or not.[1] She received a prevaricating but
distinctly unpromising reply. Nevertheless, Frederick did not
look elsewhere for a bride until after Elizabeth's wedding. It
is scarcely possible that Elizabeth was unaware of his pretensions during his prolonged stay in her country throughout
the spring and summer of 1610, but there are no signs that she
considered them seriously. A gift of a ring to her cousin is the
only record of personal relations between them[2]. A succession
of entertainments in honour of visiting princes characterize
this year, and in a contemporary account of Prince Louis
Frederick of Würtemberg's stay,[3] Elizabeth's presence, in
company with her cousin "Madame Arabella", is noted more
than once. When the prince went to take his leave of the king
and queen on the 23rd day of May at Greenwich, "the latter
was in the garden, with the Princess and Arabella".[4]

The fancy-free princess had gone on the second day of that
month to Woolwich dockyard, to inspect the *Prince Royal*,
Britain's largest man-of-war, due to be launched in the
following September. Phineas Pette, master-builder to the
navy, was unfortunately in London when she arrived on her
surprise visit, but his wife entertained the Lady Elizabeth and
her train in his house.[5] Within that week the English court was
horrified by the news of the assassination of the King of France.
Henry Stuart, who had been a warm admirer of Henry of
Navarre, was much affected, but no considerations of mourning
were allowed to interfere with the festivities arranged to
celebrate his investiture as Prince of Wales early in June.
Elizabeth, with her father and mother and younger brother,
stood in the Privy Gallery window at Whitehall to watch
Henry's arrival at Whitehall Bridge after his triumphal progress

[1] S.P. 14. 65. 144.   [2] Devon, p. 108.
[3] By Hans Wurmsser von Vendenheyn, printed in Rye, pp. 58 *et seq.*
[4] *Ibid.* p. 66.   [5] Harl. MS. 6279. 55.

down the Thames from Richmond, and on June 5th, the night of "the Creation of the High and Mightie Prince" in the Parliament House, Elizabeth took part for the first time in court theatricals.

Anne of Denmark, since her arrival in England, had discovered, in the shape of the Masque, an ideal form of entertainment. On a court Masque any amount of time and money might be spent. Very little talent was demanded from its high-born performers, and the queen was in the glorious position of being able to assign to herself the leading rôle on every occasion. In "Tethys' Festival, or the Queen's Wake", Anne was Tethys, "Queene of the Ocean, and wife of Neptune", attended by thirteen nymphs, "presiding over severall rivers, appropriated either to their dignities, signiories or places of birth". Elizabeth represented the most famous river of England, Thames. The relative who until her appearance at court had always been chief lady, was the nymph of Trent. Arbella Stuart, the Ophelia of James I's court, was attired, like her young cousin, in an amazing costume. "First their head-tire was composed of shels and corrall, and from a great muriake shell, in forme of the crest of an helmet, hung a thin waving vaile. Their upper garments had the boddies of sky-colored taffetas, for lightnes, all imbrodered with maritime invention. Then had they a kinde of halfe skirts of cloth of silver, imbrodered with golde, all the ground-work cut out, for lightnes, which hung down ful, and, cut in points underneath that, came bases (of the same as was their boddies) beneath their knee. The long skirt was wrought with lace, waved round about like a river, and on the bankes sedge and sea-weedes, all of gold. Their shoulders were all imbrodered with the worke of the short skirt of cloth of silver, and had cypresse, spangled, ruffed out, and fell in a ruffe above the elbow. The under sleeves were all imbrodered as the bodies. Their shoes were of satin, richly imbrodered."

Thus garbed, Elizabeth was discovered, lying at the feet of her mother, in a tremendous transformation scene which occurred about half-way through the performance. The seat "raised six steps", on which Tethys and her daughter were accommodated, was "all covered with such an artificiall stuff as seemed richer by candle than any cloth of gold"; and "great ornaments of relievo", including "two huge whales of silver", pillars of burnished gold, and a couple of fountains "out of which issued abundance of water", were amongst the decorations of "this great acquatick throne". Elizabeth, together with the other river-nymphs who had been languishing in "cavernes, gloriously adorned", presently descended, and "marched up with winding meanders, like a river" towards a bay-tree on a height—the Tree of Victory. Here they offered flowers in golden urns to an accompaniment of soft music and song. Tethys with her nymphs then accomplished three dances, interspersed by songs, during each of which Tethys "reposed herself on the mount". For their third dance they invited lords of the court to be their partners. The startled audience then witnessed them "sodainly vanish". Anyone, however, who imagined that he had now seen the last of Tethys and her nymphs, was disappointed, for after a lengthy invocation from Triton, "Mercury, most artificially and in an exquisite posture", summoned Zephirus—the Duke of York—to "bring back the Queen and her Ladies in their owne forme". "Hereupon the Duke of Yorke, with his attendants, departing to performe this service, the lowde musique sounds, and sodainely appears the Queene's Majesty, in a most pleasant and artificiall grove (which was the third scene) and from thence they march up to the King, conducted by the Duke of Yorke, and the Noblemen, in a very stately manner".

The author of this terrific mummery was Samuel Daniel, one of the grooms of Anne's Privy-Chamber, and like Ben Jonson,

whom she usually employed as masque-writer, an old crony of
William Shakespeare. The architect who was, as Daniel
observed, of importance in contriving the scenery for "Tethys'
Festival", was "Master Inigo Jones". Daniel was also at pains to
explain that no professional actors or even courtiers of inferior
rank took part in this select entertainment. Even "those two
which did personate the Tritons were Gentlemen, knowne of
good worth and respect". Charles, Duke of York, attended by
"twelve little Ladies, all of them the daughters of Earls or
Barons", who danced "to the amazement of all beholders,
considering the tenderness of their years", wore a short tunic
of green satin sewn with gold flowerets, silver wings, made of
lawn stretched on wires, and a wreath of many coloured
blossoms. His little garment covered one shoulder only,
and on one of his bare arms he wore a gold bracelet studded
with gems.[1] On his first arrival in England, the appearance of
the second son of their new sovereign had shocked many
ladies and gentlemen who had thought of offering themselves
to be his guardians. "When they saw how weak a child he was
and not likely to live, their hearts were down." But bold Sir
Robert Cary's equally bold lady had undertaken the charge,
and scouted James I's suggestion that the string of Charles's
tongue ought to be cut, and he must be put in iron boots.
At nine Charles's legs were not yet quite straight, and he showed
no signs of losing his stammer, which was far more pronounced than that of his elder brother.[2] But he had, to everyone's surprise, grown into a most active and demonstrative
little boy, with bright golden hair and sapphire-blue eyes.
His delighted parents spoilt him as much as possible. "Sweet
sweet brother", wrote Charles, Duke of York, in his earliest

[1] Tethys' Festival, Nichols, ii. 346–60; Somers, ii. 191–9.
[2] Both sons of James I suffered from impediments in their speech. Prince
Henry was wont to say of himself, with great good humour, that he
thought "he had the most unserviceable tongue of any man living". Birch,
Life of Henry, Prince of Wales, p. 399.

recorded letter to his slightly contemptuous elder brother, "I will give anie thing that I have to yow; both my horss, and my books, and my pieces, and my cross-bowes, or anie thing that yow would have." [1]

VI

Monday, September 24th, 1610, was the day appointed for the launching of the *Prince Royal*. Ever since Easter, when the "garnishing" of the Great Ship had begun, an incredible number of people "of all sorts" had been making expeditions of pleasure to see her. Phineas Pette, master-shipwright, had not his troubles to seek as the end of his labours drew near.

At last the great morning dawned, and the dock gates were opened, but from the first it was obvious that this was not to be a lucky day. "The wind blowing very hard at South-west, kept out the flood, so that it proved a very bad tide, little better than a neap." At eleven the king and the Prince of Wales, attended by most of the Lords of the Council arrived. James was feeling far from well after a surfeit of grapes. His unfortunate majesty was received by the Lord Admiral, the principal officers of his Navy, and his master-shipwright, and conducted forthwith to the house of a Mr Lydiard, where a banquet awaited him. Dinner was hardly over when a blast of trumpets announced the arrival of the queen, the Lady Elizabeth and the Duke of York, bringing with them a large train of "great Lords and Ladies". From a portrait of Pette,[2] it is possible to judge exactly of the appearance of the master-shipwright who greeted Elizabeth Stuart in Woolwich dockyard on that windy September day. His burly figure is clothed in a white satin doublet with an upstanding collar of spotless gauze. His bombasted breeches are nut-brown. On his noble head of curly dark hair he wears a white skull-cap exquisitely embroidered in bright light colours. Through the window of

---

[1] Harl. MS. 6986. 154.   [2] In the National Portrait Gallery.

the room in which he stands is a bird's-eye view of a Great Ship on the stocks.

"The Queen and the Royal Children, the Ladies and the Council (all railed in and boarded)" were correctly disposed in their seats. "It grew towards high-water, and all things ready, and a great close lighter was made fast to the ship's stem." Pette received the Lord Admiral's orders "to taught the crabs and screws". He had "little hope to launch, by reason the wind over-blew the tide. Yet the Ship started." She started, then "the dock gates pent her in so straight that she stuck fast". . . . And stuck she remained.

Elizabeth Stuart was not destined to witness the baptism of the Great Ship in which she was to leave her native land as a bride. At five o'clock that evening, all hope of a launch having been abandoned, the royal family, with the exception of the Prince of Wales, sadly returned to Greenwich. Henry had been on the poop with the Lord Admiral "where the great standing gilt cup was ready filled with wine, to name the Ship as soon as she was afloat, according to ancient custom". . . . For "a good while" after the disappearance of his relatives he stayed conferring with the Lord Admiral, the principal officers and the distracted Pette "what was to be done". Next day, in a furious storm, "his invincible spirit daunted by nothing", the heir of England again repaired to Woolwich, and this time "the Ship went away, without any straining of screws or tackles, to the great Comfort of the Prince's Highness". While she was being moored Henry "went down to the platform of the cock-room where the Ship's beer stood for the ordinary company, and there finding an old can without a lid, went and drew it full of beer himself, and drank it off to the Lord Admiral".[1]

In the same month that witnessed the launch of the *Prince*

[1] *Archaeologia*, 12. 201–3; Nichols, ii. 365–9; Birch, *Life of Henry, Prince of Wales*, pp. 208–9.

Royal a royal proposal arrived for Elizabeth. The King of Sweden was eager to obtain a lady of whom "he had heard such great report" as bride for his heir, Gustavus Adolphus. His offer was made in due form through ambassadors. But the King of England could not think of sending his daughter to a country so distant and at war with her dear uncle Christian of Denmark. A month later, Prince Maurice of Nassau's name was added to the list of unsuccessful suitors for the Lady Elizabeth's hand.

VII

For the past five reigns the hamlet of Kew, picturesquely situated on the east bank of the Thames, less than ten miles outside London, had been a favourite resort of courtiers. The district had an additional attraction for Lord and Lady Harington. At Twickenham Park their elder daughter, Lady Bedford, reigned as patroness of a brilliant literary circle.[1]

The site of the house at Kew in which Elizabeth Stuart lived during her early teens cannot now be identified, but Lord Harington's residence was evidently not palatial. When his son threatened to develop measles there in the spring of 1611, he flew to his pen to acquaint Lord Salisbury with the situation and ask for advice. Although none of the princess's servants were being allowed to go near the patient, yet "in respect that this house is little", her guardian deemed it might be wisest to send her to Whitehall where her lodging was always furnished.[2] No detail of Elizabeth's health was left unreported by her careful guardian. Her father was even advised of some attacks of nose-bleeding.

The year 1611 brought changes in the fortunes of two prominent figures of her father's court, startling enough to have served

[1] Ben Jonson, Daniel, Drayton and Chapman were amongst the men of letters who eulogized the learned Lucy, Countess of Bedford.
[2] S.P. 14. 62. 7.

as texts for the gravest of Lord Harington's homilies. Her cousin, Arbella Stuart,[1] vanished for ever into the Tower of London.[2] Her father's young Scottish favourite, Robert Carr, attained such eminence that he was popularly credited with responsibility for the king's angry dismissal of his first Parliament.

Robert Carr first attracted James's attention at a tilting

[1] She invariably signed herself "Arbella", though in other contemporary documents the variants "Arbel", "Arabel" and "Arabella" are to be found. Her unusual Christian name had been given her in memory of a Lennox ancestress, wife of Robert II of Scotland.

[2] Arbella Stuart was the unfortunate result of a match engineered by the ambitious "Bess of Hardwick", Countess of Shrewsbury, between Elizabeth Cavendish, a daughter of her second marriage, and Charles Stuart, Earl of Lennox, the brother of Darnley and a great-grandson of Henry VII. Whenever Queen Elizabeth wished to annoy James I, she hinted that Arbella was her rightful heir. After his peaceful succession, however, he treated his delicate, accomplished little kinswoman with favour so long as she showed no signs of wishing to marry, but early in 1610 Arbella at last wished "to taste of the forbidden tree". At the age of thirty-five she had fallen passionately in love with a gallant twelve years her junior. William Seymour, whose descent from the Suffolk line made him particularly obnoxious to James, was summoned with his lady love before the Privy Council, and there gave his oath never to marry her without the royal consent. Arbella was restored to favour, but on July 9th was arrested and detained in a house at Lambeth. Seymour was sent to the Tower. They had been secretly married for sixteen days. Her second arrest took place on board a French vessel in the Straits of Dover. She had disguised herself in truly Shakespearean manner, "by drawing a pair of great French-fashioned Hose over her Petticoats, putting on a Man's Doublet, a man-lyke perruque with long Locks over her hair, a blacke Hat, black Cloake, russet Bootes with red tops and a Rapier by her syde". Seymour, who had also escaped, but failed to meet her, reached Ostend safely. James, exasperated and convinced that they had been plotting with Rome against his throne, then sent Arbella to the Tower. She languished there for four years, growing gradually more hysterical, writing endless and increasingly illegible letters, and performing elaborate needlework which James refused to receive. Early in the year that saw her cousin Elizabeth's happy marriage Arbella was said to be "distracted". Her reason seems to have been always most delicately poised, and it is possible that the frustration of her autumnal love-match did impair it. She ordered "four new gowns whereof one cost above £1,500" in wild hopes of an invitation to appear at Elizabeth's wedding. But James had been too badly frightened to forgive. Her last letter is that of a broken-spirited but not a mad woman. She died in the Tower on September 20th, 1615. Birch, *Court and Times of James I*, i. 124; Winwood, iii. 279.

match during the King of Denmark's visit in 1606, when he was thrown from his horse and broke a leg in the royal presence. He was the son of a poor Scots knight, a little above middle height, flaxen-haired, blue-eyed, fair-complexioned, . and not without courage and intelligence. Henceforward, until the departure of the king's daughter from England, and for two years after that date, Carr was James I's arch-favourite. What Elizabeth thought of the bold adventurer, whose downfall was to provide the darkest chapter in the chronicles of her father's court, is not on record, but all contemporary writers agree that her beloved brother, Prince Henry, detested him. Three indeed [1] tell a scandalous but not incredible tale that the idealistic prince's hatred of Carr arose from the fact that they were rivals in love. According to them, Lady Essex, born Lady Frances Howard, the most unscrupulous beauty of a society in which "the holy state of Matrimony was made but a May-game", fixed upon the king's favourite as her victim only after she had ascertained that the king's heir was not going to offer her marriage. She was at this time eighteen, of an angelic, infantile, blonde type, and still nominally the wife of the lethargic and bewildered young Lord Essex, to whom she had been contracted in childhood.[2] Whatever Henry's feelings

---

[1] Sir Anthony Welldon (*Secret History of James I*), Sir Simonds D'Ewes (*Autobiography*) and Arthur Wilson (ed. Kennett).

[2] Lady Essex obtained a decree of nullity on the grounds of her husband's incapacity and, in December 1613, was married to Carr with great splendour. He was created Earl of Somerset shortly before the wedding. In May 1616 the couple were tried on the charge of having murdered the learned and accomplished Sir Thomas Overbury, a friend of Carr, who had opposed their marriage. The lady, who cut a very poor figure after her arrest, pleaded guilty, but Carr, although pressed by James, steadfastly refused to do so. Both were condemned to death, but eventually pardoned, and died in obscurity and mutual loathing. A number of persons of lower rank, convicted of having been their accomplices in administering poison to Overbury, were executed, and a wretched apothecary's assistant under interrogation (S.P. 14. 87. 74) babbled "that Somerset never loved the Prince or the Lady Elizabeth" and that he had been offered £500 to go to Elizabeth's court. His last dark saying is explained by the fact that the prince's sudden death was attributed by enemies to Carr, and Elizabeth was

towards her may have been, he "disdained the least notion" of an alliance between her brother, Lord Howard of Walden, and his sister.[1]

Another foreign princeling had been rejected as too poor a match for Elizabeth. "The 23rd of June, arrived Prince Otto, sonne and heire unto Morris, Langrave of Hessia, attended with thirtie persons, and accompanyed with the young Countie of Nassaw. This Prince was very honourablie entertained of the King, Queene, and Prince of Wales. . . . He was seventeen yeeres of age and demeaned himselfe in all things very princely and bountifully. He returned the third of August." [2] September brought a proposal from the Duke of Savoy for a double marriage between his two eldest children and those of James I. This was more seriously considered, for ever since the death of Henri IV the chances of a double marriage with his eldest children had been diminishing. Marie de Medicis, the widowed queen-mother, was determined on alliances with Spain.

By an odd stroke of fortune, no sooner had hopes of seeing his daughter Queen of France been relinquished by James I, than a possibility arose of her becoming Queen of Spain. Philip III was well acquainted with Elizabeth's desirability, for he had been engaged in supporting the suit of his young nephew, Victor Amadeus of Savoy. Finding himself suddenly left a widower, he instructed his ambassador in London to enquire, with the utmost secrecy, what chances there were of her changing her religion. Don Alonzo de Velasco got to work, and found the princess's mother so much a Catholic at heart, and so flattered by the prospect he offered, that he waxed indiscreet. Within three weeks of the Queen of Spain's death,

---

expected to be the poisoner's next victim (*State Trials*, ii. 786–866 and 991–1020; *Narrative History of King James I*, Chapters IV–XXXIV; "Truth brought to Light," 1651; *Cabala* 36. 38. 54; *Journal of Sir Simonds D'Ewes*, pp. 68–80; Winwood, iii. 453–75; Nichols, i, 707–45; S.P. 14. 72. 120; Kennet, ii. 686 *et seq.*).

[1] D'Ewes, p. 48.   [2] Somers ii. 424.

E

Englishmen in both Madrid and London were openly discussing the rumour that Philip the Pious wanted their princess
"for himself".[1] He was eighteen years her senior, and reputed
to be so virtuous as hardly to have committed a venial sin.
But he was also reputed to be entirely under the dominion
of his favourites, and without the capacity which would have
qualified him to manage a small country estate. Englishmen,
headed by the Prince of Wales and the English Ambassador in
Madrid, were loudly indignant in consequence of complacent
Spanish reports that their princess was perfectly prepared to
abandon Protestantism for a crown. Elizabeth never received
a formal offer from Philip III. When Don Pedro de Zuniga,
Ambassador-Extraordinary, arrived in England, he found the
situation by no means as it had been represented by Velasco.
He was fully empowered to demand the princess for his master,
should her father raise no objection to her changing her religion.
But articles for her marriage with a Protestant suitor were
already being drawn up. Don Pedro made the best of the affair
in his despatches home, hinting that the lady herself was willing,
but that her brother, "a great heretic", had publicly announced
that whosoever should counsel his father to give her to a
Catholic prince was a traitor. Since the Spanish Ambassador
had refrained from demanding her, the much inferior match
with a Protestant prince was to be concluded. It is very likely
that Henry did make some of the unguarded remarks attributed
to him by Don Pedro, for he was already in cordial communication with the Protestant candidate for his sister's hand
mentioned by the Spanish Ambassador. And at some time
during these months when her fate was being settled, he
comforted Elizabeth by planning with her, in secret, a scheme
that should unite their future fortunes. After her marriage he
would conduct her "on her way into Germany to the utter-
most boundaries of the States" and with her guidance choose

himself a Protestant bride. To please his father, he was still appearing to consider the prospect of marrying the second daughter of France, but as old Lord Salisbury had predicted,[1] "our brave Prince may find Roses elsewhere, instead of this Olive". The German rose on whom, according to his confidants, his fancy was set, was a sister of Prince Otto of Hesse.[2]

Sir Walter Raleigh was still a prisoner in the Tower. "None but my father", said Prince Henry, "would keep such a bird in a cage!"[3] The prince sent to the prisoner, asking for his advice as to the wisdom of accepting the Duke of Savoy's proposals, and Sir Walter set himself down to express a considered opinion which covered many pages. He described the much-courted Elizabeth enthusiastically, as "by nature and education endowed with such princely perfections, both of body and mind, as may well deserve to be reputed a worthy spouse for the greatest monarch in Christendom". As far as Sir Walter Raleigh could see, "this excellent young princess, the only daughter of our sovereign, the dear beloved sister of our prince and one of the brightest jewels of this kingdom", had nothing to gain by allying herself with "a poor popish Duke of Savoy". Amongst the great Elizabethan captain's reasons for despising the Duke of Savoy was one truly characteristic. "The duke hath no Port (his ditch of Villa Franca excepted, which is only capable of a few galleys)", and a prince without a port could "neither stead us in time of war nor trade with us in time of peace". He painted a gloomy picture of Elizabeth "removed from her native soil, far from her nearest blood, both by father and mother, into a country as far estranged from our nation as any part of Christendom, and as far differing from us in religion as climate. . . . And this also we may be assured well of, that if she should have any issue by the Prince of Piedmont, they must all be bred and brought up contrary to her conscience." His lengthy document

<hr>

[1] Winwood, iii. 291.   [2] Winwood iii. 410.   [3] Coke, i. 71.

drew towards its close with hopes, expressed in courtier-like language, that his Highness would not ask his opinion as to what prince would be likely to make the princess happy. It ended by giving exactly the advice which he had humbly begged to be excused from offering. Some overtures had, Sir Walter believed, been made on behalf of the Prince Palatine of the Rhine. "Certainly he is as well born as the Duke of Savoy and as free a prince . . . of our religion. From the little judgment God hath given me I do prefer the alliance of the prince of the Rhine and the house of Nassau more than I do the alliance of ten Dukes of Savoy."

This was the alliance favoured by Henry for his sister, and, what was more important, the one on which their father had decided.[1]

VIII

On a June day in 1611, a black-robed lady seated in the castle of Heidelberg wrote anxiously to a gentleman at Sedan—"I fear that our delays will make us lose this beautiful princess, and that while we trifle and palter, Savoy will carry her off."[2]

She wrote an elderly, scratchy hand, and looked more than her age, which was six and thirty. Her severe black damask gown and stiffly wired widow's head-dress set high on a massive brow did not become her, for though her figure and features were marked by dignity and determination, both were homely. She secured her letter with black silks and a black seal, bearing a coat of arms of many quarterings and the initials L. I. P. C. Louisa Juliana, widow of Frederick IV, Count Palatine of the Rhine, and daughter of the late William, Prince of Orange, surnamed "the Silent", was a princess of many virtues but few personal attractions. Like many another important

---

[1] *Sir Walter Raleigh's Works*, viii. 234 *et seq.*; Birch, *Life of Henry, Prince of Wales*, p. 329; Somers ii. 231.
[2] S.P. 78.58.19.

parent in Europe, she had decided that no prince was so worthy of the Princess Royal of Great Britain as her beloved first-born son. For some time past she had been goading every influential male relative she possessed to help her to her desires. Her martial brother-in-law, the Duke of Bouillon, to whom she was now addressing herself, had already done much on her behalf. In the previous February he had forwarded to the King of England a description of the young Count Palatine, which, if partaking somewhat of the nature of an inventory, had at any rate the merits of its defects. To future biographers of his nephew it was to prove invaluable.

Frederick V, Elector Palatine of the Rhine was, declared his uncle by marriage, of perfectly virtuous morals, and physically free from blemish. He had a dark complexion—*le teint noir.* His countenance was agreeable. He was of a prompt spirit and well-trained in bodily exercises, particularly horsemanship. He was an advanced Latin student and spoke French admirably. He possessed several palaces and parks, "some of the prettiest places that can be seen". At the age of eighteen he would attain his majority, and take up his duties as first Elector of the Holy Empire. As far as dependants went, he had a younger brother and three sisters.[1]

Three months after receiving his sister-in-law's anxious letter, the duke found himself in Paris. He seized the opportunity, while he was in the capital, to have a long, intimate talk with the English Ambassador, the pleasant and accomplished Sir Thomas Edmondes. The duke could speak with authority on the subject of the young Count Palatine, for the boy was being educated under his own eye at Sedan. Louisa Juliana had primed her deputy with three leading questions to put to Sir Thomas. All needed tactful handling.

Firstly, she was a little disturbed that the English princess was

[1] "Memorial from the Duke of Bouillon on the state of the Elector Palatine." S.P. 81.11.30.

so near to her son in age. Frederick had been born on the 15th of August, 1596, Elizabeth on the 19th. They were both, therefore, just fifteen. But at such an age a girl is notoriously more mature than a boy. Would the King of England be prepared to wait a little for the consummation of the marriage?

The Electress was also vexed by reports that an offer from Savoy, for the princess's hand, previously rejected, had been renewed and was receiving re-consideration. Unless her son's suit was likely to meet with "good acceptance" she would prefer that his guardians did not proceed to a formal proposal on his behalf.

Her third question dealt with the princess's exalted rank. Was it likely that the young lady would expect "a more chargeable entertainment, in respect of the eminence of her birth, than would stand with the constitution of their state to bear?" The prospect of this marriage had given great satisfaction to the Count Palatine's subjects, but they, headed by his mother, were naturally apprehensive lest the princess "by reason of her great birth" might wish to introduce customs unknown to them, "which would be of too high a flight".

Edmondes was most sympathetic and encouraging. He believed that the answers to the Electress's questions, all of which he would instantly forward to his master, would be satisfactory. But before parting from the duke he would like to be given a more exact notion of what high-flown ideas the princess might be supposed to entertain. The duke then mentioned with great earnestness the number of the retinue that she might bring with her. It was much hoped that she would restrict her train to the number allowed to previous foreign brides of Electors. Germans, he quite unnecessarily reminded Sir Thomas, were "very strict and formal" with a great regard for tradition. . . .[1]

Edmondes was as good as his word, and the result was so

[1] S.P. 78.58.161 et seq.

reassuring that the painstaking duke proceeded to his next task, getting the King of Denmark to second his nephew's proposal. Unfortunately, since Frederick was still a minor, the consent of the Princes John and Maurice of Nassau and Christian of Anhalt Bernburg had to be obtained before every advance in the negotiations, and presently it appeared that the King of England was not inclined to keep his daughter disengaged unless a proposal in form was ventured. Other candidates, he disagreeably intimated, had not hesitated to make offers because they were uncertain of acceptance.

Nevertheless James had made up his mind. The Count Palatine of the Rhine might not be a reigning monarch, but he was not a suitor to be scorned. As far as lineage went, his family ranked, in the opinion of contemporaries, as "the third if not the second Family of Christendom derived from a masculine extracted prince". The house of Mecklenburg was given first place by these genealogists, and that of Bourbon second.[1] Moreover, the Elector's maternal grandmother had been a Bourbon. The first Count Palatine of the Rhine had been an officer of the Imperial household in the tenth century. His descendant was the premier prince entitled to elect the Emperor—the Elector-Prince, the Palsgrave, or Palace-Count.[2]

[1] D'Ewes, p. 53.

[2] The Pfalzgraf was, before the dissolution of the Imperial power in the thirteenth century, one of the Empire's chief officials, administering districts held directly from the crown but not belonging to the Emperor. The Emperor had usually been a duke of Saxony, Franconia or Swabia holding paternal rights in them, distinct from his rights over crown lands not in his duchy. When the empire began to disintegrate and such hopeless candidates as Richard of Cornwall, Alfonzo of Aragon, William of Holland, etc., were nominated, the family, which at the moment included the "Comes Palatii", retained as much of their lands as they could hold by force. A tract extending on both sides of the Rhine to the borders of Alsace on one bank and to those of Würtemberg on the other, with Heidelberg as its capital, was called the Lower Palatinate. A larger tract called the Upper Palatinate was north of the Danube, west of Bohemia. With typical medieval German folly, the Counts Palatine cut off scraps of their property for younger sons—Neuburg, Simmern, Sulzbach, etc.

And his title was not nobler than his domains. Best of all, the young count would in time take his place as recognized head of the Evangelical Union founded by his father to protect the interests of Protestantism. James had decided that the time had come for him to give one child at least to a Protestant mate, and to enter into a defensive alliance with the Protestant union of German princes. The King of Spain and the Queen-Mother of France had been distressingly distant of late, and his faithful Commons were very present and increasingly tiresome. The marriage of the Princess Royal to a virtuous young Calvinist would be popular. Once James had made up his mind, the alliance moved steadily, though not rapidly, towards its conclusion. The Duke of Bouillon, attended by the Elector Palatine's representatives and "divers other young Gentlemen of Quallitie", arrived in London at length, and on May 16th in his presence, articles for the marriage of his nephew and the Princess Elizabeth were drawn up. Her father assured the duke that "since the first speech and overture" from the Count Palatine the princess had been kept "from so much as once hearing the style of love". The Papist Prince of Piedmont had been rejected. "To make her Queen of the World the King would not so abandon her."[1] Forty thousand pounds was the portion assigned with the bride, to be paid within two years of her marriage. The dowry settled on her by her bridegroom was to be ten thousand per annum in case she survived him, and for the present fifteen hundred a year for her minor expenses. Thirty-six men and thirteen women of her suite from England were to be provided for by him. Her father would pay the expenses of her journey as far as the town of Bacharach on Rhine.

The elder line at Heidelberg died out in 1559, and Simmern (the nearest cousin) succeeded and reunited his property to the main body. Frederick V held the duchy of Nussbach in North Bavaria, and is styled in all contemporary documents as a duke of Bavaria, but his family had been, since the Reformation, at deadly feud with the Duke of Bavaria proper, a Catholic Wittelsbach ruling from Munich.

[1] Winwood, iii. 272.

As she was to receive a marriage portion no larger than that brought by previous electresses, her father would augment it by annual donations which would enable her to live in the style to which she was accustomed. Nine Englishmen and six Germans sat in conference over this treaty. The chief German was the Prefect of the Palatinate, John, Count of Solms. "Out of a German jealousy," the Palatine representatives did all they could to negotiate without the duke;[1] however, at last all details were arranged. For the security of the princess's dower, Neustadt, Germersheim, Oppenheim and some other lesser Palatinate towns should be put in possession of her trustees. She should have her own chaplain, and be allowed to worship according to the rites of the church in which she had been reared. She should be at liberty to reside where she chose. If her union should be blessed with children, the King of England's consent must be obtained for their marriages.[2] (The Prince of Wales was still a bachelor, the Duke of York still delicate, and it was six years since the queen had borne a child.) The princess herself expressed a desire as to one clause in her marriage treaty. Hearing that it was proposed to pay part of her revenues in produce, not specie, she intimated that she would much prefer this German custom to be followed. She fancied that by such regard for their traditions, she would be likely to win the hearts of her future subjects.[3]

In July the Count Palatine's Steward of the Palace, Colonel Schomberg,[4] arrived in England with letters from his master for the Prince of Wales and the Lady Elizabeth. Everyone was amused that by mistake he presented to the prince a *billet doux*, and to the princess a letter hailing her as a future brother-in-arms.[5]

---

[1] Winwood, iii. 365.   [2] Devon, p. 157.

[3] Landsdowne MS. 160.129.149; Foedera, vii. II. 183–6; Harl. MS. 5112.119.

[4] Colonel, Count Meinhard von Schönberg always signed his surname so, but both his French and English contemporaries called him " Schomberg ". As Elizabeth herself generally followed this fashion, it is here adopted.

[5] S.P. 14.70.38.

The count returned to Heidelberg with enthusiastic descriptions of the promised bride. To the Electress, soon to be dowager, he confided fears that her son might not cut a sufficiently dignified figure in the sophisticated English court. Louisa Juliana sent to the "magnificent" Duke of Würtemberg, and his dancing-master was borrowed for a month, to instruct the Count Palatine of the Rhine in deportment and the latest dance-steps. On August 29th a letter to *"Ma digne Princesse"* begging her to accept as a suitor one upon whose soul her merits were indelibly engraved, and whose eyes hoped soon to behold her, was despatched to London.[1] On September 17th the widow's son left home. Somewhere on his journey to the Hague he was met by an extremely high-flown note of compliment from Elizabeth, dated Richmond. The assurances of devotion sent to her by the Elector were cherished by her with the more affection, said the princess, because the commands of a father, whose will was to her law, enjoined her to accept them. This document[2] was evidently considered a pattern by the bridegroom's aunts, for the Duchess of Bouillon sent a copy to her sister, the Duchess of Thouars, who preserved it in a château in Anjou. From Holland Frederick sent one more polite epistle in a large, carefully schooled hand-writing to the Prince of Wales, and one more love-letter to the Lady Elizabeth. Her royal highness's very humble, very obedient and very passionate suitor was delighted to hear that she approved of the match arranged for her by her very honourable father. He longed for a favourable wind.[3] Frederick landed at Gravesend at 11 P.M. on October 16th, after a ghastly passage, attended by his uncle, Prince Henry of Nassau, Count von Solms, Colonel Schomberg, six other counts, seven privy councillors and a train numbered at about a hundred and fifty persons.[4]

[1] Aretin, vii. 143.   [2] *Archaeologia*, 39.150.
[3] Aretin, vii. 144–5.   [4] S.P. 81.112.18 & 141.

IX

In England, all "the best affected" had long wished for "the Palsgrave of the Rhine in good Devotion".[1] Frederick was popular before he set foot on English soil. Friendly crowds gathered along his route towards London to behold "this German enter". A contemporary poet, whose work bears strong evidences of familiarity with *Venus and Adonis, The Rape of Lucrece* and *A Midsummer Night's Dream,* declares that scholars ran from their books, smiths from their hammers and suitors from their mistresses to catch a glimpse of young Frederick, descendant of Charlemagne. Since this author's description of Elizabeth's first meeting with her suitor is supported by more prosaic eye-witnesses, there is reason to hope that the other anecdotes which he relates in his Nuptial Ode are founded on fact. The second book of his narrative opens "above Neckar's cleare floode". There, in a chamber of his gorgeous palace, young Frederick, fair as Ganymede, lies wrapped in dreamless slumber. The prince's appearance is so disarming that Cupid remorsefully relinquishes the dart which he has prepared to shoot, and instead anoints the sleeper's bare breast "with juice of myrtle-hill". On waking, Frederick feels strangely melancholy, until, wandering in his picture-gallery, his moody eye lights upon a portrait of the Princess Royal of Great Britain. Henceforward a frenzy of energy possesses him, and he can think of nothing but "my journey towards Elizabeth". His sea-passage is described, far from truthfully, as having been most auspicious. Cupid is at the helm of the galleon, which is assisted on its course by an odd collection of benevolent inhabitants of the Ocean—"the Daulphin swift, the sea-calfe, hugely-throated, the Lobsters bold, the mullets merrily running, the Turbuts soft and Scaves, for fatness noted". The bride awaiting Frederick is fully as enchanting as her portrait.

[1] Winwood, iii. 301.

"As violets excell the bramble briar, Lilly the viollets, that the Rose disgraceth, Eliza so doth Virgins." Her beauty, in fact, as she advances, "with her golden tresses dangling, clad with rich tissues" is so dazzling that "th' amorous Palatine" loses the use of his limbs and remains "trembling cold as ice", until "her rosie lips" meet his. "Fair Elizabeth" calmly salutes her suitor, and "a modest-mannered kisse, nectarine-sweet, revives the daunted Rhine". There is witchery in the air though, for no sooner has Elizabeth thus greeted Frederick than she begins to feel herself troubled by sensations hitherto unknown to her. " 'Aie me!' quoth shee, 'what sodaine motion's this? How is my breast clogg'd with a bitter sweet.' " She finds herself unable to sleep. "To look at what she loves she lifts her eye, but dare not look for feare some other spy." Her Mother-Queen says with a knowing smile, "Our Daughter is in love". [1]

X

When the imposing Duke of Lennox, attended by several nobles, appeared at Gravesend to congratulate the Elector Palatine on his safe arrival and conduct him straightway to London, they found a well-mannered, athletic young Rhinelander much dismayed. The fact was that out of his fleet of eight ships, three had been so badly injured in the North Sea that they had been obliged to put back to Holland. The luckless youth, who had been provided with many fashionable attires in which to do his courting, had been left with no clothes except those in which he had suffered his dismal first experience of sea-travel. However, the sixteen-year-old suitor replied "merrily" that although he knew that he should have presented himself to his mistress loaded with false glitter, he

[1] "Most Auspicious Marriage between the High and Mightie Frederick, Count Palatine of the Rhine, Chief Server to the Sacred Roman Empire, Prince Elector and Duke of Bavaria, and the most illustrious Princess, the Lady Elizabeth, her Grace. Joannes Maria de Franchis." London, 1613.

would show his devotion by hastening to her in humble guise.[1]
He was soothingly assured that his host was prepared to greet
him not as a visiting prince, but as a member of his own
family.

Accordingly, on the cold, wind-swept evening of Sunday,
October 18th, a salute of eighty guns from the Tower announced to the princess that her suitor was drawing towards
her at last, and Elizabeth joined her parents and brothers in
the torchlit new Great Chamber of Whitehall Palace. She had
arrived from Kew the day before. "A great barge" had trans-
ported her "trunckes and other necessaries" to the Cockpit,
where scented juniper branches were being burnt in her maiden
chamber "against her coming thither".[2]

The Palsgrave, who had ordered that, in spite of the inclement weather, the windows of the barge carrying him
should be left open, received an ovation all the way up the
river, and was greeted on the water-steps of the Palace by the
twelve-year-old Duke of York. The lessons that the bridegroom had received from the Duke of Würtemberg's dancing-
master had left their mark, and eagle-eyed courtiers agreed
that as he passed through their midst towards their master, he
was "bold and manly". "His approach, gesture and countenance were seasoned with a well-becoming confidence."
James advanced several steps from his chair of state to embrace
his future son-in-law, and Frederick, after baring his head and
performing a "due reverence", told the king, "amongst other
compliments, that in his sight and presence he enjoyed a great
part (reserving it would seem the greatest for his mistress) of
the end and happiness of his journey". He delivered himself of
this carefully rehearsed speech in French, and in so low a voice
that it was scarcely audible, but James caught enough of its
drift to interrupt him with hearty *bonhomie*, "Say no more
about it! Suffice it that I am anxious to testify to you by deeds

[1] Nichols, ii. 463.   [2] P.R.O. E. 407.57. (2).

that you are welcome!" Frederick next bowed before the
queen. Anne of Denmark, who had longed to see her daughter
a Catholic queen, had been indisposed when Colonel Schomberg had sought to visit her during his mission to England. The
contemporary poet before quoted describes how the young
Elizabeth would "oft unto her mother queen sweetly commend
this prince's pedigree. How oft would she have blushing ready
been, to tell the titles of his emperie".[1] But Anne was not prepared to be impressed by the titles of the Count Palatine's
emperie. She had tried to put her daughter against the match
by telling her that "Goodwife Palsgrave" would henceforward
be her title.[2] To this Elizabeth, secure in her favourite brother's
approval, had replied with spirit that she "would rather be the
Palsgrave's wife than the greatest Papist Queen in Christendom".[3]

Now that she had him before her, Anne "entertained the
Palsgrave with a fixed countenance, and though her posture
might have seemed (as was judged) to promise him the honour
of a kiss for his welcome, his humility carried him no further
than her hand". Frederick turned with relief to Henry, Prince
of Wales, whose failure to meet him at an earlier point of his
progress had been much noted, and Henry exchanged courtesies with him in "a familiar strain". At last the suitor was at
liberty to end his greetings "where his desires could not but
begin—with the princess". Naturally, her demeanour had been
the subject of close scrutiny to-night. Many present had
noticed that until the moment in which Frederick approached
her personally Elizabeth had not "turned up as much as the
corner of an eye towards him". She waited motionless, with
downcast lids, until she became aware that he was before her,
"stooping to take up the lowest part of her garment to kiss it".
The princess then began a great curtsey, noticed to be as grace-

[1] Elizabeth took great interest in pedigrees and was proud of her
Plantagenet blood. Wendland, 165. 169.
[2] Howell, i. 165.   [3] Coke, i. 73.

ful, but lower than those she usually performed. She stretched out a hand to prevent her suitor making "that humblest reverence" which he was proposing. She thus "provided him, as he rose, of a fair advantage". This advantage "th' amorous Palatine" took, and kissed her with *aplomb*. The blonde princess saw the "*visage agréable*" of "*teint noir*" promised by the Duke of Bouillon. The prince saw "my soul's star".[1][2]

XI

Frederick was provided with lodgings at Essex House, Strand, and in Whitehall. On the day after his arrival he paid an early call on Elizabeth. She received him in her apartments in the Cockpit, which had been newly hung with tapestries representing the history of Abel. During the evening he called upon her again, and thenceforward no invitations from the Prince of Wales to tennis, rides or "running at the ring" could lure the Palsgrave from attendance on his princess. He seemed "to take delight in nothing but her company and conversation", and Londoners heard with satisfaction that "the speach is the yonge Princess lykes him well".[3] On the second evening of his visit, "as he sat to supper", a message arrived from Elizabeth, asking him to accompany her to a play performed by her own servants. The next day they were "all day together" at the queen's dower palace of Denmark House, famous for its waterside flower-garden with luxuriant rosemary hedges.[4] Throughout the week that followed the young couple met continually "without curiosity of bidding".[5]

Thursday, October 29th, had been chosen for a banquet at the Guildhall in honour of the Palsgrave. The Prince of Wales was expected, but "he failed". Frederick, after witnessing a

[1] Two eye-witnesses accounts of the first meeting of Elizabeth and Frederick exist. Ellis, III. 4.170–3; Dupuy MS. Bibl. Nat. 648.213 (245).
[2] Aretin, vii. 188. [3] Ellis, III. 4.173.
[4] These were noted by the Prince of Anhalt during his visit to England in 1596. Rye, p. 204.
[5] Birch, *Court and Times of James I*, i, 198, 201.

City pageant, was escorted to the feast, throughout which he discoursed gravely in Latin with the Archbishop of Canterbury. The cultured but morose George Abbot, who had known Elizabeth since she was seven, and favoured the young Calvinist prince's pretensions to her hand from the first, now entered upon a genuine friendship with him. "After dinner the Lord Mayor and his Brethren, in the behalfe of the Cittie and Cittizens of London, for testimonie of hearty welcome and love", delivered to the Palsgrave a noble gift of silver-gilt plate. Frederick made a good impression on all present, and his courtesy in going to pay his respects to his hostess, the Lady Mayoress, and her train, at the conclusion of the entertainment, was particularly commended. In the evening a water pageant on the Thames was marred by stormy weather.[1]

Naturally the Prince of Wales's defection caused astonishment. He enjoyed solemn feasts, and had himself been host at "the most magnificent and best ordered that ever was seen" only a few weeks before, in the park of his palace of Woodstock. He had sat, with his sister beside him, "in a great summer-house of greene boughs" at this last *fête champêtre* of 1612, and only broken off festivities at Woodstock so as to haste "home again to Richmond, because of the news of the Palsgrave's approach, whom he intended to grace with all possible honour".[2] An announcement was made that an attack of fever had prevented the Prince of Wales from attending the Guildhall banquet, and the performance of a play fixed for Sunday night at Whitehall was cancelled. On Sunday afternoon the king, queen, princess and Palsgrave "with divers others of the court", all visited the invalid and left him "reasonably cheerful". Next morning he was reported "somewhat amended". Many people learnt now for the first time that he had been ill for a week. On the preceding Monday and Tuesday he had been observed playing cards with his brother and Prince Henry

[1] Nichols, ii, 466–7.   [2] Somers, ii, 232.

of Nassau, but it now appeared that he had risen from bed to do so. In spite of reassuring reports, disquieting rumours began to spread. Members of the prince's household were well aware that for some time past their young master's health had not been satisfactory. There had been insomnia, headaches and fainting fits. He had been over-working himself, and, what was worse in contemporary opinion, had been exposing himself to night air, delighting "many times to walke late at night by the river's side, in moone light, to hear the trumpets sound an echo". His custom of bathing in the Thames directly after supper had long been a source of anxiety. Little more than a week before, on a sharp October day, he had played a particularly vigorous match of tennis "in his shirt, as though his body had beene of brasse". Nobody had been able to dissuade him from rising repeatedly from a sick-bed, with fever upon him, to entertain his sister's future relatives. The princess, happy with her suitor, was foremost in Prince Henry's mind as he lay abed at St James's, with "deep-sunk eyes", crazy with thirst and headache, "calling for his cloak and rapier", "he must be gone". Still courtiers did not realize that his "tertian fever" was serious, and the principal discussion at Whitehall was as to who should succeed Lord Salisbury as Secretary. Sir Henry Wotton, poet and diplomatist, a close friend of the prince, was held to have "lost his chance by an epigram". He had declared that an Ambassador was "an honest man, sent to lie abroad for the good of his country".[1]

On Wednesday, November 4th, the king was persuaded by the prince's physicians not to enter an infected sick-chamber. He found St James's besieged by visitors, and before he retired issued orders that none "save those who of necessitie must tend upon him" should be admitted to the patient. After that, only the Archbishop of Canterbury and the Dean of Rochester obtained entry. A lady who came more than once from Whitehall

[1] S.P. 14.71.28.

F

to St James's after dark was repulsed in the king's name. The Princess Elizabeth had disguised herself in a vain attempt to reach the prince's side.[1] She had paid a pound to a coachman and two footmen belonging to the household of her little brother, for escorting her on her secret errands.[2]

On Thursday, November 5th, a dismal procession set out from Whitehall for Theobald's Park. The king, having given Theodore Turquet de Mayerne, chief court physician, authority over all the other doctors attending a case now pronounced hopeless, left the capital. Henry, Prince of Wales, died quietly, after a succession of fainting fits, a little before eight o'clock on the following evening. His last words, spoken "in good sense", were "Where is my dear sister?" The first announcement that he was unwell had been made only eight days before, and it had been succeeded by reports that he was better. Consequently "in many places near the city" people heard of his serious illness and his death together. Inevitably the cry of "Poison!" was raised.[3]

XII

On the morning of Monday, November 9th, an equipage containing three young creatures in deep mourning drew up outside the Kensington mansion of Sir Walter Cope. Prince Charles, Princess Elizabeth and the Palsgrave, "all together in one coach", had come to condole with the bereaved James I. Their experiences during the next few hours were terrible, for James loathed the sight of mourning, and affliction did not ennoble him. He complained that "the wind blew through the

---

[1] S.P. 14.71.31.   [2] P.R.O. E. 407.57(2)7.

[3] Birch, *Court and Times of James I*, i. 201–5; *Life of Henry, Prince of Wales*, pp. 334–58; Somers, ii. 231–44; Nichols, ii. 466–89; *Archaeologia*, 15.19; Dupuy MS. 648.213 (243). James and his favourite, Robert Carr, were accused by scandal-mongers of having caused the prince's death by poison. Dr. Norman Moore's pamphlet *Illness & Death of Henry, Prince of Wales in 1612, an Historical Case of Typhoid Fever*, London, 1882, demonstrates that this accusation was unfounded.

walls" of his host's house, so that "he could not lie warm in his bed".[1] Young Frederick bravely quoted consolatory passages from the Bible to the scholar king, and presently James, touched by the Palsgrave's evident sincerity and surprised by his address, entered into a long conversation with him regarding the late prince's symptoms during his illness.[2] When James returned to Royston ten days later, "he carried the Count Palatine along with him".[3] Her "very faithful very obedient and very humble servitor" sent from Hertfordshire another pretty love-letter to his lady.[4]

Frederick's position was now most uncomfortable. The prince's pompous funeral could not take place for a month, and many people prophesied that after it the Palsgrave would have to depart home empty-handed. His marriage to the Princess Elizabeth would have to be postponed until the court was out of mourning. May-Day was now mentioned as the earliest possible date for a ceremony which might never take place. For now only a delicate younger brother stood between the Lady Elizabeth and the throne of England.[5] Already several persons had been summoned before the Privy Council for uttering disparaging remarks about the proposed match.

At Heidelberg, the widowed Electress was horrified by the news from England, but at present could do no more than pen a superb letter of sympathy to King James.[6] Throughout England poets and poetasters were pouring fourth elegies, many containing passages of remarkable bathos.[7] Frederick put his

---

[1] Birch, *Court and Times of James I*, i. 205–7.
[2] *Beschreibung der Reiss, etc.*, p. 16.
[3] Nichols, ii. 489.
[4] Aretin, vii. 145.
[5] Dupuy MS. 648.213 (245).
[6] S.P. 81.12.58.
[7] See "The Three Sisters' Teares, shed at the late solemne Funerals," by Richard Nicolls, London, 1613; "Great Britaine all in Blacke," by John Taylor, London, 1612, "The Laudable Life & deplorable Death of our late peerless Prince," by James Maxwell, London, 1612; and "The Period of

household into mourning at great expense, and on December 7th followed Prince Charles in the procession that bore the body of Henry, Prince of Wales, to burial in Westminster Abbey. The Palsgrave's long train of black velvet was carried by "Monsieur Shamburgh". His suite was led by Abraham Schultz, his head chaplain and Dr Christian Rumph, his chief physician, who had been called into consultation by the English court physicians during the late prince's illness. The procession began to muster at 6 A.M., and moved off four hours later. In the Abbey Frederick occupied the Dean's stall. After the service a life-size "Representation" of the late prince, in coronet and robes of estate, was left lying on the hearse which had borne his coffin, "to be seene of all", until December 19th.[1] The Ambassadors Extraordinary sent by foreign powers then began to hurry home, and those who had expected "a black Christmas" experienced a surprise. They had reckoned without their king's detestation of gloom. A private investiture of the Prince Palatine with the Order of the Garter took place on December 18th, and the ceremony of his betrothal to the Princess Elizabeth on the 27th of the same month. Frederick warmly appreciated his admission into the fraternity of the Garter, and no subsequent portrait of him [2] failed to show him decorated with its insignia. Yet the scene of his investiture cannot have been impressive. James was crippled by a sore toe, which, as usual, "must not be called or christened the gout". He received

---

Mourning," by H. Peacham, London, 1613. The last-named contains a description of the author's discovery, in a cave, of—

> "a meagre wretch alone,
> That had with sorrow both his ei'n outwept,
> And was with pine become a Sceleton.
> I ask'd him why that loathsome Cave he kept,
> And what he was. 'My name,' quoth he, 'is Death,
> Perplexéd here for Henrie's losse of breath.' "

[1] Nichols, ii. 493–512.

[2] Excepting those in which he is depicted in the character of a classical warrior.

gout.

Frederick "sitting up in his bedd; after a few wordes put the George about his neck. It was forgotten to have first dubbed him knight". However, the diamond star and ribbon which the king bestowed upon his future son-in-law had belonged to Prince Henry, and in another chamber of the palace the Princess Elizabeth and the Archbishop of Canterbury were waiting to offer their congratulations.[1]

The betrothal took place in the Banqueting-House, which had been garnished for the occasion with valuable tapestries and Turkey carpets. From an early hour in the morning the gallery overlooking the hall was packed with spectators. Frederick appeared first of the royal party, "apparelled in purple velvet, richly laced with gold lace, and his cloak lined with cloth of gold", a costume considered "very fair and suitable". "The lady, to make an even mixture of joy and mourning, wore black satin [2] with a little silver lace, and a plume of white feathers in her head; which fashion was taken up the next day of all the young gallants of the court and city, which hath made white feathers dear on the sudden."[3]

The ceremony was short and simple. James, standing under a canopy on a dais, kissed the young couple, blessed them, and "directed them to go down, hand in hand, some twenty paces or more, into the middle of that great room, where was a carpet spread on the floor for them to stand upon". There they were met by Sir Thomas Lake, proud to be deputizing as Chief Secretary, and much in hope of securing that post for life. "Swiftsure" had been his nickname in the days when he had been Walsingham's amanuensis. Unfortunately his duty to-day entailed translating into French "the formall words 'I, Frederick, take thee Elizabeth to my wedded wife, to have and to

[1] S.P. 14.71.68; *Beschreibung der Reiss, etc.*, pp. 15–23.
[2] Her gown was made of twenty yards of black satin, brocaded with silver flowers.
[3] This is the only recorded occasion upon which Elizabeth set a fashion in dress.

hold, etc.' ". His translation was so odd, and his French accent so incredible, that "an unseasonable laughter" attacked Elizabeth, Frederick and many of the spectators. The Archbishop of Canterbury did his best to save the situation by pronouncing the benediction prematurely. The king was still unwell, so did not go on to the chapel to hear a sermon preached by the Bishop of Bath and Wells, but at the ensuing supper he was noticed to be extremely cheerful. The queen did not appear at any point during the festivities. Gout was announced as her reason for indisposition.[1]

XIII

Abundant material exists from which to draw a picture of Elizabeth's last months in England. Lord Harington of Exton's accounts of her household expenditure, dated from Michaelmas, 1612, to Lady Day, 1613, are available,[2] and no contemporary news-writer could resist the temptation of filling his sheets with such popular matter as a royal wedding: full descriptions of her trousseau have been preserved.[3]

Elizabeth went hunting in Nonesuch, Hampton Court and Richmond Parks. She was seen taking the air on horseback in the parks of St James's and "Marybon" and in Hyde Park. She performed many little acts of charity. She benefacted people on the high road as she passed towards London, "the poore women that weeded in the garden at Greenwich", "a poore Scotch woman that preferred a petition", "a poore gentleman whose estate was decayed", "a poore widow with a great nomber of yonge children", "a blind harper", "a Danysh woman" and "the prysonners of the Fleete". "A Scotchwoman that offred to singe to her grace at Kewe" and "a northern boy

    [1] S.P. 14.70.170; *Beschreibung der Reiss, etc.*, pp. 49–40; *Court and Times of James I*, i, 216–17.
    [2] P.R.O. Exchequer of Receipt Misc. E. 407.57 (2).
    [3] Add. MS. 5751.27. These interesting accounts have never been published *in extenso*.

that whistled to her grace" were given ten and five shillings respectively. She stood sponsor to "a Lyttle child", and gave a pound to its nurse for bringing it for her inspection. She lost a favourite dog and a ring: both were recovered. Her evenings were gay. Payment was made to "a Turkie Jugler that shewed tryckes to her Grace and the Palatine", and to Walter Tucker "that playeth to her Grace when she danceth". Her Grace played billiards and cards, and lost a wager to Mr Edward Sackville, the handsomest man in England. Many entries are to be found of tips to servants of the Palatine, who brought her letters from their master and, on several occasions, delicacies for her table—Rhenish wine, and "a pyke, dressed after the German fashyion".

The princess bought herself seventeen pairs of silk stockings, "a very lyttle watch" and an amethyst carved in the form of a bunch of grapes. Milk in pails, for a milk bath, was ordered to her lodgings. Her lace-trimmed body linen of "cobweb lawne" and "cambricke", and her "damaske table-lynen" were washed "in conduyt water". Mr Isaac (Oliver) painted her in miniature, as a gift for Lady Chichester, the younger Harington daughter, and Mr Marcus (Gheeraedts) achieved a full-length portrait destined for Mr John Murray of the king's bedchamber.[1]

An entry in an office-book of John, Lord Stanhope of Harington, Treasurer of the King's Chamber, 1613–16, discloses one of the most interesting facts concerning Elizabeth's last amusements as a maiden princess.[2] At some date between her elder brother's death and her marriage,[3] the Lady Elizabeth, in

[1] Sir John Harington records in his memoirs that he too received a picture of the princess. There is, however, a curious absence of portraits of Elizabeth at her father's court. They probably lurk under the name of "Queen Elizabeth", having been wrongly identified, although the costume worn by Elizabeth Tudor in youth differs unmistakably from that worn over seventy years later by her namesake.

[2] Rawlinson MS., Bodleian, Oxford, A. 239. f. 47v.

[3] Elizabeth's name takes precedence of Frederick's in Lord Stanhope's memoranda. After her marriage her husband's name took precedence in all contemporary accounts.

company with her younger brother and "the Prince Pallatyne Elector", witnessed "fowerteene severall playes" at Whitehall. The author of six of them was William Shakespeare. "John Heminges", to whom payment was made for the productions, was the actor colleague to whom Shakespeare subsequently left a bequest in his will, and one of the two editors of the first folio edition of Shakespeare's plays. The six of the great dramatist's pieces enjoyed by the three young royalties were "Much Adoe aboute nothinge", "The Tempest", "The Winter's Tale", "Sir John Falstafe" (*i.e.* "Merry Wives"), "The Moore of Venice" (*i.e.* "Othello") and "Caesar's Tragedye" (*i.e.* "Julius Caesar"). A persistent legend declares that "The Tempest", a play containing the love-story of an island princess and an elaborate nuptial masque, was written, or at any rate refurbished, for production on Elizabeth's betrothal night, December 27th, 1612. But no contemporary document explicitly assigns the performance to this date. It is sixth of the plays in Lord Stanhope's list. Shakespeare himself was certainly in London this spring before Elizabeth left England, for on March 10th, 1613, he bought a house in Blackfriars, the ground floor of which was a haberdasher's shop.

No royal wedding had taken place in England for nearly seventy years. During the winter of 1612 the country became a nest of singing birds. Since the two events followed so closely upon one another, many of the odes celebrating Elizabeth's nuptials were published and bound together with elegies on her brother's death. The effect is somewhat grim, and more than one admirer of "Europe's phoenix" lamented the heartlessness of a populace that turned so readily from mourning to merriment. There is ample proof that Elizabeth, although she took part with zest in gaieties, did not forget her loss now or hereafter. A poet with an elegy and a servant of Prince Henry who brought her property that had belonged to their master, were given five pounds apiece at her command. One day during this "strangest winter that 'was ever seen for Warmth and Wet", she went by barge with Frederick to visit Westminster Abbey, where "amongst the representations of the Kings and Queens his famous predecessors", the effigy "of Prince Henry, as he went when he was alive", was still on view. On another afternoon the betrothed couple went by water to Putney.

New Year's Day, not Christmas, was the popular date for exchange of gifts. On New Year's Day, 1613, Elizabeth received many additions to her *ménagerie*. Prince Henry of Nassau sent "four Island dogges", Lord Delvin "an Irish dogg", Lady Wigmore another dog of unspecified breed. Sir Thomas Roe's man brought a strange gift from a far country—a parrot—and a servitor was sent forth to buy "canarie seedes" for its dinner. Young Sir Thomas's first voyage of discovery to the Amazon had received personal encouragement from the late prince. The Haringtons' elder married daughter sent "a phesant", Lady Dorset, a bracelet, Lady Frances Egerton, a scarf, Lady Cary, "a very fayre wrought sweete bagg, out of Devonshyre". "A great baskett of aples", "muske mellons", a "great longe cake", "dryed peares and other fruytes out of France" were also delivered by pages and gardeners at the Cockpit.

The rich young Palsgrave behaved with such munificence that finally the King had to forbid him to make any further offerings. Elizabeth's present from him was a diamond necklace, wreath and earrings, and "above all two Pearls, for Bignes, Fashion and Beauty esteemed the rarest that are to be found in Christendom". Frederick's popularity increased when it was discovered that forty thousand crowns' worth of his gifts had been purchased in England. He gave Prince Charles spurs, and a rapier set with diamonds, and Lord and Lady Harington "golden and gilt plate" valued at two thousand pounds. Elizabeth's ladies received "medalias" engraven with the likeness of their donor, and "Mistress Dudley", the Harington niece who had been Elizabeth's companion since childhood, got as well a splendid diamond and pearl necklace. Most appropriately, the Palsgrave's chief officer, Colonel Schomberg, had fallen in love with the princess's chief *demoiselle d'honneur*.

Frederick attended Christmas Day service in the chapel at Whitehall with his future relatives, and heard himself prayed for amongst the king's children.[1] Ten days later James departed from London to hunt at Royston. But before he left, he consented to fix his daughter's wedding day. The Duke of Bouillon, who understood the King of England's character, had written urgently on the subject directly after the death of Prince Henry. He had addressed himself to the arch-favourite, Robert Carr. James had replied that he thought the wedding might take place shortly, but that Frederick must be prepared to leave his bride in her native country until Whitsuntide. This scheme did not commend itself to Frederick. James's next proposal was that the wedding should take place on May-Day. If Frederick found himself obliged, by any summons from his principality,[2] to return home before that date, the wedding could always be celebrated at three days' notice. But he would have to depart alone. Frederick held out for a wedding as soon as possible, and his bride's departure from England in his company. When his doting mother at Heidelberg heard that the ceremony was at last definitely fixed for February 14th, she hastened to hold James to his promise by a letter of elevated sentiments majestically expressed. She could not sufficiently thank his Majesty for the honour done to her son. Her life would henceforward be devoted to her daughter-in-law's service.[3]

The princess's trousseau was set in hand. Her apartments in the Cockpit became crowded by merchants and tailors. Frederick spent a week hunting with her younger brother. From Hampton Court he wrote to James, reporting that he

---

[1] Winwood, iii. 421.
[2] The Lutheran Duke of Neuburg was suspected (quite correctly) of being about to turn Catholic.   [3] Bunnett, pp. 127–8.

and his "dear prince" were having excellent sport. "To-morrow, after dinner, we shall hunt again and in the evening return to Whitehall, and relate our adventures and pleasures to my very dear lady, who will greatly regret that she has not been a sharer in them."[1] On February 7th a Chapter of the Order of the Garter was held at Windsor, and Frederick was publicly installed. His banns were read there for the last time on the same day, and his bride took up residence in St James's Palace.[2] Anne of Denmark was observed to be growing so pleasant to her future son-in-law that hopes were entertained that she might after all condescend to grace next Sunday's ceremony with her presence.

The list of persons appointed to posts in Elizabeth's future household was being drawn up, and Londoners complained that it contained far too many Scots names. The Scots, for their part, having sent a wedding present of twenty thousand pounds,[3] were requesting that the bride might be styled "Prin-cess, and eldest daughter, of Scotland", not "Princess of Great Britain". What was worse, though yet unknown, was that Lyon Herald "expressly sent for" to attend the nuptials, was preparing to present himself in a coat "with the arms of Scotland before those of England."[4]

On February 11th public rejoicings began "with a sumptuous and unprecedented display of Fireworkes on the Thames". The weather, which had been "foul", took a sudden change on this day, and became "exceeding clear, sweet and pleasant", a happy state of affairs which continued for a fortnight. The complete royal family, attended by their suites, witnessed the display from "galleries and windows about Whitehall". It opened "with a peale of ordnance, like unto a terrible thun-der", which shook the earth, and the explosion, from the dusk

---

[1] Maitland Club, 20.
[2] Elizabeth's banns were also called thrice at St Margaret's, Westminster (old Cheque-book of the Chapel Royal, Whitehall, ed. Rimbault, p. 254). The ringers of St Margaret's received 2s. 6d. for ringing their bells on her wedding-day.   [3] S.P. 14.71.64.   [4] Winwood, iii. 435.

waters, of a rocket which "mounted so high into the Element that it dazeled the beholders' eyes to looke after it". A set piece, representing St George and the Dragon, continued "flying in the ayre a quarter of an hower or more", and was succeeded by "another strange peece of artificiall Fireworke", the semblance of a stag-hunt. "Hunting hounds, made all of fire", pursued a hart "up and downe the waters, making many rebounds and turns . . . as if it had beene a usuall hunting upon lande . . . to the greate delight of his Highnes and the Princess".

On Saturday night, the wedding eve, a sea-fight between thirty-eight vessels—"The Christian navy opposed against the Turkes"—was staged upon the Thames. It began at two-thirty, in daylight, and ended about six. The royal family watched it from the privy stairs of Whitehall Palace. The opposite shore was completely transformed by stage scenery. A watch-tower, and Turkish castle, "set upon craggie rocks", hid Lambeth marshes, from which ordnance thundered continually. By the time that the actor taking the part of the English Admiral "in a very triumphant manner" carried the vanquished Turkish Admiral "with the Bashawes and other Turkes, guarded" to the palace stairs, only Frederick and Elizabeth remained at their posts in the chill dusk to receive them. A disparaging account of these pageants states that the fireworks were "only reasonably well performed. The Castle of fire, which bred most expectation had worst success. . . . Likewise the Fight upon the water came short of that show and brags had been made of it". Moreover "there were divers hurt . . . one lost both his eyes, another both his hands, another one hand".[1] [2]

[1] Nichols, ii. 587.
[2] "Heaven's Blessing and Earth's Joy, or a true relation of the supposed Sea-Fights and Fire-Workes as were accomplished before the Royall Celebration of the all-beloved Marriage of the two peerlesse paragons of Christendom, Fredericks and Elizabeth," by John Taylor, the Water-Poet, London, 1613.

XIV

The outstanding feature of the document detailing Elizabeth's trousseau is the recurrence of the words "verye richẻ". The "Warrant to the Great Wardrobe on the Princess Elizabeth's Marriage" [1] covers an enormous sheet of vellum, and its items include not only her personal attire, but the costumes of her bridal train, her household, and the actors who took part in Campion's "Lord's Masque" on her wedding night. Several suites of furniture are also described, and the merchants' bills for materials are interspersed amongst those of the tailors, shoemakers, embroiderers, button-makers, hosiers, hatters, upholsterers and joiners. It is an unfortunate fact that fashions were both elaborate and unbecoming when this princess of sixteen, universally acclaimed as beautiful, chose her trousseau. Nearly all the absurdities of the Elizabethan period, in their highest accentuation, had been adopted by Anne of Denmark's court, and some had developed. Over her body-linen the court lady of 1613 wore a tightly fitting corset of whalebone and buckram, rigid and inflexible, to the base of which was attached a horizontal wire shelf, designed to display the radiating plaits around the waist of her farthingale. To this again was attached the hoop, over which were draped the petticoat and gown. Elizabeth ordered eight pairs of "whalebone bodies". They were stiffened with canvas and buckram "sized" and covered with carnation satin and crimson damask. "A proclamation against farthingales" was issued this winter, in view of overcrowding at the wedding festivities, but "to little purpose, for they rather increased than diminished". [2] Their flat, table-like edges now projected so widely that, in repose, a lady's hands must either dangle helplessly or be folded and laid upon the shelf. The "Great Ruff" had gone, but it had

[1] Add. MS. 5751.27.
[2] Kennett, iii. 279. Birch, *Court and Times of James I*, i, 228.

been succeeded by an upstanding wired lace collar, and on her exposed bosom every lady exhibited the largest possible display of jeweller's art. The hair was tortured by curling-tongs, combed upwards from the forehead and arranged over a conical wire erection, and adorned with jewels, ribbons, flowers and feathers. Elizabeth, on her wedding day, wore her hair flowing on her shoulders, in token that she was a virgin bride, but her fair tresses had been "frizled" by irons. Ladies whose locks were not abundant had recourse to quantities of false hair and pads. The hats designed to cover these "high-tired" heads naturally had to be high-crowned. Only eight hats are recorded in the "Warrant to the Great Wardrobe", four of beaver and three of felt, all trimmed with gold cord and feathers. The fashionable pattern was a tall, cylindrical crown, set in a hard, narrow brim. Since they had to be fitted over so elaborate and easily disarranged a *coiffure*, hats were not much worn. Ladies often preferred to go out of doors bareheaded, and protect their complexions with masks.

The materials of which Elizabeth's gowns were made have a lovely sound—"riche ashe-coloured silk grograine, brocaded with gold and silver", "tyssued tabine", "deer-coloured satten", "sea-green tyssue", "russet cloth of golde", "white cloth of silver, tyssued in borders, and flowers like Prince's feathers". Unfortunately there is no doubt that bale upon bale of them was ruthlessly cut up to make pointed stomachers and long, tight-fitting sleeves, with padded shoulder pieces. Yards were tightly pleated. Only in the skirt and petticoat could the beauty of a material be discerned, and even there brocades, already patterned, were further adorned with silk embroidery, and trimmed with jewelled borders, "goldsmith's work", bunches of ribbons, metal laces, fringes, tassels and spangles. Thousands of buttons of all kinds were commanded to decorate the costumes of Elizabeth and her attendants—"verye riche Barbarye buttons", "black Paris buttons", round gold Milan buttons, Compass, Bugle, Ribbon and "Highe Sugar-loafe" buttons.

The laces and ribbons used all advertised themselves as being of foreign manufacture. Venice gold chain and silver loop lace, Milan bone lace, Spanish and Venice silk ribbons and French "shag" and "muffe" are enumerated.

Many of Elizabeth's garments, including twenty-six gowns, are described in detail. She had one "Lappe Mantle and Cloake" of tawny, two-pile velvet, fur-lined, another of "silvered velvet". Two riding-gowns, of metal-brocaded satins, had tissue sleeves. Her store of petticoats was large. She had them of green satin, brocaded with gold flowers, of tawny tissue, embroidered in coloured silks, and of carnation and murray-coloured satins, lined with plush and embroidered in gold, in silver, and in both. Five of her twelve farthingales were of "changeable taphatas". Two bodices "had greate sleeves of ye Spanishe facon", and two "night-gowns,[1] tyssued very high in severall flowers", were lined with carnation wrought satin. Carnation and black were the shades most favoured by the blonde princess for her own wear, and tawny for her staff. A couple of gowns with trains were respectively of cloth of silver and of "riche tawnie clothe of golde". Both were adorned with "goldsmith's work". In the first she was married; she wore the second on her wedding night and for her triumphal entry into Heidelberg.

Over five hundred and twenty yards of "riche plaine white Florence cloth of silver" were commanded for dresses for "Bride-Maydes" and the decoration of the bridal chamber. On this apartment were further employed two hundred and sixty-one and three quarter yards of black, crimson and coloured taffetas, and four hundred and forty-five and three quarter yards of velvet. The upholsterers' and "joyners'" bills follow those of the silk-mercers, and the furniture covered by these materials is fully described. The "Sergeaunte Paynter" presented an account for gilding the woodwork of stools and

[1] A night-gown was a dressing-gown, or a *négligé*, at this date, not slumber-wear.

chairs and a "large screen, wrought to the top with a Lyon, carved, holding a scutcheon". This screen appears again in a carpenter's bill, together with charges for "little tables" and "a folding-table of walnut-tree".

The bridal "bedsteed" erected in the palace of the late Prince Henry was nobly accoutred. Its mattress, bolster and pillows were of Milan fustian, filled with down and sewn with silks. It had "two payre" Milan blankets, and four fine Spanish blankets. Its quilts were cased in taffetas. "Eighte plumes of feathers" decorated with Venice gold and spangles were used at the four corners of the canopy surmounting the great four-poster. A linen-draper's statement mentions hundreds of yards of fine Holland cloth "for curtains and sheets".

Gifts "sent to the said Prince Palatine" are entered amongst the last items of Elizabeth's expenditure. These were "a riche scarfe, embroidered all over upon carnation taffetas, both sides alike, with gold and silver and coloured silks, and sundry devices; to hang a Sworde at", and "One Sworde, curiously carved and gilded".

XV

Elizabeth arrived at Whitehall for her wedding shortly before noon, on Sunday, February 14th. Her progress to the chapel was by a route designed so that as many people as possible might behold her.

Mr John Chamberlain, a gentleman of private means and no profession, who spent his time writing chatty letters to his acquaintance, reached the palace too late, he feared, "to see the Bride go to Church". By ten o'clock the crowds were already overwhelming. However, to his surprise and delight, he found that "a whole window" in the Jewel-House had been reserved for him and his party. It overlooked the "payre of stayres" leading to the Court Gate and open gallery, so he had an excellent, but tantalizingly brief glimpse of Elizabeth "in a suit of cloth of silver, richly embroidered with silver; her train carried up by thirteen young Ladies, or Lords' daughters at least, besides five or six that could not come near it". She was preceded by Lord Harington, and escorted by two bachelors, her brother Prince Charles and Lord Northampton. She was wearing "her Hair hanging down long, and a rich coronet on her head". After her procession came that of her parents. Anne of Denmark, "all in white", was not very rich, thought Mr Chamberlain, except in jewels. The bridegroom was dressed in a suit made of the same material as the bride's gown. "We had as much view as so short passage could give, but the excess of bravery, and the continual succession of new company, did so dazzle me that I could not observe the tenth part of what I wished."

Two other gentlemen of leisure give accounts of Elizabeth "in her Virgin-robes". One, who evidently had an even better view than Mr Chamberlain, describes her costume at length. She had, he says, "upon her head a crown of refined golde, made Imperiall by the pearles and diamonds thereupon placed, which were so thicke beset that they stood like shining pinnacles upon her amber-coloured haire, dependantly hanging, playted down over her shoulders to her waiste, between every plaight a roll or liste of gold-spangles, pearles, rich stones, and diamonds, and, withall, many diamonds of inestimable value embrothered upon her sleeves". Her train was borne "in most sumptuous manner by fourteen or fifteene Ladies, attired in white satten gownes".[1] "The Prince Palatine and that lovely Princess, the Lady Elizabeth", announces Mr Arthur Wilson,[2]

---

[1] Mr. Anstis's Narrative, Leland's *Collectanea*, v. 33. The number of Elizabeth's bridesmaids is a vexed question. "The Warrant to the Great Wardrobe" mentions gowns for six "bryde-maydens" only, each gown consisting of twelve yards of Florence cloth of silver. Another contemporary account states that both the bride and bridegroom had as many attendants as the years of their age—sixteen. [2] Kennett, ii. 690.

G

"were Married upon Bishop Valentine's Day, in all the Pompe and Glory that so much Grandeur could express. Her Vestments were White, the Emblem of Innocency." His account of "her Hair dishevl'd, hanging down her back at length", under a golden crown "all over beset with precious Gems, shining like a Constellation", exactly tallies with those of other spectators, but he insists that her train was supported "by Twelve young Ladies in White Garments so adorned with Jewels, that her Passage looked like a Milky-Way".

Whatever their number, the noblemen's daughters who attended Elizabeth "like a skye of celestial starres upon faire Phoebe" had to relinquish her train to Lady Harington directly they entered the chapel. While a full anthem was sung, followed by a sermon by the Bishop of Bath and Wells, the bride sat on a stool, by the side of her mother, attended only by her governess. Opposite them on the same "stately stage or scaffold . . . about five feet in height and about twenty feet in breadth" sat the king, Prince Charles, the Palsgrave, and his uncle, Prince Henry of Nassau. James was wearing "a most sumptuous blacke suit, with a diamond in his hatte of a wonderfull great value".[1] Behind him stood Lord Arundel, bearing the sword of state. The dark young bridegroom wore on the breast of his silver suit the diamond George which his bride had presented to him. The chapel "in Royall sort adorned" had amongst its hangings, a set of tapestries interwoven with gold and silver, representing the Acts of the Apostles;[2] its altar was loaded with gold plate. The steps leading up to the raised platform were covered with oriental carpets, and the railings enclosing it were draped with cloth of gold. "The extraordinary care of the Earl of Suffolk, Lord Chamberlain" in guarding the chapel doors so that "not one person but of

[1] Later during the day, when discussing the "braverie" exhibited at his daughter's wedding, James estimated the jewellery worn by himself, his wife and his son at nine hundred thousand pounds sterling.

[2] Duplicates of a set at the Vatican, designed by Raphael for Leo X.

honour and great place came into it" was much commended. No contemporary relates the feelings of "the young Lords and Gentlemen of Honour, and younge Ladies and Bridewomen", who, together with "the necessary attendants upon the King and Queen", were obliged throughout a lengthy ceremony to stand "all below upon the pavement".

After the full anthem and sermon, another anthem began. During it the Archbishop of Canterbury and the Bishop of Bath and Wells retired to the vestry "to put on their rich copes". When they reappeared they took up positions in front of the altar. At last "the organ ceased", and the Archbishop and Bishop ascended on to the "stately stage". The bride and bridegroom rose from their stools and moved forwards. Dr Abbot married Elizabeth and Frederick "in all points according to the Book of Common Prayer" and the voice of James I answered the question "Who giveth this woman?" The wedding service, unlike the betrothal ceremony, was conducted entirely in English. Frederick had "learned as much as concerned his Part reasonably perfect". Elizabeth was in high spirits and entirely free from nerves or self-consciousness as the words were spoken which made her a wife. "While the Archbishop of Canterbury was solemnizing the Marriage, some Coruscations and Lightnings of Joy appear'd in her Countenance that express'd more than an ordinary smile, being almost elated to a Laughter." Superstitious persons afterwards remembered that for a bride to be so confident invited disaster.[1]

[1] Kennett, ii. 690; Somers, ii. 541–9; *Beschreibung der Reiss, etc.*, pp. 45–52; Birch, *Court and Times of James I*, i. 225–8.

CHAPTER III

THE ELECTRESS PALATINE

I

MANY engravings of Frederick and Elizabeth were published at the time of their wedding. Little trace of the romantic good looks so universally attributed to both bride and bridegroom is discernible in any of these likenesses, hurriedly executed to meet a popular demand. The young couple are eclipsed by their elaborate costumes, and do not even appear to be young. But it is impossible to discount the evidence of contemporary writers that Elizabeth was the most beautiful princess in Europe, and Frederick worthy of her. Mr Chamberlain, who made a special expedition to court to observe them, as soon as possible after their betrothal, decided that the Palsgrave who aspired to a king's daughter, looked every inch a king's son. The only trouble was that Elizabeth's inches already threatened to over-top those of her future husband. "He is much too young and small-timbered to undertake such a task".[1] At sixteen, Frederick was still, in popular parlance, "a beardless boy". But his glowing olive complexion, ardent black eyes and look of youth and health, were evidently attractive, and he had address and culture beyond his years. He was described as a prince "in whom Adonis and Achyllus met, armed with Ulyssius inward furniture". Londoners accepted "the County Palatine" with-out hesitation as an ideal young lover of the Shakespearean model. As for their king's daughter, they dowered her with all the stalwart virtues displayed by the Princesses Marina and Miranda at the Globe.

[1] S.P. 14.72.28.

Portraits of Frederick painted by Isaac Oliver, in England, and by "Michael Johnson,[1] a picturer" on the prince's homeward journey, do much to reconcile the evidence of contemporary prints and writers. The Palsgrave's features exhibit typical characteristics of adolescence: his nose is over-large and his chin is undeveloped. The dark complexion mocked by caricaturists in the days of his misfortune is faithfully indicated, but there is no trace of the "slight squint" that their malice also affirmed, nor does any other later portrait display such a disfigurement. Indeed, had it been remarkable, the Duke of Bouillon would have hardly dared to describe his nephew during early stages of the marriage project as "without physical blemish".

Elizabeth's appearance at the date of her marriage presents no problems. She had inherited her mother's large frame, but was as yet extremely slight. Her hair, described as "amber" and "golden", was not of the same hue and texture as that of Anne of Denmark, whose tow-coloured *coiffure* contrasts unhappily with her high complexion and harsh features in her later portraits. Elizabeth's hair in her teens resembled that of her brother Charles, who is represented, as a boy, with finely curling locks of a brilliant gold. By the time that brother and sister had reached their twenties their fair hair had darkened considerably. Charles, like many Stuarts, went grey prematurely, but there is no evidence that Elizabeth did so. Her last portraits show her with faded brown hair, which displays signs of having been much lighter in youth. Her complexion, too, faded. But in their early teens, both she and her brother Charles had the perfect pink-and-white complexions attributable to easy consciences, regular exercise and carefree existence in country surroundings, where the attendant farms sent up

[1] Michiel Janz van Mierevelt accompanied the royal wedding party on their journey through the States. *Life of Thomas Howard, Earl of Arundel*, by M. Hervey, p. 73.

daily to the Great House inexhaustible quantities of the best capon, cream and butter. No doubt there was flattery of Elizabeth's looks as a bride, but if a princess is not remarkable for a "lovely face", "graceful air" and "pretty feet", she is usually congratulated on other points.

II

The numerous nuptial odes and tracts published on Elizabeth's marriage have not been accorded high praise by literary critics.[1] Neither Dr Donne nor John Taylor produced anything of striking merit on the occasion, and such titles as "Cupid's Journey to Germanie" and "Great Brittaine's Generall Joyes" suggest that the poetasters achieved much that was very silly. In many of the odes mythological and historical characters are represented disporting themselves amongst the English royal family with ludicrous effect. Vulcan, summoned by Venus to overcome a hitch in the Thames-side fireworks, addresses her as "Sweet Duck", and an amazing "Three Graces" —Anne of Denmark, Elizabeth Tudor and Mary Stuart—are described "leaping and dancing" hand-linked, to entertain the bride. There is much shameless sycophancy and doggerel. "Greate Fredericke" and "Elizabelle" are compared again and again with classical deities. "Valentine" and "Rhine" are overworked as rhymes for "Palatine". The sentiment is frequently false. Mr Peacham [2] declares that the nation's anguish for the death of the bride's brother has been assuaged by the hope—

> "That one day we may live to see
> A Frederick-Henry on her knee."

Attempts are made to reconcile a blushing bride to matrimony by the reminder that—

> "Wedlocke, were it not for thee,
> We coulde nor Childe nor Parent see!"

---

[1] Nichols, ii. 624–6, prints a list of eleven volumes of tracts and odes. Oxford University produced 238 Latin epithalamia.
[2] "Nuptial Hymnes," H. Peacham, London, 1613.

Yet there are lovely qualities to be discovered amongst the
screeds of folly dedicated to "Beauty's Queen" on her wedding.
A description of her making her bridal *toilette*—

> "Nymphs of Sea and Land, away!
> Helpe to dresse our gallant Bride . . ."

suggests a Rubens cartoon. The shore-nymphs bring coral,
crystal and amber "bracelets for Alabaster wrists". "Silver-
footed girls" plait "tresses curled by Lydian art" with orient
pearls. Ruby, Emerald and Diamond, "friend of Chastity",
are captured after "search in rockie mounts". "Ebony-skinned
Nymphs of Niger" bring offerings of snowy ostrich plumes
and perfumes. Garlands of white violets and white roses strew
the scene. Another happy passage narrates the appearance of
Hymen "in starry spangled gowne of blew" startling the
February countryside. At once "Frost and Eclipse" vanish.
"Painted carpets of the spring" decorate every valley "whereon
Eliza's foote must tread".[1]

Floral tributes are scattered in Elizabeth's path by more than
one poet. An anticipatory description of her arrival in Heidelberg pictures—

> "The Rhenish husbandman, with axe in hand, Dressing his vines,"

called from his toil by

> "The Hilly-valley Nympes, so nice and neat,
> Some in their kirtles green, some in their blew."

who bear towards their new mistress a wreath containing the
most admired flowers of the Jacobean garden—

> "The Musky-rose, Mair-Gold, Lilly, Tulipan,
> Gallant Gilly-flower, Pinke, Primrose, Pensee and Daffadilly." [2]

---

[1] *Poems on the Marriage of Frederick, Count Palatine, and Princess Elizabeth,*
1613.

[2] The treasures of the herb-garden are also catalogued—Sweet Mar-
joram, Camomel, Southernwood, Thyme, Venus-Hayre, Rue and
Rosemary.

From near-by "Church Holy Ghost", the legendary naiad who
decks the hills around the Neckar with myrtle, mounts her
crowned lion to meet the flower-crowned Electress at the City
Gates.[1]

The hope that a crown of more solidity might be in store for
the Princess Palatine of the Rhine is voiced with fervour in a
poem which contains many curious astrological inferences :

> " Eliza's grace first saw fair Phoebus' raye
> The next unto St Helen's holy day.
> Great Jesu, grant to our Eliza's grace,
> St Helen's fortune and her Empress fate,
> Helen's long life, Helen's Crowne of Empire . . ." [2]

That the bride's father openly boasted of the possibilities of
the match he had made for her was stated by the Spanish Ambassador. Don Alonzo de Velasco, having heard that James had
said "he doubted not but that his son-in-law should have the
title of a King within a few years", made private enquiry,
"whereupon this his speech may be grounded". To his surprise, he discovered it to be "in respect of the Crown of
Bohemia, because they pretend it to be elective". France was
said to be secretly furthering this ambition. The astute Spaniard's comment was, "A thing almost impossible".[3]

III

On the morning after the wedding the sound of music woke
the bridal couple. The king had arrived at St James's "to visit
these young turtles that were coupled on St Valentine's Day"
and "strictly examine" the sixteen-year-old bridegroom
"whether he were his true sonne-in-law". Frederick "sufficiently assured" James.[4] The king presented "sundry jewels"

[1] *Albion's Remembrance of Frederick and Elizabeth*, J. Maxwell, 1613.
[2] *Princess Elizabeth's Happie Entrie*, J. Maxwell, 1612. Payments from
Elizabeth to this author appear in Lord Harington's accounts.
[3] S.P. 81.12.323.   [4] S.P. 14.72.30.

to his daughter, and they all sat down to a meal served in the room adjoining the nuptial chamber.[1] That afternoon there was running at the ring in the tiltyard of Whitehall Palace. "The illustrious Prince Count Palatine, mounted upon a horse of that courage which seemed to stand upon no air", managed his fiery steed "so like a horseman that he was exceedingly commended, and had many shouts and acclamations of the beholders". Elizabeth and her mother, with their attendant ladies, "placed in the galleries and windows of the Banqueting-house as eye-witnesses of these noble delights, smiled with much cheerfulness . . . especially the new-married Bride".[2]

Contemporaries thought it proper to attribute to Elizabeth and Frederick sentiments far in advance of their age. "The feastings, maskings and other Formalities were as troublesome ('tis presum'd) to the lovers, as the Relation of them here may be to the Readers."[3] But there is every reason to conclude that the young couple thoroughly enjoyed the week of uninterrupted revelry which succeeded their wedding. On their arrival at Heidelberg they deliberately planned a repetition of such gaieties.

Of course so many entertainments could not be achieved without *contretemps*, and the Lord Chamberlain's gentlemen were driven distracted. The Spanish Ambassador failed to appear at the wedding banquet, a gorgeous scene, at which the Lord Mayor presented to the bride, in the name of the City of London, ropes of Orient pearls valued at two thousand pounds. The newly built hall was arrayed with tapestries showing the defeat of the Spanish Armada. "The Spaniard was, or would be, sick." The French and Venetian Ambassadors were all too present. They wished to take precedence of Prince Charles, and were indignant that mere stools had been provided for everyone except the bride and bridegroom. Moreover, the

[1] *Beschreibung der Reiss, etc.*, p. 52.
[2] *Marriage of Prince Frederick and the King's Daughter*, pp. 12-13.
[3] Kennett, ii. 690.

wife of the French Ambassador, when the Master of the Ceremonies "squired her up amongst the Viscountesses", tried to
sit above Lady Howard of Effingham.[1] The Lord Admiral's
daughter-in-law "possesst allready of her proper place, as she
called it, would not move lower". By sheer force of character
she kept the ambassadress quiet through the meal, but directly
it was over the lady flew to her husband, who called for her
coach. She was prevailed upon to remain, and at the next banquet—supper on the same day—Lady Haddington gave place
to her without scruple. Lady Howard of Effingham firmly refusing to do so, retired, "forbearing both her supper and the
company".[2]

Next day, Sir John Finet, Master of the Ceremonies, suffered
again. The archduke's Ambassador, who had been invited to
"either dinner or supper or both", made "a sullen Excuse".
He was furious that the Ambassador of Venice, "a meane Republic, served by a sort of Burghers, who had but a handful of
territory", had been asked to yesterday's festivities.[3] A worse
disaster was that on Shrove Tuesday the gentlemen of the
Inner Temple and Gray's Inn, who arrived in many boats and
barges, at the privy stairs, ready to present their vaunted
masque "The Marriage of Thames and Rhine", could not gain
access. The Great Hall was already so full that officials declared
it could not be cleared that night. Also a number of important
ladies were penned in galleries, to which they had rushed to
witness the picturesque pageant of the actors' torchlit arrival.
Sir Francis Bacon, "chief contriver" of the masque, hurried to
entreat the king not to allow it to be "buried quick". James,
"wearied and sleepy with sitting up almost two whole nights",
was inclined to let ill alone. He replied that if the performance
took place they would have to bury him quick. "He could
last no longer." However, he dismissed the dejected company
with "very good words" and a promise that they should be

[1] Anne, daughter and heiress of John, Lord St John of Bletso.
[2] S.P. 14.72.33.　　　　　[3] Nichols, ii. 603–5.

summoned to perform on the following Saturday.[1] This was not an ideal arrangement, for the performance of a piece startlingly entitled "The Dutch Courtesan" had been prepared by the bride's own players for Saturday. Elizabeth, eventually enjoyed both entertainments on the same day, the play in the afternoon and the masque in the evening.[2]

Opinions of spectators as to the comparative merits of the three masques performed this week differ widely. All three have been printed in full,[3] but since music, dances, costumes and scenery were amongst the principal attractions of this style of entertainment, the modern reader is presented with but a wraith of the "shows", each of which was all-important for a single night at Whitehall in February 1613.

Ben Jonson, the queen's arch-masque writer, was abroad, so no contribution came from him. Dr. Campion's "Lords' Masque" shown on the wedding night was generally considered "very rich and sumptuous, yet it was long and tedious." "The Princely Bridegroom and Bride were drawne into these solemne Revells, which continued a long space." Frederick and Elizabeth danced, in company with masquers garbed in white baize and "sattin *couleur de roy*". Eight knights in silver armour were presented by Jove with clay figures, which resolved themselves into female dancing partners. There was a tremendous transformation scene engineered by "Master Innigo Jones"—"a prospective, that seemed to go in a long way". "In the middle was erected an obliske, all of silver, and in it lights of severall colours" and "statues of the Bridegroom and Bride, all of gold, in gratious postures". The show ended at a very late hour with "a lively straine":

> "No longer wrong the Night,
> Of her Hymenean right.
> A thousand Cupids call Away
> Fearing approaching day.
> The cocks alreadie crow—
> Dance then, and goe . . ."

---

[1] Nichols, pp. 589-92.   [2] S.P. 14.72.30.   [3] Nichols, ii. 550-601.

The masque offered by the Middle Temple and Lincoln's Inn on Shrove Monday was advertised as "the most novell, conceitfull and glorious Showe" ever staged in the land, and most people, including the king, do seem to have awarded it the palm. It contained an "anticke and delightful dance". "A dozen little boys dressed like baboones" performed fascinating gymnastics in connection with "a vast wither'd and hollow tree, being the bare receptacle of the baboonerie". Inigo Jones, responsible for "the special structure of the whole work", had staged a gold-mine, and the "Indian habits" designed by him for "Virginian princes" were "altogether estrangeful and Indian-like". An accomplished clown displayed abundance of "cleane jest". Afterwards, Mr George Chapman, author, was astounded to hear "certaine insolent objections made against the length of my speeches".

The postponed "Marriage of Thames and Rhine" took place "with great applause and approbation". "The music was extremely well-fitted, having such a strain of country jollity as can hardly be imagined." But most of the costumes had been observed by many people five days earlier, and in addition Mr Francis Beaumont had, most unhappily, been inspired to number both baboons and statues amongst his *dramatis personae*. Misfortune dogged this show to its close. When the king called for an encore of the statues' dance, it was discovered that "one of the statues was by that time undressed".

On Monday, February 22nd, James left London for Theobalds and Newmarket, "to enjoy this fine weather". Two days later, the bride and bridegroom attended a christening at which the queen stood sponsor. They saw the Lady Anne Cecil baptized in Whitehall chapel, and afterwards took barge, with the infant, to her parents' house, where they were feasted. On the same evening, as they walked together in Whitehall gardens, Elizabeth was surprised by the arrival of a magnificent chariot, attended by coachmen and footmen wearing her liveries.

Frederick presented to a delighted bride a gift intended for her use on her journey to her new home. A French-built chariot was a most acceptable offering to a lady at this date, and the couple ordered from Paris by the Palsgrave this winter, for his wife and mother-in-law, were calculated to have cost him over sixteen thousand pounds. In design they resembled that in which Henri IV had met his death in the streets of his capital three years previously. They were large, cumbrous vehicles, slung upon leathern braces, and capable of accommodating seven or eight passengers. Their equipment included no glass or springs, but they were luxuriously gilded, curtained and up-holstered. A picture of the one presented to Elizabeth [1] shows that its roof, supported by four pillars, which give it the look of a four-poster on wheels, was covered with brocaded cloth of gold, and its interior was attained by flights of steps which folded inside its central doors when it was in transit. The em-broidery with which it was decorated is described as having been of historical scenes.[2]

After the wedding came the reckoning, and, as may be judged from a single glance at the Warrant to the Great Ward-robe, the reckoning on this occasion was likely to be a heavy one. James had taken advantage of the custom which per-mitted the king to call for aid from his subjects on the marriage of his eldest daughter, but he had succeeded in collecting only £20,500. £53,294 had been spent, and another £40,000 must be found for the bride's portion. Further, Lord Harington, who had been empowered to order the trousseau, found him-self faced by bills for £3,500, which he had been unable to meet out of the annual allowance made to him for Elizabeth's household expenses. He was granted a licence to coin brass farthings, known as "Haringtons", but the privilege neither increased his popularity nor greatly relieved his financial

---

[1] Illustrating her arrival at Heidelberg in the *Beschreibung der Reiss, etc.*
[2] *Beschreibung der Reiss, etc.*, p. 67.

distress.[1] James, who had gloried in the "excessive bravery" of his daughter's wedding, was highly irritated when he discovered that it had indeed been excessive. His first economy was abrupt dismissal of the household provided by him for his son-in-law. This "necessity" Elizabeth "took very grievously and to hart".[2] Frederick intimated to a large number of "his own country gallants" who had accompanied him to England to enjoy his father-in-law's hospitality that they would do well to precede him to Germany. He renewed entreaties to be allowed to carry his bride home as soon as possible. But James was still unwilling to part from his daughter, and in mid-March a vague date "after St George's Day, that they may have fair Moon-light Nights at Sea" was still being quoted for her departure.[3] Frederick patiently visited the University of Cambridge, where he was entertained by a comedy which lasted "between seven and eight hours". He pleaded lack of time for a visit to Oxford, which had been suggested as "a good errand for the young married Gentleman".[4] He returned to London, took part in a tilting display with his usual skill, and went with his bride to the Tower, where Elizabeth herself took a match from one of the gunners and fired off a cannon.[5] A royal salute from the royal fortress sounded in honour of the arrival of the newly married prince and princess, and they were escorted to see his majesty's famous ménagerie. His more famous collection of political prisoners in the same building was not exhibited, but the young visitors were far from oblivious of the proximity of these unhappy beings. Colonel Schomberg had been, on behalf of Frederick, to visit one of them. Contrary to expectation, there had been no creation of peers to mark the wedding, and the bridegroom had deliberately left

---

[1] S.P. 14.72.74.   [2] *Ibid.*   [3] S.P. 14.71.74.

[4] He sent, however, to the Vice-Chancellor, a medal with his portrait and a beautiful Latin letter, and "was pleased with his own handwriting to matriculate himself a Member of the University."

[5] *Beschreibung der Reiss, etc.,* p. 72.

to the bride the choice of gentlemen to be knighted on the occasion. The king had accepted six of the names offered by his daughter and rejected two. Frederick now asked his father-in-law, as a parting gift to him, to grant liberty to one of the unhappy band of political prisoners whose lifelong detention in the Tower was a public scandal. His candidate was the least obnoxious possible. Lord Grey de Wilton, the young Puritan noble who had been condemned to death for participation in the Bye Plot, had been now immured for ten years, and his spirit was reported much broken. Frederick made his request, and caught a terrifying glimpse of a James Stuart hitherto unknown to him, not the Princess Elizabeth's "dear dad", learned, lax and loving, but the James Stuart of the Gowrie Conspiracy and Gunpowder Plot. The king expressed amazement that his ingenuous son-in-law "should become suitor for a man he neither knew nor ever saw". Frederick answered respectfully, but firmly, that Lord Grey had been recommended to him by his relatives, the Duke of Bouillon and the Princes Maurice and Henry of Nassau. Lord Grey had been wounded fighting under Prince Maurice in the battle of Nieuport in 1600. James next affected desire to show clemency, but divulged that Lord Grey was about to be brought to trial for fresh misdemeanours. One of his servants had been detected in communication with the servants of another prisoner—the Lady Arbel. "Evill practises were again on foot in the Tower, which first must be examined". Lord Grey, advised by Schomberg of "the germ of the king's answer", abandoned the idea of soliciting a letter of recommendation "from her Highness to the King". Although the German colonel tried to present the situation in the most hopeful light, the prisoner saw that the time had come for him to submit himself "to the will of my God. . . . All done from these princes that I can expect". James's eventual dismissal of Frederick's suit was well calculated to crush a nervous youth. "Son, when I come into Germany I will promise you not to importune you for any of your prisoners".[1] Frederick's discretion endured until he reached Canterbury on his homeward journey, whence he wrote bitterly to Dr Abbot complaining that his father-in-law had treated him not as a son, but as a "jüngling".

This affair may have decided James that the time had come for his son-in-law and daughter to depart for their country to live happily ever after. Preparations for their long-deferred journey proceeded apace, and within three weeks of their visit to the Tower they had left London for the coast.

The "Number and Quallity" of Elizabeth's train was much discussed, and in the opinion of the ubiquitous Mr Chamberlain, she went away "meanly attended by Ladies". The only peeresses to accompany her were Lady Arundel, who was going on to stay at her villa in Italy, and Lady Harington; the only peer's daughters two Harington nieces. The German historian of her journey, who provides a complete list of her household of ninety-seven persons, and is always at work to present everything with the greatest possible prestige, enters under the heading of "Edel Jungfrawen" the name of Louise Mayerne, who was a daughter of the court physician, Dr Theodore Mayerne. But the fact was that Elizabeth, like many princesses before her, took as maids of honour attractive and healthy daughters of gentlemen of reputable family but small fortune.[2] English peers, when they could afford to do so, preferred to market their daughters in their own country. Scottish names predominated amongst Elizabeth's male attendants—Sandilands, Keith, Livingstone, Spence, Gray, Pringle, Ramsay,

[1] Harl. MS. 7002.306; Winwood, iii. 545; S.P. 14.72.120. Frederick was not deterred from approaching the subject again, and in a letter five months later alluded to his "divers importunities" on behalf of "Le Baron Grey." All his efforts were vain. Lord Grey died in the Tower after eleven years detention, on July 9th, 1614.

[2] The appointments of Mary and Anne Boleyn to attend Mary Tudor, Queen of France, are perfect illustrations of this custom.

Elphinstone. Her shoemaker, however, was a Smith. She took one Dane with her, Erich Clemens. Lord Harington had a Welshman as a personal servant—"Morrice oop Price".[1]

On Saturday, April 10th, the royal family left Whitehall by barge for Greenwich. Guns were discharged all along the route, and the banks and bridges were packed with cheering people. Elizabeth never travelled on a Sunday throughout her long journey to Heidelberg. After attending morning service on the Sunday that she spent at Greenwich, she held a little *levée*. Enormous crowds had followed from London to catch a last glimpse of her. She stood with her young husband beside her, while many strangers pressed to kiss her hand. James bore off his son and son-in-law to hunt in Greenwich park next day, and the tremendous *cortège* bound for Margate did not take the road again until the following Tuesday afternoon. This rate of progress was a fair example of what was to follow. Her parents accompanied Elizabeth as far as Rochester, where she was presented with a gift of plate by the Mayor, and went with her husband, father and brother to inspect the dockyard.

Every member of the royal party behaved characteristically when the time came for farewells on the afternoon of April 14th. Anne of Denmark left first. She was going on a progress to Bath. The queen drove off in tears. The princess began to weep. She could not take comfort in her father's vague talk of coming to see her in her own court, or in the prospect of future visits to England. Her heart was, in her own words, "pressed and astounded". James, revelling in the rôle of heavy father, applied himself to Frederick with gusto, and Frederick, much affected, unwarily promised everything James asked. Unfortunately for the Palsgrave's future happiness, this included demands that his bride should take precedence of himself, his mother and any other princess she might meet in Germany. Prince Charles was to see his sister aboard the *Prince*

---

[1] *Beschreibung der Reiss, etc.*, p. 55.

H

Royal. They reached Sittingbourne that night, and Canterbury the next day. Elizabeth then sat six days in the Deanery at Canterbury, waiting for news of a favourable wind. She wrote to James "the king of fathers, the best and most amiable father that the sun will ever see", assuring him that she would never forget him. She also wrote to the Lord Mayor of London, recommending an elderly cook long in her service,[1] and to Sir Julius Caesar, Chancellor of the Exchequer, asking him to settle some bills for farewell presents.[2] She had prepared a large collection of rings for this purpose, but so many unexpected people had begged her for some memento that she had been obliged to apply to her jeweller for a fresh store. "It is fitting for my quality, at the time of my parting from my natural country to leave some remembrance of me, amongst my affectionate friends", wrote the princess, "but that anything employed for my use should rest unpaid does not well become my quality." Since "all these tokens" had been "given with mine own hand" her Royal Highness would not rest easy until she had Sir Julius's assurance that they were paid for.

Bold Colonel Schomberg, undaunted by bad weather reports, had taken most of his master's suite with him and sailed for Flushing. James, perhaps alarmed by his daughter's warmly expressed wish that she might return to him once more to kiss his hands, sent peremptory orders to Prince Charles not to linger any longer at Canterbury. On the 21st April the little prince sadly bade his sister farewell. On the same day Elizabeth left for Margate. Phineas Pette's autobiography takes up the story from this point. The *Prince Royal* had gone aground on her maiden voyage down from Chatham, and there were not wanting persons, "of whom my lord of Northampton was the chief, to persuade the Lady Elizabeth not to venture her person in such a vessel that had so ill a beginning". Elizabeth, however, was determined to sail in the Great Ship named after

[1] Ellis, ii. 3. 231.   [2] Add. MS. 12504.253.

her lost brother. With her husband, the Haringtons and their personal attendants, she was carried out to the *Prince Royal* lying at anchor in Margate roads, and formally received on board by the Lord High Admiral. Lord Nottingham, a veteran of Armada days, intended this voyage to Holland in charge of his sovereign's daughter to be his last official act. The remainder of Elizabeth's suite was bestowed in six other men-of-war, seven merchant vessels and many smaller boats. Her marriage contract allowed her forty-nine permanent attendants of her own nationality, but the persons embarked at Margate numbered nearly seven hundred. Orders were given for the fleet to form into a crescent and follow the Admiral's signals, and all preparations were made for sailing on the first of the ebb. Phineas's journal then reports laconically: "The 22nd, the wind getting Easterly, and likely to be foul weather, her Highness and the Palsgrave and most part of her Train were carried ashore." The luckless travellers disembarked and spent three further nights at Margate. Not until the evening of the 25th were they "all brought on board again; presently we set sail, and that night anchored without the Foreland".

A large oil-painting [1] depicts "The Elector Palatine leaving England with his Bride, 1613". The *Prince Royal*, with Royal Standard and Union Jack prominently displayed, occupies the centre of the picture. Her decks are crowded by gesticulating figures. The scene is very busy. The Admiral's barge is filled with solemn gentlemen, all attired in black suits, white ruffs and black hats. Three other barges are carrying passengers towards three other men-of-war. The waves are crystalline and luminous, the sky is brilliant, but not without cloud. Small craft are accepting last-moment arrivals and luggage and making ready to hoist sail. Some of Elizabeth's luggage must have been ponderous, judging by her coffer-maker's bills for "5 lardge trunckes, barred verye stronge, with verye stronge

[1] By Adam Willaerts, National Maritime Museum, Greenwich.

Locks",[1] and "Timberworke and bounde cases" to enclose twelve "bedsteeds, cheyres, stowles and tables".

On the morning of the 26th April, 1613, the Princess Royal of Great Britain watched the English coast vanish. On the night of the 27th her fleet anchored in view of a sleeping port—Ostend. Twenty-four hours later, after a passage deemed "short and prosperous", the *Prince Royal*, piloted by two pinnaces sent by Prince Maurice of Nassau, "cast anchor happily before Flushing". A salvo of guns greeted her, and presently a boat came alongside and eminent Dutch gentlemen began to come aboard.[2]

IV

The first soldier in Europe supped and spent the night of April 28th on board the *Prince Royal* with the Palsgrave and his bride. Prince Maurice of Nassau had been a favourite hero of the young dead prince, whose gilded likeness stared from the prow of the great British man-of-war, in which there was noble merriment in Dutch waters that spring night. Prince Maurice had gone to the worst wars in the world—against Spain—when he was seventeen. At forty-six he was prematurely aged, a dry-bearded, weather-beaten, baldish gentleman, with a harsh mouth. But his manners were paternal, and at the corners of his wise deep eyes were many little lines caused by merriment. He had never married, but was far from insensible to female charms. He had brought with him, to visit his nephew and new niece, two relatives, one of whom was already well known to Elizabeth. Prince Frederick Henry of Nassau, Prince Maurice's youngest half-brother, was twenty-nine, and a fine figure of a man, dark, full-blooded, with a fierce moustache. He had accompanied the young Palsgrave

[1] Add. MS. 5751.27.
[2] Nichols, ii. 611–13; *Archaeologia*, 12. 268–9; *Beschreibung der Reiss, etc.*, pp. 77–8.

to England, and been the helpful attendant uncle during all the latter stages of the marriage negotiations. Elizabeth's third guest was an exiled semi-royalty who had long made his home amongst his wife's family. Emanuel "Prince of Portugal" [1] was the husband of Amalia of Nassau, Prince Maurice's only sister.

Next day, after an early dinner, Elizabeth entered a barge decorated with crimson velvet, and was rowed ashore by twenty English oarsmen to an accompaniment of joyful music. Prince Maurice was now her host. "Behold here, therefore", says an anonymous chronicler,[2] "a Dutch piece, drawne to the life, no expences being spared." The entertainment provided for her during the next fortnight was indeed overwhelming, and that her progress was slow is not surprising. The "lardge trunkes, barred verye stronge", had all to be disembarked and brought up to strange quarters, where their arrival was eagerly looked for by solemn Scottish footmen and flustered English *filles de chambre*, unable to understand a word spoken by the natives of Zeeland. The princess's many new gowns of metal tissue, variable taffetas and coloured satins had to be unpacked and made ready, together with their correct accessories, for immediate use at a succession of civic welcomes and municipal banquets. Elizabeth's Paris-built coach was not much employed by her in a country famous for its waterways. She walked, hatless and uncanopied, attended by her husband, to the first feast given in her honour by Prince Maurice. Thereafter she used boats and her own feet whenever these seemed the obvious means of transport. Her ready acceptance of their simple customs gave great satisfaction to the "infinite numbers of the Dutch nation" who throughout her progress lined their narrow streets, in

[1] His father, Antonio, illegitimate son of Louis, Duke of Beja, had been unable to maintain his claim to the crown of Portugal against the opposition of Philip II of Spain.

[2] *The Magnificent princely and most Royall Entertainments given to the High and Mightie Prince and Princesse, etc.*, London, 1613.

martial or civic array, let off fireworks and staged pageants
with tireless zeal.

At Middleburgh, after a lengthy banquet in the Rathaus,
Elizabeth gave a farewell audience to Lord Nottingham, who
brought Phineas Pette with him. The sixteen-year-old princess
extended a gracious hand for the master-builder's kiss,[1] and
had ready for the white-bearded Lord High Admiral a letter
gravely commending him to the king his master.[2] This was
the sort of "noble behaviour" of which her old friend, the
Archbishop of Canterbury, heard presently at Lambeth with
great content.[3] She was playing her stately part unsupported,
for Frederick had been obliged to go to the Hague on important business. As head of the Union of German Protestant
Princes, it was his duty to attend the conclusion of their treaty
with the States General. He rejoined Elizabeth at Rotterdam
after four days' absence, and with him came an enthusiastic
lady and gentleman. Sir Ralph Winwood was the accomplished but supercilious English Ambassador to the States
General. As his detestation of Spain was remarkable, he was
delighted to see Elizabeth safely married to the Palsgrave.
Sophia Hedwig, wife of Count Ernest of Nassau Dietz, was a
sister of the young Brunswick prince who had visited England
in vain hopes of obtaining his first cousin's hand. The Princess
of Nassau Dietz had evidently heard stirring descriptions of the
lady her brother had failed to win, for she had determined to
be the first princess in Holland to bid her "near relation" welcome. Several of her Brunswick cousins had tastes in common
with Elizabeth, and Sophia Hedwig was to become a great
friend. She was a fair young woman of twenty-one, with a
look of good-humoured resolution. She had been married for
six years, and had borne four children, of whom only one
survived. She was expecting to be confined again this

[1] Winwood, iii. 459.　　　　[2] *Archaeologia*, 12. 269.
[3] Everett-Green, p. 69.

autumn. Her husband was a soldierly character. He had served under Prince Maurice "ever since he was able to bear arms". The hand of the Duke of Brunswick's daughter had been his reward for helping that martial prince "in bringing his rebellious Subjects to reason".[1]

Elizabeth's procession tacked slowly up and down the United Provinces. No town of size was neglected. At the Hague she was formally received by Prince Maurice at the head of cavalry, and conducted by a troop of burghers to her lodgings. The furniture of one of the rooms reserved for her in Prince Henry's apartments at the Binnenhof had been brought specially from Paris by the old Princess of Orange.[2] The Prince of Orange, Prince Maurice's eldest half-brother, was not present. He resided in Brussels, and never visited his relations, although he greatly desired to do so. After thirty years of captivity in Spain, he had emerged "deprived of all Desire of Liberty", and what was worse, in the opinion of his family, a Roman Catholic. He was "by no Means agreeable to the States of the Union". A French comedy had been arranged for the night of Elizabeth's arrival and a stag-hunt for the next morning. She shot down three stags with her crossbow from horseback, and rode cheerfully home to attend a concert and witness another comedy. Next day she drove out to the adjacent seaside resort of Scheveningen to see wind-chariots racing on the sands, but was disappointed. The spring day was windless. At seven o'clock on the third morning of her stay at the Hague she parted again from Frederick. He was going on to Heidelberg to superintend arrangements for her reception there. Before he left, the perfect son-in-law wrote to James I, explaining his actions and saying that his wife was in good health.[3] Elizabeth attended a military review, spent Sunday quietly as usual, and on Monday, May 10th, gave two audiences, one to the Burgrave of Alzei, representing the Administrator

---

[1] Breval, p. 4.   [2] Winwood, iii. 446.   [3] S.P. 81.12.138.

of the Palatinate, the other to a deputation from the States General who had brought her a wedding present. The Dutch merchants' gift included many diamonds and pearls "in a small cabinet of cloth of gold, betweene a perfumde cushion", a looking-glass in a silver-gilt frame, sixteen pieces of tapestry, six cases of fine linen damask, an entire suite of Chinese lac furniture for a bedroom, and a dinner service of sixty-eight pieces, also from China. At Haarlem, two days later, she received another wedding present, evidently considered by its donors most suitable for a lady who had now been married three months—a cradle and complete set of baby clothes, valued at fifty thousand florins.

Elizabeth toiled up to Amsterdam, to be greeted by bad weather, triumphal arches and a gift of gold plate, and down to the free city of Utrecht, where, with her usual energy, she mounted the tower of the cathedral. From a height of 364 feet she enjoyed a famous panoramic view of the thirty cities of Holland on a particularly clear day. She was bound for Dutch Gelderland now, a district in which there was good hunting to be had. For the present she had done with the solemn cities of Holland, remarkable for their sleepy canals, carillons, sounding strangely on English ears at every hour of the day and night, and churches from which the old Saints had been banished by hammer and whitewash. The princess, whose library included a copy of Foxe's *Book of Martyrs*,[1] cannot have slept in Leyden and Haarlem without hearing rousing and sickening tales of religious persecution.

On her first day in Dutch Gelderland, the first soldier in Europe took her out hunting, in country of pine and birch and heather. At the gates of a small walled city, Prince Henry of Nassau met her with a troop of cavaliers, who engaged in a mock fight to amuse her. The lodging to which she was led after her happy, tiring day was an old Augustinian nunnery.

[1] P.R.O. E.407.57 (2).

The Princess Palatine of the Rhine looked out that night over convent garden walls to a view of the Rhine, running through a plain containing many avenues of poplar and pollarded willows. The name of this place was as pleasant as everything else connected with it—Rhenen. Next day she passed on to lavish hospitality again in a town which held painful memories for one of her suite. Lord Lisle was a younger brother of Sir Philip Sidney. Ernest and Sophia Hedwig of Nassau Dietz were her hosts at Arnhem, a city that possessed two handsome palaces. Their ancestral home was the castle of Dietz, on the Lahn down in Nassau, but as Governor of three of the United Provinces, Count Ernest had a residence in the old capital of the Dukes of Gelderland. Sophia Hedwig presented her infant son to Elizabeth. Nearly quarter of a century later, when Count Henry of Nassau Dietz was a gallant young commander fighting in her cause, Elizabeth recollected his first introduction to her in his nursery at Arnhem.[1] From the town in which Sir Philip Sidney had died of wounds she wrote a neat and stately letter to her father. Now that she was quitting the United Provinces she must not fail to advise him of the " magnificent treatment " she had encountered there.[2] A spice of danger was now added to the novelties surrounding her. She had to pass through disputed territory. The death without direct heirs of Duke John William of Cleves, in 1609, had led to serious complications. His body still lay unburied in Düsseldorf, where the young Margrave of Brandenburg, one of the claimants to the Cleves-Jülich property, was awaiting the Princess Palatine, in company with Count Frederick of Solms, representative of the Duke of Neuburg, rival claimant. But no untoward happenings were destined to mar the Princess Palatine's homeward progress. Prince Maurice provided three troops of horse to escort her procession. On the borders of

[1] In a letter to Sir Thomas Roe, June 7th, 1637. S.P. 16.361.34.
[2] S.P. 81.12.151.

the duchy of Cleves she was met by more troops, sent by the
Council of Regency, to be her safe-conduct. At Niederwesel a
messenger from the Archduke Albert and his wife Isabella of
Spain brought letters congratulating her on her safe arrival,
and begging her to stay in their castle of Rheineck. It lay in
her route from Cologne to Coblenz, but her advisers decided
that, as the choice was between two evils, it was wiser to run
the risk of giving offence by a refusal than of accepting hospitality from a quarter so inimical. A pressing invitation from
the magistrates of Cologne, however, was accepted. Since
their train had now swollen to the number of four thousand,
Elizabeth and her uncles left all their soldiery outside the walls
during their three days' visit to Cologne. The Princes Maurice
and Henry were in close attendance upon Elizabeth while she
made an exhaustive tour of the sights of the celebrated cathedral city, but when news of her intrepidity reached England
it caused wagging of beards.

The month of May was now drawing to a close. Near
Mondorf, a small village four miles north of Bonn, a form of
entertainment hitherto inadvisable owing to weather conditions
awaited the travellers. The young Margrave of Brandenburg
had prepared a magnificent " morning meal " for the Electress
Palatine and her train, " in the open fields spread on the green
sward". Feasting in the open air in the country, accompanied
by a galaxy of courtiers and local gentry, had been a favourite
custom of Elizabeth Tudor, and the picnic enjoyed by her
young Stuart namesake outside Mondorf must have resembled
in many respects those in which the Virgin Queen is depicted
as the central figure. The waggons bringing up hampers of
cold viands, and barrels and flagons of wines, the discomfort
of ladies in farthingales seated on the ground, the flurries and
courtesies of attendant pages and gentlemen in charge of plate
and napery, must have been much the same.[1] But the scene

[1] There is an excellent illustration of such a picnic in Turbeville's *Noble
Art of Venerie*.

was not set in the greenwoods of Merrie England under spreading oaks. Here the background was a wide and smiling plain, running to immense horizons on which were silhouetted the towers and spires of distant towns. In the foreground flowed an enormous and famous river. The peasantry, surprised by the arrival in their fields of four thousand foreigners, were Rhinelanders, driving pale-coloured oxen with large and wondering eyes. So many cold capons and subtleties had, beyond doubt, never been seen by beast or man before in the fields without Mondorf.

This was the place at which the Princess Palatine must embark upon one of the vessels sent by her bridegroom to fetch her, and the Dutch uncles turn home, their duty done. "The much-announced ship ordered from Heidelberg for the Electoral Princess had arrived." George William of Brandenburg handed her on board a vessel garlanded with laurels and bearing her arms and those of Frederick emblazoned on the mast. To her surprise, the accommodation prepared for her in this ship of the Rhine was far more luxurious than the Great Cabin of the *Prince Royal*. A spacious saloon and with drawing-rooms hung with glowing velvets and gold-threaded tapestries, and " a Silver Room hung with green cloth, having a window on one side only", gave access to a fourth apartment designed for her private use. On deck, columns painted to counterfeit marble supported a canopy under which she could repose herself to practise patience and the appreciation of Rhine scenery.[1]

V

The bridal fleet of thirty-four vessels began to move slowly up the wide river. Gradually the scenery changed. Antique fortresses, perched on rocks amongst wooded heights, began to draw in sight. The Princess Palatine of the Rhine learnt the names and legends of Nonnenwerder Islet, Rolandseck and

[1] *Beschreibung der Reiss, etc.*, pp. 86–7.

the Seven Mountains with their "three faire Castles, in one of which the people of the country report that the divell walkes, and holdes his infernall revels". On the first night of her water-progress she reached a picturesque riverside village called Ober-winter, where she was welcomed ashore by the Archbishop of Cologne and led to a nunnery. She landed every night on the west bank of the river, but only the most important of her many attendants could share her opportunity of stretching cramped limbs. The majority had to get what sleep they could couched in their various crafts. Next night a dark-red fifteenth-century castle was the princess's lodging. Andernach was a much bigger place than Oberwinter, but, like most Rhine-side towns and villages, it had grown up on the available level space along the water's edge. Its principal street, of ancient plaster-and-timber houses, followed the course of the river, and was pierced by a succession of small cobbled lanes, hardly wide enough to be called streets, all ending in river-views.

From the beetling fortress of Ehrenbreitstein, overlooking the meeting of Rhine and Moselle, a salvo which echoed long welcomed the Princess Palatine to the adjacent city of Coblentz. All that day's associations were clerical. The Archbishop of Cologne feasted Elizabeth on fish, the day being Friday, and she passed on to sup with the Bishop of Trier at Braubach, where the English chronicler of her journey noted with relish the fate of Bishop Hatto. "Here standeth the Castle in which, by report, a German Bishop was eaten up by the rats."

The river began to narrow and wind between heights clothed by vineyards below and forests above. Many were decorated by mediaeval castles. From St. Goar, where Eliza-beth rested all Sunday, she could see three castles, and the entrance to that shadowy gorge in which it behoved navigators to be wary lest the sweet singing of a certain Rhine-maiden should lure them to destruction. Her host in these romantic surroundings was no elderly prelate. William of Hesse Cassel was a brother of the attractive Otto who had gained such golden opinions when he had visited England in 1611. It was amongst the sisters of these young men that the late Prince of Wales had dreamt of finding himself a fair Protestant bride.

A message from her husband now promised to expedite Elizabeth's progress. As several towns on the stretch of river above St Goar were reported to be plague-stricken, the Elector earnestly requested the Electress not to land in any place where there was danger of infection. So she passed without halting below a castle called Schönberg, which was the ancestral home of the invaluable Colonel Schomberg, and alongside a castle, on an island called Pfalzgrafstein, which bore on its south side the arms of the Counts Palatine, its ancient lords. Bacharach had been mentioned in her marriage treaty as the place where her husband was to assume financial responsibility for the remainder of her journey. Hardly had she left the town behind, unvisited, when her ship was hailed by a small sailing-boat. A moment later Frederick was smiling at her. "The amorous Palatine", having hurried through his business at Heidelberg, had come to conduct her home in person. He settled himself by her side to enjoy the scenery of the Rheingau, a rich and beautiful district, famous for producing some of the finest wines in the world.

That night Elizabeth set foot for the first time in her husband's principality. Gaulsheim was only a village, but coaches were waiting to carry her and her ladies to the little Town Hall for a banquet, and next morning every member of her suite was invited to land for breakfast. Her appearance was greeted with tumultuous applause by crowds of admiring rustics. The four stately English peers who had been deputed by their master to deliver her safely in her husband's territory now came to take formal leave of her. They were easily persuaded to come on to Heidelberg as guests. Lord Harington, indeed, still had duties to perform, for he was entitled to examine and take possession of her dower lands.

The question of presents was troubling Elizabeth again. She had used up all those provided for her to bestow upon deserving persons during her journey, and shrank from applying to Frederick for money to purchase gifts intended for dispersal amongst his own subjects. She asked her most obliging jeweller, Jacob Harderet, to take into pawn some of her own huge store of jewellery, and set out cheerfully for Mainz and two days of entertainment by another Archbishop. At Oppenheim, on June 4th, however, she did come to her husband with a request. "The tedious water journey had become rather wearisome." Curtailment of her programme must cause terrible disappointment in places where elaborate pageants were being prepared, but to Frederick the wishes of the *"herz-allerliebste Gemahlin"* were commands. He gave orders for coaches to be ready to take the high road for Franken-thal at ten next morning. The remainder of the river progress must be cancelled.

At Worms, where the pageants were not ready, the prince and princess listened to a congratulatory oration without dismounting from their equipage. But when they reached Elizabeth's dower-town there was no sign that her change of plans had taken anyone by surprise. "She was joyfully received with an infinite concourse of people." Guns mounted on the battlements of the small but flourishing walled city discharged a salute as her procession came in sight. Sixty citizens, clad in blue gowns and grey hats with green feathers, marched out to fire a *feu de joie* before leading her in to take possession of her property. The Worms gate was flung dramatically open, disclosing a vista of flower-carpeted cobbles and streets decorated by birch trees and lined by musketeers attired as Roman and Turkish soldiers. Eighty green-clad boys sang shrilly under a triumphal arch leading to the market-place. The arches at

Oppenheim had been ingenious, for one of them had been surmounted by statues of Elizabeth and Frederick, and another had borne likenesses of their ancestors, Blanche of Lancaster and Louis Barbatus. But if the Oppenheim arches had excelled in historical interest, those at Frankenthal won from the artistic point of view. The one under which Elizabeth passed to the market-place was decorated on either side with huge oil-paintings, and led into a tunnel of flowers. Her route to the *"Fürstliches Haus,"* now her own, was lined by more musketeers, disguised as Moors and Indians, and a band of musicians blared from a gallery erected on its façade. Elizabeth and her bridegroom entered her dower-palace, and went out on to the gallery to bow and smile to crowds below. After dark "there was a Presentation before her of a Regall Throne, in which were lighted 100 lamps; it being a figure of that Throne of Solomon whereon he entertained the Queen of Sheba". Elizabeth spent the following day, a Sunday, quietly at Frankenthal, but for the evening the citizens had arranged a pageant called the Siege of Troy. Frederick left her to witness it alone. Etiquette prescribed that he should be in his capital to welcome her.

A lively illustration[1] depicts the scene that took place outside Heidelberg on Monday, June 7th, 1613. The plain is crowded by many tents, cannon discharging puffs of smoke, and innumerable soldiery. Elizabeth, wearing a tall scarlet hat, a spreading lace collar and a farthingale of embroidered cloth of gold, has just alighted from her chariot. Her attitude is extremely dignified, but the chroniclers report that she "sprang down" to meet her bridegroom. Frederick, bareheaded, is literally running towards her. His day, since he had ridden down from his castle at noon, had not been without anxieties. The weather had disobligingly become exceedingly doubtful. He had prepared a banquet in a tent for his bride, and she had intended to make her entry on horseback. However, a crimson

[1] In the *Beschreibung der Reiss,* etc.

velvet coach and six, even more showy than that in which she
had arrived, had been hurried down to the plain. Elizabeth
mounted into it, followed by Lady Arundel and Lady Harington, and drove off dinnerless, through dense clouds of smoke
which hung over the parade-ground for more than an hour
after her departure. The crimson velvet chariot was open on
all sides, an arrangement most welcome to spectators, but
daunting to its occupants on an afternoon when the skies
threatened a thunderstorm. Frederick, accompanied by his
brother-in-law the Administrator of the Palatinate, the Margrave of Ansbach and the Duke of Würtemberg, rode immediately in front of his wife's chariot. They came in sight of a
rather bright red sandstone castle, with several large round
towers and a great many glinting windows, set some way up
a hillside covered by brilliantly green trees. That castle was
Home, but a wide and flashing river and a city full of pageants
still lay between it and its new mistress.

There was an aquatic pageant by fishermen below the bridge
over the Neckar, and Frederick sent the jolly fellows good wine
in which to drink his bride's health. Guns sounded all along
the river and from every tower on the walls, as the procession
entered the town. Every house of the Speyerische Strasse had
tapestries or coloured cloths hanging out of its windows, and
garlanded doors. The burgomaster had, at his own cost,
erected an arch from which a royal crown was to have been
let down upon the head of a princess on horseback. It was
lowered to perch for a moment on the roof of her carriage.
The University had run to four arches, all loaded with learned
allegory and musicians. Under the second waited the Rector
at the head of a deputation of professors and students, ready
with a Latin oration. Elizabeth bore up well. "The amiable
cheerfulness of her brow" was remarked with eager approval.
When the Rector had finished she prompted the efficient Schomberg to reply in her name. Presently her blue eye lit upon

something that did look to her altogether admirable. A small boy was propelled forwards to make her an offering. He piped in French : "Madame, the goddesses Flora and Pomona greet you, and wishing you every blessing and felicity, they present to you this basket." The basket was filled to the brim with luscious figs, dates, cherries, oranges and citrons. To the delight of its donors, the gift was not handed to a lady-in-waiting and forgotten. Elizabeth was sixteen and felt hungry. As her chariot moved on, the golden-haired princess, in her formal gold gown, was perceived to be partaking "merrily" of show specimens of dessert fruit.[1]

Towards six o'clock the procession began to ascend the steep and winding road up to the castle. After all, the rain had not come, and the evening was one of "lovely sunshine". Elizabeth passed over a covered drawbridge leading to a dark tower. Its gateway was surmounted by more than life-sized figures of prancing lions, holding up a coat of arms, and mailed knights, with long curly plumes in their feature-shrouding helmets. The varied architecture of the great courtyard of Heidelberg Castle was for the moment eclipsed by a glaring temporary archway, sixty-five feet high, decorated by statues of past Palatine rulers. The historians had been busy. Louis Barbatus and Blanche of Lancaster were there again, and Henry the Lion and the Empress Matilda. Neither of the English princesses depicted had been lucky, for legend affirmed that Henry the Lion had enlivened his sterile second marriage by wife-beating, and Blanche of Lancaster had perished in childbed in her seventeenth year. Elizabeth's chariot jolted to a standstill below a highly ornamented entrance attained by two flights of stone steps. Frederick leapt from his horse and hurried round

---

[1] There is an illustration in the *Beschreibung der Reiss, etc.*, showing the boy waiting under the archway with his basket. He is bareheaded, rosy and robust, and attired in ruff, bombasted breeches, padded doublet and laced cloak, but appears to be not more than four years old.

I

to hand her into a lofty reception hall, where no less than twelve German princesses, all relations, were waiting with their attendants drawn up in a long line. The "princely ones, counts and ladies" who had "stationed themselves in elegant order" were so numerous that their ranks extended the whole length of the Great Hall to the door of the adjoining "Silver Chamber", one of the most famous of the many luxurious apartments of Heidelberg Castle. Elizabeth impulsively flung her arms around the neck of the first lady presented to her. Frederick's mother said heavily, but with deep feeling, that since the death of her late husband, she had never tasted a pleasure so sincere as that with which she welcomed her royal daughter-in-law.

VI

The day after Elizabeth's arrival was marked by thanksgiving services. In the castle chapel Dr Abraham Schultz officiated. Since it was fashionable for the learned to Latinize their names, Frederick's preacher was generally known as Scultetus.[1] "About six thousand persons" feasted at the expense of the open-handed young Elector in Heidelberg Castle and city on the day following his bride's home-coming, and while Elizabeth and her guests were dancing that evening in the famous Hall of Mirrors, they were surprised by the noise of trumpets. They hurried out on to the open gallery of round-headed arches overlooking the courtyard below and a page attended by five mounted trumpeters solemnly summoned them to a tournament on the morrow. Next noon a procession of coaches descended from the castle on the hill to a riverside pleasure-garden in the "Fore" or "New" town,[2] where

[1] Abraham Schultz was a Silesian by birth. After studying at Wittenberg and Heidelberg, he became parson of Schriesheim and chaplain to the Elector Frederick IV.

[2] The "new" town had been built in the end of the fourteenth century.

the lists had been prepared "both for Tilt and Tourney".[1] Elizabeth, with her mother-in-law and a bevy of German princesses, was installed in the upper storey of a covered stand. In its lower storey sat the judges of the day's sport. Thirty-two knights in armour took part, their three companies being commanded by the Duke of Würtemberg, the Margrave of Ansbach and the younger brother of the Administrator of the Palatinate. When dusk came there was a discharge of fireworks from three mock castles mounted on boats moored in the centre of the river.[2] Two days later, Elizabeth again repaired to the tournament ground, this time to watch running at the ring, a sport in which her bridegroom was expert. Frederick carried off twenty-nine of the ninety-four prizes offered, before hurrying away to disguise himself in classical costume. He reappeared in the character of Jason, "in a ship, bearing with him the Golden Fleece which Jason fetched from Greece", and from the gilded mast of his vessel an invisible speaker prophesied optimistically as to the result of the theft by a "young lion, sprung from the royal race of lions" of the "royal lamb" from an island kingdom. Frederick's bark was the last equipage in a procession of appropriate chariots bearing Juno and Jupiter, Neptune and Arion, surrounded by mermaids, centaurs, sea-unicorns, a dragon and the Seven Deadly Sins. Every deity saluted Elizabeth and addressed her in verse. "The second Day shone more glorious in Courtly Honors, Showes and Pastimes", for this pageant was succeeded by another, presenting Mars, Hercules, Victory, Venus and Cupid, and Diana "in a chariot made like a forrest set out and adorned with living birds and beastes". Knights, virgins, nymphs with bows and arrows, and satyrs, "playing on musicke wildely", closed this day's show. Next day the tireless Frederick was again Jason, but his companions were Apollo, Orpheus,

---

[1] The Bismarck Platz and Garten now occupy this site.
[2] There is a fine illustration of this display in the *Beschreibung der Reiss, etc.*

Bacchus "in a chariot drawne by dogges" and Midas "setting on an asse, he himself having asse's eares".[1]

On the Saturday of this week of revelry an equestrian procession descended from the castle and turned eastwards. The princess, attended by her husband, many German princes and the English lords who had brought her to Heidelberg, was going hunting. The Prince Palatine's capital boasted a hunting-palace near the slopes of the lower Hardt, certainly not as large and luxurious as his father-in-law's Thames-side palaces of Hampton Court and Sheen, but excelling them in tonic air and picturesque seclusion. The brilliant train of nobles and ladies rode along a country highway, bordered by wild plum trees, running across the plain between the Rhine and Neckar. Lovely views of forest country stretched on either side. At the end of six miles they came to a moated castle of two tall, flat-faced towers. Schwetzingen had been famous for its "black waters" since the eighth century, and had been the property of the Counts Palatine since the middle of the twelfth century, but the hunting-palace which Elizabeth saw for the first time on June 12th, 1613, was comparatively modern. It had been erected about seventy years before by the Elector Louis V, a great builder. Its banquet-hall, and its gardens rich in nightingales, glow-worms and asparagus, were celebrated, but the chief pride of its princely owners was its forest, divided into six districts and abounding in wild deer. In the Palatinate it was the custom to hunt the deer with lances, but Elizabeth "chased the deer after such a fashion that it was marvelled at, and in this country even seemed somewhat strange. For her Grace shot twelve deer with her cross-bow, and at last, from her horse, she shot at a stag of the second head, struck it in the ham and brought it to the ground; whereat the Elector and the princes were much surprised." At five o'clock when they

[1] Original sketches for some of the masquers' costumes and chariots are to be seen in the Palatine Museum, Heidelberg.

had "taken about thirty stags and deer, the hunt closed, and their Electoral and princely highnesses, with the illustrious princes and ladies, rode home again".

Next day was Sunday, but after Elizabeth had attended divine worship, "a merriment was presented to her of mad fellowes with tubs set upon their heads, apparelled all in straw, and sitting on horsebacke". The tilting of these encumbered gallants "made excellent pastime to the beholders". One more tilting display took place, on the 19th June. On the 4th of July Frederick received a congratulatory deputation from the University, and Elizabeth gave many formal receptions in connection with the transference of her dower lands. But by this time she had bidden a long farewell to many friends. On the 14th of June there was a great exodus from the castle. Stout Lord Lisle left for a German watering-place, the stately Arundels for their villa near Padua, and the Duke of Lennox on an Ambassadorial visit to Paris. Carpenters began to take down the glaring triumphal arch from the great courtyard of Heidelberg Castle, and Elizabeth was at liberty to inspect her new home in its everyday guise, and to suffer from acute homesickness and also from an occasional unfamiliar bodily malaise, which passed, but seemed to presage stranger things.[1]

VII

Heidelberg Castle had originally been designed as a fortress, but by 1613 its walls already enclosed a collection of palaces, built at different dates. From the town below, however, the whole structure still appeared essentially defensive, for nearly

[1] The preceding account of Elizabeth's journey and arrived at Heidelberg is taken from the *Beschreibung der Reiss, etc.*, pp. 72–159; *Triomphes et Entrées, etc. pour le Mariage de Frédéric et Elizabeth*, both published at Heidelberg, 1613; *The Magnificent, Princely and most Royal Entertainments given to the Highe and Mightie Prince and Princesse, etc.*, London, 1613; *Mercure Français*, 1613, and Everett-Green, pp. 66–86.

all architectural ornamentation had been lavished on the inner façades overlooking the *Schlosshof* or great courtyard of arrival.

Elizabeth and her husband lived in the most modern part of the castle, the *Friedrichs Bau* and the *Otto Heinrichs Bau*. These palatial wings were connected by the *Neuer Hof*, containing the Silver Chamber or Hall of Mirrors. They were roofed with slate and built, like most of the castle, in the local red Neckar sandstone, but the many statues on their inner façades were of yellow sandstone from the town of Heilbronn about forty miles distant. All the statues were brilliantly coloured, silvered and gilt. The Elector Otto Heinrich had decorated his building with an odd collection of characters, including King David, Hercules, Faith, Hope and Charity and the seven planets. Elizabeth's deceased father-in-law had kept to relations. His set of statues began with Charlemagne and ended with himself. A couple of Justices and some nudes on the roof gables were the only outsiders. To the young Swiss sculptor who had accepted his contract after much haggling, the late Elector had appeared as a stout bearded gentleman in plate armour, decidedly too massive and grave-looking for his thirty-three years. A Bavarian lion with a singularly fatuous expression attended him. Elizabeth passed beneath the likeness of Frederick's father every time she went out from the *Schlosshof* on to the Altan. This enormous stone balcony, the size of a tennis-court, was attained by a cobbled passage leading under an echoing archway. It was an ideal place on which to while away a hot summer's day, sewing, reading or taking a gentle promenade, attended by distinguished guests, for it faced north, and its view was famous throughout Europe.

The prospect from the Altan was, indeed, of breath-taking romantic beauty. Opposite rose the Mountain of the Saints, which Romans had fortified, and long before them unknown peoples who had enclosed its double peak by two ring walls.

But it was so densely wooded that except upon its lowest slopes, along which ran "a pleasant walk called the Phyloso-phicall way", little trace of man's hand was visible. From the range of which it was part, many hidden streams hurried to-wards the Neckar. The other great river of the lower Pala-tinate, the Rhine, could only be seen as a silver streak in a distant sunlit plain. The Neckar filled the middle distance of the picture, flowing from east to west as far as eye could see. It was a nobly wide and swift river, dotted by sailing-boats, rafts and barges whose busy occupants appeared as pigmies to observers from the castle. Its great bridge, which was roofed with timber, was guarded by drawbridges and fortified towers at either end.

Squeezed between the castle hill and the river lay the old town, in which the University buildings, the market-place, the Church of the Holy Ghost, and a smaller church, dedicated to the patron saint of fishermen, were outstanding features. Most of the principal buildings, including several mansions belonging to noblemen and rich burghers, were constructed in the local sandstone, but Heidelberg, viewed from above, did not appear as a red town, for its streets and river-banks were packed with plaster and timber houses. Even up in the castle, the wing erected by the Elector Louis V for the ladies of his court, and containing the great Königsaal, was partly of "black and white". From the base of the Altan a steep, cobbled footpath descended to the town. It was called the Burgweg, and when a great expedition was planned at the castle, a messenger had to be sent flying down to summon chariots and horses stabled on level ground, beside the Riding-School, on the water's edge. Many retainers, too, had to be accommodated outside the castle walls. There were pages' quarters on the slope of the hill, supplied by rations from the castle. Heidelberg, indeed, already consisted of three towns: the Old Town, originally a fishing village on the Neckar, the

Fore Town, west of it, and the Mountain Town straggling up towards the protective castle.

Elizabeth's apartments were of splendid architecture and splendidly furnished. Two Rubens glowed upon her walls. Turkey carpets were strewn upon the floors of rooms hung with red and brown gilded leather. She was surrounded by wrought-iron work from Nürnberg, heavily carved furniture covered with velvets and silks or elaborately inlaid, and many exquisite *bibelots* of ivory and goldsmith's work. Her table was adorned with massive silver plate and Munich and Bohemian glass, through which glowed red and amber Rhine wine. But there was enough unfamiliarity of design around her to enhance her sense of exile.. The figures in the tapestries and on the plate and furniture were not like those displayed in her father's palaces. A German craftsman's grotesque or knight or saint did not much resemble one made in England.

The wing built by Otto Heinrich contained the hall into which her husband had led her on her first arrival at his home. The whole ground floor of the late Elector's wing was occupied by the new chapel, remarkable for its florid mural decoration. The dining-hall came above it, and on the second floor were many bedrooms all looking over the Altan to the celebrated view. Close to the Friedrichs Bau, in an underground chamber specially built for its reception, lay another of the sights of Heidelberg, the Great Tun, for which the Elector Casimir was responsible. This "mighty cask, such as was none other on earth", was capable of holding enough Rhine wine to fill one hundred and thirty-two thousand bottles of litre measure. In the diary of Elizabeth's father-in-law was to be found more than one melancholy entry of over-indulgence in the treasure of the Great Tun.

All books belonging to an Elector, even prayer books and cookery books, passed on his death to the world-famous Bibliotheca Palatina. This was housed in three places. The

library in the castle was a beautiful chamber with an oriel
window. Down in the town, the Church of the Holy
Ghost and the University possessed many more volumes of
inestimable value. Some were chained to long desks, and no
one except the Elector and his eldest son was allowed to borrow
them.

There were other important features of her new home which
it is unlikely that Elizabeth visited often after her first tour
of inspection—the kitchens, the soldiers' quarters, the various
towers, the old chapel built by Rupert I in the fourteenth
century, and the Gothic palace built by the third Palatine
Rupert, greatest of his name. Over its entrance was carved
a garland of roses borne by two angels, in token that this
house had been commended to the care of the Blessed
Virgin.

Within two months of her arrival, her husband's subjects
discovered with surprise that Elizabeth was not prepared to
find all her entertainment within the walls of her new home.
"The princess takes more pleasure in the fields than in this
castle of Heidelberg, although its situation, air, view and
environs are exceedingly healthy and pleasant." The castle
possessed a garden, but the English Electress preferred to take
strenuous exercise on horseback. The castle was situated on the
Jettenbühl, a spur of the heights known as the Königstuhl, so
nearly all excursions must be made up or down a steep hill.
The gentlest ride in the immediate neighbourhood was eastwards along the hillside to the Wolfsbrunnen, a distance of
about two miles. According to tradition, an enchantress
called Jetta had been killed on this spot by a wolf. There was
a little hunting-lodge set in green shade here, and the stream
which ran down into the Neckar was conveyed through the
mouth of a bronze wolf. The woods that clothed the Königstuhl were lovely and varied. Spanish chestnut, beech, mountain ash and oak grew on its lower slopes; above fir and pine

predominated. The undergrowth was thick and contained many brilliant mosses, broom, ling, harebells, wild straw-berries, brambles and much of the bilberry from which the town below took its name. The soil was the same colour as the local sandstone, a moist red, reminiscent of that found in the English west country. But the exiled English princess had never seen the counties from which the Elizabethan heroes had sailed to the New World. The Wolfsbrunnen became one of her favourite haunts, but when possible she preferred to go further afield. During her first months at Heidelberg she visited her dower-castle of Friedelsheim, which stood west of the Rhine, near Frankenthal, in country renowned for its wine, and possessed a vineyard in its garden. Friedrichsbühl, a luxurious hunting-palace, also west of the Rhine, but south of Heidelberg, in the woods between Bellheim and Zeiskam, she described approvingly as "the foremost of all the hunting-places".[1] "Madame", wrote one of her new courtiers, "takes her pleasure in hunting and is become a second Diana of our shady Rhine-side woods."[2]

In England the Globe Theatre had been burnt to the ground, and Lady Essex had presented her petition for divorce. At Heidelberg the Haringtons began to make preparations for departure. Her marriage contract had expressly stated that no eminent English should be included in the Prince Palatine's permanent household. Questions of precedence were likely to be difficult enough, and a married princess no longer re-quired a governor. The Haringtons' duty was done. In-cidentally they were ruined. A few days before they took

[1] Nothing now remains of these two country residences beloved by Elizabeth. Friedelsheim, first mentioned in 1416, destroyed and rebuilt 1578, was subsequently destroyed and rebuilt no less than three times before it finally vanished in the war after the French Revolution. Friedrichsbühl, built by the Elector Frederick II in 1552, was destroyed in the Thirty Years War and never rebuilt.

[2] S.P. 81.12.189.

their leave an unfortunate incident occurred. Seven years earlier Frederick's father had built a citadel at a little place called Mannheim, on the right bank of the Rhine near its confluence with the Neckar. Elizabeth determined upon an expedition to inspect the thriving town springing up there. As the late July day drew to its close, tempers grew short. She was seated in her coach, prepared for her homeward journey, when her ears were assailed by the sound of angry voices. Sir Andrew Keith, her Master of the Horse, dismounted from his carriage, and coming up to her, in a tearing rage, informed her that Lord Harington had cheated her in an exchange of horses. More than fifty people witnessed his outburst, and Lady Harington, the most correct of women, was seated by her hostess's side. The English peer's wife tremulously defended her husband's good name, and was rudely shouted down by the Scots knight. In vain the piping tones of a youthful mistress commanded her Master of the Horse to silence. Lord Harington hurried up, dignified but ineffective. One of his esquires, a Mr Corbet Bushell,[1] challenged Sir Andrew on the spot. Mercifully the invaluable Schomberg heard Elizabeth crying to him not to let the gentlemen fight. The imposing German colonel stalked after the would-be combatants, and represented that a royal lady whose wrath was to be feared was within earshot. The procession reached home without further incident, but next day Heidelberg was buzzing with fresh scandal about the Electress's countrymen. Sir Andrew, attended by retainers, had lain in wait for Corbet Bushell and struck him several blows with an oaken cudgel. A Harington retainer had rushed to Mr Bushell's rescue. Many other persons, spoiling for trouble after weeks of too much rich fare in hot weather, had joined in a free fight. The result was a long casualty list headed by the name of Corbet Bushell

[1] The Junker Buschel appears as "Stall-Meister" in the list of Lord Harington's train in the *Beschreibung der Reiss, etc.*

with fourteen wounds.[1] Colonel Schomberg arrested everyone he considered culpable. The Electress sent orders that her
impossible official was to be kept in duress. The Elector referred the whole matter to the King of England.[2]

The Haringtons departed with heavy hearts. Before them
stretched a dismal career of retrenchment in the country. For
nine years they had devoted every hour of their existence to
the production of an ideal royal lady. Now the Lady Elizabeth
must begin to act for herself, and they could not tell how many
of the lessons taught at Combe would be remembered at
Heidelberg. Actually, the Protestantism preached to an infant
princess by John, First Baron Harington, had left an indelible
impression. His wife's influence was equally noticeable in his
pupil's after-career. Lady Harington, who had been the model
of an English gentlewoman, had known where to draw the
line, and drawn it firmly.

The Haringtons were not destined to end their days as they
had expected. In mid-August some of the inhabitants of a
bustling Rhineside city learnt that an English nobleman,
homeward bound, had been taken ill in their town. Lord
Harington died of fever at Worms on August 23rd, 1613, and a
distracted widow was left to undertake the remainder of a
long journey alone. The new Lord Harington met his mother
at Calais.

VIII

The Princess Palatine had been pregnant before she left
England. On June 25th, 1613, Mr "Will" Trumbull, British

---

[1] Fifteen years later Corbet Bushell was still in Elizabeth's service, and
she warmly recommended him to her brother, since her finances were low.
S.P. 81.35.16.

[2] S.P. 81.12.189.196.198.202.698; Birch, *Court and Times of James I*, i.
265–6.

Resident in Brussels, wrote to Sir Ralph Winwood at the Hague—

"Sunday last, a gentleman of the Elector Palatine's pass'd this way towards England, in Post, to acquaint his Majestie with the safe arrival of our Princess at Hydelbergh. Her Highness's Physitians do report that in all appearance she should be with Child. I pray God they prove true Prophets and that with the New Year her Highness may be the joyfull Mother of a fair Prince."[1]

The messenger arrived in London, and his news spread quickly. "Her Grace is with child. . . . There wants not the concurrence of all such tokens and probabilities as are usually observed in women in that state and condition."[2]

But at Heidelberg her Grace could not be persuaded to admit knowledge of the strange adventure that was to befall her in a strange country. The gift of a *layette* as a wedding present may have offended her. She cannot have been ignorant of the "great hopes" published more than once by the Haringtons' beloved elder daughter, without result.[3] All the "physitians" who interrogated her were Germans. Although she had been allowed to take her own cook, furrier and shoemaker with her, it had not been considered advisable that an English doctor should attend the Princess Palatine. She may have nourished fears of miscarriage. She may have decided that it was wisest not to dwell on mysteries which scared her. Whatever her reasons, Elizabeth would not discuss her condition or even take any precautions. She continued to hunt, to make expeditions and to entertain visitors.

When the last of the wedding guests had gone, two important ladies of the House of Nassau arrived to stay at Heidelberg

---

[1] Winwood, iii. 407.   [2] Nichols, ii. 671.

[3] Lucy, Countess of Bedford, miscarried October 1611 and November 1612 (Birch, *Court and Times of James I*, 140–1,211), and eventually died without issue. In 1619 the words "if God had continued me a mother" appear in one of her letters. Cornwallis, p. 62.

castle. Elizabeth de la Tour d'Auvergne, Duchess of Bouillon, and Charlotte de la Trémoïlle, Duchess of Thouars, were Frederick's aunts. The Duchess of Bouillon was the blooming wife of the helpful duke who had done so much to further the English alliance. The Duchess of Thouars was, like her sister the Dowager Electress Palatine, a widow. But her Paris weeds were the height of elegance.[1] She had quick, black eyes, set in a somewhat heavy, pale face and a grand manner. She was the bearer of a letter from the Queen of France, congratulating the Princess Palatine on her marriage and arrival in Germany. The French aunts would have been so sympathetic, so flattered, had their new niece confided in them her expectation of an event so natural and so much to be desired. But Elizabeth never alluded to a fact which was common knowledge in her court. Nevertheless, the aunts departed to sing her praises at the court of Marie de Medicis.

After her sisters' visit Louisa Juliana withdrew for a holiday at Neuburg, on the north bank of the Neckar, about a mile and a half east of Heidelberg. A Roman fortress on this spot had been succeeded in the twelfth century by a nunnery of the Benedictine Order. Many ladies of the Electoral house had been inmates of Stift Neuburg, and some had attained the rank of abbess. The Elector Frederick III had suppressed the house and allotted it to Dowager Electresses as a private residence. It was indeed a charming place of retirement for an elderly lady, for it faced south, and in front of it brilliant lawns sloped to convent walls pierced by a river-gate known as the "Haarlass" in memory of the many high-born damsels who had said farewell to the world there after arrival by boat.

Elizabeth and her husband gladly made a visit to the Dowager one of their many excursions this summer. Louisa Juliana did the honours of her dower-house in style. She invited her

---

[1] A portrait at Herrenhausen represents her in black draperies relieved by a collar of many petals of transparent white muslin.

son-in-law John, Duke of Zweibrücken, to act as her *Maître d'Hôtel*, and brought forth, to amuse her young guests, two cups presented to her by the late Elector. She drank "Welcome" to Elizabeth in the cup which was shaped like a nun, and to her son in the one shaped like a monk. The banquet which followed was described as both dainty and delicious. The afternoon was spent in making a tour of the property. After viewing fountains, gardens, orchards, the picturesque stream which arose in the grounds, and the antique mill, the guests were led to a building in which "my lady dowager" took especial pride—"the cow-house, which is marvellously well fitted up, clean and polished like a handsome room". Elizabeth, thoroughly enjoying her day in the country, insisted on giving some grass to the cows "with her own hand". A table, well furnished with confectionery, had been prepared at this point, the end of the entertainment, and the princess and her band of English girls, all of whom were young enough to confess to a sweet-tooth, feasted and romped heartily. "There was a great deal of laughing".[1]

A care-free day was becoming a novelty to Elizabeth. In mid-July witty Sir George Goring had sent Sir Thomas Edmondes, British Ambassador in Paris, a doleful account of the Princess Palatine's servant troubles. "At the end of six months she will not have six persons; for some she likes not, others not the countrye." Her *Maître d'Hôtel*, Sir James Sandilands, was an elderly dodderer, "thrust upon her" because some recognition of his long service to the crown had been overdue. Her Master of the Horse, the egregious Keith, was most distasteful to her. "She hath not one with her who is able upon any occasion to advise for the best. Some inferiors have will but want wit, others wit but noe will, and a third kinde voyed of both. What this may grow to I leave to your lordship's better judgment".[2]

[1] Archives des Affaires Étrangères. *Correspondance politique Palatinat*, 2.29.
[2] Stowe MS. 174.91.

Colonel Schomberg had been appointed by James I British Agent to the Protestant Princes of the Union. He thoroughly deserved his first year's salary of £400. Fortunately for him, he was the owner of a handsome mansion down in the town of Heidelberg,[1] to which he could repair when his many troubles threatened to unseat his reason. He wrote dozens of letters in a small over-driven hand, to his Majesty the King of England, and his Majesty's favourite, Robert Carr, Viscount Rochester, Acting Secretary of State. But not all the colonel's problems could be committed to paper. Anne Dudley, Elizabeth's chief maid of honour, whom he had courted since he had first met her in London, had decided to refuse his suit. She talked of resigning her post and returning to England. Up at the castle he was disliked by his own countrymen as an English pensioner. The princess's attendants blamed him for the enforcement of every unfamiliar German custom, and wrote home that he was inconsiderate and arrogant. Moreover, the princess —"Madame", as he always wrote of her—although personally charming, had not the slightest notion of controlling either her expenditure or her household.

There was trouble over the question of her precedence. The colonel knew that, if he wished to keep the favour of James I, he must take a strong line here. He wrote to Lord Rochester that he had settled this matter. His countrymen had been given to understand that their new mistress took precedence of everybody, indoors or out.[2] His next authoritative action gained him more unpopularity. Over a hundred faithful English, who had accompanied their princess to Heidelberg, but performed no duties in her service, were still in the town. The officials at the castle refused to board and lodge them, and citizens were becoming tired of foreign guests who showed no inclination to pay or leave. The presence of a hundred unemployed English

---

[1] It was situated on the N.E. corner of the present Haupt Strasse and Universitäts Platz.   [2] S.P. 81.12.166.

lingering in her husband's capital was clearly damaging to Elizabeth's prestige, and she was persuaded to take an interest in the situation. She drew up a list of the people with whom she did not wish to part, and delivered it to Sir James Sandilands, with orders to dismiss all persons whose names did not appear in it. The senile Sir James brought the list helplessly to Schomberg, who painfully provided all the supernumerary English with money and transport to carry them to Cologne, whereupon Mr Elphinstone, her Royal Highness's secretary, complained to his mistress of the German colonel's unwarrantable interference in matters which did not concern him :

"I am doing my best to put Madame's train and affairs in good order", wrote the harassed colonel to Lord Rochester, " but I fear that I shall not have great success. Madame allows herself to be led by anyone, and is almost afraid to speak for fear of giving offence. This makes some of her attendants take upon themselves a little more authority than they should do."[1]

To the king he pleaded :

"Your Majesty must consider that I have to satisfy a young prince and princess, an Administrator, mother-in-law, sisters, aunts and all their trains. Everyone wishes to govern, everyone suspects me of partiality." [2]

Madame's servants refused to carve for anyone but their mistress, and refused to allow her cup to be handed to her by members of the Palatine aristocracy. This custom had always obtained at great banquets, the cup-bearers being all persons of noble families—members of the houses of Nassau, Solms, etc. Schomberg had represented to Madame that the formality need only be observed on two or three occasions. "Madame would gladly have agreed, but not so her servants."

"Is not this a miserable life!" enquired the colonel rhetorically, before embarking on his long catalogue of "little

[1] S.P. 81.12.175.   [2] *Ibid.*, 81.12.223.

K

dissensions with which it is scarcely pardonable to trouble your Majesty".[1]

In the end of August 1613 Colonel Schomberg offered his resignation to the Administrator of the Palatinate, but the 14th of November found him still at his desk, acknowledging instructions from the King of England. He added without comment in a postscript to his letter of this date, that the prince and princess were not at the moment in the castle. They were out boar-hunting.[2]

In London people credited a ghoulish rumour that the princess who would take no care of herself had miscarried, but on November 20th Privy Counsellors were solemnly discussing which noble English matron, out of a list of five, was most suitable to attend the Electress Palatine in her confinement. Lady Borough had been their first choice, but she had fallen ill. Sir Edward Cecil's lady had many points in her favour. She was already in the Low Countries, and she was an old friend of the princess. Lady Cecil, who was a Harington niece, was chosen. On December 8th Lord Suffolk wrote to Sir Thomas Lake :

GOOD SIR THOMAS,

I have received this morninge a packet from you, by which I find that his Majestie's pleasure is to have a skillfull Englishe Midwife sent to Heidelbergh, to attend my Ladye's Grace's bringing to bed. I can heare of none more fitting for this imployment than Mrs Mercer who hath in this Cittie an excellent good report, both for skill, carriage and religion.

The skilful Mrs Mercer was allowed no less than six attendants.[3]

Christmas found a French envoy at the Elector Palatine's court. The Elector received M. de Sainte Catherine, and

[1] S.P. 81. 12.248.   [2] *Ibid.* 223.   [3] S.P.D. 14.75.18.24 & 37.

accepted congratulations on the prospect of an heir. Elizabeth was not present at this audience, neither did she appear to banquet in public on New Year's Day. The French gentleman, who must report to Paris, learnt with amazement that "although Madame la Princesse must be, according to calculation, very near her *accouchement*, she will not have a word said about her pregnancy". He added, in his despatch of December 29th, that on this account he had deferred delivering his royal employer's felicitations to Madame herself. Fortunately for M. de Sainte Catherine, after the New Year's banquet Frederick invited him to pay a visit to his hostess, in her private apartments. When he had penetrated there, the envoy expressed in flowery terms his hopes that at an early date in the new year he should see her a joyful mother. Elizabeth replied in most stately language, thanking their Majesties of France for their special favours in remembering her. She smiled "in a gay manner" as she added—"Since they consider that I am *enceinte*, that helps me to believe that I am so". She passed on rapidly to hope that the Queen-Mother and King of France were in good health and their country in a state of tranquillity.

M. de Sainte Catherine retired baffled. Nevertheless, his was the pen destined to transmit to history the fullest account of Elizabeth's first experience of child-birth. That very night Heidelberg was startled by the news that the Electress was in labour. Nobody had dreamt that the indisposition which she had averred as her reason for absenting herself from the day's festivities had indeed been the beginning of her trial. She herself confessed that she had not expected to be confined so soon. The noble matron of her own nation, so carefully selected to support her, had not arrived, nor—which was worse—the skilful midwife. However, Dr Christian Rumph and his satellites were perfectly competent, and their patient was young and strong. Now that the hour, all thoughts of which she had suppressed for so many months, had come upon her, the princess summoned "prodigious courage" to meet it. Her sufferings were less prolonged than is usual at a first birth. The child born between twelve and one on the morning of Sunday, January 2nd. 1614, showed no signs of having been brought into the world prematurely, and he was the Frederick Henry whom the English poets had longed to see. When Elizabeth was told the sex of her infant, "a beautiful young prince very like M. l'Electeur", "she rejoiced" and uttered an heroic wish that a salute should be fired. While the cannon on the ramparts of the castle of Heidelberg sounded repeatedly, informing delighted multitudes in the town below that an heir had been born, the young mother endured the sound with "contentment". Her spirits rose, and she wished to join with her husband in composing the letter telling her beloved father of the happy event.[1] Letters poured forth from the castle of Heidelberg that day. Frederick wrote personally to Sir Thomas Edmondes. He felt it his duty to inform a gentleman who had done so much to further the marriage of the Prince and Princess Palatine, that they were now the happy parents of "a little son, very healthy and large".[2] Count Albert of Solms, in a charming note to Sir Thomas Lake, announced mother and child doing well. "The midwife will find the job, thank God, well done, whereat she will be much vexed, but I rejoice to see this young and beautiful plant in which Germany and Great Britain have participated (the one for the conception the other for the bringing into the world). One doubts which of the two should be called the real country." [3]

The birth of an heir to the Prince and Princess Palatine aroused delirious enthusiasm in their own principality, in the United Provinces, and especially in Great Britain. James I could not do enough for the daughter who had made him a grandsire. He immediately settled a pension of two thousand

[1] MS. Français Bibl. Nat. 4113.42.   [2] Stowe MS. 174.205.
[3] S.P. 81.13.1.

pounds per annum upon her. At the next meeting of Parliament a bill was passed naturalizing Prince Frederick Henry,[1] and declaring him lawful successor to the throne of England after his mother. The heir apparent was considered so delicate that doubts were entertained of his continuing the succession.

The messengers bringing the news "that the Lady Elizabeth was brought to bed" travelled with great speed considering the severity of the weather this New Year. By January 8th the bells of St Margaret's, Westminster, were ringing a joy-peal and bonfires were ablaze in the City of London.[2] The inhabitants of Edinburgh celebrated the birth of "the little Palatine" with more enthusiasm than they had displayed when an heir had been born to Mary Stuart in their own capital. "Coals and Tar Barrells" were dragged up to Arthur's Seat; Holyroodhouse had an independent illumination, and a hundred and thirty-four pounds of powder were shot off from the castle. The provincial towns of Scotland also had their solemn revelries. From Venice the English Ambassador wrote elegantly to his *confrère* in Brussels: "I thank you very much for the happy News of our Princess's Delivery, to whose Perfection it belongeth to bless the World with such a New-Year's Gift."[3]

Frederick Henry's baptism took place on March 6th. The sponsors were the King of England, grandsire, the Electress Dowager, granddam, the Duke and Duchess of Zweibrücken uncle and aunt, the Prince of Orange and Prince Maurice of Nassau, great-uncles, and the free knights of Swabia, Franconia and the Rhine, future brothers-in-arms. The Prince of Anhalt, representing the King of England, was received outside Heidelberg by the proud father at the head of two hundred horse, and lodged at the castle in the Gothic palace erected by Rupert III—"the Emperor's building". Carpenters had been

---

[1] Cotton MS. Titus C. vii. 70. [2] Nichols, ii. 746.
[3] Winwood, iii. 491.

at work again in the great court, which was transformed by a temporary gallery along which the christening procession passed to the chapel. "Organs and voices expressed the thankfullness of that happy day." "The great bell" was rung three times. "There was sounding of trumpete, sagbots and sundry other instruments of music", and "a great peal of ordnance" was discharged at appropriate intervals. The ensuing "Plays, Masks and Hunting" continued "8 daies after". Princess Catherine, the infant's young maiden aunt, was allowed to carry him to the font. Master Scultetus, his Highness's chaplain, preached. Most of the christening presents were principally remarkable for their ostentation, but one was both artistic and unusual. Prince Maurice of Nassau sent his godson a crystal ship.[1]

A contemporary engraving, a copy of which is exhibited in the museum of Elizabeth's dower town, Frankenthal, shows her first baby in a richly embroidered round cap and swaddling bands, surrounded by congratulatory verses in French, German and English. The English ode opens "Grow blessed babe!" A broad smile is visible on the countenance of the infant. His fair mother, oblivious of the old stable adage that the sire gives colour, was astonished to find that she had borne what she described as "a black babie". Prince Frederick Henry had inherited "*le teint noir*" of his young father. When he was four months old he had an illness lasting three days, described by Schomberg as measles,[2] but thereafter the heir never gave anyone a moment's anxiety. "Verie leane and paile", but "skin and bone", was Elizabeth's unflattering description of her own appearance after her accouchement.[3] She was generally reported to have had a perfectly normal first confinement, nevertheless for some weeks she continued to feel extraordinarily ill. And she had still one unpleasant duty to perform: she must mollify all the near relations likely to have been

---

[1] Nichols, ii. 756–8.   [2] S.P. 81.13.41.   [3] *Archaeologia*, 37.239.

affronted by her policy of secrecy. A letter dashed off to the Duchess of Thouars was singularly humble and involved:

MADAME MY COUSIN,

No one yet who has congratulated me on the event which has occurred to me by the blessing of Heaven is more dear or agreeable to me than yourself. As there will never be a day in my life when I do not recognize the divine favour of such a benefit, so ingratitude shall never so much gain the upper hand of my better intentions that I will not show myself most grateful for all your kindnesses.

The little dissimulation must be imputed to my inexperience, and that it is not my way to entertain the world with doubtful hopes. The very happy event has shown they were genuine. There is nothing so distasteful to my naïve disposition as making a show when I am uncertain of the result. You shall know the details when occasion offers.

God grant that the son which His bounty has given me may one day, by His grace, bring the happiness which I desire to all his relations, and especially to your house which has so particular an interest in him, and may make me so happy as to remain in your opinion, in the position, my Cousin, of your very affectionate cousin to do you service

ELIZABETH.

Heidelberg Feb. 10. 1614.[1]

Presently, tiring of medicines in which she had no faith, the young mother determined to take her cure into her own hands. Her treatment of the pain which reminded her of an experience that she wished to forget was characteristically drastic. "I rumbled it away with riding a'hunting."[2]

---

[1] *Archaeologia,* 39.155.   [2] *Ibid.,* 37.239.

*HUNTING
A PASSION*

IX

After the birth of her first child, Elizabeth entered upon nearly six years of light-hearted happiness, marred by minor worries. Her debts and the dissensions amongst her staff would have oppressed a less buoyant character, but except when such sordid and distressing matters were forced upon her attention, she disregarded them. In vain Colonel Schomberg pointed out that true charity did not consist in granting the requests of people who were lachrymose, or unpleasant, or otherwise slightly alarming and boring. The princess listened gravely, agreed that it was unbecoming for a royal lady to be so "facile", and directly his back was turned, went on just as before. Anne Dudley continued to refuse him. The colonel left Heidelberg for the wars of the Cleves–Jülich succession. He hoped bitterly that he would be missed. While affairs in her household went from bad to worse, Elizabeth entertained lavishly and made innumerable hunting expeditions. She never had a riding accident, but her companions were not so lucky. Frederick nearly broke his neck on one occasion. The Landgravine of Hesse Cassel broke her arm, most unfortunately at a time when she was keeping the Electress company while their husbands were absent at Heilbronn attending an assembly of the Protestant Union of Princess.

Heilbronn was a free Imperial city on the Neckar, a long day's ride north-east of Heidelberg. Frederick caught fever in this picturesque old town. He would not allow his wife to be informed of his illness, and continued to transact business from his sick-bed. The head of the Protestant Union had reason to be troubled. "On Sunday last, the 15th of this month", wrote Mr Dickenson, English resident at Düsseldorf, "the Prince Wolfgang Willyam did publicly become a member of the Roman church". The Prince of Neuburg's defection was a serious blow. Frederick threw off his fever, in spite, as his attendants complained, of summoning lawyers, not doctors, to his bedside. But he came home moody.[1] At eighteen the Elector Palatine of the Rhine seemed to possess every blessing upon earth. He had made a splendid and entirely congenial marriage. He had recently obtained independent control of a principality which was in a flourishing condition; he had a healthy heir. Elizabeth confided her mystification and alarm to Sir Ralph Winwood, recently appointed Secretary of State, and the following very oddly expressed and spelt, but most carefully penned little note in a large, juvenile handwriting, safely performed its long journey from a red castle set in reddening woods above the Neckar, to London, where it now rests amongst the German state papers of the year 1614, surrounded by many highly formal epistles, couched in Latin, from the various princes of the Protestant Union to his Majesty the King of England.

SIR,

The Electour sending this bearer to his Majesty, I was desirous to let you understand something of his estate, as of this place. Himself, at this late Assemblie, gott an ague, which, though it helde him not long, yett hath it made him weake and looke verie ill. Since his fitts left him he is verie heavie, and so extremelie melancolie as I never saw in my life so greate an alteration in anie.

I cannot tell what to say to it, but I think he hath so much business at this time as troubles his mind too much. But if I may say truth, I think there is some that doth trouble him too much. For I finde they desire he shall bring me to be all Dutch,[2] and to theyre fashions, which I neither have binne bred to, nor is it necessarie in everie thing I shoulde follow.

[1] S.P. 81.13.77.283.

[2] "Dutch" here means German, "Deutsch". It was customary at this date to describe German as "High Dutch" and the language of the North Netherlands as "Low Dutch".

Neither will I doe it. For I finde there is, that would sett me in a lower rancke than them that have gone before me, Which I think they doe the Prince wrong in putting into his head at this time, when he is but too malincolie.

He that hath the best hand to ease his mind of this, and sett all things in a good way, is not here (the Colonel Schonberg) who hath binne this four months in Cleve, and is yett. But I should be extreme glad that his Majesty, by you, would command him to retourne as soone home as he may. For since his going all goes not soe well as they have done, and I find none so treuly careful of me as that man.[1]

Heidelberg, Oct. 1614.

"That man", however, was not disposed to return yet awhile to the difficult English ladies at Heidelberg. Colonel Schomberg was happy under the banner of Prince Maurice of Nassau, dating his weekly letters to England "from Camp".[2]

Elizabeth wrote to her father that, by the grace of God, M. l'Electeur was very much better and had gone to visit his mother for a few days.[3] Louisa Juliana had definitely retired from her son's court, "well contented", in her daughter-in-law's opinion at least, to spend the remainder of her days at her dower-residences.[4] Frederick returned from his little visit to his devoted parent having reconsidered the question of his consort's precedence. He was now inclined to think that in future his wife would have to be content with the usual status of an Electress Palatine. Her mother-in-law had been the "some" darkly hinted at in Elizabeth's letter to Winwood, who wished the Princess Royal of Great Britain to become "all Dutch", and who put disturbing ideas in the Elector's head when he was already "but too malincolie". The situation was saved for the moment by the sudden reappearance of Colonel

[1] S.P. 81.13.242.
[2] S.P. 81.13.215.
[3] *Letters to James VI*, Maitland Club, p. 14.
[4] S.P. 81.13.69.

Schomberg. Down in the Low Countries the colonel had trysted with Sir Henry Wotton, sent by James I to urge the return of a faithful servant to the side of a young and troubled mistress. Two gentlemen famous for their tact discussed at great length "things not fit to be committed to letters", and the result had been a speedy journey by the colonel to the banks of the Neckar.

Schomberg found his "*deux jeunes mariés*" flatteringly in need of him, and set to work upon a heavy task with zeal. He reminded his prince of the promises regarding "Madame's" precedence exacted by her father at Rochester. It was true that the king had broached a difficult subject at a moment of confused and high emotion, nevertheless promises had been made. The colonel represented further to his young master that it is part of a prince's duty to make public appearances at times when he may have no taste or spirit for company. A gloomy, preoccupied countenance or a brusque manner, on such occasions, is impermissible. "I am afraid and ashamed when any one comes here. Judge, Sir, whether any well-bred cavalier will remain in this court!" [1] Having done his best to prevent the Elector from becoming a picturesque recluse, Schomberg turned to the Herculean labour of setting the Electress's house in order. It was not necessary for him to suggest the dismissal of most of her principal officers. Too many had already taken their leave. The princess who could not say "No" was without a secretary, a Master of the Horse or a *Maître d'Hôtel*. She was suffering, in consequence, some amazing inconveniences. The footmen who should have been rigid at her doors had fallen into the habit of standing about her apartments, where they flirted with her maids under her scared nose. When she wished to converse privately with anyone, she weakly retired to her own dressing-room, or even bedroom. Since her doors were unguarded, strangers, and, what was worse, ambassadors,

[1] S.P. 81.13.297.

surprised the Princess Palatine of the Rhine, and themselves, by finding her unattended as befitted her rank. Naturally everyone hurried with complaints to so accessible a mistress; even the stable-boys ran after her to pour out their grievances. Anyone who had over-spent himself had only to mention the word "homesick" to find ample money for a journey to beloved England supplied without question by an English lady in exile.

With Teutonic thoroughness and despatch, Colonel Schomberg drew up three documents which he hoped might be of assistance to a most distressed princess, aged nineteen. Some of his suggested reforms show that the Haringtons, a couple regretfully described as *"fort sages"*, had lamentably failed to instil some primary rules of behaviour for a royal lady.

"Never grant anything on the first request, but answer to all 'I will consider—I will think of it—I will see.'

"You brought three thousand pounds' worth of linen from England, and have bought a thousand pounds' worth here, yet Mrs Dean complains that you are ill provided. This makes me think that there must have been some abuse somewhere, arising from inventories not having been strictly kept.

"Your Highness should never be teased into countermanding an order. . . . Prevent gossiping between servants of all grades. . . . Never allow reports of one about another, nor importunate solicitations, nor care when they take offence. . . . Let Order and Reason govern your Highness, not the prattle of maids or valets by whom you are now enslaved. . . . Be generally more severe; Liberty causes presumption; Indifference in time spoils even the good, and all the suite of your Highness and of the Prince too, believe that you dare not take offence whatever they do. . . . Let it be known that you will be ruled by Reason, that you abhor disobedience, flattery and lying . . . that you will have no flirting in your presence. . . . As to visits, games, walks, conversation, etc., try to leave a good impression, that you may be everywhere admired and applauded. . . . This is the only way to prosper and be in repute in England and Germany. This is true satisfaction, and God will bless your Highness and the world will honour you, which is all that you should desire." [1]

Elizabeth set her hand to the list of inflexible rules for the government of her household provided by the omniscient German colonel, and sadly prepared to be feared, not loved. The touching sight of a Royal Stuart bending from the saddle to give gracious ear to the plaint of a persecuted stable-boy was seen no more in the Schlosshof of Heidelberg. On the other hand, the Electress Palatine presently found herself free of debt and spared much unnecessary fatigue by a couple of principal servants, who, most fortunately, were man and wife.

In the spring of 1615 she wrote jubilantly to the Duchess of Bouillon, "I have married Dudley to Colonel Schomberg".[2]

X

On July 14th, 1614, M. Solomon de Caus was appointed "Master of the Gardens, Fountains and Grottoes of Heidelberg Castle", at a salary of £100 a year, and assigned a house upon the south wall of the upper terrace on the Kohlhof road. The Elector Palatine had summoned the greatest expert in Europe to design a garden more upon the scale to which the English-born Electress was accustomed. M. de Caus was not unknown to Elizabeth, for he had undertaken works at Richmond Palace for her late brother, and in 1611 had designed a French garden at Greenwich for James I.[3] He brought with him a French artist, who "took Madame's portrait in black".[4] De Caus's schemes for the Hortus Palatinus entailed enormous cost and labour. The ground surrounding the castle on the south and east rose steeply. The expert was faced by the dual

[1] S.P. 81. 14.221.223.   [2] *Archaeologia,* 39.156.
[3] Devon, 153.   [4] S.P. 81. 13.324.

problem of a light soil and sharp drainage. He combated these difficulties by planning five terraces raised on arches of solid masonry. The Elector and Electress surveyed and passed thirty sheets of designs for an elaborate formal garden, replete with a maze like that at Hampton Court, a timber corridor to enclose orange trees, much topiary, grottoes ornamented by artificial stalactites, mosaic pavements, pleached alleys, parterres, fountains, sundials and garden seats and statuary. All the flower-beds were of intricate pattern, some of the fountains were beautiful. One cascade sprayed a plump Venus supported by dolphins with knotted tails, another arose from a rocky islet decorated by a miniature forest, a third played upon the back of a smiling boy with a leash of hounds. Every grotto had its cascade, and the entrance to the Great Grotto was surmounted by lively figures of deer, lions, apes and chamois.[1] An army of workmen were set to demolish the existing garden and prepare the much larger area which was to contain the new one. Presently teams of horses dragged heavy parcels of rare plants and nodding loads of shrubs and trees up the castle hill, and the Hortus Palatinus began to take shape. A pleasaunce for the Electress's private use was arranged on a site already levelled, to the west of the castle. The grim cannon mounted in days when Schloss Heidelberg had been a fortress, not a palace, were swept away to give place to beds and borders of English flowers. The "Stückgarten", now re-named the English garden, commanded the famous river view, and was attained by a path leading under a lofty rococo gateway of sandstone. Its pillars were carved to resemble knotty tree-trunks garlanded by clambering ivy; its arch was surmounted by reclining goddesses bearing cornucopias, the inevitable Bavarian lion holding up the orb, and an inscription in Latin, "Frederick V to his beloved wife Elizabeth, 1615". The persistent legend that this entrance

[1] De Caus's designs, accompanied by an introduction addressed to his royal patron, were published at Frankfurt in 1620.

to her pleasaunce was erected in a single night as a surprise for Elizabeth, is not refuted by inspection of its construction.[1]

Although by the date that this gift was made to her, Elizabeth had been Electress Palatine for two years, she had never yet visited her husband's eastern territories.

"His Highnesse Countrey", wrote a contemporary English author, "is neither so small, unfruitful, or meane, as is by some supposed. It is in length about two hundred English miles, the Lower and the Upper Countrey. In the Lower, the Prince hath twenty six walled townes, besides an infinit number of good and faire villages, and twenty two houses. The land is very fruitfull of wine, corne and other comfortable fruits for man's use, having the Rheine and Neckar running through it. The Upper Countrey hath not so many walled townes, and Princely houses, but those that are bee generally fairer than in the Lower, especially Amberg and Newmarket. Wherefore let envy, malice and ignorance cease ever henceforth to carp at that they cannot parallel . . . and all honest mindes rest satisfied herewith." [2]

In the spring of 1615 Elizabeth and Frederick announced their intention of visiting Amberg. Elizabeth's suite, still smarting under Schomberg's reforms, displayed a last flicker of spirit by opposing the expedition, which was indeed a considerable undertaking, since the Upper Palatinate was separated from the Lower by five days' journey through land belonging to other princes, and at its eastern extremity it bordered upon the wild Forest of Bohemia. But the rebellious English hastily exchanged their attitude for one of submission when they

[1] The Elizabeth Gate still stands, and its inscription is still clearly legible. But its aspect is now extremely melancholy, for one of the goddesses has lost her head, and the surrounding area is clothed by ground ivy and heavily overshadowed by many trees. The garden overlooking the shining river-scene, to which a dusty path leads through green dimness under the battered Elizabethen-Thor, no longer contains a single flower.

[2] Nichols, ii. 621.

discovered that their mistress was perfectly prepared to dispense with their services. In the end, the smallest possible number of her personal servants were chosen to accompany the Electress. The young couple entrusted their son to his grandmother, who was delighted to have him, and set off in high spirits. Louisa Juliana seized the occasion of her grandson's stay to pen one of her tactful letters to the King of England. She described the eighteen-months-old princeling as the tallest, finest and prettiest boy the heart could desire. "I often wish that he could have the honour of being seen by your majesty, for I am sure that he would soon enter into your good graces." [1]

The shadow of James I hung heavy over the court of Heidelberg. When Elizabeth wished to attend a service in "the Great Church" of her husband's capital, so as to impress upon his subjects that her creed differed from theirs only in degree, she wrote first to ask her father's permission. Rumours of her unmanageable household had penetrated to England, and James heard with alarm that some of her principal jewellery was in the possession of her jeweller, Jacob Harderet, and that a lady who had recently retired from her service had arrived in London bringing in her luggage a set of ruby buttons which the King of England had reason to know well. The Privy Council ordered a search of Mrs Frances Tyrrell's lodgings, and the buttons were found. Mr George Calvert, afterwards first Lord Baltimore, was despatched to Heidelberg to institute enquiries, and Elizabeth found herself obliged to offer very awkward explanations. She had pawned some of her jewellery to Harderet, without her husband's knowledge, on her wedding journey, and had never yet found herself in a position to redeem it. Mrs Frances Tyrrell, who had been in attendance upon her since her first arrival at Combe Abbey, had received the ruby buttons as a parting gift on her retirement after ten

[1] S.P. 81. 14.120. An engraved plaque by Simon van der Passe, afterwards court engraver to the King of Denmark, represents Frederick and Elizabeth with their first-born. Its date is 1616, but it represents the infant prince in a feathered cap, as a child of not more than a year old.

years' faithful service. Since the Electress had understood that the buttons—of which there had never been more than twenty-two—were worth three hundred pounds at the most, she had not considered the gift excessive. She was aware that the buttons had originally belonged to her mother, the Queen of England. Her Majesty had given them to her in exchange for a pearl necklace which had been a present from his Majesty to his daughter. If his Majesty desired her to do so, his daughter would be very glad to send Mrs Tyrrell three hundred pounds, and beg the return of her gift. She was convinced that Mrs Tyrrell would make no objection.

Amongst the questions which Mr Calvert had been deputed to put to the Electress was what jewels were in the charge of Anne Dudley, now Countess of Schomberg, and whether it was the custom in Germany for a principal maid of honour to be married. Elizabeth answered with some asperity, direct to her father : "She hath nothing but some plate, that was given to me since my coming hither, though I assure your Majesty I have nothing to keep that I would not put sooner into her care and trust than any creature, having never had other cause. . . . Since your Majesty desires to know if it be the custom that the dame of honour should be married, to this I can answer—Yes, that it is the fashion." She added that her husband the Elector and all his council had desired her to further the marriage of her principal lady to Colonel Schomberg, and, as his Majesty would remember, he himself had written urging the match. The Schombergs were the best servants she had.

Not unnaturally they took high umbrage when they got wind of Mr Calvert's questions, and offered to retire from her service. Calvert paid a second visit of investigation to Heidelberg during Elizabeth's absence in the Upper Palatinate, and caused more annoyance.[1]

[1] S.P. 81. 14.17.73.75.105.

The progress of the young Elector and Electress through their High Country, at a leisurely pace in midsummer weather, was a complete success. They won golden opinions everywhere, and the States of the Upper Palatinate voted Frederick a welcome subsidy extraordinary of £160,000. Joachim Ernest, Margrave of Ansbach, entertained them on their outward journey; they reached Amberg, which was to be their headquarters, on June 18th. Amberg on the Vils was a beautiful town, encircled by strong walls pierced by picturesque gates. It had a splendid Rathaus with an open four-arched porch and panelled chambers, a fifteenth-century church dedicated to St Martin, containing the tomb of the second Rupert, Elector Palatine, and a smaller church dating from the eleventh century and dedicated to St George. The ancient Electoral castle was comfortable, for it had been completely rebuilt thirteen years before. Frederick had been born at Amberg. His father had removed Louisa Juliana there during a severe outbreak of the plague in 1596. The air of his birthplace suited the young Elector. Elizabeth joyfully reported him: "Verie well in health. I hope his malincolie is so past that as it will not returne in that height." [1] After ten days' stay in their "principal town", as she termed it, they made a three-days' tour of places of lesser importance. The Electress's spectacular coach jolted over roads of very bad surface, through remote villages whose inhabitants had never thought to see such handsome and gracious Princely Ones. Elizabeth was a cheerful and tireless sightseer. On their return to Amberg she represented to her husband that, since they were so close, they had better take the opportunity of seeing the Danube. They left most of their train behind and paid a flying visit over their frontier to Ratisbon.

They reached home in time for the pompous celebration of Frederick's twentieth birthday, and Elizabeth had a rapturous

[1] S.P. 81. 14.75.

reunion with "mon petit black babie".[1] Her homecoming was not entirely unclouded, for her unemployed staff had been quarrelling. Anne Dudley, now the Countess of Schomberg, and an expectant mother, had fallen foul of her old colleague Elizabeth Apsley, still a blushing maid of honour. Their mistress took pen in hand to assure Lady Apsley in England that she was supporting her daughter, and that although she was very fond of the Countess, "if she does ill she is not to be excused". Elizabeth added that she would be very loath to lose her maid of honour. "I hope one day to bring her and myself to you in England, then you shall see how much she is mended. For she is now a little broader than she is long and speaks French so well as she will make one forsweare that toung to hear her. Her nose will be in time a little longer, for my little one doth pull hard at it." News of another of her maids well known to Lady Apsley concluded this pacificatory letter. "Bess" Dudley was the best German scholar amongst the Electress's English suite, but so far, to her mistress's regret, "ne'er a count will byte". Nevertheless in time Bess Dudley was to become a German countess, and her fish was a big one, the Count von Löwenstein.[2]

XI

To kiss the hand of the Princess Palatine at Heidelberg had become the agreeable duty of fashionable Englishmen travelling to Italy. In the autumn of 1615 Sir Edward Herbert turned aside to receive "much good usage" from Elizabeth and her husband on his road to visit the English Ambassador at Venice, after serving in the Low Countries under Prince Maurice of Nassau. A few weeks later the Ambassador himself, recalled to London, appeared to pay his respects to his master's daughter. Elizabeth entrusted him with a letter to her father,

[1] S.P. 81. 203.   [2] Everett-Green, pp. 418-19.

in which she said that Sir Dudley Carleton would inform his Majesty "of all that passes here. Therefore I will onelie assure your Majestie of the Prince's health and of the little black babie's, who grows verie well." [1]

Sir Dudley Carleton was the son of a wealthy Oxfordshire gentleman. Westminster and Christ Church had provided him with an excellent education, which he had completed by five years of foreign travel. His career as secretary at the Paris Embassy had been of short duration; he had been unable to find himself in agreement with the British Ambassador. He had passed on to be secretary to Lord Northumberland, and very nearly shared his employer's fate at the time of the Gunpowder Plot. After that sobering experience, he had become a diligent member of Parliament. In 1610 he had been appointed to succeed Sir Thomas Edmondes at the Hague, but at the last moment the king had changed his mind, and the dismayed Sir Dudley had found himself ordered to Venice to replace Sir Henry Wotton, a gentleman for whose talents he had no admiration. His Britannic Majesty's representatives on the Continent at this date were by no means all the best of friends. Edmondes, Wotton and Winwood had competed against one another in 1612 for the post of Secretary of State. Carleton and Edmondes were firm allies, and both were on cordial terms with their painstaking colleague "Will" Trumbull at Brussels. Winwood, who was sarcastic and not in their opinion a gentleman, they disliked exceedingly, and Carleton's nickname for the accomplished and popular Wotton was "Signior Fabritio, Father of Lies". Signior Fabritio's young half-nephew and secretary, Albert Morton, was, much in the Shakespearean style, always "the young Fabritio" in Sir Dudley's correspondence. Sir Dudley, at forty-two, was distinguished for his *sangfroid*. He had an attractive face of pinched features, curly hair receding from a fine brow, and thoughtful eyes. He wore

[1] *Letters to James VI*, Maitland Club, p. 14b.

modish moustachios and a *pique-devant* beard. He was sympathetic to the homesick princess, for he had felt his late exile deeply. "I profess a greater desire of seeing England than any other Quarter under the sun, finding little Taste in forreign Pleasures and Curiosities, in comparison of enjoying the Conversation, or rather Discourse of Friends and kindred, and living at our Naturell Home, be it never so plaine and homely." [1] He had recently carried through the very delicate task of concluding the Treaty of Asti, whereby the war between Spain and Savoy had been brought to an end. His achievement had been an important contribution towards the peace of Europe, and he was approaching home in good spirits. Moreover it was very necessary for an astute diplomatist to acquaint himself with the rising star at his master's court. Young Sir George Villiers, "whose favour increaseth", was receiving daily riding lessons under the eye of James I at Newmarket. Robert Carr, Earl of Somerset, was in the Tower, awaiting trial for murder. The old favourite had fallen with such a crash that echoes must have reached Heidelberg and Venice. Colonel Schomberg, who had reported to Carr weekly throughout the latter part of 1613, cannot have failed to note his decline and fall with deep interest and horror. The colonel, however, continued to report imperturbably to England, though to a new official—"Their Highnesses, God be thanked, are very well and love one another more than ever. Madame is, at this moment, playing with and caressing her little prince." [2]

Elizabeth's next important English visitor was none other than "Signior Fabritio". Sir Henry Wotton, on his road back to take up his old post at Venice, stayed for a week at Heidelberg. Sir Henry was six years older than his rival, Sir Dudley, an Old Wykehamist, a poet, and somewhat impecunious. He had first made the acquaintance of James I in the year before

[1] Carleton to Trumbull, Winwood, iii. 491.   [2] S.P. 81. 14.196.

the old queen's death, when he had arrived in Scotland from Sweden, travelling as "Octavio Baldi, an Italian gentleman". Sir Henry had strong dramatic tastes. He had subsequently courted the Prince of Wales, whose premature death had been a blow to his hopes of preferment.

Elizabeth received her brother's friend with great pleasure, and confided her latest troubles to him. She had just returned from a visit to Stuttgart, where she and her husband had been sponsors at the christening of the Duke of Würtemberg's son. The festivities had been highly ceremonious, and she had succeeded in fulfilling her father's commands to take precedence of everybody. But she had since been given to understand that the many other German princes and princesses present had given place to her from courtesy, not conviction, and Frederick now declined to discuss the subject with her. She asked the bold Sir Henry to approach her husband and ascertain his desires and intentions. Sir Henry did so, and discovered that Frederick's silence was due to a decision that his wife must henceforth be content to rank as his consort and no more. In vain Sir Henry pointed out that Elizabeth was heiress presumptive to three crowns. Frederick replied with dignity that king's daughters had matched with his house before, and that "in Germany he did compete with the Kings of Denmark and Sweden". After a last attempt to soften the heart of the Elector by a reminder that the princess in question was the mother of his heir, the poet diplomatist retired from the conflict. "Seeing him for the present otherwise resolved, I besought him to represent his reasons unto your Majesty by Colonel Schomberg." [1]

"Several disputes with M. l'Electeur concerning my rank" [2] were duly reported by Elizabeth to her stormy sire this April. Another great family gathering on the occasion of a marriage was about to take place at Heidelberg. George William of Brandenburg, the handsome young prince who had handed

[1] S.P. 99. 21.73.   [2] S.P. 81. 14.298.

Elizabeth on board a Rhine vessel after a *fête champêtre* on her
wedding journey, was to become her brother-in-law. The
engagement of this agreeable, weakish youth to Frederick's
sister Charlotte had given great satisfaction in the Palatinate.
Wotton, who was on the spot early in the year, noted that
there was no appearance of friction between Frederick and
Elizabeth. In public their behaviour to one another was
marked by dignified formality, but "amorous demonstrations"
would not have been in keeping with the tone of their chaste
and somewhat over-solemn court. He learnt on the best
authority, "from her highness herself", that the Elector was
"otherwise" when they had no audience, and that it was not
his nature to be "froward and impliable". If he ever seemed so
it was entirely due to "the infusions of others, particularly of
the old Electress".

Sir Henry's despatch to England included descriptions of
his host and hostess. In his opinion the Elector had not grown
much since his wedding, either in height or breadth, though
most persons at his court affirmed that he was taller. "*Par
boutades* he is merry, but for the most part cogitative (or as
they call it here melancolique)." On the subject of his hostess
Sir Henry waxed lyrical. "My lady, your gracious daughter,
retaineth still her former Virginal verdoure in her complexion
and features, though she be now the mother of one of the
sweetest children that I thinke the worlde can yielde." [1]

The second problem discussed by Elizabeth with Wotton
concerned a vacancy in her household. She had suddenly and
unexpectedly lost her lady of honour. Schomberg's English
bride had died in the tenth month of their marriage, a fortnight
after giving birth to a son. Within the year her husband was
to follow her to the grave. Elizabeth hoped pathetically that
her father might consider her tastes when selecting a new
principal attendant for her. She said that she would prefer

[1] S.P. 99. 21.73.

someone of no lower rank than "Dudley", as she still called her lost friend, and not much older, because an elderly dame, besides being unable to accompany her in her disports abroad, might "perhaps be less plausible at home".[1] After a delay of more than a year, James appointed a widowed peeress stricken in years, but his choice gave entire satisfaction to his daughter. A fluttered caravan, consisting of a frail dowager in deep mourning, a cavalier of elaborate manners and thirty liveried English attendants, embarked for the port of Calais on Thursday, December 13th, 1617. Lady Harington had leapt at the chance of returning to Heidelberg, "to wait on the Princess Elizabeth as the first lady of honour in her chamber". The appointment of someone so elderly had caused considerable gossip in England. Mr Chamberlain wrote to Sir Dudley Carleton, now happily established in the British Embassy at the Hague, warning him to expect Lady Harington, squired by Sir John Finet, Master of the Ceremonies, on her road towards Germany, "by the way of Flanders and Brabant". He added his doubts whether the old lady, who was known to be disastrously poor, had been recommended for a post said to be worth five thousand pounds, or whether she had herself asked for it, "she being thought an ambitious woman".[2] Lady Bedford, on the other hand, affirmed "my Lady Elizabeth's extreme ernest desire and the King's commandment" as her mother's reasons for undertaking "so cruell a jorney" at such a season, and declared that she must suffer anxiety until she received news of her parent's safe arrival. "But her affection to her Highnes keeps her from being frightened with any difficultie, and her spiritt caries her body beyond what almost could be hoped att her years."[3]

Her old *gouvernante* had an additional reason for hastening towards Elizabeth this mid-winter. The formal announcement

[1] S.P. 99. 21.73.   [2] Birch, *Court and Times of James I*, i, 436, 444, 446.
[3] Cornwallis, pp. 26, 41.

of the Princess Palatine's pregnancy had been greeted with enthusiasm in London in July, 1617. "Never princess more deserved good wishes." Little Prince Frederick Henry would be about to enter his fifth year by the time his brother arrived. The Princess's doctors had been getting anxious.

Her new lady of honour did not arrive in Heidelberg in time for Elizabeth's second confinement, but her new secretary very nearly did. Sir Henry Wotton had secured for his clever half-nephew the double post of English Agent to the Princes of the Protestant Union and Secretary to the Princess Palatine, which had fallen vacant on the death of Colonel Schomberg. Mr Albert Morton, "the young Fabritio" of Sir Dudley Carleton's letters, set out much elated five days before Lady Harington. When he reached Gravesend he wrote himself down "a great part of the way, being freed of these incombrances I fellt at London".[1] His uncle had thoughtfully provided him with a detailed description of the Palatine Court. At the end of his journey the future Lady Morton awaited him, in the person of plump Elizabeth Apsley, maid of honour to her Highness, but this romance was not to flower for many a year.

He arrived in Heidelberg on December 26th, to find his royal mistress "in perfect health, and likely by the goodness of God long so to continue". She had been safely delivered of a second son between 4 and 5 A.M. on "the Monday before St Stephen's day" (December 22nd, 1617).[2] Elizabeth's favourite child had been born. He was another "black babie", but he was not a fine baby. He received the names of Charles, after his mother's brother, and Louis, after his father's brother. This infant "somewhat weake and very little",[3] roused in Elizabeth passionate maternal instincts which had been un-stirred by the child of her startled immaturity. She had desired him. She had realized that a princess who can only give her husband one heir is a comparative failure. Many prayers for

---

[1] S.P.81. 15.56.   [2] *Ibid.*, 81. 15.62.   [3] *Ibid.*

the princeling, "who was but a little and weake one when he came into the world", were offered up in Heidelberg, and to the general relief he began to thrive so remarkably that little over a fortnight later experts declared they had seldom seen a more promising infant.[1] Frederick prepared to leave his capital for Amberg and his mother for Kaiserslautern. The birth of Charles Louis brought to an end all bickerings between his mother and grandmother. Louisa Juliana had been pleased to receive a special invitation from Elizabeth to attend her second confinement, and on her arrival, a welcome far more spontaneous and affectionate than any previously accorded to her.[2] Since she had herself borne eight children within eleven years, and lost three of them, she was well able to sympathize with a young mother's anxiety over an under-sized baby. At heart Elizabeth had always recognized the sterling qualities of her solid and ceremonious mother-in-law. She now began to make efforts to please her. She sent word to James I, asking him to write a letter of thanks to the Dowager Electress for the "paynes and care" shown to his Majesty's daughter during her late ordeal. If the king had no other deputy in mind, she suggested that he should appoint the Dowager Electress to represent the Queen of England as sponsor at the forthcoming christening.[3] Louisa Juliana, highly gratified, made a great gesture in return. Although she had just heard of the death of her entirely undistinguished and regrettably Catholic half-brother, the Prince of Orange, she refused to take official cognizance of the fact until after the christening on March 3rd. No extra crape adorned her widow's costume or the liveries of her suite until the baptism ceremony was accomplished.

Within a few weeks of her departure she received news which increased her satisfaction with her beautiful and high-spirited daughter-in-law. All but four years had elapsed

[1] S.P. 81. 15.67.   [2] MS. Français 4113.2712 Bibl. Nat.
[3] S.P. 81. 15.67.

between the births of Elizabeth's first and second child. She was now making up for lost time.[1]

XII

Her third pregnancy upset Elizabeth's most cherished plan. Throughout the dark months preceding the birth of Charles Louis she had buoyed herself up with hopes of a visit to England as soon as she was able to travel. Nobody except herself had approved of the scheme. Frederick very naturally did not relish the prospect of another expensive and protracted stay in his father-in-law's domains. He consented to the idea, but told his wife's secretary to ask if the Elector Palatine would be allowed to take precedence of Charles, now Prince of Wales. On his last visit he had made no effort to precede Henry, Prince of Wales, but at that time he had still been a minor. James I found himself hoist with his own petard. In answer to his daughter's many letters, expressing her "earnest desire" of beholding him, he replied vaguely or not at all. George Villiers, newly created Earl of Buckingham, "the handsomest-limbed man in England", filled the eye and drained the purse of his king these days.

Her countrymen had not forgotten their princess, but Mr Chamberlain voiced the sentiments of many when he wrote to his crony, Sir Dudley Carleton—

"The Lady Elizabeth, we hear, makes great means to come over hither after she is fully recovered of her child-birth, and is so bent to it that she will hardly be stayed. I see not to what purpose it is, nor what good can come by it to either side. For

[1] On July 2nd, 1614, only seven weeks after Elizabeth's first confinement Dr. Thomas Lorkin reported "the news from Heidelberg is that her Grace is with child". Birch, ii. 332. Lorkin is usually a good witness, but nothing further is heard of this pregnancy. Charles Louis, in middle age, declared that his mother took a course of the famous waters of Schwalbach directly before his conception. Bodemann, p. 366.

unless here were a more plentiful world she will not find that contentment she hath done hertofore and expects." [1]

In March Sir John Finet turned homewards. He had enjoyed a month of Elizabeth's hospitality, after bringing safely to her Lady Harington, "who in the winter, both of the yeare and of her Age, hath performed such a pilgrimage in devotion to our Lady of Heidelberg". Elizabeth entrusted Sir John with fifty letters to English friends.

The days lengthened towards spring, 1618, and no definite invitation arrived from London. The Princess Palatine became more melancholy than ever her new secretary had seen her. English-born Sir Albert hoped that when she was allowed out in the open air she might feel better. It was over five weeks since she had given birth to Charles Louis, and she had not yet been permitted to quit her lying-in chamber. [2]

The christening brought her husband home to her, and at last the King of England professed his desire to entertain his daughter and son-in-law during the forthcoming summer. But in the end of April all the news sent to England by Sir Albert Morton was of illness. The aged Emperor Matthias was so sickly that he was having to be carried by attendants in a chair. Sir Albert himself had been laid low for a fortnight with an alarming set of symptoms—a terrible pain in his head, total deprivation of taste and smell and of all sensation down the left side of his body. [3] His mistress, too, was considering her symptoms with apprehension. But hers were not unfamiliar to her. Her visit to England would have to take place next year, not this year.

As usual, she had conceived in the spring, to bear with the snows. The infant Princess Elizabeth Palatine did not in the least resemble her namesake and mother. She was, like her father's family, dark of hair, complexion and eye. After her

---

[1] Birch, *Court and Times of James I*, i. 389.
[2] S.P. 81. 15.89.   [3] *Ibid.*, 137.

birth little more was heard of her parents' projected journey to
England. "The combustions which are yet likely to continue
in Germany" made such an expedition inadvisable in early
1619, and in England that season the court was in deep
mourning.

Contrary to the last, but much to the satisfaction of Archbishop Abbot, Anne of Denmark had acknowledged herself on
her death-bed a member of the Church of England. When the
news of his mother-in-law's death, of dropsy, at the age of
forty-five, reached Heidelberg, Frederick himself broke it to
Elizabeth. He sent an express embassy of condolence to
James I, and Elizabeth wrote that she knew she should regret
this bereavement all her life. "It is to me an affliction so great
that I have no words to express myself. . . . Sadness weighs
down my heart." [1] Lady Harington, who had been just about
to leave for England to attend the wedding of her only grandchild, put off her departure so as to console her mistress. Lady
Harington knew what bereavement meant, for soon after the
sudden death of her husband she had lost her only son. Smallpox had carried off the young Lord Harington. The new
peerage which had given so much satisfaction was now extinct.
The grandchild who was to be married this year was the
daughter of Lady Chichester. In May, when Lady Harington
said what was to prove her last farewell to her beloved pupil,
Elizabeth was still grief-stricken, but comforted by hearing
that her father, whom pessimists had expected to follow her
mother to the grave, was convalescent. "God has had pity on
me, not wishing to overwhelm me by two such great losses at
once." She had taken a step which would have gained the hearty
approval of the deceased. A Parisian lady, Madame de Bérig-
non, had been empowered by the Princess Palatine to choose
and forward suitable *toilettes* for a daughter to wear on the
death of a queenly mother. Elizabeth heard too late that a

[1] S.P. 81. 16.15.

much greater authority on such a subject, her widowed aunt the Duchess of Thouars, was also at the moment resident in the centre of fashion. The duchess, although unable to direct the choice, sent detailed advice, and Elizabeth was "very pleased" with her French mourning.[1]

Anne of Denmark was known to have possessed "a world of brave jewels", and a rumour spread that a casket of valuable jewellery had been bequeathed by her to her daughter. This proved to be untrue. Anne had left no directions as to legacies, and only on her death-bed given verbal assent to the suggestion that her son should inherit all her property. Her neglect of her only daughter caused little surprise in England, where many people believed that the queen's disgust with the German match had diminished her affection for the Lady Elizabeth, "so that she would often call her Goody Palsgrave. Nor could she abide Secretary Winwood, ever after, who was one of the chiefest instruments to bring that Match about." [2]

At the time of his daughter's marriage, James I had boasted that "he doubted not but that his son-in-law should have the title of a king in a few years". Six years had now passed, and Elizabeth, rising three and twenty, and the mother of two "young masters" [3] and a daughter, was still no more than Princess Palatine. The Duchess of Thouars, who felt that her royal English niece needed more scope, sought to comfort her by a prophecy that she should be a queen.[4]

XIII

Throughout 1618 and early 1619 the hills above Heidelberg echoed once more to the sounds of hammer and chisel. True to the traditions of his ancestors, Frederick was adding a

---

[1] Trémoïlle Letters, *Archaeologia*, 39.156–7.   [2] Howell, i. 165.
[3] Sir Albert Morton often alludes to the little princes as the two " young masters".
[4] *Archaeologia*, 39.158.

building to the castle. There was no room left in the Schlosshof, so he chose a site upon the old ramparts, between the large round tower known as the Dicker Turm and the building containing the Great Tun. Amongst his expensive alterations was the conversion of the Dicker Turm into a ballroom. His new wing harmonized in style, and was connected by corridors, with the most modern part of the existing castle, the palace built by his father. A more than life-size statue of Elizabeth's husband was erected to preside over her private garden. Frederick at two and twenty made a charming subject for a sculptor. He was depicted clean-shaven and bareheaded, in an attitude full of youthful dignity, attended by a hirsute Bavarian lion. The young prince wore his Garter at his knee, and the collar of that order over the ermine cape of his electoral robes.[1]

The northern façade of the English or Elizabeth building possessed a pair of gables, and two dozen round-headed windows, from which the famous view of river and town could be obtained. On its south side, the palace built to please Elizabeth overlooked her private garden, the moat and wooded heights.

She had settled, like many a princess before her, to uncomplaining exile, and seemed happy enough with her children and her garden and her hunting and her pets, "obliging all hearts that come near her, by her courtesy, and so dearly loving and beloved of the prince, her husband, that it is a joy to all that behold them".[2] Increasing her *ménagerie* delighted her, and she received many "presents that eat". Archbishop Abbot sent her Irish dogs, and Sir Dudley Carleton a couple of monkeys. Her monkeys caused her perpetual amusement, for her old one refused to take the slightest notice of the newcomers.

[1] The English wing suffered most severely in both the Thirty Years and Orleans wars. A replica of Frederick's statue still presides over his wife's garden. The original, somewhat damaged, is still to be seen in the castle chapel, and gives a very favourable impression of his looks and bearing.
[2] S.P. 81. 15.56.

The princess instructed her secretary and her lady of honour and one of her maids in waiting to write and tell Sir Dudley how much his present was appreciated. Thereupon old Lady Harington wrote a formal note in a pointed hand to the British Ambassador at the Hague, telling him that her Highness accounted the monkeys as jewels,[1] and Sir Albert Morton scribbled that no travellers had been so welcome in this court for a long time,[2] and Elizabeth Apsley sent a very merry letter, informing their donor that the monkeys were now so conceited that they would come to nobody but her Highness, who played with them in her bed every morning, together with her son and heir. Frederick Henry, at the age of four, announced that he desired nothing in the world so much as a monkey like those owned by his mother. "You could have sent nothing would a' been more pleasing", ended the maid in waiting, whose mistress had bestowed upon her the title of "The Right Reverend Mrs Elizabeth Apsley, chief governor to all the monkeys and dogs".[3]

The Princess Palatine had ceased to have "disputes with M. l'Electeur concerning my rank". The question of her precedence had been settled, but in a way agreeable to nobody except James I. Frederick now paid visits to other German princes unaccompanied by his consort. He wrote cheerfully from Berlin, telling his wife that he wished she had been by his side hare-hunting this morning. At the reception this evening he had worn the tremendous diamond George given him by the Princess Royal of Great Britain. A certain Electress had remarked chillingly that she preferred small stones. "But I think she was being like the fox who said the pears were sour".[4] Elizabeth refused an invitation from the Landgravine of Hesse Cassel on account of the distance and bad weather; she was unable to attend the christening of the Duke of Zwei-

---

[1] S.P. 84. 83.268.   [2] Ibid., 81. 15.137.
[3] Ibid., 84. 83. 78.   [4] Aretin, vii. 195.

brücken's son because at the date fixed for that ceremony she must be taking a cure at Schwalbach Spa. Such excuses would not serve when the Empress was her would-be hostess. Elizabeth resolved to go to Ratisbon when the Imperial Diet was appointed to be held there in July, 1618. But even that expedition was frustrated, and in an extraordinary manner.

Just after she had received the Empress's invitation, which was addressed to her and to her heir, an English soldier of fortune arrived in hot haste in Heidelberg town. According to his own account, Captain Henry Bell told her Highness's secretary that two years previously the Elector of Brandenburg had received secret intelligence from Vienna that an atrocious plot, designed to imperil the English alliance with Protestant Germany, was in train. If the Princess Palatine and her heir went to Ratisbon to meet the Empress, "they should never go back again alive". The Diet of 1616 had been postponed on account of the Emperor's illness, so the Elector had kept silence, but now the captain had come "with all speed" to warn the princess of her danger. Sir Albert Morton bore his startling visitor up to the castle. When she had heard the story, Elizabeth took the Empress's letter out of her pocket and gave it to Bell. With uncommon calm, she then commanded him to rest himself until she had written to her father. This business occupied her two days, at the end of which time she urged her champion to make all possible speed into England to show the Empress's letter to her father. She assured him that until she heard from England she would not stir from Heidelberg, and she generously presented him with "a very costly ring, adorned with eleven rich diamonds". Captain Bell found the King of England in his garden at Theobalds, attended by the Prince of Wales. As soon as James saw Bell, he asked eagerly if the traveller brought news of the Empress's letter to the Princess Palatine. Bell replied dramatically that

M

he had the fatal document upon his person, but an anti-climax ensued when he presented it to James, who could not read a word of "Dutch". However, the king who never disbelieved in a plot led his guest to a privy chamber, where Bell translated her Imperial Majesty's invitation out of the "High German" into the English tongue.[1] When the translator had done, James gravely, but disappointingly, commanded him to keep the document safely in memory of the service he had done. But better reward followed, for Bell presently received the grant of a patent office worth £300 a year.

Over eighteen years later, when Captain Henry Bell presented one of many petitions for release from the Gatehouse prison to Elizabeth's brother, he detailed this stirring tale of service to the Princess Palatine. He piteously asserted that he knew of no reason for his arrest, except that owing to the revocation of his grant and his large expenditure upon his Majesty's business, he had fallen into debt. He complained bitterly of an official search of his papers, culminating in the seizure of the Empress's letter, which his persecutors declared to be, like his plot story, of his own fabrication.

Captain Henry Bell makes his last appearance in State Papers Domestic, still a prisoner and still petitioning for money, for a trial and for sustenance at his Majesty's "expense either in or out of the Gatehouse". Letters from the Elector of Brandenburg, asserting his belief in the plot, are certainly to be found in the German State Papers of May 24th and September 6th, 1618, but Bell's story and fate are typical of the unsuccessful "secret agent."[2]

[1] This seems a weak spot in Bell's narrative. Formal letters from European royalties of different nationalities to one another were at this date invariably written in French or Latin.
[2] S.P. 16. 218.61. *Ibid.*, 346.

XIV

"Much too young and small-timbered to undertake such a task", had been the pronouncement of Mr. Chamberlain after critical inspection of the Princess Elizabeth's bridegroom.

Frederick's tendency to melancholy dates from his first attendance, after attaining his majority, at a meeting of the Protestant Union. Hitherto he had been a success in everything he had attempted. At the age of sixteen he had travelled to England and obtained the hand of the principal Protestant princess of Europe, not without difficulty, and to the surprise of many. But for such an undertaking he was suited by nature. Unfortunately the very virtues and faculties which made him an excellent husband and father, and a popular ruler of a prosperous principality, unfitted him for the post of head of the Union.

At Heilbronn, in the autumn of 1614, he realized for the first time, and with horror, that a task far beyond his experience or strength awaited him. He fell ill, but struggled, with high fever upon him, to fulfil his duties. The object of the meeting was to strengthen the financial basis of the Union and develop its foreign alliances. Nothing was achieved, except the formal ratification of the defensive treaty already existing with the States General. Gustavus Adolphus of Sweden was approached, but as yet he was not actively interested in Germany. Frederick returned home, shaken in health and spirits, and the events of the next four years did nothing to restore his confidence or mould him into the man of destiny required to lead the Union through the forthcoming storm. He worked hard with his energetic secretary, Mauritius, he travelled much upon visits to fellow-princes, but at times despair overwhelmed him. Deep-seated disturbances in the religious, political and social life of Europe were making for war, whatever he did. As the years slipped by, and the storm still continued to mutter at a distance, he sometimes yielded to the temptation to devote himself to work he could do well—planning an artistic new palace and garden for the beloved consort, who strove to drive away his melancholy by organizing fêtes and inviting guests to their court.

How much Elizabeth understood of the problems that distracted her husband during these years is doubtful. Her letters, and those of Frederick to her, reveal that they discussed leading events. Their comments upon them at this date, however, are mainly confined to personalities.

In 1615, at Nürnberg, the Union offered to meet the League to consider a composition of their differences, but the Catholics held aloof. In April 1617, the Union, already weakened by the secession of Neuburg, lost the support of Brandenburg in all but name. At this second Heilbronn meeting the purposes of the Union were restricted. Henceforward it was to be a purely defensive alliance. A few months earlier, Ludwig Camerarius, a leading Palatine councillor, had paid a significant visit to Prague. The League was not without its troubles, and these were now centring in Bohemia.

The childless and failing Emperor Matthias, a Catholic and a Habsburg, desired to be succeeded in all his honours by a prince of his own family and religion. He was Archduke of Austria by hereditary right, Emperor, and King of Bohemia and Hungary, by election only. In 1617 he began to take steps to secure the crowns of Bohemia and Hungary, as hereditary possessions, to his cousin and heir, Ferdinand of Styria. The Archduke Ferdinand, in his fortieth year, was the pattern prince of the Counter-Reformation. His organized attacks upon Protestantism in Styria, Carinthia and Carniola had been most effective. Many of his subjects, faced with the choice of conversion or exile, had left his domains. His enemies painted the portrait of this prince, pupil of the Jesuits, in dark colours. Actually Ferdinand was a singularly uninteresting character.

The Catholic party in Bohemia, although in the minority, held most of the prominent posts at court, and in July 1617 Ferdinand was crowned in Prague. Theoretically his power was only nominal during the Emperor's lifetime, but he began at once upon a repetition of the measures which he had employed with so much success at home. The Protestant Bohemians had in 1612 obtained "Letters of Majesty" from the brother and predecessor of Matthias, according them complete liberty of conscience. They deemed that their new ruler had violated his coronation oath. Having appealed in vain to the Emperor, they decided to revolt.

The Hungarian Diet, after two months of debate, grudgingly consented to accept Ferdinand as an elected king, and he was proclaimed on May 16th, 1618. A week later, in Prague, the representatives of the Bohemian Protestants, headed by Count Matthias Thurn, proceeded to the Hradčany palace, and after a violent scene, cast the absent king and Emperor's two principal advisers, Jaroslav Bořita of Martinice and Vilém Slavata, out of the palace windows into the moat below. Fabricius, secretary to the royal council, who attempted to remonstrate, soon followed. The distance which they fell was reckoned to be close on sixty feet. Martinice and the secretary presently arose, but Slavata lay inert, and as Martinice staggered towards him some shots were fired from the window above. That all the victims escaped with their lives was attributed by their coreligionists to Divine interposition. The word "defenestration" was added to the English language. The Bohemians established a provisional government, and raised an army, the command of which was given to Count Thurn.

In July, Austrian Imperial troops entered Bohemia, but were repulsed. In November, Thurn's army entered Austria, but was obliged to retire, owing to weather conditions. At Heidelberg the Elector Palatine was closeted for many hours with his advisers and signed innumerable letters. The Emperor had asked two Protestant princes, the Electors of the Palatinate and Saxony, and two Catholic, the Elector of Mainz and the Duke of Bavaria, to mediate between him and the Bohemians. John George of Saxony, a bucolic prince, who spent his days hunting, and his nights carousing, was Lutheran by creed, and the policy of his family had always been Imperialist. He professed himself ready "to help to put out the fire". The Elector Palatine, who was by no means so certain that this fire should be put out, hastily despatched Baron Christopher Dohna to represent the situation of the Bohemians to the King of England. The only satisfaction obtained by the baron was the king's consent to prolong his alliance with the Union. James, like John George of Saxony, wished "to finish the business peaceably and quietly". He informed the King of Spain that if he found the Bohemians tractable he would "feel it very deeply" were they nevertheless "destroyed and ruined". On March 10th, 1619, the Emperor died suddenly, in a fit.

Englishmen now began to take an intense interest in the "hideous fires that are kindled in Germany, blown first by the Bohemians", and to prophesy "a War without end. For the whole House of Austria is interested in the Quarrell, and it is not the custom of that House to set by any affront or forget it quickly.". A thrilling report that the Imperial crown was likely to pass to the young husband of the Lady Elizabeth was not generally credited in London. The election of Ferdinand was indeed, almost a certainty. The Electors numbered seven, and no Protestant candidate could hope to gain more than three votes. Maximilian of Bavaria, whose candidature Frederick had been prepared to support, in the hope of dividing the Catholics, refused to be nominated. A complicated secret negotiation with the versatile Duke of Savoy had ended in failure. Prince Christian of Anhalt Bernburg had gone to the length of paying an incognito visit to Turin. An inopportune attack of illness had necessitated his summons of physicians and apothecaries. The prince "did boldly pull off his maske, and as soone as he had recovered his health, he did shewe himself in publique". But the duke, who had sent mercenaries to aid the suffering Bohemians, was now chiefly interested in the prospect of adding Milan or Genoa to his domains. He gloomily suspected "that the Princes of Germany do only serve themselves of him to beat the bush, and that they entend to keepe the birds for themselfes, if any may be gotten".

James I's attitude during these critical months was characteristic. He began by pointing out that he had engaged himself in a purely defensive alliance. He wrote privately to his son-in-law that he was at the moment impecunious, but was expending a large sum on a pacific embassy to the Emperor. James Hay, Viscount Doncaster, did not leave England until after the death of the Emperor. "A tough piece of worke" was his own description of the task set him by his cautious royal master. At Brussels he had an odd interview with the Archduke Albert, who replied to his French speeches in Latin, and did not seem "much to favor King Ferdinande's election". On his arrival in Heidelberg, in mid-June, he discovered that the Prince Palatine was absent at Heilbronn, and was, moreover, preparing to lead into the Upper Palatinate an army raised by the Union "under colour of defence thereof". When this news reached the English court at Greenwich it roused an unexpected would-be volunteer. Charles, Prince of Wales, now nineteen, and still a suitor for the hand of a Spanish Infanta, wrote to his father's ambassador:

DONCASTER,

I am verrie glad to heer that my brother is of so rype a judgement and of so forward an inclination to the good of Christendome as I fynd by you he is. You may assure your selfe that I will be glade not onlie to assiste him with my countenance but also with my person, if only the King my father will give me leave.

But, on second thoughts, the young prince sadly crossed out the second "will" in his letter, and substituted the less hopeful "would".

Frederick returned to Heidelberg and joined with his wife in welcoming a flamboyant, euphuistic gentleman. Lord Northumberland had haughtily opposed the marriage of his daughter, Lucy, to James Hay, a penniless and obscure Scot, but Viscount Doncaster was now flourishing and famous, if only as the originator of a social novelty known as "double-suppers". He brought in his train to Heidelberg Dr John Donne, who duly preached a sermon to the Palatine court in the castle chapel on the apposite text, "For now is our salvation nearer than when we believed".

Doncaster, who rightly described himself as "a white paper to receyve impression from his Highness", sent home enthusiastic accounts of his host and hostess: "His Highnes—muche beyond his yeirs, religious, wise, active and valiant. Her Highnes—the same devoute good sweet princess your Majestie's daughter should be." He was greatly struck by Frederick's "lively" exposition of the European situation. "Never since its foundation", said the prince, had the Protestant Union been in such danger. All the Ecclesiastical princes were already in arms, determined, he feared, "to bring it to a Warre of Religion". "The fire being so near his house", he was inevitably concerned in the Bohemians' struggle. The best hope entertained by his counsellors was that the election of the Emperor might be deferred for a breathing-space. Contrary to his instructions from England, Doncaster decided to cut out a projected call upon the Elector of Saxony, and make on at once to King Ferdinand with proposals that he should deal with the Bohemian problem before presenting himself for election.

The "mediator Ambassador" passed on to Munich, where he found Maximilian of Bavaria most attentive but, "in respect

of his sickliness and consequently love of a retired life, altogether alienated from the ambition of being Emperor". At
Salzburg Doncaster succeeded in meeting King Ferdinand, *en
route* for Frankfurt and his election. "Finding his Majestie's
answere more kinde than particular, I humbly prayed him to
speak cleerly to me." Ferdinand referred the English Ambassador to a counsellor, who kept him waiting "a Dutch houre",
which proved "as long as their mile". When the Ambassador
begged the counsellor to declare "upon what condition his
Majesty would be pleased to agree to a cessation of armes", so
that they might be proposed to the Bohemians before the
election, his Majesty's official "was startled, rubbed his fingers,
sayd it was a new proposition and now out of all reason and
season, his Majesty having the Bohemians, as it were, in his
power". He finally took refuge in the excuse "that his Majesty
had no counsellor about him here to advise him on a matter of
that importance".

Ferdinand's election took place at Frankfurt on August 28th
(N.S.). A deputy represented the Prince Palatine. From
Amberg, five days earlier, a young and untried general, happy
at the head of his army of defence, sent thanks to his wife for a
"dear letter". "Believe me, my dear heart, that I often wish
myself near you; it seems long to that happiness. Meanwhile,
love me, I beg, for ever." The Prince of Transylvania had
offered to bring an expedition in aid of the Bohemians into
Hungary. The Prince Palatine had written to the Bohemians,
entreating them to submit to mediation, but heard nothing
from that country for a week—an ominous sign. "It looks as if
Ferdinand, instead of gaining a crown at Frankfurt, may lose
two." With less than his usual good humour, the Prince Palatine commented, "God grant it! What a lucky prince he is to
have the pleasure of being hated by all the world!"[1] Elizabeth's feelings on hearing of Ferdinand's election were expressed

[1] Bromley, p. 2.

to Sir Dudley Carleton in startling terms: "They have chosen heare a blind Emperour, for he hath but one eye, and that not verie good. I am afraid he will be lowsie, for he hath not monie to buy himself clothes."

But already the new Emperor had fulfilled part of her husband's predictions. On August 19th the Bohemians had formally deposed Ferdinand and declared their crown elective. They had then considered various candidates, but none appeared to them so desirable as the young Elector Palatine, whose upper country bordered upon their own, and who was head of the Protestant Union and son-in-law of the powerful King of England. By August 27th the walls of Prague ´were echoing to the discharge of cannon and the pealing of joy-bells in honour of the election of Frederick, King of Bohemia, and messengers bearing letters begging his acceptance of a crown were on the road for Amberg.[1]

On a late August day, Baron Christopher Dohna arrived at Heidelberg post haste, *en route* for England. It is probable that a letter from Frederick brought to her by Christopher Dohna, first informed Elizabeth that gentlemen in "the château of Prague" were ready to salute her by the title of "Serene and Puissant Queen".[2][3]

[1] Lord Doncaster believed the election had taken place on Frederick's twenty-third birthday, August 25th (N.S.), and noted that the news reached the king-elect on his wife's birthday, the 29th (N.S.). Other authorities give 16th–26th as the date of the election, but all agree that Frederick received the news on the 19th–29th. (*Relations between England and Germany*, ii. 52.)

[2] S.P. 81.16.266.

[3] All the letters quoted in the foregoing part, unless otherwise annotated, have been printed by the Camden Society in two volumes entitled "*Letters and Other Documents Illustrating the Relations between England and Germany at the Commencement of the Thirty Years War.*" A comprehensive list of authorities on the Thirty Years War occupies 152 pages of the *Cambridge Modern History*, vol. iv.

CHAPTER IV

THE QUEEN OF BOHEMIA

I

"My Lord,"

wrote the Princess Palatine to the Marquis of Buckingham, on September 1st, 1619 (N.S.),

"This worthy bearer will inform you of a business that concernes his master verie much; the Bohemians being desirous to chuse him for their King, which he will not resolve of till he knowe his Majesties opinion in it.

"The Baron of Dona will inform you particularlie of all. The King hath now a good occasion to manifest to the world the love he hath ever professed to the Prince heere. I earnestlie entreat you to use your best meanes in perswading his Majestie to shew himself now, in his helping of the Prince heere, a true loving father to us both.

"I am so assured by manie testimonies of your affection to us both, as I make no dout but you will lett this bearer have your best furtherance in this business, I therefore recommende it to your care and am ever

your most affectionate friend

Elizabeth.

"I am intreated by the Prince of Anhalt, for feare he shoulde be censured in concilling the Prince to the warres, to intreat you not to beleeve of him anie thing hardlie, but to be assured he will councell nothing but what shall be for the Prince's good."[1]

[1] Tanner MS. 74.219.

Christian of Anhalt Bernburg subsequently escaped much censure that he richly deserved, but to her grief and surprise, blame for having urged, for purely selfish reasons, a decision which proved fatal to her husband's fortunes, was unhesitatingly bestowed by contemporaries upon Elizabeth.[1]

Towards the end of July, she had written to Frederick that she believed she was childing again. Frederick had answered that he was glad, but would be gladder when he heard more definite news. Whether she was *enceinte* again or not, she could not be more dear. Letters from Frederick to his wife flowed in to Heidelberg during August and early September. On August 13th, writing from "high up in the little tower of Neumark", he mentioned in a postscript that an alliance between Bohemia, Moravia and Silesia, not likely to be agreeable to Ferdinand, had been concluded. He had other "important things" to tell his wife, but owing to the disturbed state of the roads dare not write them.[2] From Amberg on August 24th he told her that he had heard from Achatius Dohna at Prague that he was likely to be elected by the Bohemians. The documents carried by Christopher Dohna, explaining the situation to the King of England, and asking what support James was prepared to give, had been drawn up by Christian of Anhalt Bernburg. Five days later, having heard definitely of his election, Frederick expressed himself much troubled, and asked his wife to forward the news to his mother. "I don't suppose that this can be

[1] Later critics have represented Elizabeth as using every means in her power to compel Frederick to accept a crown. This fiction is fully discussed by Dr. J. G. Weiss, in an article, "Some questions concerning Elizabeth Stuart, etc." (of which a copy is to be found at the Institute of Historical Research, University of London), and by Mrs Lomas, in her introduction to Mrs Everett Green's *Elizabeth of Bohemia*. These authorities agree that the story of Elizabeth telling her husband that she "would sooner eat sauerkraut at a king's table than feast on delicacies with an Elector" is not to be found in any contemporary document, and that although Elizabeth rejoiced in her husband's eventual decision, she used no violent importunities to secure it.

[2] Aretin, vii. 146–8.

kept a secret for long."[1] On the same day[2] he wrote to the Margrave of Ansbach and sent copies of the invitation from Prague to his Palatine counsellors, who were still at Frankfurt attending the Imperial Diet.

He received his wife's comment on his news in the romantic little town of Rothenburg, to which he had hastily summoned a meeting of the Union. Elizabeth wrote that, since God directs all, He had doubtless sent this thing. She would leave the decision to her husband. But should he decide upon acceptance of the proffered crown, she would be ready to follow the divine call, to suffer what God should ordain, and if necessary, pledge her jewels and what else she had in the world.[3]

Before she saw her husband, Bohemian envoys had arrived in Heidelberg, and were asking for an audience with their queen-elect. The Bohemians proved unalarming. They were two brothers of the name of Müller. They brought a letter written in French, informing "your Majesty" that by the singular providence of God, Messieurs the Directors of the Realm of Bohemia, with the Ambassadors of the Countries of Moravia, Silesia and Upper and Lower Lusatia had, after much counsel and consideration and amongst great applause, elected as King of Bohemia "Monsieur, your husband". Elizabeth sent them on to see her husband at Rothenburg.

According to James I, Christopher Dohna bore him Frederick's solemn assurance that "untill the election was past" the Elector Palatine had been "utterly ignorant" of the Bohemians' intention.[4] Hopes of a larger destiny for the Prince Palatine had always been cherished by his uncles of Bouillon and Nassau. At the date of his marriage, his expectations of becoming King of Bohemia, a country conveniently adjoining his own principality, had been openly mentioned. Last year,

[1] Aretin, vii. 148.
[2] Which he calls Elizabeth's birthday, since he reckoned O.S.
[3] Moser, *Patriotisches Archiv*, vii. 47.
[4] S.P. 81.16.266.

his Chancellor, Christian of Anhalt, and his fellow-Elector, the Margrave of Ansbach, had discussed with Charles Emanuel of Savoy the division of the spoil in the event of the duke's succession to the Imperial throne. Bohemia had then been suggested as the Prince Palatine's share, but Charles Emanuel had been inclined to keep Bohemia for himself, leaving Hungary to Frederick. The desirability of annexing Alsace and even part of Austria to the Palatinate of the Rhine had been considered.[1] If Frederick remained in blissful ignorance whilst such projects were discussed by his Chancellor on his behalf, he must be convicted of lethargy or inefficiency. As he was both talented and sensitive, it is far more likely that the knowledge of such schemes was amongst the reasons for the recurrent melancholy which afflicted the young head of the Protestant Union. When his enemies heard of his election they hotly accused Frederick of having intrigued to obtain it, and of having deliberately deceived the Emperor by the announcement that he had sent Albrecht of Solms to Prague only to urge obedience upon the Bohemians. No evidence is forthcoming that Solms or Achatius Dohna intrigued with, or without, their prince's knowledge at Prague, but Christian of Anhalt Bernburg rests under suspicion of having intimated that Frederick would accept the Bohemian crown, nor was the Chancellor of the Palatinate mistaken in his reading of his young master's character. Frederick, who had been bitterly disappointed when Ferdinand succeeded to every honour, may well have been taken by surprise by the turn of events in August 1619, but the surprise was not wholly unpleasant to him. Lord Doncaster, on his road to take a cure "at the Spaw" after his fruitless embassy, wrote, on the very day that Frederick was being elected at Prague, that he had "apprehensions" the Bohemians might proceed to elect a king. On parting from him, some of them had hinted mysteriously at a "brave resolu-

[1] Lundorp, *Acta Publica*, iii, 596–621.

tion their masters had taken". When Christopher Dohna delivered to him a letter from Frederick, announcing his election and his intention of asking advice from England, the English Ambassador expressed his belief that "the Count Palatine hath a disposition to accept of that crown."

Frederick arrived home in late September. His counsellors had assembled to meet him; his mother had arrived from Kaiserslautern. His wife had heard from the Archbishop of Canterbury, whose opinion she had solicited. Archbishop Abbot unhesitatingly advocated acceptance of the Bohemian offer. The Dukes of Bouillon and Zweibrücken shared these views. The Prince of Orange was preparing fool's livery for all who should attempt to dissuade his nephew from embracing the Bohemian offer. In Paris the English Ambassador said, "God forbid he should refuse it." But amongst all the Palatine counsellors, only one, a brother of the late Schomberg, advised unconditional acceptance, and at Rothenburg, among all the members of the Union, only the Margraves of Baden and Ansbach had given the same advice. The Dowager Electress was opposed to her son's endangering his hereditary domains to assist a foreign country.[1] Maximilian of Bavaria warned the Prince Palatine openly of the risks he must run. Four reasons for acceptance and fourteen against were finally adduced by Frederick's council, while the Bohemians pressed for their answer, pointing out that delay was fatal to their cause. Frederick had now, like Caesar, thrice received the offer of a kingly crown, which many held him to be loath to wave away. But, unlike Caesar, he had not thrice refused. Christian of Anhalt, a famous soldier, old enough to be his father, was at his elbow, advocating a bold course. His chaplain, Schultz, was calling upon him to arise as the Champion of Protestant Germany. Frederick decided that God had called him to a throne. "I can say with truth that I have not aspired to it, but

[1] Spanheim, *Mémoire sur la vie de Louise Juliane,* p. 142.

always sought my happiness in what God has given me, and rather tried to impede than to advance this election. This makes me the more assured that it is a divine vocation which I ought not to reject." [1]

On September 28th he wrote privately to Prague, agreeing to meet Bohemian deputies upon the borders of the Upper Palatinate. If he found the conditions which they offered acceptable, he would proceed at once with them to their capital. On October 6th this decision was formally made known in several of the courts of Europe.

II

Although she was childing again, his loving consort would not desert the King of Bohemia. A worried young husband confided his difficulties to Lord Doncaster, hurriedly summoned from Frankfurt by Sir Albert Morton. Lord Doncaster went to Heidelberg as privately as possible. He was justifiably nervous as to what might be his master's feelings towards a son-in-law who had acted before receiving advice from the Solomon of Europe. He presented himself at the castle at an early morning hour, attended by one servant only. When he was ushered into the presence of the young king-elect, he explained at once that he was "unable to say anything as a publique person". His future Majesty gracefully intimated that he was addressing a friend. "He was distracted." Should he leave his wife in Heidelberg, send her to England, or "lead her up with him into the Upper Palatinate, and as farr further as the importunity of the business drew him"?

To his great relief, after a very little conversation with the queen-elect, Lord Doncaster was able to assure her husband that "her owne vehement inclination and almost inexorableness to the contrary, drew her to accompany him. . . . To leave

[1] *Mercure Français*, vi. 135.

her at Heidelberg tooke from her the occasion of that which she estimated her greatest happiness, to expresse her love to him, and her desire to participate all his fortunes." Lord Doncaster was convinced that a visit by his hostess to her native land would at present be most inadvisable.

The king-elect, having announced that eight hundred horse should guard his consort on her journey, "descended to the second occasion of his calling me", which was to discuss his father-in-law's attitude. He entreated Lord Doncaster to use every endeavour to persuade his Majesty of Great Britain to assist him in an enterprise "into which he protested, with very much and credible zeale and fervour, that no levity or ambition, but only a desire to be an instrument of God's glory, had embarked him".

Action suited Frederick. There was no trace of melancholy or diffidence about him as he explained his situation and intentions to the English Ambassador-Extraordinary. He proposed to set out for Prague within two or three days. He was entrusting the civil government of the Lower Palatinate to the Duke of Zweibrücken, and the military to Count John of Nassau. Heidelberg and Mannheim were both reliably manned and munitioned. The infants, Prince Charles Louis and Princess Elizabeth, were to be left with their grandmother, the Electress Dowager, who would take up residence at Heidelberg, but the heir, Prince Frederick Henry, who was nearly six, would accompany his parents. Frederick enumerated rousingly the names of the puissant gentlemen who had already rallied to him—the Margraves of Baden and Ansbach, the Duke of Zweibrücken, the Landgrave of Hesse and Prince Christian of Anhalt Bernburg. The Duke of Würtemberg should reach Heidelberg to-day; the King of Denmark had offered a loan to the Union; the King of Sweden had given "good hopes of his assistance". "From the other side of the countrey" the Prince of Transylvania had sent an express embassy, advising

N

the Bohemians "to forbeare the hazzard of a battel" until he could come up to their aid.

In vain Lord Doncaster begged his host to remember also "the number and quality of his ennemies". Frederick closed the interview by a tactful message to "a nobleman of merit, and my friend", the Marquis of Buckingham, now Lord High Admiral. On his return to Frankfurt, the dismayed Ambassador-Extraordinary received a further "commandment" from Heidelberg, "to present to his Majesties gratious consideration" his son-in-law's desires regarding the Venetians. Would the King of England ask the Venetians to assist the King of Bohemia to the tune of two hundred thousand crowns; to assign to him henceforward his regal title, and, in the event of their permitting troops to pass through their territories "to the prejudice of the Bohemians", to communicate first the numbers, and rate of advance of the invaders? Fatherly favour would, his son-in-law expected, induce the King of England to act "with all hast and expedition".[1]

The great exodus from Heidelberg took place on Monday, October 7th. The weather had broken. Yesterday, when Frederick, leading his heir by the hand, had attended a farewell morning service in the principal church of his capital, the heavens had wept as if in sympathy with his deserted subjects. The departure from the castle was effected as early and quietly as possible. Fortunately there was no question of having to pass through the town on an eastward journey. Before eight o'clock in the morning most of the luggage had been loaded upon a hundred and fifty-three waggons. Some of it was very heavy. Both their Majesties were great readers. A folio first edition of poor Sir Walter Raleigh's *History of the World* was going to Prague.[2] Another weighty coffer held all their gold

---

[1] *Relations between England and Germany*, ii. 46–52.

[2] This volume, which is to be seen in the British Museum (Press Mark C.38.i.10) had romantic adventures, detailed in Latin manuscript notes by

plate, including a gold box in which reposed the bond for a life-pension of four hundred pounds granted by the States General to the little prince.[1] Larger but lighter trunks contained his Royal Highness's toys and lesson-books and little suits, and her Majesty's farthingales and laces and tall hats, and all the swaddling-bands and linen and pap-bowls that would shortly be needed by Hans-in-the-Cellar, as the jolly Dutch coyly called the little-one-that-is-to-be.[2] Their Majesties' attendants descended into the Schlosshof, prepared to mount horse and chariot. His Majesty's chaplain, Dr Abraham Schultz, was very ready, clad in his long black gown and flat cap, his pale face alight with spiritual exaltation. Her Majesty's resolute English ladies, cloaked and hooded, were in charge of her jewels and the pets which she esteemed as jewels. Jacko the monkey from Venice, gift of Sir Dudley Carleton, was going east with his indulgent mistress. Upstairs, the Queen was saying good-bye to her infants and her mother-in-law in her recently completed English apartments. Anxiety had made the Dowager ill. When the royal couple and their heir appeared, their expressions were closely noted. Frederick had "such a cheerful assuredness in the faith and promises of Almighty God imprinted even in his countenance, as promiseth all good successe". He was known to have given away his hounds. The

---

various hands, on its title and following page. The first writer, Father Henry Fitz-Simon, S.J., relates that this book belonged to the library of "the pretended Queen of Bohemia", and that when, "on account of her misdoings", she was driven from Prague, it became the property of the Spanish Imperialist commander Verdugo, "the deposer from the throne of Frederick of the Palatinate—Henry Fitz-Simon being eye-witness". On the recapture of Prague by the Swedes in 1648 the book was recovered in the Hradčany by one John Klee. A nameless follower eventually presented it to Elizabeth's son, "Prince John Philip, my most clement master", for return to its owner.

[1] Bromley, p. 3.

[2] This expression was so popular at this date that even Lady Buckingham's expected heir was so termed in a letter to her husband. *Fortescue Papers*, CXXV.

arrival of a very young king bringing with him all the equipment for pleasures of the chase would not have produced a
good impression amongst persecuted Bohemians. Frederick,
who had always looked young for his years, had begun to
grow a beard. Although he was so dark, the result was not very
successful. His air as he took farewell of his depressed subjects
that depressing morning was considered to contain just the
right mixture of modesty and ardour. The extraordinary grace
and charm of "that hopeful young Prince Henrie" recalled
forcibly to English observers memories of his namesake, their
late Prince of Wales. "Queen Elizabeth, for so now she is",
left Heidelberg in tears. Her bearing, as she stepped towards
her waiting carosse, bowing and smiling, but "with teares
trickling downe her cheekes", "ravished" her audience. She
was to become the mother of a fourth child within nine weeks,
but her look of youth was still remarkable. As he watched her
mount the first carriage of the long procession bound to
succour Bohemia, an impressionable chronicler remembered
with emotion: "It is the manner of the Moors, in their most
deadlie battayles, to make choice of one of their chieffest and
fayrest virgins to goe before them into the field." [1] The
tremendous *cortège* began to move off along the moist and
shadowed hillside road leading east, followed by "strong cries,
prayers, well wishes and acclamations". The Dowager Electress, watching from a window of the castle, gave vent to a
Cassandra-like utterance treasured by her listeners, "*Ach! nun
geht die Pfalz in Böhmen!*" [2]

III

Elizabeth had looked her last on the home of her early
married life. On wet early autumn mornings the mist moves

[1] John Harrison, "A Short Relation of the Departure, etc." S.P. 101.27.
News letter from Heidelberg Oct. 14th–24th, 1619.
[2] Söltl, *Der Religionskrieg*, i. 157.

slowly across the wooded heights that back that tremendous red-sandstone structure of many watching windows. Her husband's capital held poignant memories for the weeping queen-to-be—her arrival there as a bride, "Madame, the Goddesses Flora and Pomona greet you!"—her dreaded first confinement, "A beautiful prince who strongly resembles himself to Monsieur l'Electeur!"—her summons to the death in child-bed of her English dame of honour, poor "Dudley" bright-eyed with fever, gasping out her hopes to meet her dear master and mistress again in Paradise.[1] She had also known many hours of utter happiness in the friendly Pfalz, many happy returns, flushed with exercise and forest air, along the road, bordered by flowering plum, that led to Schwetzingen and good hunting, many cosy winter evenings up in the castle, when, after curtains had been drawn, shutting out the view of silvered Christmas trees and town-lights reflected in the Neckar, her Highness's laughter would startle "*ma bonne mère* Harington" and Sir Albert Morton from their low-voiced English conversation about her Highness's finances, because, by the fireside, plump, good-natured Apsley, dandling Prince Frederick Henry, was once more caught by the nose. Twice a year there had been the excitement of hearing the mule-train come jangling up the castle hill from Frankfurt Fair. All German princes sent their agents to make purchases for them at this famous fair. Sometimes they went themselves, incognito. Schomberg had gone on behalf of his "*deux jeunes mariés*", and brought back ten thousand pins in a paper for Madame, who, he calculated, could afford to order twenty-four new gowns a year and six hundred pounds' worth of stockings, ribbons and laces. Her best laces, however, had been obtained for her by a Strassburg merchant, from Italy.[2]

The first stages of Elizabeth's long pilgrimage were familiar to her. She saw, across the river, Stift Neuburg, where she had

[1] S.P. 81. 14.207.   [2] *Ibid.*, 13.324.

fed her mother-in-law's prize cows. From Neckargemund the main road led down to Sinsheim, and up to the ferry near Neckarelz. Thence the east-bound procession wound its way by the small towns of Mosbach and Adelsheim, down to Halle and Crailsheim. The benevolent Margrave of Ansbach had entertained Elizabeth before when she had been bound for the capital of her husband's upper country. But the weather during her visit in 1615 had been more favourable for travelling. In October the best roads of Central Franconia held terrors for the occupants of the large and lumbering carriages of the early seventeenth century. As Elizabeth's chariot charged down a steep hill towards Ansbach, one of its wheels struck up a large stone which leapt into the carriage and hit her on the leg. The shock and pain made her faint. An accident already was a daunting experience for ladies who had before them the unnerving prospect of negotiating a road through the Bohemian forest. A halt was called at the nearest inn, but the queen-elect insisted on continuing her journey. She lay sideways along the seat of her chariot. On her arrival at the court of Ansbach her spirits were noted to be excellent.[1]

At Amberg an Imperial envoy asked for immediate audience with the Elector Palatine. Ferdinand II, by the mouth of Count Fürstenberg, adjured his vassal to refuse the requests of Bohemian rebels and repair to a Diet for discussion of the situation. But Frederick had ceased to hesitate. He answered that he had pledged himself to meet Bohemian deputies, and must keep his word. The king-elect, who had no military experience, was well satisfied with the appearance of the troops who had mustered to meet him in the capital of his Upper Country. He ordered a thousand of them to accompany him on the remainder of his journey.

[1] Everett-Green, p. 135.

IV

On October 23rd, 1619, much unusual traffic converged upon a small town on the border of Bohemia, between the Ober Pfalzewald and the Fichtelgebirge. Waldsassen had possessed a Cistercian monastery since the twelfth century, but no event of European importance had ever been staged there. The first arrivals in the bleak frontier town that autumn day were a large party of preoccupied gentlemen, who asked for news of the roads with obvious anxiety, and settled themselves down to wait with impatience. The speech and imperious bearing of some of them clearly announced them as large Bohemian landowners. Towards nightfall a travel-stained caravan of innumerable horsemen, baggage-waggons and carriages, strongly guarded by troops, toiled up towards the castle of Waldsassen. On the night of the 14th Frederick, king-elect of Bohemia, gave private audience to twenty-one Bohemian deputies, who assured him that even most of the Papist nobility of their country were determined to support him in preference to a tyrannous Habsburg.

Early next morning, in a chilly and obscure fortress, far from the land of her birth, her ladies arrayed Elizabeth Stuart for her first audience as a queen. Charming little Prince Frederick Henry was dressed and sent downstairs. While the Bohemian gentlemen offered his father a crown, he was to stand in attendance with his father's young brother, the Duke of Simmern, and the martial Prince Christian of Anhalt Bernburg. Eighteen coaches were toiling up from the town to the castle of Waldsassen. The first three vehicles contained the deputies of Bohemia, the fourth those of Moravia, the fifth the Silesians, the sixth the Lusatians. At length all the commissioners and their attendant officers were disembarked and ready to enter upon an historic interview.

The young and slight king-elect received his guests standing
and bareheaded. Without apparently any preliminary greetings, a venerable nobleman stepped forward and made a speech.
"Joachim André, Comte de Schlick, Chef de l'Ambassade", as
he is described by a contemporary French chronicler of this
Shakespearean scene, solemnly announced the deposition of the
Emperor Ferdinand II from the throne of Bohemia, and the
election in his stead of Frederick V, Prince Palatine of the
Rhine. He therefore begged his serene Electoral Highness to
accept forthwith the titles of King of Bohemia, Margrave of
Moravia, Duke of Silesia and Margrave of Higher and Lower
Lusatia. Frederick then spoke briefly, but with such frankness
and obvious deep feeling that tears sprang into the eyes of
several of his listeners. He returned thanks for his election, and
declared that, since he was convinced that the voice of God and
none other was calling him to assume these dignities, he would
do so. He was resolved to govern like a Christian prince. He
proceeded to present his son, his brother and the General of his
forces to his new subjects, and the commissioners solemnly
advanced to kiss the hand of their new master and salute his
attendant princes. Frederick played the king with *aplomb*.
"Amongst other hortatives", he had been reminded that "if he
had the courage to venture upon the King of England's sole
daughter, he might very well venture upon a sovereign
crown".[1] The same bearing which had carried him to success
at Whitehall at the age of sixteen had been remarkable in him
ever since he had made up his mind to mount a throne. Lord
Doncaster at Heidelberg had been struck by the high spirit,
authoritative and withal prudent air, of a prince who seemed
clearly "on the way to achieve greatness".[2]

The commissioners next asked for an audience with their
queen. A nobleman well known to her by name was spokes-
man of the procession introduced to Queen Elizabeth. Baron

[1] Howell, i. 83.   [2] *Relations between England and Germany*, ii. 81.

Vilém Václav Rupa had been one of the managers of the demonstration at Prague Castle last year. After assisting at the expulsion of Martinice, Slavata and Fabricius through the council-chamber windows, he had become head of the provisional government to defend the religious liberties of the Bohemians. Rupa's eloquence was very generally held to have turned the scale in favour of Frederick's election. The nobleman who was the first to kiss the hand of Queen Elizabeth of Bohemia at Waldsassen did not pay for his privilege so dearly as his colleague who first saluted her husband as king. Rupa's eventual reward was merely exile and death in sordid poverty; he escaped by flight the savage sentence performed upon the aged Schlick.

All the principal actors in this day's business, however, carried themselves with lofty disregard of their probable fate in case of its failure. The stalwart Baron Rupa, addressing in polished French a fair and smiling northern princess, thanked her for the services which she had already done to her new subjects by persuading her lord and master to become theirs too. He prayed that she might reign long over a people whom he commended to her regard. Elizabeth's answer, also spoken in French, was perfect for the consort of a Protestant champion. "Sir, what I have done for the honour of God and the good of our religion has been done whole-heartedly. Rest assured that in future my love and affection shall not be found wanting."

The King and Queen of Bohemia then descended to the town, attended by all their court and the commissioners, to implore God's blessing on their reign. After the service they returned to the castle through streets lined by enthusiastic troops. They feasted the commissioners by torchlight. Dr Abraham Schultz preached that day's sermon, taking as his text words from the twentieth Psalm—"In the name of our God we will set up our banners. . . . Some trust in chariots and some in horses; but we will remember the name of the Lord our God." Next day Frederick and Elizabeth crossed the frontier into their new country.[1]

V

The King and Queen of Bohemia proceeded towards their capital up the wildly picturesque valley of the Eger. The old industrial town of Eger (Cheb), situated at the foot of one of the spurs of the Fichtelgebirge, was their first halt over the border. Its castle boasted a massive black tower built of blocks of lava. The royal procession, which was reckoned to contain between a thousand and twelve hundred horses, wound its way upstream to the castle of Falkenau. The roads are reported to have been in poor condition. Every day the queen and her ladies, crouched in their unwieldy carosses, beheld fresh views of crystalline torrents dashing between granite cliffs clothed by "tall Fir trees, fit to make Masts for Ships" amongst which antique castles peered down upon river and road. Between Falkenau and the famous Hussite town of Saatz˙ (Žatec) they deserted the banks of the Eger for a space. At Maschau, on the morning of October 27th, they enjoyed an open-air banquet offered by a neighbouring landowner of the name of Steinbach. It had never been the custom of the Prince and Princess Palatine to travel on a Sunday, but it behoved the King and Queen of Bohemia to reach home as soon as possible. Christian of Anhalt's field-chaplain preached a sermon after the feast. Saatz on Sunday afternoon greeted a Protestant king and queen with gunfire and the ringing of joy-bells. At the gate of the town a deputation of councillors presented their keys to Frederick, and a gathering of matrons and maidens addressed themselves to Elizabeth. After listening to a Latin

[1] Abelin, *Theatrum Europaeum*, i. 242; Häusser, ii. 314; Khevenhüller, ix. 610–12; *Mercure Français*, vi. 142–4; *Mercurius Gallo-Belgicus*, xiii. 71; *Relations between England and Germany*, ii. 44.

oration, the royal couple were escorted to their lodgings through streets lined by troops clad in blue and white. Laun, another old Eger-side town, was their next halt. They then turned south-east, and tasted the hospitality of a wealthy Bohemian nobleman noted as the Herr von Colobrat, owner of the beautiful château of Bussierat (Busantierad). At this castle, a gentleman, riding post, was hurried to their presence. Christopher Dohna had missed his lord and lady at Heidelberg. The tidings brought by him were not all that had been hoped, but might have been worse. The King of England had kept his son-in-law's envoy waiting ten days for an answer to his request for advice. During this period a second messenger from the Palatinate had arrived with the news that the Palsgrave had accepted the crown of Bohemia. "Britain burned towards Frederick and Queen Elizabeth." Londoners had lit bonfires and rung joy-bells. "There was not a soldier, or an officer, or a knight that did not beg to be allowed to go to the help of Bohemia." But chilling orders from Theobald's Palace had speedily forbidden public rejoicings or prayers for King Frederick and Queen Elizabeth. His Majesty could not give the Elector Palatine the title of king until he was sufficiently assured of the legality of this election. The King of England was sending to ask the opinion of the King of Spain on the matter. He had "returned Baron Done home with a request unto his sonne that til he can heare again from Spain, the whole busines may be continewed with as much peace as may be".

From Busantierad the approach of the King and Queen of Bohemia to their capital was "for the most part through fruitful hils of corne, the rest through Rockes and Mountaines planted with Vines". Their entry into Prague took place on the last day of October, 1619, and was well staged to impress both their Majesties and their subjects. The ceremonies began at a hunting-lodge in a walled park on a spur of the Bílá Hora (White Mountain), west of the river Vltava. The Hvĕzda

(Star) Palace was so called because it was built in the form of a six-rayed star, and surrounded by converging avenues of trees "planted in the figure of starres".[1] This first palace of their kingdom to be occupied by Frederick and Elizabeth was of unusual beauty. Its roof was covered by burnished copper, its walls were plastered white. Within, its echoing hall and fine double staircase displayed many classical statues, posed in niches. The ceilings of its reception-rooms, necessarily of peculiar shape, bore exquisite reliefs, representing gods and goddesses, birds, beasts and a notable collection of sea-monsters, attended by Naiads and Tritons. The views from its windows, on three sides, were of whispering woods. West-wards the ground sloped sharply, revealing a wide view of cheerful beauty. Spacious stables and an Italian garden were amongst the amenities of the "Star" hunting-lodge six miles from the Bohemian capital. To this "little faire house" on the morning of Thursday, October 31st, Baron Boruslav Burka, Grand Chamberlain of Bohemia, and the burgesses of Prague, repaired to meet their new master, attended by a brilliant assembly of Bohemian, Moravian, Silesian and Lusatian gentle-men on horseback and in carriages. Baron John of Tallenburg opened the proceedings by a speech in Czech, which was trans-lated for the benefit of their majesties by Baron Rupa. "To the great contentment" of all present, Frederick did not depute Rupa to return thanks, but condescended to answer personally. Nearly all his principal listeners could speak German, but at such a moment patriotism dictated to them the use of their native tongue, not one word of which could be understood by their new king. Representatives of the great families of Bohemia next advanced to kneel on the greensward, first in front of Frederick, then in front of his wife. When the Grand Chamberlain had concluded his presentations, Frederick

[1] The "Star" hunting lodge still stands, its park is a favourite summer resort of the citizens of Prague.

mounted a charger, and Elizabeth a chariot decorated in gold and silver and attended by footmen in liveries of maroon velvet. She took no companion in her gorgeous equipage, neither did Frederick take any gentleman to ride on his right or left hand. This arrangement had been designed so that their subjects should have no difficulty in distinguishing the king and queen.

The entry of Frederick and Elizabeth into Prague is reported to have resembled a Roman triumph, and to have occupied three hours, yet to reach the castle they did not have to pass through the "three towns" of their capital. These lay on the east bank of the Vltava. All the festivities of October 31st took place on the plateau and slopes of the White Mountain and Hradčany hill, on the west side of the river.

As the royal procession approached the Strahow gate of the Hradčany, it encountered a party of four hundred peasants marching under a tattered banner. The colonel of this force delivered himself of a "brave speech" in Latin, at the close of which "all the clowns cried out with a loud voice 'Vivat Rex Fredericus!'" They were armed with "scythes, flails, hatchets and targets", and they "made such a tintamarre in clattering of their weapons together that their Majesties could not forbear laughing". But the clowns had no intention of amusing their Majesties. Their uncouth antics were inspired by spiritual emotion. They were members of a religious sect, "Taborites", descendants of the men who had fought for the liberties of Bohemia under the Hussite leader Žižka.

Within the walls of the Hradčany the crowds were unmanageable. They manifested their loyalty with such exuberance and abandon that the dark young king, becomingly attired in a suit of brown and silver, turned in his saddle to issue an order forbidding the firing of any more *feux de joie* lest any of his subjects should be injured."

The home to which Frederick and Elizabeth were brought after darkness had fallen resembled the Kremlin, in that it was not a single royal residence, but a fortified walled enclosure containing several palaces, churches, monasteries and even taverns. The royal procession toiled by torchlight up steep cobbled inclines and across wind-swept squares adorned with statues and fountains and dominated by spires and towers. Elizabeth's chariot halted at last outside an imposing Italian Renaissance entrance. A party of ladies, richly, but to her eyes most barbarously attired, dropped on their knees to raise the hem of her hoop skirt to their lips. The chief lady addressed her fluently, and evidently flatteringly, in Czech. The comparatively modern palace built by the late Emperor Rudolph II had been made ready for her Majesty. But Queen Elizabeth would not be parted from King Frederick. His Majesty had been lodged in the Královský Hrad, oldest part of the Hradčany. This ancient fortress of the Přemyslide kings of Bohemia had been largely rebuilt by the Luxembourg Emperor Charles IV in the fourteenth century. No Habsburg ruler of Bohemia had ever slept there.[1]

VI

On the day after her arrival in Prague, the Queen of Bohemia wrote to the Marquis of Buckingham to tell him that her husband and she had been received in their capital "with a great show of love of all sortes of people. The King hath stayed Morton by him till he and I be crouned. I will write to you more at large, for now I am in hast. I pray continue still the good offices you doe me to his Majestie. I am ever your affectionat frend ELIZABETH."[2]

[1] *Theatrum Europaeum*, i. 243–4; *Mercure Français*, vi. 147–50; Harl. MS. 6815.64; Khevenhüller, ix. 614.

[2] Hist. MS. Commission, 10th Report, Appendix 1, pp. 89–90.

To conciliate the King of England's favourite was of first importance.

Next morning Frederick and she emerged from the Královský Hrad and proceeded on foot across the square which contained the Cathedral of St Vitus, and an equestrian statue of St George, which had been sadly damaged in the great fire of 1514, and again on the occasion of the coronation of Maximilian II. The coronation of Frederick I was to take place in two days' time, and inside the cathedral officials and workmen were busy. The king and queen were on their way to inspect one of the most famous sights of Prague, the collection of art treasures made by Rudolph II. This prince, patron of chemists, alchemists, astronomers and astrologers, had despatched agents all over Europe to secure "curiosities" for the decoration of the great gallery which he had built in the north-west corner of the largest courtyard of the Hradčany. English-born Queen Elizabeth was observed to display knowledgeable pleasure as she beheld statues of bronze, marble and stone, coins, cameos, watches, clocks and several hundred canvases by leading Italian, Dutch and German masters. A particularly fine painting represented the Virgin and Child bestowing crowns of roses on the Pope Julius II and Emperor Maximilian I. The "Rosenkrantzfest", by Albrecht Dürer, had been carried over the Alps from Venice to Prague by "four stout men".[1] The new queen laughed as she remarked to the gentleman attending her, "Really, Ferdinand has left us many beautiful things!" "These things are no longer his, Madame", was, according to his own report, the smooth reply of this courtier.[2]

Early on the morning of November 4th, a deputation of "the chiefe of the kingdom" arrived in Frederick's bedchamber, to invite him to accompany them to the cathedral. Arrangements

[1] This picture is one of the few "curiosities" of Rudolph's collection still to be seen in Prague.
[2] News Letter from Prague, Nov. 4th, 1619. S.P. 101.41.

for the coronation of a Calvinist king in Prague had not been accomplished without difficulty. The deposed Ferdinand had been crowned in St Vitus, with great pomp, little more than two years before, so many officials and clergy were well versed in the procedure of such an occasion. It was obviously desirable that the coronation of Frederick should be performed with all the impressive rites hallowed by custom, but it was unthinkable that he should receive his crown from the hands of a Catholic archbishop. This problem had been solved by the appointment of two leading Bohemian Protestant clergymen, but the question whether Frederick should be anointed was much more vexing. The Calvinists and Taborites had cast away holy oil together with holy water and graven images. On the other hand, to Lutherans and Catholics the unction was an essential feature of a coronation. Frederick wisely decided not to run the risk of being stigmatized by any sect as an unanointed and unconsecrated king. His Calvinist chaplain thereupon abstained from assisting at so Papistical a service, whilst his Lutheran subjects regretted the appearance of their cathedral on November 4th. Many a carved and gilded figure, long venerated by them, had been removed from the scene. The High Altar bore six candlesticks only—"ny croix ny saincts".

Elizabeth witnessed her husband's coronation from a gallery specially erected for her use. Since the name of Prince Frederick Henry is not mentioned in the list of six princes for whom chairs were set in the vicinity of the throne, it appears that the young heir sat with his mother and her ladies. The unrehearsed, unusual and hastily ordered ceremony, although shorn of some of its ancient rites, was of inordinate length. The music is said to have been of a remarkably high quality. Frederick was duly led in royal robes from the chapel of St Wenceslaus to the High Altar, where he was blessed by one of the two clergy "executing Episcopall function". Prayers were followed by music, and the royal robes were laid upon the Altar. Whilst a sermon was preached a Litany sung and a lesson read, the king occupied his throne. He was then again led to the Altar, where the chief Burgrave of Bohemia administered the coronation oath. The disputed unction was performed. The king re-assumed his robes, "but first was the anoynting done on the tope of his head". The sword, the ring, the sceptre and the orb were delivered to Frederick I. He stood while the crown was bestowed upon him "in a triumphant manner" by the two principal clergy and two principal laymen of his realm, with the words, "Receive the Crowne of the kingdome O King-Elect, which is set upon thy head in the name of the Holy Trinity, and out of the free consent of the States and chiefe of this kingdome, through the providence of God". The homage was performed in a manner striking and novel to English eyes. After the king had been escorted back to his throne, the Chief Burgrave invoked the congregation in Czech—"All ye that can, come neare unto the Royall Chayre and lay two fingers on the King's Crowne: the rest put up your fingers!" "Instantly there was seene all the chief of the kingdome, with an excessive joy, thronging to touch the King's crowne: the rest put up hands in token of a willing obedience and faithfull oath." The service was brought to a close by a prayer opening, "O Lord our God, looke heere in Thy presence stands Frederick, our lawfull chosen and crowned King".

Three days later a second gorgeous religious ceremony and banquet took place in the Hradčany. Queen Elizabeth's coronation was arranged to occupy less time than that of her husband, but its appointments were fully as splendid. The arrival in Prague before his mistress, of the Queen's chief physician, sent to collect medicaments in view of a royal accouchement in the capital "round about the feasts of Christmas", had aroused interest and sympathy which Elizabeth's personal appearance, marked by "sweetness and humanity",

o

had much increased. She was reported to have won "in particular the hearts of the ladies". The remarkable child with whom Elizabeth was quick, as her ladies attired her for her coronation, was to make an appropriately dashing entry into the world within six weeks. Nevertheless, her spirits were high as she prepared to receive, by grace and favour of a husband who had long been disparaged as her inferior in rank, the crown of a queen consort. "The queen showed herself very joyous in going to the church." The cobbles of the square across which she passed on her short route from the castle were covered by rich carpets. At the door of "the by-chapel called by the Romanists the Sachristi" she was met by the two principal prelates who had officiated at her husband's coronation. The stately building in which Elizabeth Stuart was crowned Queen consort of Bohemia little resembled the small and primitive rotunda raised on the same site by St Wenceslaus early in the tenth century. The light and lofty Gothic cathedral planned by the Emperor Charles IV had been adorned by architects from Arras and Gmünd with the likeness of many a smooth-faced saint and benefactor. After the great fire of 1541, the Emperor Ferdinand had added to a damaged and unfinished building a Renaissance Great Tower and double choir. The marble "Tomb of Kings" which faced the High Altar displayed fine recumbent effigies, the work of a Dutch sculptor. The chapel of St Václav, however, to which Elizabeth was led to assume her royal robes, was altogether Bohemian in character and, although it had been rebuilt in the fourteenth century, of a gloomy and barbaric magnificence. Its upper walls bore a spirited series of mural paintings representing the life and martyrdom of the national patron saint; its lower walls were entirely covered by an inlay of Bohemian semi-precious stones, amethysts, jaspers, chrysoprases, agates and cornelians. Other glittering treasures which surrounded the golden and jewelled shrine of the Prince-Saint were his bust, in silver, his helmet and coat of mail, and a candelabrum of rare beauty, containing a gilded reliquary in the shape of a tower.[1] Many candles lit the close and over-crowded chapel on the morning of Thursday, November 7th, 1619 (N.S.), and the clergy who attended the queen were of dignified appearance and clad in rich materials of glowing colours. "The Administrator and State-Holder of the Bishoppricke of Prage, by name Georgius Dicastus Mirzcovinus", was remarkable for his sonorous voice and long grey beard. His robes were of violet velvet. His colleague, "Johannes Cyrillus Trebicensis, Elder of the Consisterie", wore the blue velvet mantle and blue taffetas hat of a Bohemian Brother.

The procession which went before the queen to the High Altar of St Vitus' Cathedral included many blue- and violet-robed Bohemian clergy, and a string of hereditary crown officials, bearing tokens of their offices. The Chief Sewer carried two loaves of bread, one silvered, the other gilded; the vessels in charge of the Chief Cup-bearer were also of gold and silver. The queen's "scepter or staffe" was carried by the Chief Secretary; the Chief Judge bore the orb, and the Chief Burgrave the crown. Elizabeth was supported by the Administrator on her right hand and the Elder of the Consistory on her left. After both had uttered a solemn prayer, "answered by organ and choir's 'Amen', all kinde of Musicke was sung through the Church". The ceremony which followed resembled that performed three days before, with one important exception. After the queen had arisen from silent prayer in front of the High Altar, she was joined by her husband, who presented her to the Administrator, saying in Latin, "O Reverend Father, we request that thou wilt deign to bless this our consort, joined to us by God, and decorate her with the Crown Royal to the praise and glory of our Saviour, Jesus Christ."

[1] The splendours of the chapel of St Wenceslaus have survived many scenes of violence and are in the main preserved intact to-day.

Elizabeth sat on a throne draped in cloth of gold, set opposite
a pulpit, whilst a sermon was preached, a Litany chanted and a
lesson read. The lesson, which was taken from the second
chapter of the First Epistle of St Paul to Timothy, stopped short
at the seventh verse. Elizabeth's attire, as portrayed on her
husband's coronation medal, was a striking example of the
very "broided hair", "costly array" and decorations of gold and
pearls denounced by the apostle in verse nine as unfitting for a
modest woman. A lengthy prayer that the queen might become
a nursing mother of the Church and enjoy a long and happy
life, followed the lesson. "This prayer being ended all kind of
instruments were played on, with sweete melodies and
musicall voyces." The Burgrave of Karlstein, custodian of the
regalia, then advanced from the Altar, bringing the royal
insignia, and the "ancien pasteur" proceeded to anoint the
queen on both brow and breast, using the following words:
"Most gracious queen, seeing that also in the Church of old
Queens were annoynted (which annoynting was a signe of
God's lawfull calling, wherewith God hath sealed godly and
faithfull queens to the life which is prepared for us in Christ
Jesus), so the said God annoynt thee with His holy spirit, that
thou, as a true annoynted of God, mayest accomplish His holy
will and councell, through Jesus Christ Our Lord." The orb
was delivered to Queen Elizabeth with a prophetic reminder.
"Receive the Apple, the which, as it doth signifie the power of
kings and queens of this world, so also betokens the fickleness
of Kingdoms and Empyers." Elizabeth Stuart was crowned
with the crown of St Elizabeth, a beautiful and simple circlet
of archaic design, with double arches surmounted by a cross.
As the crown of the royal saint was bestowed upon her namesake, an appropriate prayer was uttered that it might be succeeded by a wreath of immortality. The service, advertised as
much curtailed, in view of the queen's hopeful condition, wore
on. Elizabeth occupied her throne throughout the singing of a

Te Deum and a prayer containing an exhaustive list of the noble women whose names are recorded in the Scriptures. At last the Administrator announced: "Long life to our Queen Elizabeth, with our most potent and gracious King Frederick and all their children and all their illustrious house, through Thy grace and mercy, O Lord our God, Almighty Father who, with the Son and the Holy Ghost reignest one God world without end, Amen."

A burst of colour and noise greeted the queen as she emerged from the cathedral. Bells were ringing from every tower of the three towns over the river, cannon were being discharged from city and castle walls. The Hradčany was packed by throngs of Bohemians in brilliantly coloured national costume, singing musically in chorus. The people of Prague prepared to celebrate the coronation of "Isabella" as they had done that of Frederick, with "great joy and jollities" and "all kind of Shewes, triumphs and fires". The queen's bounty to her subjects consisted of a liberal distribution of bread and wine. At her husband's coronation, medals had been scattered amongst the crowds. The great and costly banquet, attended by Elizabeth herself, took place in the Vladislav hall, or Hall of Homage, within the precincts of the old palace. The Westminster Hall of the Kings of Bohemia was one of the largest buildings in Europe.[1] Its vaulted roof was adorned with the coats of arms of many a Czech and Hungarian monarch. The heralds had been busy since the election of a king of the house of Wittelsbach. Within the Hradčany, emblems of the House of Habsburg had been hastily removed from hangings and furniture. Elizabeth's coat of arms now displayed several impressive additions—the lion rampant of Bohemia, the crowned eagle of Silesia, the eagle of Moravia, the wall of Lower Lusatia and the ox *passant* of Upper Lusatia. The queen was observed to look very happy "in the street leading to the palace

[1] It is 263 feet long, 52 feet wide and 43 feet high.

having the crown on her head; as she was also at table". She was served at her coronation banquet by ladies only, the wives of court officials, and, unlike her high-born countrywomen at her wedding feast, the court ladies of Bohemia appear to have behaved with restraint and dignity. Their duties were despatched "in such fine order that never before had anything more fine or magnificent been seen". Judging by contemporary engravings of her husband's coronation banquet, that of Elizabeth was attended by many sympathetic hounds and energetic trumpeters. Such English as were present to cry "Vivat Regina Elizabetha" rejoiced in "the sacred memory of that precious name, never to be forgotten, now revived again to God's glory and the general good of His Church". But no English eye-witnesses's report of the coronation of Elizabeth of Bohemia is forthcoming. No official representative from Great Britain had attended the ceremony. Sir Albert Morton was there as a guest, only because the king had "stayed him" by a personal request. The father of Queen Elizabeth still forbade his subjects to salute her by any other title than that of Princess Palatine.[1]

VII

Twelve days after their new queen's coronation, two coach-loads of citizens' wives, dressed in their best, crossed the noble bridge over the Vltava built by the Emperor Charles IV. They

[1] *Mercure Français*, vi. 150–6; *Theatrum Europaeum*, i. 245–7; "Relation of the Coronation of the King of Bohemia, etc., with the Ceremonies and Prayers," *Mercurius Gallo-Belgicus*, xiii. 97–104; S.P. Foreign News Letters, 101.27 & 41; News Letter from Nürnberg, Nov. 4th and from Prague, Oct. 20th, Nov. 4th and Nov. 10th, 1619; Harl. MS. 6815.64–7; *Actus Coronationis Friderici, Com. Pal. Rheni et Elizabethae Britanniae Magni principis etc. in regem et reginam Bohemiae Prague*, 1619; Khevenhüller, ix. 628–9. A contemporary engraving, representing Frederick and Elizabeth in their coronation robes, was entitled "The Triumph of Protestantism", and bore beneath it the words "This is the Lord's doing and it is marvellous in our eyes". To the left of the royal couple Calvin, Luther and Huss were shown, united in study of the Bible. To the right, the Catholic clergy fled into ominous darkness.

were going to the castle to see the queen, and their bearing was marked by all the gleeful importance peculiar to those who are in charge of a present which is a surprise.

The beautiful legend of St Elizabeth of Hungary, patron saint of queens, tells that the royal saint gave so bountifully to the poor as to leave her own household needy. On a winter's day her lord and master encountered her with her lap full of something, and demanded sternly what she was carrying. "Only flowers, my lord", replied the scared saint. When she disclosed her burden, the many loaves of bread which she had been carrying to the poor had been miraculously converted into a wealth of summer flowers. The memory of this pious princess, who had died nearly four hundred years past at the early age of four and twenty, was tenderly cherished by the women of Prague. Although few of them were still Catholic, they still persisted in the old custom of baking delicate bread shaped to resemble her miraculous flowers.

The entrance into the royal apartments of a group of respectable women who wished to make a presentation to the new queen was not opposed. The beaming deputation attained her Majesty's presence and the spokeswoman duly made her little speech, wishing Queen Elizabeth many happy returns of her name day. The St Elizabeth commemorated on November 19th (N.S.) was actually the mother of St John the Baptist, not the Queen of Hungary, for whom July 8th was reserved. However, the name was the great point. The appropriate gift was produced. But from this moment the interview limped towards a tragic finish, for the fair and majestic lady who found herself suddenly the possessor of a quantity of oddly shaped confectionery failed to display the deep emotion confidently expected by its donors. Baron Rupa thanked the good wives of Prague for their gift, in their queen's name,[1] adding that she

[1] Khevenhüller's account says that 'Müllner, then Vice-Chancellor' undertook this duty.

hoped that ere long their language would not be a dead tongue to her, but it was obvious to them that this Queen Elizabeth, so strangely attired in skirts distended by wires and a bodice which displayed her white bosom, took no great account either of her name day or the memory of St Elizabeth Regina. Or perhaps she scorned their gift as of small cost. The homely deputation could not even be certain that she had understood its significance. Confusion seized them, and they made a precipitate exit. In Prague over the river that night a dire story spread that the foreign queen had permitted her pages to gambol derisively in her presence with the little flowers of blessed St Elizabeth stuck in their hats and round their arms. "Before the queen, and the eyes of the women, who were made a laughing-stock, it was smashed and trodden upon." The stranger queen was reported to have no regular hours either for church or meals.

Great allowances, however, are made for a royal lady who is about to present her country with a prince, and presently a second deputation crossed the Vltava bound for the Hradčany. This time the gift for the queen was of suitable magnificence —an ebony and ivory cradle studded with gems, and a casket to match, containing a complete set of infant's clothes of finest lace and lawn from Cambrai. This time things went much better. The queen, to her subjects' surprise, seized and wrung their right hands, after the custom of her own country. She spoke a sentence of gratitude in Czech. She was evidently desirous to please, and exactly a month later she confirmed a good impression. Between nine and ten on the night of December 17th (O.S.) the Queen of Bohemia gave birth to a strong male child.[1] The citizens of Prague had much hoped that the infant born in their capital might prove little Prince Přemysl. They learned next day, as they filed past the presentation cradle ostentatiously exhibited in the queen's antechamber,

[1] S.P. 101. 27.177.

that the swarthy baby boy within was Prince Rupert. He had been named in honour of his ancestor, Rupert III, Elector Palatine, who had been elected Emperor and King of Bohemia on the deposition of Wenceslaus IV in the year 1400.[1]

<h1 style="text-align:center">VIII</h1>

Frederick had gone back over the frontier into the Upper Palatinate directly after his wife's coronation, bent upon a serious effort to combine the Calvinists and Lutherans of Germany. But the Lutheran princes had not even answered his summons to an assembly at Nürnberg. As soon as Elizabeth had recovered from her confinement, her husband set out on his travels again. Her heart had always sunk when the Elector had left her to attend one of his eternal conferences of the Union in some friendly German town. To be left in Prague while the King of Bohemia went on a mid-winter progress to try the temper of his new subjects was clearly a much more enervating prospect. The familiar scene took place attended by more than usual emotion. Frederick, between ardent kisses, promised to write if not every day, as often as possible. Elizabeth, in deepest dejection, promised not to give way to gloomy fancies. Frederick went on his way over the Moravian heights, and after some dark winter days had passed, a messenger arrived in Prague from Brno. His Majesty wrote from the capital of Moravia in high spirits. The country here was more beautiful than Bohemia, the noblemen's houses finer than any he had seen ever, except in Munich and Heidelberg. Last night he had been lodged with a Baron de Leip, whose house contained quantities of the finest tapestries. He enumerated an odd collection of presents for his queen, brought to him in this old industrial town—a most graceful wrought-iron bedstead, fur gloves, many fine steel knives and a service of pottery. He had

[1] Häusser, ii. 318; Gindely, pp. 160–1; Benger, 2.5; Strickland, 8, 107–8 ; Khevenhüller, ix. 660–4.

the best of news from his ally the King-elect of Hungary, but doubted whether the hopeful rumours of her father's attitude which his wife reported could be true, for he had heard nothing from Dohna, who was still in London. His busy Majesty was coming home as soon as possible. Meanwhile he begged his wife to remember her promise not to be so melancholy.[1]

But Queen Elizabeth, experiencing her first Bohemian winter aloft in the Hradčany, was extremely melancholy. She had for company her two sons, aged six and two months, her English suite—a band much thinned by time—and a number of Palatine ladies, all desperately homesick and by no means enchanted with Bohemia. She had no immediate prospect of hunting or of guests. Her long-projected trip to England was relegated to the dimmest of futures. The only important visitor expected by the King and Queen of Bohemia was, like themselves, a newly elected monarch. Frederick wrote that he held Bethlem Gabor to be a most honest man. The choice of this gentleman as a sponsor for Prince Rupert seemed to some people a little surprising, for a very general belief existed that the Prince of Transylvania and King-elect of Hungary was at heart a Moslem, and the story of his rise to power certainly had an Oriental flavour. He spoke his native tongue and Latin, an awe-inspiring prospect for an English hostess. But even Bethlem Gabor was not coming to Prague for several months.

The Jesuits had coined a disquieting nickname for the new King of Bohemia. They called him The Winter King. With the snows, they said, he would vanish. The Winter Queen sent her husband—who did not write nearly often enough—a beautiful yellow pen,[2] and applied herself to answering letters of congratulation. Her reply to the Duchess of Thouars' reminder of that old prophecy that she should be a queen was so resolutely cheerful that its postscript read strangely—"I shall never cease to love you whatever misfortunes overtake me—

<hr />

[1] Aretin, vii. 149–51.   [2] Aretin, vii. 150.

Elizabeth".[1] Nobody, except the King of Bohemia, must get gloomy letters from his queen, who, now that her infant had arrived and her husband had departed, had ample leisure to survey and reflect upon her new possessions.

The Hradčany was noticeably rich in gruesome legends. An epigram made during the reign of Rudolph II declared that if Libuša, the soothsayer, ancestress of the house of Přemysl, had built a town of wood on this site, Rudolph had transformed her foundation to marble, but golden.[2] Rudolph had been responsible for most of the modern apartments of Elizabeth's new home, but even these displayed dull leathers and dusty tapestries, for they had been entirely uninhabited for over two years before her arrival and not much used before that. Rudolph himself had always preferred to live—and even give state audiences—in his new stables. He had kept his astrologers, and the alchemists who were going to discover the Philosopher's Stone for him, in the north wing of the old castle. Those who proved unsatisfactory were consigned to the Daliborka, a tower which possessed a series of underground cells into which serious offenders were lowered by ropes through trap-doors. Even the cathedral within the Hradčany had its tales of violence, for it contained, in addition to the shrine of St Václav the martyr, the shrine of John Nepomuk—"a Bishop who, being the Queen's Confessor, was cast into the Molda, because he would not reveal her confession to her husband".[3]

On the bank of the river opposite the Hradčany, rose the "Great Side" of Prague. This consisted of "a little City of the Jewes, encompassed with wals" and "the City called new Prage; both which Citties are compassed about with a third, called old Prage". Although the capital was so lavishly walled, a well-travelled English observer [4] at the close of the

---

[1] Trémoïlle Letters, *Archaeologia*, 39.158.   [2] Lützow, *Prague*, p. 103.
[3] Wenceslaus IV, who ordered the martyrdom of John Nepomuk, was the brother of Anne of Bohemia, first queen of Richard II of England.
[4] Fynes Moryson, i. 32.

last century had expressed "small hopes in the fortifications", and his fears that "except the stinch in the streetes drive back the Turkes", Prague must fall an easy prey to the invading infidel. "The streetes are filthy. There be divers large market-places; the building of some houses is of free stone, but the most part are of timber and clay, and are built with little beauty or Art, the walles being all of whole trees as they come out of the wood, the which with the barke laid so rudely as they may on both sides be seen." [1] The three towns, in fact, contained many historic and impressive buildings worthy of inspection, but Queen Elizabeth, like the Austrian queens who had preceded her, knew little of the Great Side of her husband's capital. The Hradčany had, for many years, been considered to contain all that was necessary for a royal lady's comfort and pleasure.

The "King of the Snows" turned north towards the mountains of Silesia. He wrote that three letters from his wife had been delivered to him just as he was stepping into his coach to quit Sternberg. He was saddened to see that in spite of his prayers she was still melancholy. One must put one's trust in God. He thanked her for the beautiful pen, but it seemed to him that he was already writing three or four times a week. "Certes, you have no reason to think that I have forgotten you, or that you are a moment out of my thoughts." [2] At Breslau, "the next best town to Prague" in his dominions, he was greeted by the reassuring sight of a triumphal arch. He mentioned this to his wife, but did not divulge that a local seer [3] had prophesied that he saw an imperial crown on the brow of his new king. Scultetus, a Silesian by birth, preached a rousing sermon in the great hall of the old castle. The perfect husband sent his queen descriptions of the "very brave" jewelled and embroidered costumes worn by the Breslau ladies who

---

[1] Fynes Moryson, i. 32.　　　　[2] Aretin, vii. 154–7.
[3] Christopher Kotter. A wise woman, "Christina", made the same prophecy.

thronged to his receptions. The weather was terribly cold, but he had suffered no return of his earache. Spring was coming, and he had learnt that there were two excellent hunting châteaux close to Prague.[1] He was sending to Heidelberg for his hounds.[2] He had done his best to discover if the Count of Löwenstein had serious intentions towards her Majesty's maid of honour, Elizabeth Dudley. The count, summoned and asked the direct question, had replied, somewhat unsatisfactorily, that his thoughts at present were of war, not marriage. The entry of the King's younger brother had cut short this scene. "If only", sighed Frederick, "God would give us a good peace".[3]

On the 13th day of March Elizabeth heard that her husband would be home again to-morrow. She set herself down to answer the last of her congratulatory letters. Needless to say, Lady Harington's elder daughter had been amongst her warmest well-wishers.

DEARE BEDFORD,[4] (wrote the Queen of Bohemia),

I see by your lines that you are still the same to me in your affection. . . . I would that others were of your mind. Then I hope there woulde be taken a better resolution for us heere than yett there is; for I ame everie way assured of the peoples love, which is more than I can yett deserve.

I think I can easilie guesse who it is that doth chieflie hinder the King in resolving, but I am sure that though they have English bodies they have Spanish hartes.

The King heere comes home tomorrow. He hath bene in Moravia, Silesia, and the hie and low Lousnitz to take their othe of allegiance, which they have done with much testimonie of theire love. I shoulde have gone too, but that I lay in. They have given us both very faire presents in Moravia—the

---

[1] Aretin, vii. 159–60. [2] Bromley, pp. 5–6. [3] Aretin, vii. 154.
[4] Elizabeth always called her ladies by their surnames or titles, and generally called her artists by their Christian names. "Mitens" was the only artist whom she addressed by his surname. Hervey, p. 310.

noblemen's lands that were confiscated before our comming hither, and many other things besides.

This is a verie good countrie, but the ladies goe the strangeliest drest that ever I saw. They weare all furred capes and furred clokes, and great Spanish ruffes. Their gownes are almost like Spanish fashion, but no fardingales. The citizens and the better sorte goe alike.

The King hath biden Bethlem Gabor, the Prince of Transilvania, to cristen this little boy. He will not yet be called King of Hongarie,[1] though all that Kingdome hath sworne allegiance to him. He hath the croune by him, but will not yett be crouned, and onelie calls himself Prince of Hongarie and Transilvania. He will doe no other till he hath settled that countrie. He is altogether of our religion and a verie brave gentleman. I tell you this because manie putts it out that he is halve a Turk. But I assure you it is not so. I hope I shall see him this sommer, heere or in Moravia. The languish heere is not understood by the Dutch. It is like the Sclavon toungs. But allmost all the better sorte speeke Dutch and their owne toung.

I will say no more at this time. I pray commend me to my deere mother and yours.[2]

IX

On Sunday, March 31st, Prince Rupert was christened in the same cathedral which had been the scene of his parents' coronation. The day was one of dazzling sunshine. The pageantry was decidedly Bohemian. The arrival of each great personage was announced by trumpets, and each entrance was heralded by flourishes on kettledrums and hautboys. The

---

[1] A News Letters from Prague, dated Nov. 10th, had announced that Bethlem's coronation was expected to take place the next day. But Bethlem did not put himself outside the pale of Ferdinand's forgiveness by accepting a crown.

[2] Historical MSS. Commission, Supplementary Report, Hamilton MSS. 9. The spelling of the above transcript follows the original, but the punctuation has been augmented.

queen was escorted to the cathedral by her brother-in-law, Prince Louis, and the Duke of Saxe Weimar. Behind her came the wife of the Chief Burgrave of Bohemia, carrying the baby. Count Turzo, Bethlem Gabor's deputy, presented himself at the font clad in Hungarian national costume, and wearing a steel helmet. The black-eyed infant was handed by the Chief Burgravine to Count Turzo, who uttered the name "Rupert", and thence in turn to the representatives of Moravia, Silesia and the Lusatias, all of whom were in full armour. Every important lady present was then allowed to take the child in her arms for a moment. Even some casual spectators succeeded in holding the Bohemian-born princeling. When the procession emerged from the cathedral, the King of Hungary's gift to his godson was formally presented. Bethlem Gabor's offering was a wildly neighing Turkish courser, wearing a saddle, bridle and housings ornamented with gold and jewels. The ensuing feast took place in a temporary banqueting-hall on the river-banks within the walls of the Star Park. It lasted seven hours, and was followed by dancing in a silken pavilion where the fair queen presided in the light of many torches. Prince Rupert's christening was a brilliant success. Even the Jews, who do nothing unadvisedly, had sent him a valuable gift. Out of the mysterious walled Josefská Třílda had come a lovely silver alms-dish in the shape of a ship.

The christening festivities proved the opening of a series of gaieties quite in the old Heidelberg style. Three days later an important wedding took place up in the Hradčany. Since the bride was a Solms daughter and the bridegroom one of the Dohna brothers, both Frederick and Elizabeth attended the ceremony in state.[1] After the wedding came a tournament. The king's hounds arrived from Germany. Their Majesties began to hunt. Elizabeth wrote to her Trémoïlle aunt that the Prince of Anhalt, at the head of the strong army of the Protestant Union, meant to give battle to the Imperialist General

[1] Spanheim, *Dohna*, 226.

Bucuoy at the earliest opportunity. "There is nothing else for news here."[1] In clement weather her new home disclosed many attractive features outside the walls of the Hradčany— the Gardens of Paradise, which contained the Singing Fountain, and the little summer pavilion which bore the monograms of the Emperor Matthias and his consort on its weather-vane, and the *ménagerie* in the Lions' Court, and St. Václav's vineyard, and the riding-school and the tennis-courts. The Belvedere built for Anna Jagellowna, wife of Ferdinand I, was the most beautiful structure of its kind north of the Alps. Italian artists had decorated its colonnade on the ground floor with a frieze of graceful foliage and many a medallion, one of which showed its builder presenting flowers to his queen. Its broad balcony commanded an unequalled view of the castle and the towers and spires of the Great and the Little sides of Prague. With spring, fruit-blossom flowered below the Black Tower, where in Jelení Příkop, the Stag's moat, dappled fawns drank from the brook Brusnice.

On April 12th the Estates of Bohemia acceded to their newly elected king's request that they should nominate his eldest son his successor. Prince Frederick Henry was publicly proclaimed Crown Prince of Bohemia. Thunder rattled as the proclamation was read, but this was defiantly construed as a happy omen. The Estates proceeded to bestow upon the Queen the suzerainty of Arlingen and the domain of Kinsky. In the same week word arrived from Ferdinand II that unless the Elector Palatine resigned the crown of Bohemia within the month, he would be placed under the ban of the Empire. Frederick replied that it was for him as Elector Palatine to judge the Emperor, not for the Emperor to judge him.[2] On May 19th a correspondent at the Hague reported no news from Prague but that the king was very happy, continually hunting with his wife, the young

[1] *Archaeologia*, 39.159.
[2] *Mercure Français*, vi. 119; Bethune MS., 9774.98. Charvériat, i. 184.

prince and his court. His Majesty appeared perfectly unmoved by menacing messages from the Emperor, Bavaria or Saxony. He was confident in the justice of his cause and the support of every good German.[1]

Midsummer came to Prague, bringing no more alarming visitor than his Majesty's mother. Louisa Juliana dutifully undertook the long journey from Heidelberg. She had yet a daughter to marry. The Princess Catherine of the Palatinate lacked the arresting qualities which had made her elder and younger sister brides in their teens. A suitor for the hand of the King of Bohemia's sister was forthcoming at Prague, and rumour announced that the wedding of the Princess Catherine to the Duke John Ernest of Saxe Weimar would take place in the cathedral of St. Vitus.[2] The princess, however, returned home with her mother, at the close of their visit, not yet betrothed. She was destined to die a spinster and one of the most innocent victims of the Thirty Years War.

Prague became very warm, and her inhabitants indulged in their time-honoured custom of mixed bathing in the waters of the Vltava under the celebrated bridge which united the "Great Side" of the capital to the "Little Side". The young new king, who was an expert swimmer, joined in his subjects' sport. His fair queen looked on. The people of Prague were surprised and somewhat embarrassed by such behaviour on the part of royalty.[3] The King of Bohemia, for his part, was entirely taken aback when one of his most important nobles—Count Schlick—arrived panting in his presence, to tell him that an indignant mob was on its way to the castle. Frederick had long since empowered his chaplain to banish from the town all pictures and statues offensive to Calvinist eyes. He learnt with bewilderment that the people of Prague would not brook the removal from their bridge of the large gilded bronze crucifix with attendant wooden figures of the Holy Mother and St

---

[1] Harl. MS. 7015.34.   [2] *Ibid.*, 7015.336.   [3] Fitz-Simon, p. 101.

P

John, which was one of its salient features. Scultetus, well aware of the disapproval provoked by his ruthless iconoclasm in the cathedral and churches, had taken the precaution of superintending the banishment of this "brazen serpent" under cover of night, but with dawn the people of Prague had discovered their loss and sprung to arms. Schlick assured his master that "unless the order for pulling down the bridge statue was revoked Bohemia was lost". It appeared that the citizens, regardless of creed, set a high value on a national monument which had never been touched by the fiercest Taborites or affronted by the Jews. A crucifix had certainly stood on this spot from time immemorial, but the present monument was not very old. It had been erected by Rudolph II. Feeling indeed a foreigner, Frederick consented to cancel an order which had produced such undesirable results, and Schlick hurried to assure the mob that their new king would always be guided by native opinion in such matters. The storm died down, but not without mutterings, in which the queen's name was involved. The infrequency of her visits to the Great Side had always been resented and remembered. At first delicate health, and later delicate feelings, had been announced as her reason for neglecting greater Prague. The foreign queen, it had been said, was shocked by the spectacle of Bohemian mixed bathing. Now another explanation of her avoidance of the three towns of the east bank was affirmed. She had sworn never to cross the bridge while an idolatrous abomination remained upon it.[1] When a fanatic Irish Jesuit priest arrived in the capital five months later, he heard this story with appalling additions—"The ex-Queen would never drive over the bridge of Prague because, as she said, she did not wish to look at the naked bather who was on the battlements. This bather was a crucifix, representing Him who bathed our souls in His blood! Good lady, did you not gaze on

---

[1] Riccius, *De Bellis Germanicis*, p. 15; *Mercure Gallo-Belgicus*, pp. 97–104; *Theatrum Europaeum*, i. 280; Khevenhüller, ix. 661.

Frederick bathing, with the scum of the people, near the mill-race, to the indignation of all?"[1]

Elizabeth continued her unlucky efforts to win popularity. On the next public feast day she was served at table by Bohemians only. The experiment was not a success, for the servitors chosen by Scultetus were all Taborites, who performed their duties most unhandily. Her cup-bearer poured wine over the Queen's skirts, her sewer presented her with an empty plate from which the meat had slid during his passage from the buffet, while a third attendant, in charge of the sugar, dropped his bowl and fled with a yell when one of her Majesty's amusing monkeys suddenly helped himself to its contents.[2]

Elizabeth was without a secretary in Prague. She answered in her own hand, this summer, a series of cheering letters from an English gentleman for whom she had a particular regard. Sir Thomas Roe was an example of the best type of Elizabethan *nouveau riche*. He fastened his letters with an elegant seal, displaying the head of a roe. He had been an esquire of the body to Gloriana, and on his first voyage of discovery sailed further up the Amazon than any previous explorer. His grandfather, the first Sir Thomas, merchant-tailor, had been a Lord Mayor of London in the great queen's reign, and his grandmother was a Gresham. Young "Thom" had married a high-spirited niece of the childless Lord Grandison. He had been a close friend of the late Prince of Wales, and in the year of her marriage sent to the Lady Elizabeth a parrot from the Orinoco. In the same month that the Electress Palatine quitted Heidelberg for Prague, Sir Thomas Roe landed in England "rich from India".[3] James I had employed him as ambassador to Jehangir, Mogul Emperor of Hindustan. At the age of forty Sir Thomas's black eyes still retained the slightly startled expression noticeable in those who have looked over-young into

---

[1] Fitz-Simon, p. 101.   [2] Benger, ii. 13–14.
[3] He accompanied Elizabeth on her honeymoon-journey to Heidelberg. S.P. 16.361.34.

the brighter eyes of danger. He was afire in the cause of her "most glorious majesty" of Bohemia, and doing all that he could to aid her husband's ambassador in London. He expressed his hopeful belief that James I, an "affectionate and good father" but "a wise and wary prince", was "inwardly glad" of her elevation. So far, James's affection had manifested itself in pedantic enquiries as to the legality of Frederick's election, and a most grudging consent to his son-in-law's request to be allowed to raise a regiment of English volunteers at his own expense. Sir Thomas, who had been educated at Oxford, produced a pamphlet explaining the righteousness of the Bohemians' actions, and sent a copy to her Majesty.

"HONEST THOM ROE,"
wrote Elizabeth, "I see your journey hath not altered you in your true professing of your love to me. I understand by the Baron of Dhona and Williams how diligentlie you labour in furthering anie thing that is for the good of our Bohemian affairs. If ever I have means and occasion to shew you my thankfullness, assure yourself I will. For I have ever wished well to Thom Roe, and will doe so as long as I live.

"I thank you for the book you have written concerning the Bohemians. It is exceeding well done. I shewed it to the King. He likes it verie well and commends him to you. He says you doe so much for him as he knowes not how to requite you. For me, be ever confident that I am constantlie

your most assured friend,

ELIZABETH.

P.S. I pray commend my love to your good wife. Your old friend Jack, my monkey, is in verie good helth and commandes al my woemen pages with his teeth."[1] Prague, June 19th.

Sir Thomas's answer was couched in high romantic style:

"I am ready to serve your Majesty to deathe, to poverty,

[1] S.P. 81. 17.62.

and if you shall ever please to command, I will be converted to dust and ashes at your Majesties feet. . . . Perhaps here I may blow up fires or doe somewhat. . . .With all humility I beseech you give me leave to kiss the hands of his Majesty, whose acceptance of my little labour in the defence of his cause in writing cannot farther oblige mee, for I am as ready to dye in his cause as any man living, and rather to shed blood than inck. I have this reason, besides that he is your Majestie's, that I thinke him the bravest Prince on earth."[1]

Sir Thomas Roe was not the only English knight to use an accomplished pen in championship of the Queen of Bohemia this mid-summer. Sir Henry Wotton had been ordered to Vienna to approach the Emperor, on the Bohemian question, with pacificatory proposals. Before he departed on his fruitless embassy Sir Henry achieved a poem destined to rank amongst the first efforts of its kind in his native language and be an imperishable monument to the lady whose merits it celebrates. The following lines, according to the testimony of a gallant naval friend of their author,[2] were composed on a summer's day of 1620 in Greenwich Park.[3]

Sonnet of the Queen of Bohemia, by Sir Henry Wotton, Kt.

> You meaner beauties of the night,
> That poorly satisfy our eyes
> More by your number than your light,
> You common people of the skies;
> What are you when the moon shall rise?
>
> You curious chanters of the wood,
> That warble forth Dame Nature's lays,
> Thinking your passions understood
> By your weak accents; what's your praise
> When Philomel her voice shall raise?

---

[1] S.P. 94.

[2] Sir Henry Mainwaring; see *Life and Works of,* by G. E. Manwaring, i. 78–9.

[3] S.P. 14. 115.69.

You violets that first appear,
By your pure purple mantles known,
Like the proud virgins of the year,
As if the spring were all your own;
What are you when the rose is blown?

So, when my mistress shall be seen
In form and beauty of her mind,
By virtue first, then choice, a Queen,
Tell me, if she were not design'd
Th' eclipse and glory of her kind.

X

In mid-August Sir Albert Morton's successor arrived in Prague. The Queen of Bohemia's new English secretary possessed every essential qualification for his post, except tact. Sir Francis Nethersole, who had received knighthood on his appointment, was a man of learning. He had been a prominent tutor and Public Orator at Cambridge. He was accustomed to foreign travel and courts, for he had, for a year past, acted as secretary to the magnificent Lord Doncaster. His despatches from Prague, which swell the file of German State Papers for the latter half of 1620, throw a flood-light on the last months spent by Elizabeth in Bohemia. Hitherto English well-wishers might have gathered no more than that their princess was playing her new rôle to admiration, and that she was happy, hunting every morning in a Star Park, or dallying with her ladies and children in a sunlit Garden of Paradise, overlooking one of the most beautiful cities in Europe. The note of Nethersole's despatches is that of an alarm bell. Within ten days of his arrival, he reported "the dangerous and almost desperate state of the affairs of this kingdom".[1]

The observer fresh from England noticed in the King of Bohemia's court "two divers sortes of discourse, according to the diversity of the hearts and heads of those that make them".

[1] S.P. 81. 17.315.

"The first sorte", who seemed to him to have "more wit than courage", had been convinced a month past that the movements of Maximilian of Bavaria's and John George of Saxony's troops signified no more than "a wise Provision for the defence of their countryes against all sudden dangers that might arise in these troublous times". The worst they could imagine of the Archduke was that "he might possibly attempt the taking in of some towne in the skirtes of the Empire, as he did Wesel and Aix heretofore". That their king would ever be attacked in his own capital, they refused to consider. Prague was "so long a march".

The other sort of counsellors, described by Nethersole as people of "age and experience in the world", were frankly defeatist. They believed that the four armies of the Catholic League, which had been steadily increasing their strength since the spring, were liable at any moment to attack Frederick, and that his ally Bethlem Gabor would then have no choice but to "call in the Turke". "The difference between the Emperor and the King of Bohemia is so irreconcilable that in the end one of them must, of necessity, be ejected out of the Empire."[1] Maximilian of Bavaria was already on the Bohemian frontier, and the Imperial General, Charles of Longueval, Count of Bucquoy, was marching to meet him.[2]

This despatch was set on the road to England a day later than a letter from Heidelberg which confirmed one of its gloomiest prophecies. Louisa Juliana, who had returned to the care of her grandchildren, wrote in grief-stricken horror to James I: "It is now too late to doubt whether Spinola's large force is designed against us; it is already at our gates". The army of twenty-five thousand Spaniards, practised in the wars of the Low Countries, and commanded by the famous Ambrogio

[1] S.P. 81. 17.273–8.
[2] A joint Bohemian and Hungarian embassy set off for Constantinople a few weeks after Maximilian of Bavaria crossed the Bohemian frontier.

Spinola, Marquis de los Balbases, which had long been mysteriously inactive in the south Netherlands, had begun to move. "Your Majesty", wrote the desperate dowager, "will know also in what sorrow the queen your daughter is, and that she is about to be entirely surrounded by enemies. The state in which I lately left her makes me doubly pity her."[1] Elizabeth was about to give another hostage to fortune. As usual, she was expecting a child with the snows.

On August 28th Spinola entered the Lower Palatinate and proceeded rapidly towards Heidelberg. Louisa Juliana, taking the infant Charles Louis and his sister Elizabeth with her, fled precipitately to the protection of the Duke of Würtemberg. On September 5th Nethersole reported to England that he had "presumed, ex-officio" to represent to Frederick's counsellors that they must "provide in time for the safety of the queen, my master's daughter, and her son, by removing them hence to some place of safety". He considered Prague perfectly undefensible should any army that shall become master of the field approach it, moreover he was convinced that the capital harboured many persons ill-affected. The Palatine counsellors thoroughly agreed with him. They were themselves sending away their wives and children. The families of de Plessen and Camerarius were leaving that day. The Countess of Solm and her daughters were packing. The eldest Solms daughter, married to Christopher Dohna in March, expected her baby with the New Year.

Nethersole assured James I that Frederick was distracted at the thought of Elizabeth's danger. "The King himself hath this thought both in his heart and head day and night, and is more troubled therewith than with all the other thorns of his crown." ... A sad little scene had already taken place early that morning in the queen's apartments. The Crown Prince of Bohemia, aged seven, plainly dressed for a long

[1] Balfour MS. A.433.56, Advocates' Library, Edinburgh.

journey, learnt from his mother that he was going on a delightful visit to kind cousins in Holland, accompanied by his nineteen-year-old uncle, Prince Louis. He might even, perhaps, be
going to cross the sea to England.[1] A number of bulky parcels
were surreptitiously removed from the queen's bedchamber,
and carried downstairs, to be carefully stowed amongst the
young princes' luggage. A strong plain carriage, slenderly
escorted, set off at top speed for the Silesian frontier. Seventeen
days passed before Elizabeth knew that her first-born and her
jewels had arrived safely in Berlin. Nethersole, seated in his
lodgings in the "Small Side" of Prague, scribbling a despatch
for England, heard the good news just in time to add it in a
postscript as the clock struck "the Poste houre". The secret of
the Crown Prince's departure had been jealously guarded.
Nethersole had not mentioned the project until it had been
successfully accomplished, and even then had not divulged the
child's destination. "My next shall tell yr lordship to what
place, for as yet I dare trust it to no cipher for fear his Highness
might be intercepted."

Nethersole meant well by "this queen, my most gracious
mistress", but it is easy to see that his reports of Frederick's
precarious position in his new kingdom were little likely to
induce James I to make giant efforts to establish his son-in-law
there. The threatened loss of the Palatinate touched James
more nearly. He did not wish to be obliged to support Frederick, Elizabeth and their progeny for life. But the small body
of English troops despatched for the defence of the Palatinate
in July had been hopelessly hampered by stern instructions not
to attack Spinola.

Nethersole had heated interviews with Elizabeth on September 4th and 5th. Her majesty was "irremovably resolved, out
of her rare and admirable love to the king her husband", not
to leave Prague. "It were a pleasant thing", reflected her

[1] Harl. MS. 7015.87.

secretary "(and I trust in God will be, herafter, when the danger is overpast) to recount the loving conflicts that have been between their majesties on this occasion." Elizabeth gave as her reasons, firstly that her departure might produce a discouraging effect in the capital, especially when Frederick was obliged to join his army, and secondly that whichever way she looked she could see no prospect of a safer place. She said that since Spinola had not been afraid of offending her father by refusing the request of English Ambassadors to refrain from attacking the Palatinate, she could not imagine that he would hold her person sacred. Nethersole disagreed with her, but seeing "the settledness of her disposition" retired at length, begging her permission to inform her father that no efforts had been spared either by her husband or himself to preserve her from disaster.[1]

On the day that they heard of their heir's safe arrival in Berlin, Frederick and Elizabeth partook of Holy Communion after the fashion that so much scandalized the Catholics and even the Lutherans of Bohemia—seated in chairs at a long "dinner-board" adorned by nothing but a white table-cloth. The king then left Prague to join his army in the field, "with as cheerful a face and as resolved a heart as, it may be, prince of his age ever bare, so near the end of a game wherein his honour, fortune and all worldly contentments were at stake". Frederick had taken every possible precaution for his queen's safety during his unavoidable separation from her. He had disarmed all Catholics who had refused their oath of allegiance, summoned three companies from the troops commanded by the Duke of Saxe Weimar, and left behind all his chief officers of state and even his personal bodyguard. Nethersole had the curiosity to go across the river and mingle with the crowds of the "Great Side" to judge for himself how Frederick I was received by his people as he rode out to war. There were whispers that the

[1] S.P. 81. 18.2.

young German king's efforts to ingratiate himself with his Czech subjects had been misinterpreted. In vain his Majesty had danced with citizens' daughters, bathed in the Vltava, and ridden through his capital at an early hour, dressed plainly for hunting, attended by a single groom. Such informalities had been regarded as undignified. On his return from seeing the king "to the town's end" Nethersole was able to assure Elizabeth that "a great number of people of all conditions" had lined her husband's route, and that his reception "(as far as can be judged from outward expressions) might have made a native, hereditary, aged king think himself very happy". Typically, Nethersole could not resist the unhappy rider, "It was much more than I expected to have found".[1]

The autumn rains came down, and Elizabeth entered upon her third and worst experience of sitting in Prague waiting for news of the King of Bohemia. Letters from Frederick began to arrive. As usual, they were filled with lover's messages and exhortations. "My dear and only sweetheart, I kiss your lips, your hands, in imagination, a million times. . . .[2] For the love of God have a care of your health, if not for your own sake for mine, for our dear children, and for your dear little creature-that-is-to-be. Do not give way to melancholy. . . .[3] Such bad news as must inevitably reach her he did not attempt to suppress. One by one the Rhineside towns which had greeted her with triumphal arches on her honeymoon journey were falling into the hands of Spinola. Bacharach had surrendered, Caub was taken. . . . Frederick did not tell his wife that he had found his army ill clad, ill fed, short of ammunition and almost mutinous owing to lack of pay, that Count Thurn refused to serve under Count Hohenlohe, that an order for a parade at 6 A.M. had been greeted by bold Bohemians with murmurs that men must be allowed some time for rest and recreation.

[1] S.P. 81. 18.117.   [2] Aretin, vii. 162.
[3] Bromley, p. 9.

Still he can hardly have hoped to raise his wife's spirits by such a story as the following :

"Last night I left here, taking the greater part of our cavalry, with the intentioning of surprising the quarters of the Duke of Bavaria. But the skies were so overcast and the roads so bad and narrow that by daybreak we had advanced only one league. We returned here having effected nothing. We have since been told that the Duke of Bavaria and the Count of Bucuoy were waiting ready to engage us all night. From this one may judge that we do not lack traitors in our camp."[1]

On October 14th Frederick returned to Prague on a flying visit. For the first time since his acceptance of a crown, English Ambassadors were waiting upon him. Elizabeth entertained Sir Edward Conway and Sir Richard Weston for four days before her husband appeared. On the night of their arrival she sent her state coach, and a deputation of eminent officials, to greet them, and invited them to call upon her the next afternoon. She was disturbed that, owing to lack of funds, she could not offer them hospitality of suitable magnificence. Frederick wrote that it would be best not to attempt to lodge them, but to ask them to dinner as frequently as possible.[2] The Ambassadors' first audience opened somewhat awkwardly, for they had dire instructions from their master to salute his daughter as Princess Palatine, no more, and they had just heard that Elizabeth was wrath with Sir Henry Wotton for beginning a letter to her with "a solemn protestation" that he gave her the title of queen as a private person, not as an Ambassador. Elizabeth, however, was so relieved to see English Ambassadors at all that she disregarded their form of salutation. Conway and Weston were feeling personally well disposed towards their Majesties of Bohemia. James I, who still

[1] Bromley, p. 7.   [2] *Ibid.*, p. 8.

believed that his son-in-law's problems might be settled by statecraft, had sent them on a series of fool's errands to Catholic potentates, who had treated them with little consideration. At Dresden, his Britannic Majesty's diplomatic representatives had been subjected to the unprecedented indignity of having their trunks searched, lest they were carrying gold to aid rebellious Bohemians.[1]

A single interview sufficed for Frederick to assure the English Ambassadors that although in his anxiety for peace he would consent that Ferdinand should be titular King of Bohemia for life and enjoy certain revenues, he would never relinquish his own title or possession. The king returned to his fortified camp at Rakovitz.[2] Sir Edward and Sir Richard retired to their lodgings to write to England and to Sir Henry Wotton at Vienna. Their labours were enlivened by the sound of distant gunfire. Sir Francis, also writing to England, but from the Hradčany, reported, "There are daily skirmishes, and we can in this town hear the cannon play day and night, which were enough to fright another queen. Her majesty is nothing troubled therewith; but she would be if she should hear how often there have been men killed very near the King, with the cannon, and how much he adventureth his person further than he is commended for." [3]

During the last days of October Frederick wrote to Elizabeth, thanking her for a beautiful scarf, and telling her that her black horse, which had been ill, was better. The weather had suddenly turned bitterly cold. "We are now very close to the enemy. I trust that God will not abandon us." On November 1st he reopened the question of her leaving Prague. "God grant that it may not be necessary . . . but it is best to prepare for the worst. Tell me, don't you think it might be better for you to

[1] Gindely, p. 228.
[2] Rakovitz, on the river Rakovitza, is about 33 miles west of Prague.
[3] S.P. 81. 19.132–3.

withdraw in good order, while you can, rather than wait until the enemy comes too close, in which case your departure would rather resemble a flight? I would not urge you to leave against your will. I merely give my opinion. . . . You are", a lover reminded her, "so bad at making up your mind."[1][2] But he had already issued orders to Elizabeth's secretary for "necessaries to be put up in a readiness to be removed upon any sudden occasion", and a certain amount of her furniture and luggage had gone ahead to a spot chosen in September to be the scene of her confinement, should the enemy winter in the country. The name of the place had been kept an utter secret, but a rumour that the queen was leaving Prague caused alarm in the city, which was now packed with refugees. Nethersole informed the Secretary of State for England, "Concerning '11' whom I mentioned in my last, there is yet no full resolution taken therein, but I think she will go to. . . ." A galaxy of numerals decorates his despatch at this point. Above them the London decipherer has written "Breslau, in Silesia" and above "11" "The Queen of Bohemia".

XI

On November 5th the Imperialists decamped under cover of night from Rakovitz, in an attempt to get between the Bohemians and their capital. Bucuoy had been disabled by a slight wound, and his place had been taken by the dashing Walloon cavalry general, Count Johann Tzerklaes von Tilly. Anhalt and Hohenlohe, however, brought up their forces with speed, and at three o'clock on the afternoon of November 7th, Frederick appeared "with a countenance of glee", to tell his wife "that the enemy was within eight miles of Prague but his army of twenty-five thousand was betwixt them and it".

[1] Aretin, vii. 164, 169, 170.   [2] Bromley, p. 10.

By 1 A.M. next morning, Bohemians, who had been moving up all night, were encamped in the Star Park on the White Mountain. "That night", records an English eye-witness, "we slept securely, as free from doubt as we supposed ourself quit from danger."

The morning of Sunday, November 8th, dawned foggy. In spite of news that the Bohemian cavalry "upon the outflanks of the army did skirmish", the general opinion within the walls of the Hradčany was "that both the armies were apter to decline than give a battle". The enemy had been short of food for four days. The king had invited the English Ambassadors to dine. People went to church as usual. "There was confidence enough."[1]

About the hour that Elizabeth's ladies arrayed her to entertain her father's ambassadors of peace, Maximilian of Bavaria was enquiring of the omens from a Dominican Friar. "He, after going a ceremonious time apart, returned with an encouragement to them to fight, assuring them that a troupe of Angels was over them for their defence." During dinner Elizabeth arranged with the Ambassadors that they should escort her that afternoon to inspect the troops entrenched in the Star Park. Frederick had already risen from table "to go to horse to see his army", when ominous sounds startled the feasters left with the queen. "Before the King could get out of the gate, the news came of the loss of the Bohemian cannon, and the disorder of all the squadrons, both of horse and foot." The Battle of the White Mountain, which lasted not much more than an hour, was already half over before information reached Frederick that Tilly had attacked. The king, at the head of a small body of horse, pressed his way through streets packed with apprehensive citizens, who had been wakened from their Sunday afternoon sleep by the sound of cannon. Congregations emerging from the cathedral churches stared at

[1] S.P. 81. 18.6.

the sight of crowds of people all running towards the Strahow gate. Frederick dismounted at the gate, and from its tower perceived that the worst had happened. His Generalissimo, Christian of Anhalt, and George Frederick of Hohenlohe, "more pale than death could have made them", were amongst those below, clamouring to be admitted into the Hradčany. The Bohemians were surging down from the White Mountain in hopeless panic. Their only idea now was to put the river between them and the enemy. Frederick ordered the gates to be opened, and a tornado of terror-stricken soldiery swept through the courtyards of the palace in which he had left his wife. A message was brought to Elizabeth that the king desired her to follow the general example and seek safety in the "Great Side", but she did not stir until she saw her husband before her. One glance at Frederick was enough to tell her that the moment had indeed come for her to leave the Hradčany. His nerves are said to have been severely shaken by the shrieks of the Bohemian women, who expected a lurid fate at the hands of the Cossacks of the Imperial Army.[1] The queen's coach was summoned, and she mounted into it without further demur. The victorious enemy were reported to be in hot pursuit. Elizabeth descended towards the river through scenes of wildest confusion.

Much frenzied packing was done on that dark November afternoon, but Frederick's chamberlain, on a last progress through the deserted royal apartments, discovered something important which had been left behind. He picked it up, and hurrying down to the courtyard, was just in time to catch the last coach drawing away from the palace doors. Not until the bundle "thrown in" by Christopher Dohna rolled from the "boot" on to the floor of the carriage and burst into a roar,

[1] Ferdinand had, with the permission of Sigismund of Poland, enlisted on Polish territory 800 Cossacks. These troops were known in Bohemia and Austria as "the bloodhounds".

did his astonished fellow-travellers discover that the infant Prince Rupert was amongst them.[1]

The string of coaches and cavaliers accompanying the Winter King in his flight stretched in an unbroken line from the Hradčany over the bridge, into the Great Side, as far as the old Town Square.[2] Catholic pamphleteers noted afterwards that Frederick's defeat was effected in the Star Park, where he had begun his triumphal entry into Prague, that the battle took place on the Octave of All Saints' Day, consecrated to the blessed company whose images he had banished from his capital, that the gospel for that day contained the text "Render therefore unto Caesar the things that are Caesar's", and that his queen, on her flight, was obliged to cross the bridge deemed abhorrent to her, because it was decorated by a crucifix. "Whither goest thou now, Elizabeth? Whither but over that bridge. . . . Unsanctified! Unbeliever! Now art thou carried whither thou wouldst not go . . ."

Elizabeth's first halt was at "a principal citizen's house" on the Brückenplatz. As her husband handed her out of her coach he said with a heavy sigh, "Now I know where I am! We princes seldom learn the truth until we are taught it by adversity."

No day is so long as the day of defeat. Elizabeth's view that Sunday evening, until fog and dusk closed down upon it, was of the stately tower, adorned by the figures of Bohemian saints

[1] Warburton, i. 39. The "boot" of a seventeenth-century coach was not a receptacle for luggage in the rear of a vehicle. It was the uncovered space on or by the steps projecting between the front and back wheels, and was furnished with extra seats. The boot seats of a coach, although occasional, were not ignominious. Henrietta Maria took the French Ambassador in the boot of her coach to see the Lord Mayor's Show (Bassompierre, 81) and Louis XIV allotted boot seats in his equipage to the Duke and Duchess of Orleans on the occasion when he drove en famille with his grandson, the newly proclaimed King of Spain, beside him (St Simon, iii. 173).

[2] A wood relief depicting this scene, carved by George Bendl (1630) decorates the Ambulatory opposite the Archbishop's chapel in the cathedral of St Vitus, Prague.

and kings, guarding the sixteen-arched bridge over the shining river. While the streets below resounded to the exclamations of alarmed civilians, the staggering tread of fugitive soldiery, and the grinding of waggon wheels, she assisted at a conference between her stricken husband and his supporters. After two hours, the English Ambassadors, "pressing through a confused multitude", were announced. Conway and Weston found Frederick "accompanied with his blessed undaunted lady and all the Chiefs of his army and council". Naturally feeling amongst the discomfited generals was running high.[1] Eye-witnesses' accounts of the Battle of the White Mountain are strongly marked by racial prejudice. "An English gentleman there present" attributed "the losse of Prague", which he describes as the last wonder of the age, to the cowardly flight, before five hundred Imperial horse, of six thousand Hungarians,[2] and "the unanswerable and unparalleled unworthiness of the Prince of Anhalt, General of the foot, and of Count Hollock (Hohenlohe) General of the Horse", who "at the first appearance of danger left the field and never returned to try if they could againe rallie some troups which were but disordered". His praises are for Anhalt's son, "who to wash out, as I conceive, his father's leprozie of cowardize, shedd much bloud, fought gallantly and is now the Ennemies wounded prisoner", and "the Grav von Thurn, an old gallant noble, who, till the day shutt down shutt not himself into the citty". The Moravian foot, he says, "bore the honour of their deaths carved on their

[1] Christian of Anhalt wrote, by desire of Frederick, a lengthy despatch, detailing the movements of the army under his command on November 8th and for several days before, but does not offer an entirely convincing story. He is anxious to show himself as having failed to achieve the impossible. According to his account, he was not surprised by Tilly's attack, a statement which reflects on Frederick's absence from the battle-field, and even after the battle had opened badly he still hoped for a decisive victory. He displays the typical disdain of a cavalry officer for infantry and of a foreign commander for an unruly staff.

[2] Another author says that the undisciplined Magyar horse, after a successful charge, began to plunder the Bavarians' baggage.

bodies in large characters". All accounts agree in admiration of the Calvinist Moravians, who held out around the Star hunting-lodge long after their companions had deserted them. Their corpses were found lying twelve deep next day around the walls of the pretty miniature palace where Frederick and Elizabeth had arrived in triumph almost exactly a year previously.[1] But the flight was responsible for far more casualties amongst the Bohemians than the actual engagement. "Our foot . . . leapt down hastily to their own ruin." Hundreds who had forsaken their arms were drowned in the Vltava attempting to cross a ford near the present suburb of Smichow. A second English witness declares that the Bohemian army was so ill-disciplined and discontented that he marvels that the unpopular German generalissimo held it together at all.

The reputation of the king who had been feasting ambassadors of peace whilst his army was attacked received a fatal blow on November 8th. Elizabeth's own attendants afterwards assured a countryman at the Hague [2] that "but for her" Frederick would have been in the field, and that the unfortunate man professed himself "very sorry for his absence from the army, the day of the battle, which fell out by his going to see her, and in the meantime the enemy marching in a mist towards Prague". Even Nethersole, doing his unhappy best to present Frederick's absence as providential "considering the hazard his too great adventurousness must needs have put his person into", admits "there is no question but that his presence would have had much power to make his men stand better". "The king", he explains, "the night before having made an escapade to see the queen with a few of his chamber and all the English volunteers, by this means, going forth the next day, immediately after dinner, he came to the

---

[1] In the cellars of the Star Palace to-day are to be seen the bones of many victims of the Battle of the White Mountain.
[2] S.P. 84. 89.70.

end of the fray (it deserveth no other name) whether fortunately or not is hard to determine." Contemporary opinion
decided unhesitatingly that no amount of conjugal affection or
conviction that a military action was not imminent excused
Frederick's absence from his camp.

The night of the defeat wore on in consultation and dispute.
Eight thousand men sent by Bethlem Gabor were expected
to come up at any moment. The bolder spirits amongst the
Bohemian nobility were all for defending their capital. The
less optimistic considered that Frederick should retire no
further than the impregnable mountain fortress of Glatz on
the Silesian border. Christian of Anhalt, disgusted with his
command, declared that the mutinous condition of the troops
rendered it impossible for him to induce them to face the
enemy again. Conway and Weston, justifiably dubious of
the wisdom of attempting to hold Prague, advised that all
available men and stores should be scrutinized before such a
decision was taken. They were at length empowered to send
to Maximilian of Bavaria and Bucuoy, asking for an interview
to discuss terms. "Time was to be won, for the better fashion-
ing and assuring of the blessed lady's retreat." At a late hour
that night, no answer having come from the enemy, the king,
the queen and the generals retreated further into the town.
Elizabeth's night clothes could not be found.[1] She spent her
last night in Prague in the mansion of a citizen who held an
important position in the iron trade. Herr Kirchmayer was a
Protestant and a wealthy man. He possessed two houses in
the capital. His private residence was an antique and palatial
building. Its cellars dated from the eleventh century. It stood
on the Malýrynk, "Small Square", which together with the
Velkýrynk, "Great Square", surrounded the Town Hall.[2]

[1] S.P. 77. 14.251-2.
[2] This house still stands, but historians are not in agreement as to which
of Kirchmayer's houses was occupied by Elizabeth and Frederick on the
night of November 8th, 1620.

The queen resolutely refused to seek safety while her husband held his capital against siege. The feeble light of a November dawn grew upon the cobbled market-place which was the very heart of old Prague. The twin towers of the Tynský Chrám, chief church of the Hussites, became visible, silhouetted against skies of an ominous hue. The English Ambassadors despatched another trumpeter to the Imperialist camp. Maximilian of Bavaria had spent the night in the Star hunting-lodge. Nine o'clock sounded from the elaborate great clock on the south side of the Town Hall, and still no answer had come from the victorious enemy, and the queen refused to enter her waiting coach. The hopelessly involved Bohemian nobles, who during the small hours had urged wild schemes of defence, fell silent. Presently two seniors, Thurn and Rupa, advised the king not to try "the fortune of resistance in the town".

The appearance at the west gate of the old town of a cavalcade headed by the king riding beside a coach containing his wife and the infant prince born in Bohemia, roused the citizens' alarm. There was a tedious wait before the gates of the Powder Tower were opened. Frederick made a short impromptu speech. But his subjects, who only understood that he was deserting them, grew so clamorous that the Bohemian officials attending his Majesty had to explain that they were merely escorting the royal procession a short distance and would be back at their posts in a few hours. A mile outside the town the queen's coach halted. Young Count Bernard Thurn had been ordered back to the city "to dispute the passage of the bridge, to secure the queen's retreat". With his regiment of Moravian infantry he reckoned that he should be able to hold the old town for twenty-four hours. As he bent over Elizabeth's hand in farewell, he recommended her Majesty to God, and wished her a safe journey and a triumphant return. Speaking in French, he assured her that he would do the work he went for, or die in the attempt.

Amongst those who accompanied the queen on the first stage of her long journey, "six great leagues, to a town called Nimberge", were the English Ambassadors and her secretary. Nethersole considered that he could be of little immediate service to his mistress, and ought to make an effort to collect his correspondence, half of which was in his office in the Hradačny and half in his lodgings. The Ambassadors' last report of their master's daughter and son-in-law was cheering. "Truly the king bare himself through all the passages of this disaster with more clearness of judgment, constancy and assurance than any of the chiefs of his army, and indeed as well as could be looked for in such an unexpected change, and, as man may say, total disorder. But his incomparable lady, who truly saw the state she was in, did not let herself fall below the dignity of a queen, and kept the freedom of her countenance and discourse with such an unchangeable temper, as at once did raise up in all capable men this one thought—that her mind could not be brought under fortune."

On November 10th the slow-moving procession, which included three hundred heavily laden vehicles, faded from the anxious Englishmen's view, and they turned back to Prague, which surrendered to the Imperialists that day. Next morning, three days too late to save Bohemia for King Frederick, the first snows of that winter began to fall.

The white flakes fell fast as the Winter King's *cortège* approached the mountains of the Silesian frontier, and presently the roads were blocked by drifts through which no wheeled vehicle could pass. Some unfaithful attendants began to plunder the queen's stationary baggage-waggons. The Winter Queen dismounted into the snows from her lumbering equipage. A young English volunteer, fresh from a few months martial training in Holland after education at Oxford University, was the possessor of a well-trained steed which would carry two. A tantalizingly terse note in the margin of a contemporary life of Captain Ralph, afterwards Lord Hopton, records, "He carried the Queen of Bohemia behind him, after the sad battel of Prague, forty miles".[1]

The iron veil of war had descended at several frontiers. Indignant Protestant housewives in England and the North Netherlands asked imperatively for news of a princess whom they remembered as a sweet bride. She was known to be expecting a child round about Christmas, and her children generally took her by surprise. The demand for news produced a supply. In the streets of London, citizens stopped one another to discuss the tragic end of the Lady Elizabeth—dead in childbed, after giving birth to a still-born infant. Prints of her hearse and funeral procession were on sale in Antwerp. The report of her premature confinement and death was so widespread and well authenticated that Sir Edward Villiers, half-brother of the Marquess of Buckingham, despatched from England with a New Year's gift for the King and Queen of Bohemia, hesitated in Flanders whether to proceed further.[2][3]

[1] Lloyd, p. 342.   [2] S.P. 77. 44.266.
[3] The authorities for the preceding account of the Battle of the White Mountain and the events immediately following it are—*Mercure Français*, vi. 418–26, vii. 1; Khevenhüller, ix. 104–6; *Theatrum Europaeum*, i. 409–11; Letter addressed by Prince Christian of Anhalt to the King of Bohemia, dated Jan. 1st, 1621, printed in Moser, vii. 123–36; Riccius, pp. 45–7; Spanheim, pp. 163–5; Harl. MS. 1580.281–7 (Conway and Weston's despatch). *Ibid.*, 389, 1 ("Relation of the manner of the losse of Prague by an English gentleman there and then present".) S.P. 81. 19. 188.190–1.196 (Nethersole's despatches). Nieuwe Tydinge vyt Oostenryck, Bohem, etc., Nov. 10th, 1620. Hurter, i. 87 *et seq.*; Lützow, pp. 347–54; Charvériat, i. 227; Häusser, ii. 332–3.

Theatrum Europaeum, vol. i., contains engravings showing the disposition of the troops, and the battle at various stages, and Moser's *Patriotisches Archiv*, vol. vii., has a plan as frontispiece.

Fitz-Simon, *Diary of the Bohemian War of 1620*, tells the story from the Imperialist side. He was chaplain-in-chief to the Imperialist army.

XII

The Queen of Bohemia, however, was not dead. On
December 5th she had reached Frankfort on the Oder, attended
by Christopher Dohna and sixty horse. Her husband, who had
stayed in Moravia to rally his subjects, wrote earnestly entreating the Elector of Brandenburg to grant her hospitality during
her approaching confinement. George William of Brandenburg, who had recently succeeded to his father's territories,
read his brother-in-law's letter with dismay. No tender
memories of the fair Princess Palatine whom he had entertained at a *fête champêtre* before handing her on board a Rhine
vessel, visited his brain. He was obsessed by the notion that
he must not offend the victorious Emperor. His position was
already delicate. To please his wife, a sister of the Winter
King, he had abandoned Lutheranism for Calvinism. He
replied at length that neither of the castles near Berlin suggested
by his brother-in-law as possible havens were at all suitable
for a lady in Elizabeth's condition. At Spandau she would be
exposed to intrusion from the Elector of Saxony's troops, at
Cüstrin she was likely to be starved. His description of
Cüstrin was calculated to shake strong nerves—its walls were
devoid of tapestry, its cellars empty of wine, and its granaries
without corn. Her Majesty's attendants would doubtless be
annoyed when they discovered that she had been allowed to go
to a place where there was neither food and fuel for man, nor
fodder for horse. As a finishing touch, George William
announced that Cüstrin castle did not possess a kitchen or any
apartment suitable for conversion into one.[1]

His next news of his sister-in-law was that she had reached
Cüstrin. At first hopes were held out that her stay there would
not be prolonged. She was awaiting an answer from her
cousin, the Duke of Brunswick, to whom the two Palatine

[1] Von Gallos, pp. 13-15.

counsellors, Plessen and Camerarius, had been sent with a request that she might lie-in at Wolfenbüttel. But it presently appeared that, although the duke, once her rejected suitor, was willing to be her host, he must first consult his mother, the Dowager Duchess, and she was unfortunately absent from home. Actually Elizabeth had resigned herself to the prospect of being confined in the "fortress" so pessimistically described by George William before she set eyes on it. On her arrival in Berlin, the second town in the Mark of Brandenburg, she had found neither host nor hostess, no preparations made for her reception and not a word of welcome. She foresaw that her Brunswick relations meant to employ the time in "goings and comings" until all danger of her being able to accept their lukewarm invitations was past. The weather was appalling. The only consolation was that the wind and frost and snow must be inconveniencing the enemy almost as much as her Majesty, whose child was due to appear within the month now. Her last experience of labour had been short. She dared not risk the possibility of the conquered King of Bohemia's fifth child being born in a coach or a wayside hut. She occupied herself during her last weeks of pregnancy, inaction and anxiety amongst the snow-covered north German flats, with the painful business of writing explanatory letters to friends and relations. On the Battle of the White Mountain the Queen of Bohemia did not dwell. "I have no doubt that you have heard some time ago of the misfortune that has come upon us, and that you will have been very sorry; but I console myself with one thing. The war is not yet ended. I hope that God has only done all this to try us, and doubt not but that for the love of His church He will yet give us the victory." [1] To her father, during the one night that she spent at Breslau, before parting from her husband, she had prefaced an earnest request for immediate assistance, "otherwise I know not what will

[1] *Archaeologia,* 39.160.

become of us", by the simple statement, "the Baron of Dhona will not fail to tell your Majesty of the misfortune that has befallen us, and by which we have been compelled to quit Prague".[1] To Sir Dudley Carleton she wrote from Frankfort, "I am sure by this tyme you have had the unwelcome newes of our armies' defeat, which forced the King and me to leave Prague not without danger to have bene taken by the ennemie if they had followed us, which they did not. I have left the King at Breslau in Silesia where he has assembled the States. They and the Moravians hold fast to us. I am now in the Elector of Brandenburg's Countrey. Tomorrow I goe to a fortresse of his, where I shall winter. The King sent me hether for feare the ennemie should invade Silesia. I am not' yet so out of heart, though I confesse we are in an evil estate, but that (as I hope) God will give us again the victory. For warrs are not ended with one battle, and I hope we shall have better luck in the next."[2] The Duke of Thouars received matter in the same vein from Cüstrin. Only to her favourite aunt did the Queen of Bohemia admit, after a dignified announcement of her prospect of wintering in North Germany, "I feel that I am an exile here".[3] Cüstrin probably was very uncomfortable. The castle, which had been built above a small and obscure village about a hundred years before by the Elector Joachim I, had been the residence of a branch of the Brandenburg family for a short period, and since suffered neglect. Seven waggon-loads of timber were brought up to warm it during the first three weeks of Elizabeth's stay there. Then the supply failed, and her absent host found himself charged for firing brought from a distance.

Four days before Christmas, according to the Old Style, in which the Protestant Queen reckoned, she was surprised during dinner by sounds of horsemen arriving at her gloomy abode. Although she had been right in thinking that the war in pro-

[1] Ellis II, iii. 112.   [2] S.P. 84. 98.84.   [3] *Archaeologia*, 39.160.

gress could not be ended by one battle, Bohemia, it appeared, could be lost thus easily. Her husband had returned to be with her in her hour of trial. The story that Frederick had to tell was tragic. He had been well received in Moravia, but no sooner had he gone back to Silesia, than the Moravian Estates had declared their secession from the Bohemian confederation. The sudden appearance of Bucuoy's army in their country had taken them unprepared. They had no word from the elder Count Thurn, who had gone to hasten Bethlem Gabor's promised Hungarians. The Silesians, finding themselves threatened on all sides, had proceeded to beg his Majesty to retire to some safer place than their capital. They had accompanied their unwelcome suggestion with a gift of eighty thousand florins. Frederick had replied that in deference to their wishes he would winter elsewhere, but that with the spring he would come again. They then divulged that the Elector of Saxony, whose forces were overrunning Lusatia, had heartily advised them to lose no time in opening negotiations with the Emperor. In the town which had welcomed him with a triumphal arch last winter, a king who had lost but one battle realized that he was rejected of all men. "I did not constrain them to choose me , . . . I could have lived contentedly in my own lands . . ." [1] Londoners learnt on January 26th that for several days after hearing from her husband's own lips of the succession of disasters that had overtaken him during his separation from her, the Queen of Bohemia had appeared "more affected than by all that had before fallen out". A conquered king had been observed to shed tears as he took leave of his Silesian subjects, quoting the words of David fleeing from Absalom, "If I shall find favour in the eyes of the Lord, He will bring me again". "Yet God be thanked", continued the newsletter so eagerly scanned in London, "she was notwithstanding, safely delivered upon our Twelfe Day of a large and goodly

[1] Courante vyt Italien, Duytsland, etc., Feb. 1621.

son." [1] Elizabeth had indeed been wise in deciding not to attempt any further mid-winter travelling. Nethersole, who had hurried up from Magdeburg to rejoin her, added in a postscript to a despatch which occupied him for two hours, that her Majesty was the speedier worker. Her fifth experience of labour lasted little over an hour. [2] Her choice of a name for her infant showed Europe that she had recovered her spirits. The dark child born at Cüstrin on January 6th (O.S.), 1621, was christened four days later after his martial great-uncle, the Prince of Orange—"Maurice, because he will have to be a fighter". [3]

XIII

The feelings of the King and Queen of Bohemia were not spared directly after their flight from Prague. Placards in Brussels and Vienna offered a reward for news of "a King, run away a few days past—age, adolescent, colour, sanguine, height, medium; a cast in one eye, no beard or moustache worth mention; disposition, not bad so long as a stolen kingdom does not lie in his way—name of Frederic". [4] A flood of caricatures of Frederick and Elizabeth, so numerous as to arouse the suspicion that they were the result of paid propaganda, appeared during the winter of 1620-21. Some of the engravings were printed in the Archduke Albert's territories and forwarded to those of Maximilian of Bavaria for the addition of rhymes in the Bavarian dialect. The majority present a combination of picture and explanatory text, generally in verse. From a short study of the collection in the Bodleian Library and British Museum more intimate information can be gathered concerning contemporary opinion of the Winter King and Queen at this stage of their fortunes than from many

[1] Harl. MS. 389.2.   [2] S.P. 81. 20.22.
[3] "Courante", Feb. 1621. MS. français 4122.46. Bibl. Nat.
[4] Fitz-Simon, p. 103.

an hour spent amongst the despatches of their adherents, all of whom wished to present their situation with the least possible loss of prestige.

Amongst the valuables captured by the victors of the White Mountain in the King of Bohemia's deserted baggage-waggons was a well-worn velvet garter embroidered with the words "Honi soit qui mal y pense". The King of England's son-in-law was well known to have been particularly proud of his inclusion in the fraternity of the "most noble" Order. The great joke about the king who ran away and lost his garter is repeated again and again in the lampoons published by his enemies. Frederick is represented in many humiliating attitudes —imprisoned in a bee-hive with a barred window, through which he pushes pathetic letters begging Spinola to refrain from invading the Palatinate; riding on the famous Heidelberg tun, for economy's sake. "He might", suggest onlookers, "be made King of Lappland, Winter is long there." He is shown climbing up a Wheel of Fate, from the top of which he falls into an ocean of troubles, to be hauled ashore by Dutch fishermen, who will display him as a new monster. "His kingdom was not of this world", runs the impious inscription. "God help poor Frederic! He will never recover."

By what name Elizabeth commonly addressed her husband in their private life no letter or anecdote discloses. Hundreds of his letters to her survive, all signed "Frideric". On one occasion he alludes to himself as "your poor Celadon",[1] but "Celadon" was the stock romantic name for a lover at this date, and Frederick and Elizabeth had doubtless read "L'Astrée" of Honoré d'Urfé, published in 1610. In later life the queen had a favourite dog so named. Their caricaturists unhesitatingly represented Elizabeth calling her German husband by the homely *petit nom* "Fritz". Not a single letter sent by Elizabeth to Frederick after their marriage is forthcoming, although

[1] Bromley, p. 22.

from internal evidence in his many replies it appears that she showered epistles upon him during his absences. It seems likely that, since she was the survivor, she destroyed her share in their correspondence.

Upon the whole, "the king's daughter who chose that her spouse should buy a kingly title, cost it ever so dear", is more roughly handled than her husband. Frederick is depicted as a runaway soldier. Though all his generals try to draw it from its sheath, the King of Bohemia's sword will not emerge. He wears the Order of Misery round his neck, and is tormented by Spanish gnats, whilst his children eat pap out of an inverted crown. "Blame Fate!" says the broken-spirited ex-king. Sterner accusations are made against Elizabeth. She is repeatedly shown as the lioness with many cubs. When she urges her lethargic mate to get food for their over-numerous young, he replies, "Let me be." Frederick, on his knees, confessing his sins to Scultetus, announces, "What my wife did, by her provocation, only the devil can describe!"

The likenesses of Frederick and Elizabeth are evidently intended for portraits, but most of the artists had not been furnished with up-to-date material. Their Frederick is frequently round-faced and clean-shaven. For Elizabeth's figure, the portrait painted by Mierevelt on her honeymoon journey towards Heidelberg seems to be the source. Her elaborate costume is that in vogue when she chose her trousseau, and she wears the unbecoming "high-tired" coiffure abandoned by ladies of fashion three seasons past.[1]

Naturally, the homeless situation of the Winter King and Queen offered their ill-wishers ample material for sarcastic

[1] Lady Anne Clifford's diary notes, under date May 12th, 1617, "I began to dress my head with a roll, without a wire". The medal of Elizabeth reproduced facing p. 144 shows that she too had by this date put aside the conical support over which the locks were combed upward into a tower, adorned with feathers, flowers and many jewels, and begun to wear her hair in the simple and more becoming new fashion.

speculation. The pilgrim Frederick, staff in hand, is shown addressing himself to his brother-in-law of Brandenburg. George William tells him that he may stay for six weeks, until his wife is delivered. Then they must move off, Elizabeth carrying the baby, Frederick following with the cradle. Frederick next applies himself to the kind, rich cities of the Hansa League, offering as security the whole Palatinate, over which, unfortunately, Spinola, the spider, has spun his web.[1] The Hansa merchants reply, "You expect us to give you money! In the past you played us a lout's trick with your loans on our treasury." His father-in-law is Frederick's next hope. "Yes", agrees Elizabeth, "had you not lost your Garter!" When she takes the infant Maurice to offer him to her father in place of the insignia lost by "My Fritz who is not here", James drives her out. "O Fritz!" wails the unprotected lady. Frederick's last supplication "on my knees, which I have not done before", is to the Dutch States, "the land of dried fish." "We are", the Dutch replied, "too weak to help you. But if you wish to make yourself at home here we will not chase you out." So in the last caricatures the King of Bohemia is exhibited trying to earn an honest living—as a carter, as a mason, as a woodcutter, as a road-mender, as a Dutch cheese-vendor. But in every occupation he is impeded by his stockings, hanging down over his shoes, "because he has lost his garter".[2]

The caricaturists were correct in their forecast. The North Netherlands were the only available future home for the Winter King and Queen. Suddenly the background of Eliza-

[1] In many of the pictures the contending parties are represented by birds, beasts, etc. A bear symbolizes Bavaria, the Catholic League and occasionally the Dutch States. Spinola is a tireless spider, Bucuoy a devouring dragon, and Tilly a cunning serpent. A group composed of Christian of Anhalt, the stag, Bethlem Gabor, the fox, and the Dutch States, the bear, are shown vainly attempting to overset a column on which the Habsburg eagle is seated.

[2] A collection of caricatures of Frederick and Elizabeth, with an introduction, notes and translations, by E. A. Becher, was published by the O.U.P., 1928.

beth's life was to be Dutch quietude. She was inescapably bound for a countryside of immense changing skies and eternal green fields where the west wind drove windmills, and sailing-ships tacked up and down rush-bordered waterways haunted by gulls and plovers and herons. Henceforward the only towns seen by her were to be those rich in light, unadorned churches, and houses of bland magnificence screened by limes and provided with gardens of geometric tulip-beds and clipped alleys. Their sleepy canal-sides were crowded by the stalls of the fishmonger and the fruiterer, and also of the picture-monger, who offered to wealthy citizens the likenesses of placid beeves, and flowers and fish and fruit, and well-scrubbed kitchens and polished parlours where well-liking ladies bent to catch the sunlight on a letter or to touch the virginals.

XIV

While Elizabeth was still confined to her lying-in chamber, a doleful scene took place in another apartment of Cüstrin castle. Her husband set his name to a document offering to resign the crown of Bohemia if, in return, the Palatinate was restored to him. He asked also that the Imperial ban might be removed from his name and from the names of the principal followers. These terms had been drawn up by James I.[1] Sir Edward Villiers, who had nearly turned home on hearing of the death of his Majesty's daughter, was much relieved to find her so well and her husband so ready to listen to reason. As soon as he had signed the humiliating document, Frederick set off for the Hanseatic ports, in quest of money. His wife's uncle, the King of Denmark, was to be found at Segeberg near Lübeck. Frederick broke his journey at Wolfenbüttel, where his wife's aunt, the Duchess of Brunswick, expressed herself delighted

---

[1] S.P. 81. 19.294.

to make his acquaintance. Her son had been obliged to leave home two days before. Frederick wrote dully to his wife that Wolfenbüttel, which was a very pretty place, possessed fine pictures but no tapestries. The Dowager had entertained her guest by a display of her jewels. "They don't compare with yours." Talk of jewels filled the unfortunate Winter King's letters from Wolfenbüttel. He thought that the pearls which Elizabeth had forwarded for his inspection were very expensive and not very large, but if she considered that they would be suitable for his three-year-old only daughter, he would be willing to purchase them for her.[1] His hasty departure from Cüstrin had been accelerated by the painful fact that a number of distressed Bohemian nobles had arrived at Frankfurt with their families. The Burgravine, who had carried Prince Rupert to his christening, was desirous to sell her pearls to the Queen of Bohemia. The tremendous ropes of pearls presented by the City of London to the Princess Royal of Great Britain on her marriage were safe in Holland, but her Majesty, who never could refuse a pathetic personal request, graciously bought the Burgravine of Prague's little necklace for the future Abbess of Herford.

The Winter Queen had entered upon a business at which she was to become expert—keeping up appearances against fearful odds. Her secretary supported her stoutly. Even her degrading Christmas-tide progress " round about the Empire" in search of a byre in which to lay her babe, was represented by the indefatigable Sir Francis as providential. The royal mother had conquered all hearts in every place through which she had passed. "I confesse I am rapt with the greatness of her Majesties' spirit, and the goodness of her disposition and I am not alone in it." No hints of the discomforts she was enduring at Cüstrin, or of her friendless situation, were allowed to appear in his despatches. The old Duchess of Brunswick was exceeding

[1] Aretin, vii. 174.

R

in kindness. Two messengers enquiring for her Majesty's health had already arrived, and no doubt, since the news of Prince Maurice's birth must by now have reached Wolfenbüttel, a third envoy bearing congratulations was even now on the roads. The Elector of Brandenburg had done more than had been asked or could be expected of him. Her Majesty—somewhat surprisingly in view of so much good cheer—intended to leave her present residence as soon as she could get up, the Low Countries being her probable destination. "Scarcity of matter for news in this retiredness" was offered by her secretary as his reason for a brief letter.[1]

Elizabeth was "on foot again" exactly a week after her confinement, and stood sponsor to the Dohna baby who had been born at Cüstrin a few days after Prince Maurice. Christopher Dohna had been extremely anxious, but his young wife, who was attended by her Majesty's own doctor, Christian Rumph, "an accoucheur of the highest ability", made a good recovery.[2]

The King of Bohemia had humbled himself to no effect. Ferdinand II was going to make an example of the vassal who had defied the house of Habsburg. Ambassadors from the King of England, who had hastened to the German Princes of the Union, the Archduke Albert, and the Emperor, with proposals of peace, were finding themselves "laughed at for their pains". The Elector of Brandenburg had received an Imperial mandate, "requiring him not to harbour the King in his dominions, nor to suffer the Queen to stay in them longer than he could truly excuse it upon her Majestie's inability to go on".[3] George William did not ask Elizabeth to arise from her sick-bed. He merely complained of the inordinate amount of food devoured at Cüstrin in three weeks—"Thirty one baskets of oats consumed by horses, forty barrels of butter,

---

[1] S.P. 81. 20.24 & 81.   [2] Spanheim, *Dhona*, p. 301.
[3] S.P. 81. 20.202.

twenty two casks of table wine.". . . Even the geese, hens
and eggs which had been the diet of the invalid queen were
enumerated by her bucolic and absent host, who, according to
the testimony of an indignant subject, had been known to give
a sum three times their worth to a witty buffoon in a drinking
bout.[1] Berlin on February 19th was Elizabeth's first halt,
and when her train resumed their journey it was without the
youngest member. The pilgrimage his mother was about to
undertake would be beyond the strength of Prince Maurice.
Elizabeth left her six-weeks-old son in the nursery of her
sister-in-law, George William's spouse, and struggled on to
meet her husband. The Elbe was full of ice. For several days,
until a thaw allowed the passage of ferry-boats, she was obliged
to sit staring at a snowscape. Frederick wrote from Lübeck
that it seemed already years since he had seen her.[2]

The Winter King and Queen were reunited in Upper
Westphalia in mid-March. A convoy of nineteen troops of
horse was awaiting them at Bielefeld. The Prince of Orange
had sent this escort to conduct them safely into his country.
His invitation, which was warm, mentioned that a town
residence at the Hague was already furnished for their reception. A palace at Breda would be available as a summer
residence for her Majesty when her husband took the field
again. But there were wearisome delays even after this cheering news reached the exiles. Frederick was averse from
retiring so tamely and far from the scene of conflict. He
replied with a counter-suggestion that he should go into the
Palatinate, leaving his wife at Cleves or Arnhem. He believed
that the King of England would approve of his making every
effort to recover his hereditary domains with the greatest
despatch possible. His father-in-law, in fact, was mainly
perturbed by a report that the mission of Sir Edward Villiers
to Cüstrin had been misinterpreted. A popular rumour was

[1] Von Gallus, p. 15. [2] Bromley, p. 14.

spreading in London that Sir Edward had been the bearer of a message calling the King and Queen of Bohemia home to the arms of their loving father. "God forbid!" was James's comment. "May it please your Lordship", wrote Sir George Calvert, Secretary of State, to Lord Buckingham, on March 13th, "I presume to trouble you with this letter enclosed, from his Majesty to Sir Dudley Carleton, because I know not whether his Majesty would have any else acquainted with it. He gave me the order for it yesterday, and it is for the stay of his daughter the Queen of Bohemia from comming into England. Your Lordshipp may please to procure his Majesty to signe it and to returne it me inclosed in some other cover by this bearer." [1] Elizabeth first heard of her father's determination not to receive her by means of the Dutch Ambassador, who informed her confidentially of the unpleasant fact. She forthwith announced to her suite that although her husband was urging her to return to her native country, she had "no inclination" to do so, and she had empowered Sir Edward Villiers to explain her reluctance to her father.

The Prince of Orange was sending word that Cleves was not a safe residence for the Queen of Bohemia; [2] that the delay of the royal couple in unfriendly territory was dangerous, and that the States General were becoming resentful at the long detention of their convoy. From Bielefeld, in the last week of March, the King and Queen of Bohemia sent to the Prince of Orange a grateful acceptance of his generous invitation and a list of the attendants who would be accompanying them to the Hague. They then set out on the last stages of their long journey. Their travel-worn procession skirted the walls of Münster. More than quarter of a century was to pass before the peace which ended the present war was to be signed in that city. At Wesel they came in sight of a broad and noble river. Henceforward they retraced exactly the route which had been

[1] *Fortescue Papers*, p. 151.   [2] S.P. 84. 100.46 & 100.

"THE PEARL OF BRITAIN"

Elizabeth Stuart before her marriage, aged about fifteen.

By Nicholas Hilliard

FREDERICK V
ELECTOR PALATINE
Aged 16

By Isaac Oliver

ELIZABETH STUART

'The picture of the King's sister when she
was young, in her high-tired, past-fashioned
hair-dressing. By Isaac Oliver.' Van der
Doort's catalogue of the collection of
Charles I

'Les deux jeunes mariés'

SILVER MEDAL
OF THE ELECTOR AND ELECTRESS
PALATINE

THE KING AND QUEEN OF BOHEMIA

riding with the Princes of Orange
on the Buitenhof at the Hague

By H. A. Pacx

'Though I have cause enough to be sad, yet I am still of my
wilde humour to be as merrie as I can in spite of fortune'

THE QUEEN OF BOHEMIA

Aged about 30

detail of a portrait by Daniel Mytens who was travelling in
Holland, August 1626–March 1627

FREDERICK V
ELECTOR PALATINE, KING OF BOHEMIA

By Honthorst

FOUR OF THE CHILDREN OF THE
QUEEN OF BOHEMIA

By Honthorst

The records of the Deanery of Winchester, where this picture long
hung, state that it was presented to Dean Bramston in 1883, and came
from the collection of Lord Fitzwalter, of Wanstead House. Frederica,
wife of the last Earl Fitzwalter, was a great grand-daughter of Elizabeth
of Bohemia: the child of Meinhardt, third Duke of Schomberg and
Caroline Elizabeth, daughter of Charles Louis, Elector Palatine

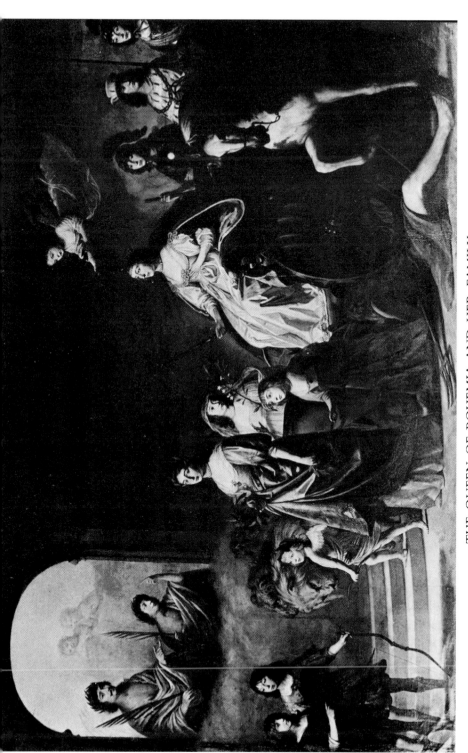

THE QUEEN OF BOHEMIA AND HER FAMILY

This picture forms part of the large collection of Palatine family
portraits at the Palace of Herrenhausen, the home of the Queen of
Bohemia's youngest daughter, Sophie

WILLIAM,
FIRST EARL OF CRAVEN

By Princess Louise

SOPHIE

Youngest daughter of Elizabeth of Bohemia
and mother of George I, King of England

By Honthorst

From the Queen of Bohemia's collection
inherited by William, First Earl of Craven

followed by the Prince and Princess Palatine of the Rhine on
their honeymoon journey seven years past. At Emmerich
they received a pleasant surprise. Ernest of Nassau Dietz had
brought the little Crown Prince of Bohemia over the Gelderland frontier to meet his parents. Young Frederick Henry's
arrival in the Nassau Dietz household last autumn had been
singularly inopportune, for Sophia Hedwig had been in
hourly expectation of her confinement when the unexpected
addition of a German cousin had been made to her nursery.
The strange princeling, however, had settled down very
happily amongst the kind Dutch.

Kindness was the predominant note of the welcome which
greeted the weary king and queen as soon as they entered the
country which was to be their new home. No trouble or
expense had been spared to make their reception as dejected
exiles as much of an occasion for festivity as their honeymoon
visit. The burghers and garrison of Rotterdam put themselves
in arms for two days, and entertained and banqueted the royal
procession at the town's expense. "The whole way, as well by
water as land" between the environs of Delft and the centre
of the Hague resembled "a continued street" so great was the
press of people, "from the highest to the lowest", eager to
testify to the Winter King and Queen that their feelings had
not been "changed by the change of these princes' fortune".
There was something gruesome in finding the end of their
flight turned into a prolonged triumphal progress, but Elizabeth showed herself appreciative of the intention under-
lying her host's efforts. Her happy remark as she stepped on
board the barge sent by the Prince of Orange to carry her to
Rotterdam was noted with satisfaction—"This hour repays
me for the past!" [1]

[1] S.P. 84. 100.108.122.138.

CHAPTER V

THE QUEEN OF HEARTS

I

THE Hague, 'S Graven Hage, "The Count's Enclosure" or
"Hedge", had been in the thirteenth century no more than a
hunting-lodge of the Counts of Holland. Floris V had set the
example, followed by his successors, of residing there, but the
eighteen towns of the Dutch Republic who sent representatives
to the national assembly guarded their privileges jealously, and
in 1621 the Hague was still resolutely denied a vote or the title
of "town". It was "the largest village in Europe", and was to
continue a village in name for nigh on another two hundred
years. Its plan was easily to be comprehended by strangers, for
it was built in the shape of a cross, a design which gave scope
for the Dutch love of broad and handsome streets of substantial houses, and long avenues of trees guarding stretches of
placid picturesque water. "On all sides without the Village",
except upon the north "where the sandy downes of the Sea
lie neere", the eye of the visitor was delighted by the sight of
"faire pastures and fruitfull corne fields". Within the Hague
the majority of the houses were "faire, built of brickes", some
few were "stately built of freestone". The most spacious and
imposing square, containing both the Town Hall and the
principal church, was the Fish-market. Only in by-streets was
thatch to be detected.[1] The western quarter of the Hague was
distinguished by being situated on higher and more sandy

---

[1] An order of 1629 insisted on tiles being used for roofing, but the change
was made gradually.

soil than the rest, and the south by "the water that leadeth to Delft. "The East side, comming in from Leyden," was generally awarded the palm for beauty, for its environs included the celebrated Haagsche Bosche, "a most pleasant Grove, with many wild walkes, like a Maze", and, "neerer the houses", another "very pleasant walke, set round about with willowes", leading to "the publike house for excercise of shooting in the Peece and Crossebow, which hath a sweet prospect into a large greene plaine, where they use to spread linnen clothes in the sunne; and here, certaine rowes of trees, being planted, yeeld a pleasant shade to them that walke therein".[1] The most important of these avenues, the Lange Voorhout and the Vijveberg, ran parallel and were connected at their western ends by the Kneuterdijk, once the jousting field. The Vijverberg took its name from the "Vijver", fish-pond, of the old castle. The fish-pond, which reflected the backs of some of the important buildings of varying dates which now surrounded the Prince's residence, was already, by 1621, a carefully regulated sheet of water, decorated by an ornamental islet inhabited by many swans. The "Buitenhof", outer court, of the original castle lay to the west of it. The "Binnenhof", inner court, still attained by antique gateways and "compassed with a dry ditch", was the centre, topographically and historically, of the Hague. Its Great Hall, hung with flags and other trophies captured from the Spaniards was pronounced by English visitors "not much inferior to ours of Westminster". Its gardens were "full of ornament, close-walks, statues, marbles, grotts, fountains and artificiall musiq".[2]

The apartments assigned to the King and Queen of Bohemia on their arrival were those in which they had stayed seven years before as bride and bridegroom. They belonged to Prince Henry of Nassau. Prince Henry, who was now seven and thirty, was still, like his brother the Prince of Orange, a bachelor,

[1] Fynes Moryson, i. 109–11.   [2] Evelyn, i. 26.

but since it was obviously undesirable that he should be deprived of his official residence in the capital for an indefinite
period, the States set to work without delay to choose and
furnish another dwelling for their guests. Their first selection,
made on March 9th, was a house in a street south of the
Binnenhof. It had until a year before been the Swedish Embassy. On April 9th, however, they bethought them of a
better choice. Two of the palatial private mansions for which
this district was famous, situated conveniently side by side on
the Kneuterdijk at the west end of the Lange Voorhout, were
sequestered property. One was standing empty; no rent need
be paid for either. The Hof te Wassenaer, designed to be the
home of the King and Queen of Bohemia, had already a long
history of aristocratic ownership.[1] The original structure on this
site, dating from the years when every nobleman of the first
importance, attendant at the court of the Counts of Holland,
had his family residence close to the castle, had been demolished
in 1394. The Hendrik van Wassenaer whose name still clung to
it had built the nucleus of the existing house early in the
fifteenth century. From the Wassenaers the property had
passed by marriage to another noble family. The Counts de
Ligne, however, Southern Netherlands absentee landlords,
had eventually lost personal possession of the house. Count
van Hohenlohe, a son-in-law of William the Silent, had
succeeded them as a tenant of the States, who made him an
allowance to cover necessary repairs. His widow had continued to reside there until 1609, when the de Lignes, taking

[1] The two houses which accommodated the court of the exiled King and
Queen of Bohemia have suffered many changes since 1661. They are now
both occupied by the Ministry of Finance, and known as Kneuterdijk 22.
The Wassenaer Hof was hopelessly dilapidated by the time that Elizabeth
quitted it, and nine years later a new baroque house, bearing the old name,
was built in front of it, on the site of what had been its courtyard of entry.
See *De Huizen aan den Kneuterdijk, No. 22*, by A. de Vink, Haghe Jaarboek
1921–22; *Het Hof van Boheme*, by C. van Sypesteyn, and *Beschryvings van's
Graven Hage*, by J. Riemer, iii. 729.

advantage of the Twelve Years' Truce, had applied for permission to sell all their Hague property. Finally, in 1616, the Grand Pensionary van Oldenbarnevelt had bought the Wassenaer Hof on the Kneuterdijk for the sum of twenty thousand guilders. He had proceeded to establish in it his well-born and accomplished son-in-law, Cornelius Van der Myle, husband of his daughter Maria. The Grand Pensionary had himself become the owner, five years previously, of the adjacent Naaldwijk Hof.

Cornelius Van der Myle had redecorated his new home lavishly and made extensive structural alterations. In April 1621, when the States bestowed it on the King and Queen of Bohemia, Cornelius was a political exile. He had been banished to the Island of Goree. His unfortunate wife was informed that she might continue to live under her own roof, but in an inferior set of apartments. This arrangement, most trying both to the Queen of Bohemia and Madame van der Myle, proved a complete success. Elizabeth, who had the best of reasons for understanding the feelings of the wife of an exile, interceded tirelessly with the States during the next four years for her host's return. In 1625, when Henry of Nassau succeeded his brother, Cornelius Van der Myle, a personal friend of the new prince, reappeared at the Hague, and thenceforward lived with his family and the Bohemian royal family. Two years after their arrival there, the king and queen began to pay rent, and exactly forty years after she had first set foot in it Elizabeth quitted the Van der Myle mansion, taking with her to England as a lady-in-waiting, a daughter of the house.

The adjacent houses occupied by the royal exiles and their suite were dissimilar in appearance, and of the two the Wassenaer Hof was superior both in antiquity and picturesqueness. It stood back from the road within its own courtyard, guarded by a wall containing a gateway attained by several steps and surmounted by a lordly coat of arms. It was built in red brick, and judging by a contemporary sketch,[1] its façade was remarkable for many crowding gables, dormer windows, steeply sloping tiled roofs of varying heights, richly ornamented chimneys, and even a couple of towers. It had no unity of design, but its appearance was not unpleasant, for it looked exactly what it was—a large, rambling family residence, bearing obvious signs of the additions and improvements of every successive patrician owner. The States ordered some hasty interior alterations at their own expense, and sent in valuable furniture bought from the heirs of the Archduke Albert's late Chancellor Pieter Peckius. Three apartments were entirely re-decorated in a style suitable for royal occupation. The walls of the principal reception-room in which their Majesties would take their meals were covered with gilded leather; the "salet" or lesser salon, received wall-coverings of silk. The portico of the royal exiles' new home displayed impressive armorial bearings carved in oak. Many beams were visible in the ceiling of the outer hall, which was panelled in oak, and hung with Flemish tapestries and oil-paintings by famous masters. The floor was of stone mosaic; the large stone fireplace and overmantel were elaborately carved. The many narrow windows of the old house were filled with small, heavily leaded panes, containing brightly coloured coats of arms, medallions and scrolls inscribed with mottoes and proverbs in the prevailing style. Around the walls were ranged sets of chairs with well-stuffed, low seats and tall backs. Cornelius Van der Myle, who wrote several French letters expressing elegant gratitude to the Queen of Bohemia during his years of banishment, had lived in luxury.

The Bohemian exiles were not to be poor. The States were making them a grant of ten thousand guilders a month, and from England came another twenty-six thousand guilders monthly. All members of their Majesties' suite capable of bearing arms were offered commissions in the Prince of

[1] Facing page 130, *Die Haghe Jaarboek* 1921–22.

Orange's army. Unfortunately the suite, according to the testimony of the British Ambassador, was extremely numerous. It numbered two thousand persons, of whom many were old men, women and children.[1]

On April 13th a deputation from the States General paid a congratulatory visit to their guests in their new residence. For the next three days the king and queen kept open house, and were granted a special allowance to cover the expenses of this house-warming. On April 23rd the formal call paid to them by the States General was returned. Frederick made a speech, relating his sad experiences and announcing himself extremely sensible of the hospitality shown to him and his family. The States replied that they hoped better times would soon dawn for him, a sentiment with which Frederick agreed with all the heartiness consonant with civility. The lot of an exiled queen is notoriously easier than that of an exiled king. Frederick did not find his position either as guest of a new Republic or as a leading figure in his uncle's court, congenial. Elizabeth, on the other hand, found at the Hague her best opportunities for communication with England since she had left home as a bride. The English Ambassador and his lady had been ready waiting on the quay at Rotterdam to greet her. They were a most sympathetic couple. Poor Lady Carleton, always bearing and always burying, shared the Queen of Bohemia's love of pet animals, and between them, within a few months of Elizabeth's arrival, they collected an extraordinary *ménagerie*, including over thirty "little dogs and monkeys". Jack, her Majesty's old monkey, had astonishingly survived all his mistress's changes of residences and fortune, and sat by her writing-desk in the "salet" of the Wassenaer Hof on the Kneuterdijk "as knavish as ever he was" in Schloss Heidelberg or the Hradčany.[2] Sir Dudley Carleton, much to the Queen of Bohemia's surprise, did not share her enthusiasm

[1] Persons who held no office at the court lived elsewhere in the town.
[2] Roe, p. 74.

for her favourite puppy "Apollon", "the most beautiful grey-hound in Europe".[1] Sir Dudley wrote to his sister, who was desirous of sending the queen a present from London, advising her not to choose anything four-footed. "Horses be welcome here, though here be no place to ride them." He knew that her Majesty did not care overmuch for sweetmeats. The choice of dress-materials obtainable at the Hague was wider than in London; indeed he knew that many English ladies sent to the Hague for their best gown-materials. The queen was amply provided with plate and jewellery of a quality which his sister could not hope to equal.

The arrival of the Queen of Bohemia gave the English Ambassador at the Hague a welcome new subject with which to fill his despatches. The North Netherlands, freed from the yoke of Spain, and flowering into prosperity in commerce, and genius in art and literature, were far from being at peace within. A furious and unedifying war between Protestants who differed on essential articles of belief, particularly predestination, had occupied Sir Dudley's pen ever since his appointment. A shadow which had not been apparent when last his nephew and niece had visited him, now darkened the brow of the first soldier in Europe. On a spring day, not two years past, a great Dutch patriot, aged three score years and ten, had perished on the scaffold in the Binnenhof. The trial, condemnation and execution of the Grand Pensionary van Oldenbarnevelt had left an indelible stain upon the reputation of Maurice of Nassau. The court to which he welcomed the exiled King and Queen of Bohemia was cosmopolitan in character and of unrestrained morals. It exercised no influence whatever on the cultural or domestic life of the Dutch. Its language was French. The House of Orange was linked in marriage with many noble French Huguenot and German families, and the Binnenhof was crowded with the result.

[1] *Archaeologia,* 39. 167–9.

Many letters from England awaited Elizabeth at the Hague. Some, from strangers, were quite mad—urging her to come over to London, even if her father were to throw her into the Tower for doing so. Others, from well-wishers who were personal friends, were full of comfort and concern. A simple country dame, the mother of her plump maid of honour, Elizabeth Apsley, sent a confused screed evidently evoked by strong emotion. Lady Apsley's joy at hearing of her "most gracious Quene's" safe delivery of "a fourth sonn which God bles with the rest", was inextricably mixed with her horror at the many reports to the contrary, and "of your great journey", which had reached England. The Sussex dame's comment on the Battle of the White Mountain was a model of tact. "Though it plesed not God to give your worthy king the first victoary, I hope in God's great mercies he will the last, to his comfort and the good of his church." Now that her "maigesty" was, by God's grace, the mother of so many sweet children, some alas! now so far from her, "an old woman" hoped that her Majesty might sympathize with a mother's desire to see her child. When Elizabeth Apsley could be spared for a visit home, "your maigesty's to be commanded" would be "hartly glad".[1]

In several great houses of England, in town and country, this spring, untravelled ladies were nerving themselves to face a sea-voyage. Since the Queen of Bohemia could not come to London, her old playmates, who longed to see her, were all going to the Hague. Lady Bedford was going; Lady Wharton (born Philadelphia Cary) was going.

Three weeks after his mistress's arrival in Holland, Sir Francis Nethersole crossed the seas to England in "a fisher boat, no other daring hazard such a storm".[2] His business was pressing. The King of Bohemia had learnt with dismay that the Princes of the Union had perfidiously arranged a permanent

[1] Sussex Archaeological Collection, iv. 221.   [2] S.P. 84. 100.217.

peace with the Emperor, from which his name was excluded. He earnestly hoped that now his father-in-law would approve of his intention of marching without delay to the relief of his Palatine subjects. But the King of England, after much delay, did not approve. He was sending an Ambassador Extraordinary to Vienna to treat for the restoration of the Palatinate, and, if possible, some toleration for Bohemian Protestants. He must ask his son-in-law to await the issue with patience, and refrain from taking up arms. James knew that his daughter was no longer suffering physically. In the eyes of the most cautious monarch in Europe, his children had committed the worst of sins. They had been imprudent. Moreover they had asked for his advice and acted before receiving it. As a result, they had imperilled his relations with Spain and forced him to ask his most disobliging Commons for money. That his subjects were enthusiastic in the cause of the King and Queen of Bohemia, did not endear his children to the King of England.

"In Holland and some parts of Germany" the queen who had lost her crown won a new title this season. She had been vaunted as an ideal princess before she left England. But she had been but sixteen then, and all untried. Since then she had not failed those who had hoped greatly for her. It now appeared that the lady who presided as mistress of an exiled court in a Dutch setting had developed a decided character all her own. Her secretary, unflatteringly to her sex, described her as "the lady of the world that hath the least of the woman in her". He passed on to dilate on her extraordinary freedom from "woman's humours". Although famous for her personal attractions, the Queen of Bohemia was innocent of coquetry. She was entirely of the type that would sooner hear her dog bark than a man swear he loved her. She was as frank and downright as a school-boy. Like a school-boy, she rejoiced in rude health and, it must be confessed, a rude jest. Yet where more poignantly feminine princesses slew their thousands the Queen of Bohemia slew her tens of thousands. English visitors to the Wassenaer Hof began to know exactly what to expect. A friend of her Warwickshire days described a typical audience :

DEAREST SISTER,

By this you shall receive an account of the present that you left with me for the queen of Bohemia. As soon as she saw me come into the room . . . her second words were 'How doth my lady Cornwallis?' I gave her your present . . . she took the box, and before all the company that was there, did open it, and did very much commend it. . . . I saw that it was a gift very agreeable to her. The same day at my lord ambassador's house, where the king and queen and princes of Orange did dine, she took occasion to speak of it again, and said that the old love between you two must not be forgotten. I pray therefore continue this interchange to her, as often as you shall find occasion, for, upon my soul, if it lay in her power to do you a good office she would not be sparing to perform it.[1]

The nickname "Queen of Hearts" which was to be hers for life fastened upon her.[2] But in the Spanish Netherlands, and other parts of Germany, the fair royal lady who was deemed by her ambition to have brought such calamity to thousands, was bitterly dubbed "the Helen of Germany".[3]

She did all she could to refute the suggestion that from worldly and selfish motives she had goaded her husband to snatch at a crown. She realized that even her present hosts considered that, except from the domestic point of view, their nephew's alliance had not fulfilled expectations. Some of the many visitors who flocked to call upon the exiled queen were surprised one day of this summer to find a member of her household ready to read aloud to them a document left by her

[1] Cornwallis, p. 183.　　[2] Howell, i. 113.　　[3] Lützow, p. 330.

Majesty in her withdrawing-room for their edification. The
letter, which was addressed to the Princess Palatine by the
Archbishop of Canterbury, and bore a date two years old,
strongly advised her husband's acceptance of the crown of
Bohemia. Archbishop Abbot added that if the King of England would not at present advise such a step, he was convinced
that his Majesty would eventually support his children."[1]

The Queen of Bohemia had begun at last to criticize her
father. "I confess to you", she wrote to Sir Thomas Roe,
"that I do not look for anie good change of fortune for us if
my father doe noe otherwise than he hath done."[2] To James
himself she wrote, "Your majesty will understand by the kings'
letters how the Palatinate is in danger of being utterly lost if
your majesty give us not some aid. I am sorry we are obliged
to trouble your majesty so much with our affairs, but their
urgency is so great that we cannot do otherwise." She still
nourished hopes that a visit to England by her eldest son might
work wonders. The Queen of Bohemia ordered a full-length
portrait of the Crown Prince for presentation to the King of
England.[3] The artist summoned by her was no stranger.
Michiel Jansz van Mierevelt had painted the Prince and Princess
Palatine on their honeymoon journey.[4] Every prominent
member of the house of Nassau employed "Michel of Delft".
Sir Dudley Carleton, who sat to the fashionable artist this
year, considered his work elegant but cold. The patronage of
the Winter King and Queen brought a man, already over-busy,
both pleasure and pain. His son-in-law engraved his portraits
of the royal couple and sold twenty-nine copies, printed on

---

[1] Goodman, i. 236.   [2] S.P. 81. 21.30.   [3] S.P. 84. 101.154.

[4] These portraits were engraved by Bolswert in 1613 and are reproduced
in the Grangerized Pennants' *London*, xi. 57–8. Frederick presented a copy
of his portrait to the government of the Upper Palatinate in 1616. It was
still preserved in the Session Chamber at Amberg in 1824, when it was
reproduced as an illustration in Lipowski's biography of the Winter King.
Recent enquiry has failed to discover its present whereabouts.

satin, at four florins the pair, to the Estates of Holland. But twenty years after he had completed the Queen of Bohemia's first commission, the unfortunate "Michel" noted in his will that payment was still owing to him from several members of her Majesty's household for pictures delivered thirteen and fourteen years past. Even the critical Sir Dudley had "left long ago without paying" for his portrait of Mlle Harington.[1]

In return for the full-length likeness of his grandchild the King of England sent to his daughter a ring containing a miniature of himself. This disappointing result did not deter Elizabeth from giving "Michel" further employment. Until she found a younger man who worked quicker and produced more flattering likenesses she continued to rain orders upon his studio. The Queen of Bohemia's celebrated ropes of pearls confined by an enormous brooch surmounted by a jewelled crown, her great sleeve brooches and her hair ear-ring must have become as familiar to the pupils and assistants in Mierevelt's workshop as they were to their owner and her servants. No court painter had been available in Prague, and the visit of a French artist to Heidelberg had been an unusual occurrence. Since she was sixteen Elizabeth had not enjoyed such opportunities as presented themselves at the Hague. Many copies of a head and shoulders portrait by Mierevelt were ordered by her for deserving friends.[2] Sir Thomas Roe had to wait long for his copy. It was promised in May, 1621. In August Elizabeth wrote, "I will send you my picture, as soone as I can have it done, for you know, I am sure, that Michel of Delft is verie long in his work".[3] In January, 1623, she wrote to the Duchess of Thouars "The painter has been so afflicted by the loss of his son[4] that he has been unable to paint me".[5] Not until March

[1] Havard, p. 104.
[2] The descendant of her steward, Sir Charles Cottrell, possesses one; another is in the National Portrait Gallery. [3] S.P. 81. 21.30 & 217.
[4] Pieter van Mierevelt, a promising artist, died in this year.
[5] *Archaeologia*, 39.163.

S

1623, did Sir Thomas, at Constantinople, receive the gift which made "my house a Court, my chamber a Presence". The King of England had ordered one of his daughter's most voiceful champions as Ambassador to the Porte. "I am infinitely satisfied", wrote Sir Thomas, "that no adversity hath power to banish those smiles which yet smile upon us". Elizabeth had sent companion portraits of herself and her husband. Sir Thomas had not been able to resist "forcing the fight" upon the Emperor's representative by asking his opinion of the new pictures hanging upon the walls in the British Embassy. "When he had well beheld them, he asked me 'Whose they were?' I replyed 'The King and Queen of Bohemia, and are they not worthy to have a kingdome?' The Emperor's agent "rose and departed as if he had broken a tooth."[1] [2]

II

With midsummer of their first year in Holland, heartbreaking news from Prague penetrated to the exiles of the Hague. Since March, those of Frederick's principal supporters who had failed to escape with their master had been lingering under sentence of death in the Hradčany. There is no hope that Elizabeth did not see some of the flood of engravings published this summer, depicting "How by gracious order and command of his Royal Imperial Majesty, the former Bohemian Directors, Counsellors, Lords, Knights and men of the estate of citizens, were, on Monday, June 21, punished and executed on the market-

[1] Roe, p. 136.
[2] In the winter of 1621 an appearance of the romantic royal exiles to watch Dutch sports on the ice near the Hague was eagerly recorded by a young local artist, who scribbled below his sketch the words—'C'est Fréderic, V, Roi de Bohème et sa femme, dessinés d'après mature.' Hendrik van Avercamp saw Elizabeth wearing a yellow gown, a muff and a mask. The sketch is reproduced in an illustrated volume of the work of Netherlands artists by C. Ploos van Amstel, published at Amsterdam in 1821.

place of the old town". The ex-queen's last night in Prague had been spent in a house overlooking that square. The scene which took place there at 5 A.M. on June 21st was designed to impress upon Bohemians that it was unwise to revolt against the house of Habsburg. Seven squadrons of Saxon horse were brought into the town to keep order. Many of the sentences performed included torture and mutilation. The first person to suffer was old Count Schlick, who had been captured in his castle of Friedland. His wife, "as soone as she heard of the execution of her lord, for sorrow fell straitly dead". It is enough to say that the twenty-seven patriots eventually done to death that day met their ends with exemplary courage. When it is considered that many of them had been in daily attendance at the court of the Winter King and Queen and that the shadowy court at the Hague still included their closest friends and relations,[1] something may be imagined of the feelings of Frederick and Elizabeth. An observer records that the Bohemians of the Wassenaer Hof went about staring at one another, as if surprised to see their heads still on their shoulders. In Vienna Ferdinand II had torn the seal from the Bohemians' treasured Letter of Majesty and cut the document in two with scissors. The crown of Bohemia was declared hereditary in the house of Habsburg. Three-quarters of the soil of the kingdom was confiscated and either sold or presented to victorious Imperialist generals and court dignitaries. In place of the Bohemian noblemen whose heads stared from both towers of the Charles Bridge of Prague, a new landed aristocracy, mostly German, but including Spaniards and even Irishmen, all strictly Catholic, arrived to bear rule over large tracts of territory ravaged by war. The spectacular vengeance of Ferdinand II achieved its object. For nearly three centuries the history of Bohemia was that of an Austrian province.[2]

[1] S.P. 84. 100.235.
[2] S.P. 81. 21.77.82; Lützow, pp. 356–8 and *Prague*, p. 121.

III

A fortnight after the execution of the Bohemian patriots in Prague, the King and Queen of Bohemia "with their court" paid a visit to Amsterdam "to pass away three or four melancholy days". They were "most stately welcomed and feasted" in an atmosphere of profound sympathetic gloom. At a religious service attended by them, an English clergyman named Paget "went so far as to make affliction an argument of happiness". He concluded his discourse "with a prayer to God to increase our afflictions that thereby we may be known to be His children". To this "none but his own parish said Amen ".[1] The Winter Queen, safe at last amongst friends in a placid midsummer, was beginning to find herself called upon to face an enemy far more feared by her than the pursuing Cossacks of last year's snows. Her husband showed unmistakable signs of a recurrence of the melancholia which had been the bugbear of her early married life. She was back again at her old Heidelberg task of devising distractions to raise the spirits of "M. l'Electeur". Nor could she deny now that his despondent musings on "his bruised honour and fortune" and "the furie of those further storms which are threatening" were without foundation. Late in July the news that Lord Digby's efforts in Vienna had failed to effect a renewal of the truce in the Palatinate brought on a bout of black despair so alarming that she confessed her anxiety in the postscript of a letter to Lord Buckingham. The Queen of Bohemia begged the favourite in confidence to inform her father and her brother that she had never known the king worse.[2] She comforted the stricken man as best she could. In this month was conceived the Princess Louise Hollandine, most talented and difficult of the children of the King and Queen of Bohemia, a family destined to be remarkable for these qualities. The Hague in August was remarkably quiet. All families who could arrange to do so

[1] S.P. 84. 101.234b.
[2] Hist. MSS. Comm. 10th Report, Appendix i, p. 90.

departed to the country. The long, wet sands of Scheveningen were thronged by holiday crowds. The Prince of Orange had left to take the field against Spain. Spinola, who had left Brussels, was said to be advancing on Maastricht. The ex-King of Bohemia, who had been born and reared in mountain country, made up his mind about "the largest village in Europe" and its inhabitants. He particularly disliked both.

Sir Dudley Carleton had written optimistically to England, soon after the exiles' arrival, that the king was "holding himself" to the promise made to his father-in-law, and the queen was "contenting herself with her abode in these parts". His Britannic Majesty might rest assured that they would not "take any course concerning their persons or affairs than shall be agreeable to him". On August 16th Frederick took a step most disagreeable to his father-in-law. He set out with a small train to join his host's army as a volunteer. Carleton and Nethersole had done their best to dissuade him, but he was maddened by the persistent request of three friendly military commanders that he should take some action to recover his lost possessions. He was determined to adventure his person somewhere.

Unhappily for Elizabeth, Lady Bedford arrived on her long-promised visit just when the queen was preoccupied with her husband's impending departure, a project with which she was "no whit contented". Moreover such Dutch ladies of rank as were still in their capital did their best to ruin the short stay of the queen's great friend, and her Majesty's own ladies assisted them. Since Lady Carleton, from a mistaken notion of pleasing Elizabeth, gave place to her guest, every entertainment given in honour of Lady Bedford was rendered infestive by the determined efforts of Dutch and Palatine dames to take precedence of the English Ambassadress.[1] At length Frederick had gone, and Elizabeth was at leisure to enjoy the society of the lady whom she had not seen for eight years, and who had

[1] S.P. 84. 100.163–6.

taken considerable pains to meet her. James I had only permitted this visit of an important English peeress to his daughter on the condition that no other person of rank accompanied her, and Lady Bedford had been obliged to announce before she left England that she would not be absent more than a month. Although she had bravely declared that she thought not much more of crossing the sea than crossing the Thames, she had made her will before embarking on her maiden voyage.[1] The old friends had much to hear and much to tell, and much of even the guest's story was sad, for Lady Harington had died last year, and her daughter, who had given up the hope of children, was thinking of selling Combe Abbey. However, there was many a promising young "Frederick" and "Elizabeth" now—god-children of their Majesties, and well known to Lady Bedford—in the nurseries of more fortunate playmates of Combe days, and her accomplished ladyship had two absorbing hobbies typical of the middle-aged English gentlewoman. She collected antiques. "Some of those I have, I found in obscure places and gentlemen's houses, that because they were old made no reckoning of them: and that makes me think it likely that there yet may be in diverse places many excellent unknown pieces for which I lay wait with all my friends."[2] Her other great source of interest was her Hertfordshire garden, "with which I am so much in love that, if I were as fond of any man, I were in hard case".[3] Her visit to the Hague was dogged by disaster from start to finish. Scarcely had the Queen of Bohemia settled down to news of all the Russells, Talbots, Killigrews, Chichesters, Cornwallises, Haringtons, Bacons and Meautys, when tidings were brought of "the winde's suddaine coming good" for a passage to England. She could not attempt to deter a very delicate woman from seizing the opportunity of an easy crossing. Elizabeth had exactly one day of far from uninterrupted converse with her friend. Her Majesty both dined and supped at the British

---

[1] Cornwallis, p. 42.   [2] Ibid., p. 42.   [3] Ibid., pp. 50–1.

Embassy, where Lady Bedford was staying, on August 17th.[1]
Five days after she had been left "very much alone", Sir Dudley
Carleton and Sir Francis Nethersole were surprised by the entry
of the Queen of Bohemia in good spirits. She had denied herself
a further week of her "deare Bedford" all in vain. The unfortunate lady had been caught at sea by one of the worst
storms of the year. Her Majesty's father was, as she had fore-
seen, furious with her husband; one of her children—Rupert—
was far from well; she was herself almost certainly in debt
again, and with child again. But her Majesty had just heard
that an enormous fish—fourteen feet long—had been washed
ashore six miles up the coast. She had come to dinner, and to
carry the gentlemen with her, and a large company, to view the
interesting monster.[2]

Frederick returned to the Hague in October. "No great
exploits" were expected by the Prince of Orange's troops
during the next few months. Lord Digby had complained
that it was impossible for him to treat for peace at Vienna
while the King of Bohemia, and commanders employed by
him, were still in arms. Sir Edward Villiers, who had been so
successful at Cüstrin, was again sent from England to urge
obedience upon his master's son-in-law. Frederick, on his
homecoming, made for the first time a remark which he was to
repeat with increasing vehemence during the rest of his life.
"He could have wished he had married rather a Boore's
daughter than the King of Great Brittaine's." [3] Whenever he
made it, he accompanied this statement with a tender declaration of his devotion to his consort, but Elizabeth had been
proud of being Princess Royal of Great Britain.

Bethlem Gabor, "the fox", whose offers to negotiate had
been refused by the Emperor, was eager that the King of
Bohemia should endeavour to recapture that country. Another
daring adventurer, whose overtures Ferdinand had felt
strong enough to reject, had for some time been working

[1] S.P. 84. 100.786.　　[2] S.P. 81. 21.232.　　[3] Harl. MS. 389.67.

wonders in Frederick's name. Ernest, Count of Mansfeld, was an illegitimate son of Peter, Prince of Mansfeld, a commander who had fought with distinction for Spain in the Netherlands. The count himself, a Catholic, had seen his first service in the Imperial army, and tried to return to it when the cause of revolting Bohemia, in which he had been hired by the Duke of Savoy, seemed hopeless. "Mansfeld", said Elizabeth, "is a brave man, but all that glitters in him is not gold." [1] She might well say this, for after baffling Tilly, Mansfeld had come to an agreement with Maximilian of Bavaria to evacuate the Upper Palatinate, and either dismiss his troops or transfer them to the Emperor. At a moment's notice, however, he changed his mind, marched into the Lower Palatinate, effected a junction with General Vere, raised the siege of Frankenthal, Elizabeth's dower town, and arrived in Heidelberg.

The third of the trio of odd characters now calling upon her gentle husband as a brother-in-arms was thoroughly approved by the Winter Queen. Christian of Brunswick, "temporal bishop" of Halberstadt, was her first cousin and her champion. "For God and for her", was embroidered on his banners. "God's friend and the priest's foe", was the superscription on the dollars coined by him out of the silver statue of St Liborius at Paderborn. "The mad Halberstadter" and his merry men admittedly kept themselves in funds by many a deed of violence, but glamour has always surrounded the name of a Robin Hood, and Elizabeth as yet saw in her twenty-two-year-old "yong cousen of Brunswick" nothing worse than a bold oppressor of the rich evil-doer and helper of the virtuous needy. He wore her glove on his helmet, like a knight of old. Unless he had seen his lady at a moment most unflattering to her beauty, newly risen from child-bed, amidst the snows of last winter at Wolfenbüttel, it is unlikely that Christian had set eyes on her. But he had heard enthusiastic accounts from

[1] Roe, p. 146.

his sister Sophie of Nassau Dietz, and to all the younger children of the widowed Duchess of Brunswick the Princess Royal of Great Britain, who had been unsuccessfully wooed by their elder brother, Frederick Ulrich, was a romantic figure. Elizabeth herself can hardly have failed to see the series of full-length oil portraits of her first cousins sent over to her father's court in 1610.[1] The likeness of Christian at the age of ten represented him as a very plain boy indeed, with a long, pale face, lank brown hair and greenish eyes. Christian addressed himself to his "*princesse lointaine*" in a style fully as sycophantic as that employed by the courtiers of Elizabeth Tudor. The following was written after he had been attacked by Tilly while attempting to cross the Main at Aschaffenburg near Höchst, an encounter in which the Imperialists won their victory at terrible cost.

MADAME, MY DEAREST AND MOST BELOVED QUEEN,

The fault is not that of your most faithful and affectionate servant who ever loves and cherishes you. I entreat you, most humbly, not to be angry with your faithful slave for this disaster, nor take away the affection which your majesty has hitherto shown to one who loves you above all in this world. Consider that " la victoire" is in God's hands, not mine, and that I cannot challenge it. Courage will never fail me to die in your majesty's service, for I esteem your favour a hundred times dearer than life. Be assured that I shall endeavour with all my might, not only to reassemble my troops but to double them, that I may be in better case to serve faithfully your majesty, whom I love "outre le possible". Assuring you that as long as God gives me life I shall serve you faithfully and give all I have in the world for you—Your most humble, most constant, most faithful, most affectionate and most obedient slave, who loves you, and will love you, infinitely and incessantly to death

CHRISTIAN.[2]

[1] Now at Hampton Court.   [2] S.P. 81. 25.49. Copy of a French original.

Her Brunswick cousin was not the only young gentleman to vow his blade to the Winter Queen this season.

"The Lieutenant of the Middle Temple played a Game this Christmastide whereat his Majestie was highly displeased. He made choice of some three of the civillest and best-fashioned gentlemen of that House to sup with him, and being at supper, took a cup of wine in one hand and held his sword drawn in the other, and so began a health 'to the distressed Lady Elizabeth,' and having drunk, kissed his sword, and laying his hand upon it, took an oath to live and die in her service: then delivered the cup and sword to the next, and so the health and ceremonie continued." [1]

IV

On the morning of April 4th, 1622, a dark, clean-shaven young German, very simply dressed, was wandering about the streets of Paris, looking pensively at bull-pups. The British "dogue", a light brown, smooth-haired animal with a broad muzzle and a combative disposition, was the fashionable French lady's pet of the moment. He would have liked to send his wife a Parisian little dog, but to tell the truth he could not see any of greater merit than the many she already possessed. It occurred to him also that he had at present no means of sending any gift to the Hague. He passed into one of those shops which exist for the benefit of good husbands visiting the French capital for the first time, and bought several pretty bead necklaces of no value and considerable cost, and a number of little cases for scissors, thimble and needles—so many, indeed, that it seemed probable that he made his living in his own country by retailing such attractive Paris novelties. That night "Frideric" wrote to his wife detailing his disappointment over the bull-pup, and suggesting that when she had selected those

[1] Nichols, iii. 751.

of the *étui* cases which she preferred, she should present the remainder amongst her ladies. He had been to look at the Queen Mother's new palace, and thought it would be lovely when it was finished. He did not doubt that God would give him a good journey. Except that one of the travelling companions mentioned by its writer bore the name of Michalowitz, there was nothing in this letter to suggest that the ex-King of Bohemia was in Paris *incognito*.[1]

Ten days had passed since her husband, looking suddenly much younger, had taken a passionate farewell of the Queen of Bohemia in the Van der Myle mansion at the Hague, and made his way quietly under cover of night to the Brill, where a ship was in readiness "to transport him into France: which way he takes, the other, through Germany, being long and desperatt".[2] Count Mansfeld and General Vere were quarrelling. The Margrave of Baden Durlach and Prince Christian of Brunswick would accept orders from nobody. For two months past Frederick had been "absolutely and fully resolved to go up into the Palatinate without delay", and, to the great relief of Sir Dudley Carleton and Sir Francis Nethersole, they were no longer required to oppose such desires. The King of England was at last convinced that the Emperor was not peaceably inclined. The Elector Palatine had offered to renounce the crown of Bohemia for himself and his heirs and crave the Emperor's pardon on his knees. The document making these generous offers had been drawn up by the Solomon of Europe, and the British Ambassador at the Hague had spent many a weary hour urging an obstinate exile, for the sake of his wife and children, "to drink his cup off roundly and cheerfully". However, it had been possible to exert financial pressure, and at last the humiliating document had been signed and forwarded for the Emperor's consideration. That ungrateful potentate had replied that he would sooner

[1] Aretin, vii. 182.   [2] S.P. 84. 105.178.

cherish a crushed snake in his bosom than re-admit the King of England's son-in-law to his former dignities. The King of England's Parliament had gladly voted money and troops for the recovery of the Palatinate, but had passed on to make demands from their sovereign in return.

In London, after stormy scenes, Parliament had been dissolved, and at the Hague anxious English gentlemen learnt that the ex-King of Bohemia might go where he liked. Sir Francis Nethersole, as British Agent to the Protestant princes of Germany, was the possessor of a safe conduct through all countries not at war with his employer. On the night of March 25th he set off on as odd an expedition as was ever undertaken by a Public Orator of Cambridge University. He was going to Paris, accompanied by a young German merchant bound for his native land *via* Alsace. Frederick, yearning for home and action, ruthlessly sacrificed the beard which he had grown in the hopes of adding years and dignity to the appearance of the King-elect of Bohemia. Elizabeth was expecting her confinement within the month. For the first time her husband would not be with her to greet his child, and never before had he left her on an adventure so perilous. A dark, clean-shaven young German in a plain travelling costume, looking very like the prince who had come a-wooing her at Whitehall, reminded her how easily she got rid of her children. "*C'est une grande grace que Dieu vous fait.*" [1] A single carriage turned out of the courtyard of the Van der Myle mansion and bowled off down the wide, tree-shadowed Voorhout, a thoroughfare dark and deserted at so late an hour. Next morning, curious people at the Hague learnt that the King of Bohemia had gone on a private visit to England.[2]

On the night of April 7th, when Elizabeth fell into labour, she had not yet received a line or a message from her husband. But as he had prophesied, her sufferings were not protracted.

[1] Aretin, vii. 191.   [2] S.P. 81. 23.12.75 & 125.

Her pains began after she had gone to bed. Sir Dudley
Carleton sat up late that night at the British Embassy, writing
to England. The Countess of Nassau Dietz's coach had
deposited its kindly mistress at the Wassenaer Hof. All should
be well, but he was uncommonly anxious. Early on the
morning of the 8th he added triumphantly to his despatch the
familiar words "mother and child well".[1] Between 1 and
2 A.M. the queen had been safely delivered of a sixth child and
second daughter, a lovely fair infant. A princess had evidently
been desired by the absent ex-king, for her names were already
settled. She was to be Louise, after his mother, and Hollandine,
out of compliment to her godfathers and hosts, the States of
Holland. The christening of the Princess Louise Hollandine
took place when she was eight days old, and the bells rung
that spring morning were clearly heard by her mother, for the
church selected as the scene of the ceremony was that whose
walls were visible from the queen's windows. The dignified
fifteenth-century building in the Voorhout, which had
originally been the church of the Dominican monastery of St
Vincent, was now known simply as the Klooster-Kerke. The
baptism was performed "with as much solemnity as this place
can afford", and the princess received rich gifts. The States of
Holland granted her a life pension of two hundred pounds;
her other godfather, Christian of Brunswick, sent her the latest
and largest ransom extorted by him from a prisoner of war.
Since the distance between the nursery and the church was so
short, the christening procession went on foot, but it was an
imposing spectacle, for it was headed by the Prince of Orange,
"with the captains and commanders of all nations, and all his
court". "The child, following, being carried under a canopy",
was immediately preceded by the British Ambassador and her
eldest brother; the representatives of the States of Holland were
followed by the two godmothers, Sophie of Nassau Dietz

[1] S.P. 84. 106.88 & 93.

and Amalia of Nassau, "Princess of Portugal". "All the ladies of quality in this town" brought up the rear of an orderly *cortège* watched by large crowds with sympathetic interest.[1]

Elizabeth, as usual, made a quick recovery, and the first news that came from her husband was cheering. He had arrived safely in the Palatinate, after many an amusing adventure, including a carouse with some of the Archduke Leopold's cavalry, who had told him all the latest jokes about the poor King of Bohemia. His appearance in disguise in his own country was greeted by a burst of enthusiasm, and he made a dramatic entry at Germersheim just in time to frustrate the attempts of a Spanish envoy to buy Mansfeld. On the day of his daughter's christening, after repulsing Tilly at Mongolsheim, he slept in his beloved Schloss Heidelberg.

Elizabeth began to show herself in public again, and as warmer weather came, make expeditions along the coast. She did her best to appear undisturbed as vague rumours penetrated of quarrels between the Margrave of Baden Durlach and Count Mansfeld, and certain tidings of a defeat of the Margrave by Tilly. Letters from her husband arrived at longer intervals as he proceeded towards the siege of Ladenburg and a junction with Christian of Brunswick. With mid-June the black news of Christian's defeat at Höchst reached the Hague. In spite of all her efforts, Elizabeth's anxiety became so obvious and infective that her attendants began to prefer the days of the week on which no letter from the king could possibly be expected.[2] George Frederick of Baden Durlach was a cultivated and prudent man, but in Mansfeld's camp the idealistic King of Bohemia was having enlightening experiences. His letters began to display familiar symptoms terrifying to his wife. Soon her father too began to act characteristically. The King of England had great hopes of

[1] S.P. 84. 106.128.   [2] *Ibid.,* 107.65.

negotiating successfully on behalf of his children with the
Infanta Isabella at Brussels. He was indignant to hear that
Frederick, in Mansfeld's company, had made a raid into Hesse
Darmstadt, and captured the persons of the Landgrave Louis
and his heir. He desired Frederick to forward an agent to
Brussels immediately, and to forbear from further offensive
measures. Early in July, Frederick, threatened with the withdrawal of Vere's army and all means of paying his own troops,
retired reluctantly from the field. The picturesque retreat
chosen by him was Sedan in the Ardennes, the property of his
uncle, the Duke of Bouillon. At Sedan the fatherless young
Prince Palatine had received the education which had made him
an excellent scholar and courtier, but left him wholly unprepared to become a military leader. Elizabeth poured out her
feelings to her old friend, "honest Thom" Roe—"I see it is
not good in these days to be my friend, for they have ever the
worse luck, but I know that will not alter you. The prosperitie
the king hath had in the Palatinat did not last long, for he was
constrained to leave his armie, being readie to mutinie for lake
of payment." The criticism of his master conveyed in this
letter to "his Majestie of Greate Britaine's Ambassadour at
Constantinople" was outspoken. The King of Bohemia had
gone to the Palatinate "by the king my father's command".
When the unfortunate man had got there, not only had "his
majestie of Great Britaine" failed to maintain his army, he
had actually chidden his son-in-law for going in person to the
succour of his subjects. The queen was worried by speculations as to her husband's companions. "There is a speache
here that the count Mansfeld will serve the French king against
those of the religion. If he doe, I would he may be hanged for
his paynes. But I must confess I am in a little trouble what will
become of a worthie cosen germain of mine, the duc Cristian
of Brunswic, who I am sure you have heard of. He hath
ingaged himself onelie for my sake in our quarrell, and if

Mansfeld goe to the French king I know he will not follow him . . . I look every hower for newes of him and the king, who cannot stay long at Sedan for feare of a siege." The Queen of Hearts ended her catalogue of woes with a humorous description of her own situation in her mimic court, "never destitute of a foole to laugh at. When one goes, another comes." [1]

Frederick's letters were certainly not calculated to improve her spirits. The ex-king wrote that he was playing tennis [2] and bathing. He was afraid of inconveniencing his wife, but must ask for another four or five thousand florins. Living was desperately expensive at Sedan, and he could not dismiss any of his followers until he had paid them.[3] The Duke of Bouillon was afraid that the presence of his nephew in his territories would give the Spanish General Cordoba an excuse to attack him. "If so, I am in a pretty position, but where else am I to go? My thoughts are often with my soul's star, whom I love perfectly, even to death. Amongst the many afflictions which God sends to me, not the least is to be so long separated from my sweetheart, whose portrait I carry everywhere . . . If it would please God to give us a little corner of the world in which we could live happily I would ask no more. But I don't like living at the Hague at all." [4]

The Prince of Orange was attempting to raise the siege of Bergen op Zoom. On calm days the sound of his cannon thundering against those of Spinola could be heard in the Voorhout, and waggon-loads of wounded began to arrive at the Hague. Elizabeth began to make plans for joining her husband.[5] Mansfeld and Christian of Brunswick had left Sedan. They had entered the service of the Prince of Orange. They marched boldly to meet him through the Spanish Netherlands, and won battles against Cordoba at Ligny and

[1] Roe, p. 74.   [2] Aretin, vii. 188.   [3] Bromley, p. 15.
[4] Ibid., p. 16.   [5] S.P. 84. 108.25.

Fleurus. But his victory of Fleurus cost the queen's young cousin dear. On an early September day Sophie of Nassau Dietz left the Hague hurriedly for Breda. There she found her favourite brother recovering from the amputation of his left arm. Christian sent word to Elizabeth that he was "already devising how to make an iron arm for his bridle hand", and still had "one arm left to fight God's battles".[1] On September 11th Heidelberg fell to Spinola.

"*Voilà!*" wrote Frederick, "the end of the Brussels treaty! *Voilà!* my poor Heidelberg taken! All sorts of atrocities have been committed there. The whole town has been pillaged. The suburbs which were its chief beauty have been burnt . . . Were I to follow my own inclination I should now become a recluse and allow the King of England to do what he thinks best for his children. But the love you show me will not allow me to do that, and I desire to see you again, to which now no obstacle remains but the king's wish that I shall stay here. I hope he will soon permit me to leave. I think that in a few days I shall send ahead my baggage and train—neither large—so as to save trouble. You assure me warmly that I shall have a welcome home. It is a misery to have to live amongst such delightful people—but patience! I am much relieved that you promise me I shall not be plagued by creditors, for I should be very loath to take up my abode in the gate of the Hague.[2] I hope you received the letter I wrote you last Friday about the taking of Heidelberg. I do all I can to stop myself thinking about it, for it is a wound that hurts. I am rejoiced that Duke Christian is recovering, for I had certainly sooner lose an arm myself than that he should die. We owe him much and God knows that I love him as a brother. . . . Continue for ever to love your poor Celadon, and rest assured that his thoughts turn

[1] Harl. MS. 389. 232b.
[2] By "the gate of the Hague" Frederick meant the Gevangenpoort prison over the gateway leading from the Binnenhof to the Buitenhof.

T

contually to his star, and that he is, even to the tomb, your most faithful friend and affectionate servant." [1]

On the 9th October the exiled queen's household was surprised by the arrival of a jaded traveller. The king had come "home" as quietly as he had departed. "The welcome of his wife proved rather an ecstasy than a meeting", but the long strain had told upon her constitution and on Frederick's appearance. "Seeing him so greatly changed in countenance, she swounded divers times together".[2] Later on this day her cousin Christian of Brunswick presented himself before her, probably for the first time.

Within a month General Vere's surrender of Mannheim was announced to a king whose spirits were in no condition to rally from "this last heavie blowe". "Of all the ill news, which have come unto him, like Job's messengers", wrote Sir Dudley Carleton, "I have observed none since his first arrival in these parts, to drive him into so much distemper and passion as this, for which the sorrow of her highness's heart (who was present at the reading of the letters) was seen in her watery eyes and silence. God send them both patience." [3]

v

A letter from the Queen of Bohemia received by the British Ambassador in Constantinople in March, 1623, displayed so little of her wonted resolution that it caused his Excellency's lady to shed tears, and called forth from him the following rousing paragraph—

Most excellent Lady, be your owne queene. Banish all despaire and feares. Be assured the cause in which you suffer cannot perish. If God had not planted it, it had long since bene rooted out. Vouchsafe to remember the motto of our last,

[1] Bromley, 18.19.20.   [2] Harl. MS. 389.245.   [3] S.P. 84. 110.20b.

eternally glorious, Elizabeth, "This is done of the Lord, and it is wonderful in our eyes." So shall the day of your retorne bee to those honors which you, above all princes, merit.[1]

Sympathy was all that her countrymen could offer Elizabeth at present, for her father had recalled the English troops serving in the Palatinate, and few of his subjects shared James's belief that one of the happy results of a Spanish marriage for his son would be the restoration of his Protestant son-in-law. To the Dean of St. Paul's, who had sent her a copy of a sermon preached by him before her father, Elizabeth wrote with her own hand one of the most charming letters ever addressed by an English princess to an eminent divine who is also a childhood's friend.

GOOD DR D.

You lay me under a double obligation; first in praying for me, then in teaching me to pray for myself, by presenting to me your labours. The benefit likewise I hope will be double, both of your prayers and my own, and of them both to both of us. And as I am assured herof (though it hath pleased God to try me by some affliction) so I desire you to be of my thankfulness unto you, and that I will remain, upon any good occasion, to express as much as lies in the power of

yrs etc

ELIZABETH.[2]

Ten months after the King of Bohemia had surveyed the sights of Paris *incognito*, his wife's brother followed in his footsteps. But "John and Tom Smith", a couple of handsome young Englishmen wearing large bushy perukes, were more enterprising sightseers than the King of Bohemia. They penetrated to the Louvre, where they observed the King of France walking in a gallery and the Queen-Mother dining.

[1] Roe, p. 135.   [2] Matthews, p. 200.

They obtained entry to the private rehearsal of a court masque, in which the fourteen-year-old Princess Henrietta Maria was dancing " rarely well, as she could". The Prince of Wales and the Marquis of Buckingham were on their way to Spain to fetch back the Infanta. Count Gondomar, the agreeable Spanish Ambassador to London, had held out flattering hopes of the effect of a personal visit to Madrid by so irresistible a pair. Their "dear dad" had not allowed his "Baby Charles" and "Steenie" to set out on so perilous an adventure without lamentable tears and protestations. Elizabeth faced the situation with strong common sense. She wished her brother well, but she did not desire a Spanish Catholic sister-in-law. The restoration of the Palatinate was mentioned as an essential clause of the Spanish marriage treaty, but she was far from convinced that her love-lorn young brother would be capable of enforcing it in Madrid. Her English friends indeed were loud in their fears that now the wily Spaniards had the Prince of Wales in their clutches, they would be able to get his father to agree to anything. Prayers for the prince's safe delivery from the House of Rimmon were being offered up in Protestant churches. Since she was her father's next heir, the Queen of Bohemia had not much fear that any Spaniard would kill the Prince of Wales. Unfortunately she said something of the kind in a letter to an English friend. Sir Francis Nethersole was set on the road for Madrid, bearing a "most civil letter" from the King of Bohemia to the King of Spain, and a present from the Queen of Bohemia to the Infanta. The diamond pendants forwarded by Elizabeth were not very large, but they were the best she could afford, and in the note that accompanied them she addressed the Infanta as "sister".

Presently Lady Bedford wrote from England, begging the English Ambassadress at the Hague "for God's sake" to "preach more wariness to the Queen".[1] A damaging rumour

[1] S.P. 14. 122.99.

was current in London that the Queen of Bohemia had announced her intention of coming over, so as to be on the spot to advance her claims to the throne in case any accident should befall her brother. Her father, from whose brain plots were never absent, had for some time been unusually hysterical. On Twelfth Night he had leapt from his bed crying "Treason! Treason!" The loud explosion which had startled him from his slumbers had been caused by nothing more terrible than some of the artillery of the Tower, borrowed by the young gentlemen of Gray's Inn to add a striking finish to their revelries. Now his ageing majesty wandered about his palaces, embarrassing courtiers by asking them tearfully whether they thought he should ever see the Prince or the Marquis again.

The Hague, too, was vexed by cries of "Treason!" this spring. The Prince of Orange, having decorated his capital with the heads of several gentlemen whom he had convicted of an attempt against his life, invited the King and Queen of Bohemia to go on a pleasure expedition to Hellevoetsluis. Their Majesties experienced an inspection of some of his fleet, in adverse weather, and a quarrel amongst his suite in which one combatant was slain. Maurice's opinion of his guests was expressed characteristically: "The Queen of Bohemia is accounted the most charming princess of Europe, and called by some the Queen of Hearts. But she is far more than that— she is a true and faithful wife and that too, of a husband who is in every respect her inferior." [1] Elizabeth and Frederick paid two other short visits within the next few weeks. At Breda they spent five days "with much contentment, though no great cost". At Leyden they made an arrangement which showed that they expected no immediate change for the better in their fortunes.

The old convent of St Barbara, at Leyden, had been transformed into an official lodging for the Prince of Orange. The

[1] Blaze de Bury, pp. 84-5.

Prinsenhof, as it had been re-named, stood on the picturesque Papenburg; its façade commanded a pleasant view of the canal flowing past the University. It was most conveniently situated for young scholars. The Prince was willing to lend a residence he seldom occupied, and the town authorities, who owned the building, had no objection to its being used as a nursery palace for the family of the King and Queen of Bohemia. "The Prince Elector and her Highness", explained the British Ambassador at the Hague, "intend to settle the three children they have here, for some time, under the government of Monsieur de Plessen and his wife, both persons very fit for such a charge. Their highnesses are in part compelled to this course by reason of the greatness of their family, which exceeds the proportion of the small house they have here, and will increase by one more within this few months." Madame Plessen had been governess to the children's father until he reached the age of seven. The "some time" mentioned by Sir Dudley Carleton proved a long period. Eighteen years later the Queen of Bohemia presented to the Burgomasters of Leyden, in token of her gratitude for their courtesy to her family, a flamboyant silver-gilt cup.[1] Her children did not preserve grateful memories of their early years spent in a small medieval town under severe guardians. The authoress amongst them went so far as to state in her memoirs that the Queen of Bohemia kept her infants at a distance because "she preferred the antics of her monkeys and lapdogs".[2] But Elizabeth was only following the traditions of her own youth when she sent her children away from their father's court for their early education, and in her opinion regal appearances

[1] This beaker, preserved in the Municipal Museum at Leyden, bears the Hague hall mark for 1641 and the maker's mark of H. C. Brechtel. The statuette of Elizabeth, on the cover, represents her as Honthorst often painted her—in classical draperies, wearing her hair in ringlets under a small crown, and holding a sceptre.

[2] *Memoirs of Sophie, Electress of Hanover*, p. 8.

must be kept up at all costs. Discipline at the Prinsen-hof was very strict. The youngest daughter of Elizabeth of Bohemia records that she rose early every morning at seven, and received religious instruction before eight-thirty breakfast. Lessons lasted until eleven, the dinner hour. "This meal always took place with great ceremony at a long table. On entering the dining-room I found all my brothers drawn up in front with their governors and gentlemen posted behind." Before eating a mouthful the princess was obliged to make nine curtsies—a very deep one to her brothers, and a lesser one to their attendants, one in reply to her governess and another on relinquishing her gloves—"again on placing myself opposite my brothers, again when the gentlemen brought me a large basin in which to wash my hands, again after grace was said and for the last and ninth time on seating myself".[1]

The atmosphere of Wassenaer Hof was gloomy after "the three little ones" had left for Leyden "to make room here for another coming into the world". [2] Madame Van der Myle was mourning several of her relatives who had perished in the late executions. Despite his promise to his son-in-law, that if the Palatinate was not restored by the New Year, he should be supplied with an army of ten thousand, the King of England was now negotiating vicariously for a truce of fifteen months' duration. The only suggestion to which James objected on behalf of Frederick was one made by the Infanta Isabella. She had considered that it would be desirable that the King and Queen of Bohemia should remove from the Hague to Alzei in the Palatinate, where they might dwell under the surveillance of guardians supplied by the King of Spain. Frederick absolutely refused to consider the third clause in the proposed treaty, which entailed disowning his allies. Elizabeth wrote to the champion who had invoked her to be her own queen:

"Though I have cause enough to be sad, yett I am still of

[1] *Memoirs of Sophie, Electress of Hanover*, pp. 4–7.   [2] Roe, p. 163.

my wilde humour to be as merrie as I can in spite of fortune. I can send you no newes but what will make you sadder. . . . All growes worse and worse, as I know you understand by honest Sir Dudley Carleton. My brother is still in Spaine. The dispensation is come, but I know not yett upon what conditions. My brother is still loving to me: I would others had as good nature. He sent Will Crofts to see me from Spaine with a verie kinde letter and message. But my father will never leave treating though with it he had lost us all." [1]

Her nerves were about to receive a severe trial. On June 19th the British Ambassador at the Hague was obliged to admit that the King of Bohemia was missing. Her Majesty herself knew no more than that her husband had gone to try the wind-chariots at Scheveningen. He had taken luggage and two attendants. With nightfall no tidings had come from him. Her Majesty's attendants recalled ghoulishly that his Majesty's farewell to their mistress had seemed unduly emotional for one bent on an afternoon's pleasure excursion. Fears were entertained that he had gone off secretly to engage himself in some desperate enterprise in company with Christian of Brunswick, who was now at Göttingen. When Elizabeth's anxiety was partially dispersed by a letter from her husband, announcing his date of return, and describing his inspection of the art treasures of Haarlem and Amsterdam, Sir Dudley Carleton, who treasured his reputation for imperturbability, said snappishly that he thought the King of Bohemia's disposition nowadays inclined rather to dissociability than militarism. [2] The arrival of English court ladies to visit the queen was regarded by the British Ambassador as providential. "It gives new life to this good and gracious princess to see her old friends . . . which do minister some entertainment, of which (God knoweth) she hath need." [3]

[1] Roe, p. 146.   [2] S.P. 84. 112.252.   [3] Ibid., 113.179.

With late July Christian of Brunswick arrived at the Hague with his sister, Sophie, who had come to attend Elizabeth's confinement. The duke attended the king and queen to a banquet given in their honour at Delft. Such solemn festivities, the subject of many a contemporary painting in the land of her exile, were the staple entertainment offered to Elizabeth nowadays. The scene was always much the same—an honourable hall, hung with tapestries, lighted by many long windows of pale green glass and floored with cool tiles. At tables groaning beneath their load of glazed pasties and succulent baked meats, dishes piled with shell and salt fish, show fruits, glittering Venice glass, and goldsmith's work, sat scores of grave gentlemen in black best suits, growing, as the day wore towards sunset, increasingly brilliant or pallid of countenance. This occasion, however, presented one agreeable novelty. Many of the voices competing with the clatter of cutlery were English. Their Majesties' hosts were the English merchants of the East India Company resident in Delft. The martial Earls of Essex and Warwick were present. Robert Devereux had developed into an odd character. He surprised the troops whom he led into the Palatinate by punctuating his speeches at councils of war with long puffs at his long pipe. His lordship smoked tobacco incessantly. Duke Christian did nothing to add to the gaiety of the great Delft banquet. As the lengthy feast proceeded he was heard to sigh so often and deeply that guests at the other end of the room looked up in surprise. He broke out once into a disconcerting regret that he had been born a German. Her Majesty's cousin, who had lost his bridle arm in her service, was a large-boned, gaunt young man with a doomed look, entirely devoid of courtier-like graces.[1]

Too much good Dutch food on a breathless August day produced a result almost inevitable in Elizabeth of Bohemia's

[1] He is the figure on the piebald, in the equestrian group reproduced facing page 256.

household. The queen's return by water to the Hague was enlivened by a sudden contest between two of her pages, who drew their swords in her presence. The child of this year of sorrows, borne by Elizabeth "safely and quickly" the very next day, was beautiful, but displayed signs of having been brought into the world prematurely. Three months passed before Prince Louis—named in compliment to the King of France—was considered strong enough to survive the ordeal of public christening in the Klooster Kerke.[1]

At last the ultimatum dictated in Madrid was known at the Hague. Frederick would be allowed to administer his forfeited territories on behalf of his eldest son, on the condition that the boy was sent to Vienna to become a Catholic and marry the Emperor's daughter. The King of England had suggested an amendment—that the boy should be educated at the court of the Infanta when she became Princess of Wales. The Prince of Wales was still in Spain. The despairing King and Queen of Bohemia played for time. They said they would be glad to send their heir to London presently.

Christmas brought destructive floods to Holland. The King and Queen of Bohemia, who had reasons for feeling more cheerful, engaged in seasonable revelries. The Prince of Wales had returned safely to England, still a bachelor and disgusted with Spanish duplicity. He had never been allowed to address the Infanta in private, and when, after much difficulty, he had obtained permission to converse in her native tongue with Isabella of Bourbon, Queen Consort of Spain, she had warned him at once that his suit here was hopeless. He had much better apply to Paris for the hand of her little sister Henrietta Maria. The newly created Duke of Buckingham, whom the Spaniards had made the scapegoat of the unsuccessful marriage negotiations, sent private word to the Queen of Bohemia that the Spanish marriage would never take place. The King of

[1] S.P. 84. 113.179; Birch, *Court and Times of James I*, ii. 417.

England "liked not to marry his son with a portion of his daughter's tears". He was now prepared to insist on the old clause in the marriage treaty, demanding his son-in-law's restoration. Buckingham had made a desperately bad impression in Madrid, and was proportionately furious with his late hosts.

The Prince of Orange gave a banquet in honour of his guests on Twelfth Night, and on New Year's Day Prince Henry of Nassau invited them to witness a theatrical entertainment. The Dutch notion of a masque included passages to which the Winter Queen took exception, and she said so. Sir Dudley Carleton would bear her witness that she was no spoil-sport, and could enjoy a full-flavoured jest with the best, but some of this poet's dialogue had been purely wanton. "We are likely to have it againe with alterations", said the British Ambassador of Prince Henry's masque.[1] But that a guest should offer such criticism was resented by Count Henry's countrymen. The luckless Frederick, who, unlike his wife, had not danced during the recent festivities, found himself publicly censured on his next attendance at the Klooster Kerke, for rejoicing in a time of national mourning. Elizabeth replied with spirit, accusing the preacher of impiety for suggesting that God would punish poor peasants by sending water dancing over the dykes at Vianen, because an English lady at the Hague had taken "seemly recreation". A frost followed the floods, and the exiles took the opportunity of going by sledge to taste the Dutch hospitality long offered to them by the Count and Countess of Kuilenborg and the Baron of Brederode. While they were making merry at Kuilenborg, they received "an alarum of the enemy's approach". Count Henry of Berg, accompanied by seven thousand foot and thirty-five troop of horse, was making his way over frozen waters to attack the country that sheltered his Imperial master's victims. The Winter King and Queen

[1] S.P. 84. 116.11.

refused to fly from the Hague to the Brill or Delft, "because
their remove on this occasion would much dishearten the
whole country, and prove a matter of scorn and obloquy in
case it should prove unnecessary". A thaw, and the impossi-
bility of feeding his army, checked Count Henry of Berg's
advance.

On "the day of good St Davy" Elizabeth wrote jubilantly
to Constantinople. "Since my deare brother's returne into
England, all is changed from being Spanish. Buckingham doth
most nobly and faithfullie for me. . . . I leave all particulars
to Sir Dudlie Carleton's letters, onelie I will tell you that one
thing gives me much hope of this Parliament—because it began
on my deare dead brother's birthday." [1]

The Parliament of which Elizabeth had much hope voted
for war with Spain. That bold mercenary, Count Mansfeld,
went over to London to offer his services. He was not a man
after the heart of the King of England, but the Prince of Wales
and the Duke of Buckingham greeted him warmly. During
this summer was to be seen the extraordinary spectacle of
Londoners pressing to kiss the hem of Count Mansfeld's
mantle. "Long live Mansfeld! God bless you, m'lord!" was
their cry, as the celebrated general who was to lead an English
army to succour their Lady Elizabeth rode through their streets
by the side of the Prince of Wales. The count found himself
lodged in the suite of apartments in St James's Palace redecorated in expectation of a Spanish Princess of Wales. A Spanish
agent sent to London to further the marriage negotiations
made a last desperate effort to prejudice the King of England
against the Queen of Bohemia. Her Majesty had despatched her
secretary to Madrid to upset her brother's marriage. She was
in league with the Duke of Buckingham to secure the crown
of England for her eldest son, who was to be married to the
duke's little daughter. "Two of the greatest falsehoods that

[1] Roe, p. 227.

could have been invented", said Elizabeth disdainfully. The duke and the Prince of Wales angrily demanded an enquiry. The King of England decided to disbelieve in this plot, and the Spanish Ambassador presented his letters of recall.

James had told his Parliament that he would fain "like the aged Simeon, die in peace". He did not wish to lose his title of "Rex pacificus". As the campaigning season of 1624 drew on, he became less and less belligerently inclined, and more and more anxious to secure allies. The King of Sweden was offering "as much as could be desired", but the King of Denmark was "more backward than so neare a kinsman should bee". "I have", announced Elizabeth, "no hope of the Elector of Saxony. He will ever be a beast." [1] Her brother was resigning himself to the prospect of a child-bride from France. One of the terms of the French marriage treaty would be aid in recovering the Palatinate. Elizabeth's agents searched the Hague for a present suitable for their mistress to send to the Queen-Mother of France. A fashionable little dog need not be over-expensive and must, in the opinion of the Queen of Bohemia, be a gift acceptable to a royal lady. But exactly what she needed—a "lion" a few months old—was not to be found. She bought a litter of "lion" puppies, "they will grow quickly". She had, in her own *ménagerie*, a number of greyhound whelps, lovelier than any the Queen-Mother was likely to possess. But misfortune overtook those selected by her to soften the heart of Marie de Medicis. One sickened and died, another broke its leg. [2]

Christian of Brunswick was fretting to be allowed to go to England to stir up preparations there. Elizabeth suggested to her father that he should bestow the Garter upon her champion of the iron arm. To her consternation, after her letter had been despatched, Christian's reputation fell under a cloud. An ex-burgomaster of Hamburg, called Bokman, innocently wander-

[1] Roe, p. 325.   [2] *Archaeologia*, 39. 166–8.

ing near his country house, found himself suddenly "circum-vented by certain disguised persons in habits of merchants and shippers, and conducted to a small ship, into which he was brought and shut down under hatches. He had a ball thrust in his mouth to suppress his crying". The ship then sailed for North Friesland, where the unfortunate Bokman was closely confined in the house of one Kniphausen, an officer in the ser-vice of Duke Christian of Brunswick. While he languished in great pain, for he had "lost some of his teeth in the pulling out of the ball", a mysterious messenger arrived at the house of his brother, another rich Bokman, trading in Amsterdam. This messenger presented a bill of lading, with the request to pay bearer nine thousand rix-dollars. But Bokman of Amsterdam's suspicions were aroused, for he had not heard from his brother for over two years. The messenger was detained by the magis-trates of Amsterdam and identified as a servant of Kniphausen. "One Rook", who had "chiefly assisted him", proved to be "a High Dutch gentleman belonging to the Duke Christian". The Duke was known to be in financial straits. "The whole business", as Sir Dudley Carleton wrote to the scrupulous Prince of Wales, was "of very ill sound". Her Majesty begged that nothing should be done in the matter of the Garter until her candidate had cleared himself. Christian hardly did that, for although he denied all knowledge of the bill of lading, he did not disown his merry men. He "took the matter, but not the manner" upon himself. Rook persisted that his master knew about the whole affair, and feeling at the Hague waxed warm against the duke. Christian, who took "the unhappy acident" very lightly, was persuaded to leave for Denmark. Before he departed he explained that his officers had exceeded his orders, commanded Kniphausen to release the captive, and wrote apologetically to the magistrates of Amsterdam.[1] With the end of the year he arrived in London. He was far from

[1] S.P. 84. 118.45–8 & 85.

suited by nature to be a successful advocate with Elizabeth's father, or indeed with her brother and Buckingham. Nevertheless he got his Garter.

A pestilence which had originated in the devastated Palatinate had travelled down the Rhine into Holland. According to Sir Dudley Carleton more than half of the children of Leyden and Delft had succumbed to it. Prince Henry of Nassau lent the Queen of Bohemia a country house "about two houres distance" from the Hague, and there her "full colledge" from Leyden was removed. In hopes of better times, she had sent to Berlin for one of the three children still in charge of her mother-in-law. The one summoned by her was her favourite second son, whom she had not seen since she left Heidelberg. She was again "in a faire way to increase the number of princes".[1] Prince Edward was born on October 6th. Prince Frederick Henry, happy on a seaside holiday, was told to write a letter to the King of England, who was very fond of horses, and would want to know how his grandson's studies were progressing. In England "little children did run up and down the king's lodgings like little rabbit-starters from their burrows", but they were the children of the king's favourite, not his daughter.

SIRE, wrote Prince Frederick Henry, aged eleven,

I kisse your hand. I would faine see your Majestie. I can say Nominiatius, hic, hac, hoc, and all five declensions, and a part of pronomen and a part of verbum. I have two horses alive that can goe up my staires, a blacke horse and a Chestnut horse. I pray God to blesse your Majestie.

Yours Majestie's obedient grand-child

FREDERICK HENRY.

Honsholredyck. Nov. 2. 1624.[2]

A very old friend would bear this effort to England. Good-

---

[1] Roe, pp. 256, 298.   [2] *Letters to James VI*, Maitland Club, p. 16.

humoured Elizabeth Apsley, who had allowed an infant prince to wring her nose at Heidelberg, was going to get married at last. Her bridegroom, who had wooed her long, was prim Sir Albert Morton, once her Majesty's secretary. He had just been appointed Ambassador Extraordinary to Paris.[1]

At two o'clock on the afternoon of Christmas Day, 1624, "the youngest save one" of the King and Queen of Bohemia's children died. Prince Louis, who had been delicate from birth had been ailing for over a month, and since her doctors had reported that he was not benefiting by the sea air at Honsholre-dijk, Elizabeth had sent for him to the Hague. At the Was-senaer Hof "no human help" was lacking, but ten days after the infant's arrival there "God took it". In vain Sir Dudley Carleton, whose lady had never succeeded in rearing a child, pointed out to their Majesties that they still had "plentiful and hopeful issue". It appeared that they had "placed a particular affection" on this child. "It was", said Elizabeth, "the prettiest child I had." She said that she had never known what it was to lose a baby—had never known that a baby could die "onelie of breeding of his teeth".[2]

Throughout December the King and Queen of Bohemia had been anxiously waiting "for some certaine good newes out of England". Elizabeth complained bitterly that her husband and

---

[1] This match was one of the happiest engineered by Elizabeth, but Morton died within the year. His widow was promptly courted by Colonel Sir Edward Harwood, but Elizabeth did not regret her lady-in-waiting's rejection of this offer. "For the answere you give me concerning Ned Harwood, it is a verie good one, you could not have made a better, for though he be a verie honest man, yet I doe not think him good enough for you. What I writt was at his request, as you saw by the letter I sent you, and now there is an ende of it." Lady Morton, who died a few months after her husband, was the heroine of the famous couplet by Sir Henry Wotton :

"He first deceased, she for a little tried
To live without him, liked it not and died."

[2] Roe, p. 325.

she were being kept "utterlie ignorant" of what was to be done with the "therteene thousand men a-levying for Mansfelt". All Frederick knew was that he was not to be allowed to lead them. Mansfeld had demanded supreme command. Old Count Thurn had been appointed Lieutenant-General, and Christian of Brunswick General of the cavalry. His bitterest disappointment yet was about to befall the luckless Winter King. The English troops, who had been lingering inactive throughout the months suitable for campaigning, sailed for the Continent on the last day of January, 1625. They were denied permission to land at Calais, and met the same fate at Flushing. The Prince of Orange was disgusted to learn that no assistance was to be given to him against the Spaniards at Breda. Mansfeld had been expressly ordered by the King of England to restrict his efforts to banishing the Imperialists from the Palatinate. Pestilence and famine struck the vessels transporting the English army of deliverance. "Scarce a third" of the "raw and poor rascals" landed. "All day long", groaned Thomas, Lord Cromwell, "we go about to seek victuals and bury our dead."

James had spent Christmas hawking and hunting. Sir Thomas Mayerne, royal physician-in-chief, prescribed without result for his Majesty's gout. The king, who was too badly crippled to mount a horse, had himself borne down in a litter into his parks, to watch the game being driven before him. Lady Bedford paid one of her rare visits to court on a March day, and found him full of complaints and talk of his approaching end. Personally she thought that he looked rather better than he had done for a couple of years.[1] But on March 27th James died.

His orphan daughter replied to expressions of sympathy on the loss of "such a father" in suitable terms, but every letter written by her mentioned a reason for consolation. "My

[1] Cornwallis, p. 130.

U

affliction would have been much more but that I ame confident of the King my brother's love." [1] "God has left me such a dear brother. He assures me by a messenger whom he has sent express, that he will never desert me, and will help to re-establish us in our rights." [2] "I should have been much sadder, but the comfort of my deare brother's love doth revive me. He hath sent to me to assure me that he will be both father and brother to the King of Bohemia and me. Now you may be sure all will goe well in Englande." [3]

In her heart her father had been dead for some years.

VI

During the year 1628 the inhabitants of a small country town in Dutch Gelderland became accustomed to the presence in their midst of a distinguished stranger. He came in April for a month's hunting. August brought him again. His figure was often to be seen proceeding towards a viewpoint between two and three kilometres east of the town. On a grassy hillock on the north bank of the Rhine, he would sit for hours under wide and changeful skies, staring with melancholy eyes west-wards along the river. [4] In Lower Gelderland the Saxon dialect was spoken. Presently the rumour spread that the strange German visitor had taken such a fancy to the neighbourhood of Rhenen that he was going to build a house in the town. The disused fifteenth-century Augustinian nunnery adjoining the twelfth-century church was to be demolished, in order to make room for a summer palace for the King of Bohemia. The Koningshuis would have to be large, for his Majesty was the father of nine surviving children. This would have sounded promising had not all the stories from the Hague, whence he

---

[1] To the Duke of Buckingham, Fortescue MS. 163.
[2] To the Duchess of Thouars, *Archaeologia*, 39.165.
[3] To Sir Thomas Roe, Roe's *Negotiations*, 597.
[4] The "King's seat" near Rhenen, still bears this name.

came, agreed that this gentleman was one who did not pay his debts. The tradesmen of a capital in which he owed above twelve thousand pounds still politely followed their master's example of addressing him by a regal title, but in fact he did not possess a rood of land even in his hereditary dominions, and his very title of Elector had been formally bestowed more than a year since on the victorious Duke of Bavaria. When his father-in-law had died, the King of Bohemia's adherents had voiced loud hopes of better fortunes. But it had presently appeared that this father-in-law had been an extremely astute old man. The tale had always been that King James possessed the means but not the will to take action on behalf of the King of Bohemia. It was now obvious that King Charles possessed the will but not the means.

Many reasons drew the Winter King and Queen to Rhenen in Gelderland. Elizabeth had pleasant memories of the old miniature walled city in which she had been greeted by a mock fight on her honeymoon journey, and after a day's sport in healthful country of pine and heather, lodged for a spring night in an antique building looking out over convent walls to a view of the Rhine running through a placid plain containing many avenues of poplars and pollarded willows. Frederick loathed town life, and what he termed "the *canaille*" of the Hague, and the Hague was undeniably a less agreeable residence than it had been, even for his wife. Sir Dudley Carleton had been recalled to England, but no new British Ambassador had yet been appointed, in spite of strong hints that the choice of Sir Thomas Roe or Sir Francis Nethersole would be most acceptable to their exiled Majesties. A new Prince of Orange now presided at the Hague, and he had a wife. The Queen of Bohemia was still the chief female guest at every court festivity, but her hostess was "one of my woemen".[1] A few weeks before his death, the late Prince of Orange had urged his brother

[1] Roe, p. 397.

to marry. Although fine sons of Prince Maurice were visible at his court, "the boys William and Louis" had not been born in wedlock. Prince Henry would succeed his brother. Prince Henry had long suppressed a passion for a lady of noble but not royal birth—"a Countess of Solmes, daughter to Count Solmes that served the King of Bohemia at Heidelberg. I doubt not", wrote the Queen of Bohemia to Sir Thomas Roe, "but you remember him by his red face and her mother by her fatness." The queen hastened to add that the future bride was "very handsome and good", and that though "she has no money he has enough for both".[1] The third Solms daughter had never lacked suitors. A Count Sworffsky in Bohemia had been so "madly in love" that his condition had been apparent to everyone, including the preoccupied Winter King.[2] Her parents provided an awful warning of the physical possibilities awaiting Amalia of Solms, but as yet her complexion of milk and roses, limpid eyes and heavy fair hair were enough to dazzle any gentleman. Prince Henry made his love-match and succeeded his brother, and her old mistress called the new Princess of Orange "*la petite tante*" and presently stood sponsor to an infant Prince William. Michel of Delft painted a tremendous family group, in which the Queen of Bohemia and her contemporary, Sophie of Nassau Dietz, were represented seated, while the fair Princess of Orange stood, suckling her babe.[3] Nevertheless, as her husband's prospects became gloomier, Elizabeth's ladies were on the alert to mark slights

---

[1] Roe, p. 397.   [2] Aretin, vii. 153.

[3] An engraving of this group, dated 1627, is exhibited in the Palatine Museum at Heidelberg. Elizabeth and Sophie are surrounded by their families and attended by hounds. Only one figure in the picture is nameless —that of a third seated lady. Since Emmanuel of Portugal and his wife Amalia of Nassau left the Hague for the Spanish Netherlands in 1626, allured by the offer of a pension from the Emperor, and the engraving was probably made several months after the group had been painted, it seems probable that this lady is the Nassau princess, no longer an acceptable relation.

offered by their old companion. Even Sir Dudley Carleton's nephew—envoy to the Hague pending the appointment of an Ambassador—thought he detected a diminution of the former respect shown to the exiles by their hosts. "The Prince of Orange comes seldom, nor yet his wife—though she have more leisure than he—and stayeth little when they come."

To build a house of their own, in the country, to which they could gather all their children for holidays, seemed to both Frederick and Elizabeth an admirable solution of most of their problems. Frederick had never been strong. Elizabeth had recently, to her surprised disgust, found herself ailing. In her ninth confinement she suffered inordinate pain. After her tenth she caught measles. She was no longer coy about her prospects of maternity. In September 1627, a month before the birth of her seventh son, she wrote to her Trémoïlle aunt, deploring the inconvenience of being in an advanced state of pregnancy during a Dutch heat-wave.[1] She wrote to Sir Theodore Mayerne, who had known her constitution from birth. She said that she would submit to being bled and dieted, but utterly refused to swallow medicines.[2] Personally she was always a strong believer in the efficacy of violent exercise and country air. At Rhenen, where she could get both, she would recover.

That two persons, already in debt, should contemplate another source of expenditure, caused some of their well-wishers considerable trepidation. But Frederick protested that he need not touch his capital. In 1623 he had sold the township of Lixheim to the Duke of Lorraine for 130,000 rix-dollars. "Halfe was arrested by the Emperor", but the other half "paid upon the naile", had been invested in the Bank of Holland for his Majesty's children. Frederick's "sommer house at Rhenen where he maye somtimes take the aire with the Queene" was to be paid for out of the interest accruing from this sum.[3] Elizabeth warmly encouraged a scheme which her husband

[1] *Archaeologia* 39. 167–8.   [2] Ellis, II. iii. 247.   [3] S.P. 84. 146.15.

admitted would be *"toujours un divertissement"*. Plans were passed, the work of demolishing the old nunnery began. The King of Bohemia sent a little model of his "Palazzo Renense" to Sir Dudley Carleton, now Viscount Dorchester, who returned his Majesty "many humble thanks for it. For when I look upon it methinks that I wayte upon your Majesties in it, and much please myself in the contemplation." Lord Dorchester considered that the Palazzo Renense would be "exceeding fair and convenient, if the multitude of windowes—it being 'Casa molto finestrante'—doe not expose it to the extremities of heat and cold". The artistic king of England heard of the model, asked to see it and offered expert advice.[1]

Elizabeth's letter of congratulation to her brother on his accession had expressed her hopes that he might be the most fortunate of kings. So far he was bidding fair to rank amongst the most unfortunate. She was still his heiress presumptive and seemed likely to remain so. He quarrelled incessantly with his neurotic little French wife and with his Parliament. In November 1626 one "Thomas Brediman, a souldier", was summoned before the Privy Council and accused of "desperate and seditious speeches". A witness deposed that he "had heard the said Brediman saye that shortlie they should see such a skirmish with soldiers as they never sawe these many yeares. Being demanded whether they intended to kill anybody he answered they intended to kill the Duke of Buckenham and perhapps the Kinge too. Being demanded whoe should then be Kinge, he answered it may be it shall be a free State, or perhapps the King of Bohemia and the Lady Elizabeth shall have itt." [2] The Duke of Buckingham was more powerful under Charles than he had been under James. Leaflets distributed in the streets of London were asking, "Who rules the Kingdom? The King. Who rules the King? The Duke. Who rules the Duke?

[1] S.P. 84. 142.196. 80-1 & 34.
[2] Hist. MS. Comm. 15th Report, Appendix Part II, pp. 290-1.

The Devil." [1] Charles had no money to spare for his brother-in-law, for he was busy equipping a second expedition against his wife's country, to be led, like the last, by his favourite. Elizabeth had, by now, met "the great man", as she called her brother's ruler.[2] The Duke of Buckingham had been lavishly entertained at the Hague in the autumn of 1625. His visit had put their Majesties of Bohemia in a very awkward position, for although he had come ostensibly to cement England's alliance with the States General and all Protestant powers, another alliance had been his secret object. His overweening vanity led him to suppose that the penurious royal exiles of the Hague would welcome a match between their heir and his heiress. The old Spanish rumour of this amazing design had been founded on fact. He had not been encouraged to approach the subject, and had retired discontented. Elizabeth was well posted in inimical French opinion concerning him, for her aunt, the Duchess of Thouars, had sent her from Paris "Le Livre du Baiser Extravagant", an account of his supposed wooing of Anne of Austria.[3]

In August, 1628, Elizabeth and Frederick arrived at Rhenen to pass a couple of months simply lodged with a small train, in a house adjacent to the site of their future palace. They had no immediate hopes of relief from exile, rather the reverse. The "fire lighted in Bohemia" was still waxing. But the eyes of Europe were now turned upon new commanders and a new scene of battle. The victories of Albrecht of Wallenstein over the King of Denmark were now driving despair into Protestant hearts. The Helen of Germany never saw the most spectacular Imperialist leader of the Thirty Years War, but there were reasons to make the Prince of Friedland and Duke of Sagan and Mecklenburg particularly interesting to the Queen of Bohemia. He had been born a Bohemian and a Lutheran,

[1] Harl. MS. 390.415. [2] *Ibid.* 6988.113.
[3] *Archaeologia,* 39.168.

quite an obscure nephew of the Slavata family. At forty-five
he was a tall, thin, pale man, with fox-red hair and eyes of
arresting brilliancy. He consulted the stars for indications of
his destiny. The mere sound of his drums in the distance roused
the spirits of troops. His manner was overbearing; his tastes
were refined; he was seldom seen to smile; his palace in Prague
was an Aladdin's cave. As he proceeded from triumph to
triumph at the head of an army maintained at the cost of the
countries it occupied, one by one the only formidable leaders
opposed to him vanished from the field. Bethlem Gabor at last
made the peace long dreaded by his allies. Mansfeld and
Christian of Brunswick, after quarrelling bitterly, died within
five months of one another. Elizabeth had last seen her cousin
in the autumn of 1625. Christian had come to the Island of
Goree, where she was upon a hunting expedition with
Frederick, to take his farewell before joining the Danish army
moving against Wallenstein. During the last winter of his short
life the queen's unlucky champion had believed himself
scorned by her. Contemporaries—even Sir Dudley Carleton's
sober nephew at the Hague—said that he had been poisoned by
his enemies.[1] But the same had been said of the deaths of
James I and Maurice of Orange. Christian of Brunswick, who
drank water from the wells of towns which had stood siege
against him, and who had survived the amputation of a fear-
fully mangled arm by seventeenth-century camp surgeons,
probably did die of poisoning, but not of the nature suspected
by his contemporaries.

Friends in England heard with grief that the Queen of
Bohemia, who had "long had cause enough", was "marvellously dejected". "The sore travail she had of her last child"
was said to have abated her usual courage, and she appeared
apprehensive of further evil fortune. Lady Bedford made
plans for coming to comfort her.[2] But Lady Bedford within

---

[1] Harl. MS. 390.89.   [2] Ibid. 390.148

the year undertook a longer and final journey. With her Elizabeth lost an invaluable source of information as to English affairs.

While the King and Queen of Bohemia were hunting in the woods above Rhenen, an event took place in England which seemed likely to have a favourable effect upon their fortunes. On August 19th, 1628, a morose unemployed ex-officer, John Felton, set off from London for Portsmouth, where the second Rochelle expedition was mustering. He nourished a grievance against the Duke of Buckingham. In a house near the north end of Portsmouth High Street, five days later, John Felton stabbed the duke to the heart, with the words "God have mercy on thy soul!" The news of this tragedy caused "no small wonder" at Rhenen. Elizabeth said, "I am sorry for it, and especially to have him die in such a manner so suddenly." But she could not help hoping "now that the great man is gone" that her brother and his Parliament would agree better.[1] A miracle was to happen, but not that. Charles realized belatedly that the querulous, sallow girl of fourteen whom he had taken to wife three years past had developed into a fascinating brunette beauty. On Christmas Eve, 1628, an English letter-writer stated cautiously that Queen Henrietta Maria appeared to be with child.[2] The Puritans of England heard of the prospect of their Papist Queen bearing a Prince of Wales with no enthusiasm. "God had better provided for them in the hopeful progeny of the Queen of Bohemia."

VII

The eldest of Elizabeth's children reached the age of fifteen on January 2nd, 1629. Prince Frederick Henry was now considered old enough to leave Leyden and begin his military education. His parents sent for him to the

[1] Harl. MS. 6988.113 [2] *Ibid.*, 7010. 107B.

Hague. With the spring he would join the Prince of Orange's army as a volunteer. Elizabeth's first "black babie" was now only a year younger than the County Palatinate had been when he had come a-wooing the Princess Royal of Great Britain. Except in colouring, Frederick Henry had fulfilled every promise of his infancy. He was slightly fairer than his father had been at his age. He had inherited his mother's superb health and high spirits.

The Hague, when the young prince arrived there, was rejoicing in the news that Vice-Admiral Pieter Pieterzoon Hein had come to safe moorings in the Zuyder Zee with "a great prize". Hein, acting for the West India Company, had captured not only galleons laden with plate valued at £870,000 bound from Mexico for the Spanish Netherlands, but also "the Brazil fleet laden with sugars". The exiles of the Wassenaer Hof were deeply interested, for "in that West India company of Holland, the Queen of Bohemia hath one-eighth part left her by the late Maurice, Prince of Orange, in his last will and testament". Every patriotic Dutchman who could muster the fare was setting out for Amsterdam to cheer national heroes and stare at Spanish prisoners. Prince Frederick Henry "insisted" that he should be allowed a glimpse of "the sea-terror of Delfshaven" whose romantic New Year's tide reappearance had fired his boyish imagination. Elizabeth was still confined to her lying-in chamber. The delicate daughter born by her eighteen days previously had been christened Charlotte. Five days after his fifteenth birthday, Prince Frederick Henry took the road for Amsterdam, accompanied by his father and but three attendants. The little party left the house on the Kneuterdijk at 6 A.M. on a frosty morning. They reached Haarlem in time for an early dinner and, according to the official version of the day's happenings sent to England, the king hired a fast boat for the remainder of their journey. Contemporary English letter-writers afterwards expressed disgust that the King of Bohemia and his heir should have embarked as passengers in a "common boat" crowded by plebeians and merchandise. The facts seem to have been that the boat was hired in the king's name, but that since he was not prepared to pay an exorbitant sum to "buy out" the many other people demanding transport to Amsterdam, she left Haarlem overcrowded about 1.30 P.M. This fatal occasion is the only one in Frederick's career on which he is detected acting economically. The day was without a sign of storm, and the travellers reckoned to reach their destination in time to view bold mariners and Spanish treasure by the light of sunset on a Dutch mid-winter's day. As they drew near Amsterdam, however, they found their passage impeded by many other vessels of all sorts and sizes. Some bore passengers, and even crews, who had dined too well. Dusk fell, bringing an unpleasant mixture of frost and fog. Somewhere on the Haarlem Meer, about three-quarters of a league from Amsterdam, a heavy bark laden with a cargo of beer loomed suddenly out of blue gloom. In the moment before a shattering collision took place, some of the passengers in the boat hired by the king had time to notice that the craft bearing down upon them, although much superior in size and weight, was controlled by a single man and boy. As he struggled in black waters, Frederick heard his son's voice calling "Help! Help! Father!" A sailor who was a strong swimmer overtook the escaping cargo-boat, boarded her and shouted to her skipper to put about to save the King of Bohemia. A rope splashed into the waters near Frederick. . . .

Not until the next afternoon did the inhabitants of the Wassenaer Hof hear the welcome sound of the King of Bohemia's homecoming. But a long interval succeeded, and no husband or son arrived to break the quiet of the queen's lying-in chamber with thrilling descriptions of chests of gold and pearls and spices at Amsterdam. A coach from the British

Embassy drew up in the courtyard, and presently its occupant stood drooping before the queen. Her old admirer, Lord Doncaster, whom she had long since nicknamed "Camel's-face", was now Earl of Carlisle and over at the Hague on a matter of high diplomacy. An unexpected task needing great courage had been thrust upon him. Lord Carlisle gently informed the Queen of Bohemia that he was the bearer of bad news, which the king, who was being attended by his physicians, was unfit to communicate personally. Lord Carlisle performed his duty with all his celebrated tact, but nothing could make the story which he had to tell sound anything but hideous. Of all the persons who had overcrowded the King of Bohemia's fast boat, only three had survived, the king himself, "a woman and a lackey". Frederick, although bruised and wet through, had insisted on returning three times during the night to superintend frantic search around the scene of the accident. Not until this morning's dawn had a damaged boat been sighted floating peacefully, upturned on the waters of the Haarlem Meer. The body of a boy was attached to it. Prince Frederick Henry, who had become entangled in the rigging as the boat foundered, was discovered with his cheek frozen to its mast.

One of Elizabeth's ladies—Christopher Dohna's wife, also recovering from child-birth—lost the power of speech on hearing Lord Carlisle's story, with which he hastened to England. In the opinion of many, only the knowledge that her husband had need of her recalled the Winter Queen on this occasion from the gates of death.[1]

[1] S.P. 81. 35.123; Howell, pp. 177–8; Spanheim's *Life of Dhona*, p. 302; *Court and Times of Charles I*, i. 440 & ii. 7.

VIII

Elizabeth experienced sordid difficulties in connection with "the loss of my poor boy".[1] For weeks the embalmed corpse of the young prince lay in the Wassenaer Hof, while letters passed between the courts of Whitehall and the Kneuterdijk. Frederick and Elizabeth wished that the body of their heir might be temporarily interred in the church visible from their windows, until such time as it could be removed to ancestral vaults, either in the church of the Holy Ghost at Heidelberg, or in Westminster Abbey. Charles I thought that a Prince should not be buried, even temporarily, in a parish church, and suggested that Frederick Henry should be interred beside his infant brother Louis in the tomb of the Princes of Orange at Delft. But the parents, who had not sufficient ready money to buy suitable mourning for themselves, could not face the expense of a royal funeral procession to Delft. Charles I sent a thousand pounds for "blacks" for the late prince's brothers, sisters and immediate attendants, and after a strictly private service, the body of the ex-crown prince of Bohemia was laid to eternal rest in the aisle of the Klooster Kerke at the Hague.

As soon as they were able, Frederick and Elizabeth fled to Rhenen, and there Elizabeth stayed for the summer when her husband joined the army of the Prince of Orange, now engaged in besieging s'-Hertogenbosch. To Rhenen, on a July day, arrived a most welcome visitor. The stout and genial Sir Thomas Roe was on his way to negotiate between the Kings of Sweden, Denmark and Poland. The British Ambassador to the Ottoman Porte had only been allowed four months at home after his "honourable banishment". Elizabeth had not been able to secure her usual lodging at Rhenen, and her husband wrote that he feared she must be ill at ease. Sir Thomas, however,

[1] Harl. MS. 6988.113; S.P. 16. 236.44.

knew well how to cheer and distract her. Nearly seven years
"almost amongst the dead . . . secluded from the conversation
of both Christian and civill men" had, in his own words,
cooled but not quenched his spirits,[1] and he had many a
ludicrous anecdote of his embassy to relate. Bethlem Gabor's
slippery representative had been one of his greatest trials at
Constantinople—"a mountayneere that never wore band nor
cuffs, nor, I thincke, linen".[2] Then the Duke of Buckingham had
sent imperious demands for "columns, or statues in stone,
books, ancient coyns or medalls". Sir Thomas had obediently
set agents to work, but everywhere found himself forestalled
by a Mr Perry, Lord Arundel's agent. After Mr Perry had been
ignominiously shipwrecked with a load of irreplaceable
treasures designed to grace his master's famous collection, the
British Ambassador and he had become reconciled, and
eventually made their enquiries together for "old idolls",
too many of which proved on arrival to be but "newe images".
There had been the sad adventure of "the halfe lyon of white
marble", for which Sir Thomas had sent "a great way into
Asia, and when it arrived it had no grace in my eyes, for the
face was broken off".[3] Sadder still was his loss of the black
marble negress of Alexandria, "the forehead inlayd with a work
of gold". She had been captured by a French consul.[4] A
goddess from Angora, reported of divine beauty, had cost Sir
Thomas eighteen days' mule charge, and when she appeared
reminded him of nothing but a hospital.[5] . . . His homeward
passage, from Smyrna to Leghorn, had been enlivened by a
brush with Maltese galleys, during which he had been felled
by a spar which luckily checked a ball. Lady Roe had shown
great courage during the naval engagement. "Naked I came
in and naked I goe out" had been the retiring Ambassador's
comment, but the Queen of Bohemia knew that his grand-

---

[1] Roe, pp. 336, 343.   [2] *Ibid.*, p. 353.   [3] *Ibid.*, p. 343.
[4] *Ibid.*, pp. 344, 433.   [5] *Ibid.*, p. 495.

father had been a worthy merchant tailor and Lord Mayor of London, his lady a niece of Lord Grandison. The Roes would have made ideal parents, but their union had not been blessed with offspring. The Queen of Bohemia summoned one of her ladies, and Sir Thomas beheld a true classic beauty. Mademoiselle de Rupa was commanded by her mistress to tell her story. Tears soon checked the little damsel's narrative, for she was one of the eight children of Baron Václav Vilém Rupa, who had lost everything in the world in the cause of Bohemian Protestantism and King Frederick, and her Majesty had graciously written again and again to her royal brother representing the destitution of the Rupa family, but no doubt his Majesty heard of too many such cases. . . . The rubicund English milord was visibly affected. The Queen of Bohemia beheld with delight that one of her determined efforts at philanthropy was likely to succeed. Sir Thomas did not realize when he left Rhenen that he had made the acquaintance of his future adopted daughter, but his next letter to his late hostess affirmed satisfactorily that "the grecian eyes of Mademoiselle de Rupa shine yet in my wounded heart, but her tears pierced it". He engaged himself to represent mademoiselle's "pious suit" to the King of England at the earliest opportunity.[1] He wrote after a visit to the Prince of Orange's camp, and expressed his relief that Elizabeth had consented to retire to Vianen. The enemy had crossed the Yssel, and a flying attack on Rhenen was apprehended. "I will write you no news of the camp I saw", explained Sir Thomas, "for all things admirable are beyond description. But I cannot so sin against humanity as not to acknowledge the virtue of your brave king, who is so diligent to observe the royal trade of taking towns that it doth augur his taking more than Heidelberg, without a treaty. I have seen his Majesty without sense of an enemy, look upon them, and I beseech you to prevent that he look not too much,

[1] S.P. 81. 35.161b.

for no man doth more than he, that is worthy an army of men. Madam, I cannot say enough of him . . ." Sir Thomas signed himself "your Majesty's unfruitful, humble, honest, east, west, north and south servant".

s'-Hertogenbosch fell a month later, and Elizabeth was invited to behold a triumphal scene from a tented field. The battered Spanish garrison left the town by one gate while the Prince of Orange's victorious troops entered by another. Descriptions of the sight witnessed by the Winter Queen on September 7th, 1629, are strongly reminiscent of Velasquez' "Taking of Breda".

On her return to the Hague, Elizabeth was prostrated by "a feevr which took me sudainlie. . . . It made me very weake for the time. . . . I was cured by being lett blood. As soone as I was well I went to Rene to aire myself. . . . I tell you all this", she wrote to Sir Thomas, "that you may not think that I have forgotten you by my long silence, for assure yourself I will ever be constantlie honest fatt Thom's true frend in spite of the divell." The queen's account of her sport at Rhenen, which had been "verie good", included a description of Mademoiselle Rupa's progress. The little Bohemian baroness, to whom Elizabeth gave the pet name of "Queen Mab", followed her mistress "a-horseback as well as her bigger fellows", and on one occasion refused to abandon the chase although she had lost both her hat and her leather, "to the great hinderance of her ease".[1]

The work of demolishing the old Augustinian nunnery just within the Utrecht gate of Rhenen had been completed, and the King of Bohemia's new home was beginning to arise on its foundations. The northern façade of the Palazzo Renense was designed to overlook an imposing walled courtyard of entry and gain a view of a wooded eminence, behind which lay the country of pine and birch and heather in which there

[1] *Camden Miscellany*, vii. 53–4.

was a good hunting to be had. But the view to the south would be the pride of the place, for in its foreground arose one of the most beautiful towers in a country famous for stately architecture. The legendary St Kunera, to whom the church of Rhenen was dedicated, had been, like the Queen of Bohemia, an island princess. Her father had ruled the Orkneys. The fifteenth-century tower was so close to the new house that its carillon would discourage conversation. Below the church the ground sloped towards the wide waters of Rhine, running through a plain, dyked against flood, pale in colour, pea-green, shadowed blue by passing clouds at midday, hazily golden at sunset. Under avenues of noble trees, somnolent cattle awaited the advent of the milkmaid, armed with yoke and pails. No scenes could have been more typical of South Gelderland than those commanded by the many windows of the King of Bohemia's summer palace. A garden for his wife was included in his schemes. Elizabeth's garden was enclosed by the old west wall of the town. During Frederick's brief visit to Heidelberg in 1622, he had managed to despatch some waggon-loads of furniture from the castle over the border into Alsace. The long, light galleries and lofty chambers of the Koningshuis, well warmed by big fires of the peat easily obtainable in its neighbourhood, promised to be both dignified and comfortable.[1] Frederick superintended building operations personally

[1] In the summer of 1937 the sound of hammer and chisel was again to be heard in the vicinity of Elizabeth's vanished palace. The church of St Kunera was being repaired after the second disastrous fire in its history. Trams now run in front of a site occupied by two houses, containing an inn, a butcher's shop and a large garage. The inn, which was called "The King of Bohemia" as late as 1855, is now called "The King of Denmark", but a blue plaque on one of the house-fronts records, without explanation, the name of Frederick of the Palatinate. The King and Queen of Bohemia, however, are still remembered in Rhenen, and a little promenade just outside the city north wall is known as the Queen's Walk. The foundations of Elizabeth's garden wall, which included a bastion of the old town fortifications, are to be traced amongst long grass, and planes and chestnuts shadow the scene. The palace, already decaying, was converted into a barracks for French troops in 1789, and destroyed in 1812.

in great detail. Lord Dorchester wrote that he was heartily glad that his Majesty had "that entertainment whilst his fortune is now building again". Elizabeth held out promises of "verie good fooling this winter at the Hague". There were hopes that a French company of actors was coming.[1] But the truth was that neither his months in arms nor his occupation at Rhenen had produced the desired improvement in Frederick's health. The approach of the anniversary of his son's death found him fully as gloomy as he had been directly after the tragedy. On an early November day of this year, unknown to their employers, a highly significant conversation, conducted partly in Latin, took place between a couple of court officials in the Wassenaer Hof. Dr Christian Rumph had known two generations of Frederick's family. Sir Francis Nethersole had now been in Elizabeth's service for ten years, and last winter had sold his plate in order to settle some of her debts. Each official knew that the other was thoroughly to be trusted. What the king's physician "in confidence imparted to me" so much alarmed the queen's secretary that he transmitted it to paper and forwarded it to the Secretary of State for England, presuming, quite falsely, "on your lordship's care by burning this.[2] Dr Christian Rumph had closed a chronological report by saying with professional dispassion that although neither the queen nor the king apprehended "any danger of his sicknesse", and at present there was no danger of death, in the opinion of one who had known his constitution from birth, the fifth Elector Palatine was unlikely to live as long as the fourth. Frederick's father had died at the age of thirty-six. Frederick himself was now in his thirty-fourth year.

---

[1] These hopes were realized, and in spite of the objections of "all the preachers" of the Hague, the Queen of Bohemia patronized the players. The Prince of Orange crushed a deputation of divines by voicing his conviction that if they preached better, plays would be less frequented. S.P. 84. 155.255.

[2] *Camden Miscellany*, vii. 54.

Sir Francis Nethersole scribbled the words "Quod Deus avertat!" at the foot of a note which presently found its way into the hands of the King of England.[1] Charles I, like most of his subjects, had long considered that his sister had married beneath her. As he had once confided in Buckingham, he thought the grey mare the better horse.[2] He had not much sympathy to spare for his melancholic brother-in-law, who had appeared for some time to be able to do little except get into debt, sire innumerable children and forward indifferent portraits of them to deface the English royal collection. But the cold and conscientious Charles was devoted to his sister, and could not consider the prospect of her widowhood without concern. He wrote sternly to Frederick, admonishing him, for the sake of his wife and family, to make an effort to pull himself together and follow the advice of his physicians. By March 3rd, 1630, Sir Francis Nethersole was able to report that "God be thanked", the King of Bohemia was taking more notice of his doctor's orders and recovering bodily strength He was now "out of his room, but not yet out of the house".[3]. Three days earlier Elizabeth had informed Sir Thomas Roe that her husband had been suffering from a succession of minor maladies. A sore throat had been followed by a gastric attack and troublesome abscesses. "He is well againe and I hope will be abroad at Easter. He was never so evill as he kept his bed with. The physitians say that his desease is come from the misfortune he had last yeare in the water; indeed he was never well since; but I hope all is past. I write this to you because I know you will heare manie rumours of his sickness that may make you afrayed, and I am sure you will be glade to heare he is so well." [4]

The Queen of Bohemia was being cheerful for two, or rather for three. She had now no doubt that her family was to number

[1] S.P. 81. 35.263.   [2] Harl. MS. 6988.9.   [3] S.P. 81. 36.13–14.
[4] *Camden Miscellany*, vii. 76.

a dozen. It appeared incredible that she had once taken a
course of waters at a famous Spa in shy hopes of getting a
little companion for her only child.

IX

On May 29th, 1630, Charles I had a busy, happy day. Between visiting his adored wife's lying-in chamber, routing her
priests and riding in state to attend a thanksgiving service at
St Paul's, he snatched time to write a letter to the lady who
was no longer his heiress presumptive. On the first floor of the
palace of St James's, in a set of apartments overlooking a peaceful view of the deer-park, Queen Henrietta Maria lay smiling
at a perfect French baby. The enormous canopied structure in
which she had given birth to a Prince of Wales was of green
satin clogged with embroidery of silver and gold thread. More
than seventeen years had passed since the crimson velvet and
taffetas bridal "bedsteed" of the Prince and Princess Palatine
had been erected in this chamber.

The King and Queen of Bohemia gave a feast to celebrate
the birth of their nephew, and Frederick was flattered by being
asked to stand sponsor to the future Charles II. Within a few
months all his kindly feelings towards his brother-in-law had
vanished. The exiles had been aware for some time that England was treating for peace with Spain. Elizabeth reposed utter
faith in her brother's "old promise" that he would never consider a treaty "without our full restitution". Midsummer
brought an Ambassador Extraordinary to the Hague. Sir
Henry Vane, a Kentish gentleman, was no scholar, but his
cheerful disposition commended him to the Queen of Bohemia.
Sir Henry's mission was so unpleasant that his nerve failed when
the moment came for him to declare it. He paid his respects to
their Majesties, delivered her brother's letters to Elizabeth and
fled. A few hours later he was surprised at the British Embassy

by a visitor, who proved to be no less a personage than the King of Bohemia. The scene which followed fulfilled the ambassador's worst anticipations, for Frederick, having learnt that Charles was preparing to conclude a treaty without mention of the Palatinate, broke down and gave way to a terrible sobbing fit. The disconcerted Ambassador offered what comfort he could. The King of Spain had promised to do his best for the King of England's brother-in-law at an electoral Diet about to be held at Ratisbon. Sir Henry presently repaired to the Wassenaer Hof, and found Elizabeth "a little distracted betwixt the love of a husband and a brother", but ready to listen to explanations. Next morning, however, he encountered Frederick again in no easy mood. "The first word he said unto me was that he was reduced to that want and necessity by the non-payment of the queen's pension, as that, if I had not brought money with me to supply their present wants, he was resolved to put away all his servants, himself to live obscurely with a couple of men, and to send the queen by the next passage to England, to throw herself at your majesty's feet, for that he was not able to put bread in her mouth." Vane, much taken aback, expressed his surprise and regret at the inefficiency of Lord Treasurer Weston's officials. Frederick embarked upon a further tirade, during which he mentioned that he had at the moment exactly two hundred pounds in his possession. Elizabeth, "with tears in her eyes", desired her brother's representative "if it were possible (to avoid further disputes) that I would engage my credit and take up four thousand five hundred pounds for the three months that they were in arrear".

It was perfectly true that the ten thousand pounds promised to the exiles in July 1626 had not yet arrived. But Charles, who had himself inherited a quarter of a million of debt from his father, had not been idle, for he had pawned some of the Tower ordnance in an attempt to help his sister. That transaction had been mismanaged, and for the last year Elizabeth's pension had been paid most unpunctually. Her creditors, who were becoming desperate, were stopping her in the streets of the Hague with demands for their money. Sir Henry hastily took upon himself the responsibility of agreeing to her suggestion. He judged "nothing so unfit at this time as to hazard the publishing of these particularities". The exiles, gloriously relieved, restored him to favour, and invited him to be one of their first guests in their new palace. The Ratisbon Diet, in July, was attended by an agent on their behalf, empowered to agree to any terms considered suitable by the King of England. Frederick was offered prospects of some revenue from the tracts of the Palatinate occupied by Spain and the removal of the Imperial ban. He remonstrated, but Charles signed the peace treaty.

The Palazzo Renense was habitable at last. Workmen were still busy in one of its courtyards, and Elizabeth's garden was yet to be made, but on a mid-August day the King and Queen of Bohemia took up residence. Sir Henry Vane was with them by September 10th. "I am now att Renen visittinge the Kinge of Bohemia's new house which is exquisitely builte.[1] . . . The situation is agreeable, and both their Majesties take greate delighte therein. Hee complaines of the charges. . . ." [2]

Frederick indeed was still full of complaints. Elizabeth valiantly continued to be his hourly companion. "They are hunting as hard as they can, and I think I was born for it, for I never had my health better in my life." She lingered at her remote country house as long as she dared, too long for the peace of mind of Sir Henry Vane, who advised Lord Dor-

[1] John Evelyn wrote that in 1641 he had visited Rhenen, "where the Queen of Bohemia hath a neate Palace or Country-house built after the Italian style, as I remember" (Evelyn, i. 23). But Mr Evelyn remembered incorrectly. Many engravings testify that the Koningshuis at Rhenen was a fair example of 17th-century North German or Dutch Renaissance architecture, characterized by poverty in scale and overlaid with meaningless ornament. It was shoddily built and soon in need of repairs.

[2] S.P. 84. 142.19B.

chester that when she reappeared at the Hague on October 3rd, he believed her to be within "ten or twelve days of her terme". She had performed the journey from Utrecht that day, "forty English miles, in Coach, without any shew of wearinesse".[1] On the evening of October 13th, 1630, her Majesty dismissed her secretary at seven-fifteen. Shortly after nine a beaming midwife surprised Sir Francis with the words, "Shee is, thanks bee God, as well as any one in her case can bee—a goodly Princess!"[2]

Frederick had desired a Frederick Henry, to be named in memory of the drowned lad whose voice he still heard calling to him in the night watches.[3] The Winter King and Queen experienced some difficulty in finding godparents for their twelfth hope. All the available royalties had been complimented by them years ago. They hit upon the solution of writing a number of fashionable girls' names on slips of paper and drawing lots. The first to turn up was "Sophie". All that remained was to think of godmothers bearing this name. They chose the Countesses of Hohenlohe, Kuilenborg and Nassau Dietz.[4] The only drawback was that Sophie of Nassau Dietz had been used already for Louise Hollandine.

The baptism of the Princess Sophie was long delayed. A month after her birth her ailing father's physicians refused to pronounce until January "whether he be curable or not".[5] Their treatment produced favourable results, but on January 27th a funeral procession set out by torchlight for the Klooster Kerke. "After a long and languishing sicknesse . . . Madame Charlotte, a child of no more than two years of age" was laid to rest beside her brother Prince Henry. The Princess Sophie was christened very quietly three days later in the same church. She was the twelfth child and fifth daughter of her parents. Henrietta Maria, already the proud mother of a Prince of

[1] S.P. 84. 142.124b. [2] *Ibid.*, 140. [3] Spanheim's *Dhona*, p. 133.
[4] *Memoirs of Sophie Electress of Hanover*, pp. 3–4. [5] S.P. 84. 142.152.

Wales, was to produce seven more children. Nevertheless a
son of Sophie was destined to ascend the throne of Great
Britain and found a dynasty.

X

On January 16th, 1632, the Queen of Bohemia heard the
familiar sound of her husband's luggage being carried downstairs. The Winter King was going on another long journey.
But his consort had never had reason to feel more hopeful and
less apprehensive. For at last, beyond all doubt, the Protestant
cause had found in the martial King of Sweden a great states-
man who could unite Calvinists and Lutherans, and a great
general to lead them to victory. The landing of Gustavus
Adolphus in Pomerania eighteen months before had not
aroused great alarm in Vienna, and at the Hague the Prince
of Orange had forborne from encouraging his guests to expect
too much. His memories of Mansfeld's last campaign were still
depressingly clear. But the King of Sweden had refused to go
into winter quarters and advanced into Mecklenburg. As, one
after another, Frankfort on the Oder, Landsberg and Magdeburg fell to his arms, the Imperialists realized that their troops
were feeling the loss of Wallenstein, whom Ferdinand had dismissed in the previous September. On the field of Breitenfeld
Tilly lost his reputation as a commander. The Elector of
Saxony, "that beast", in whom Elizabeth had reposed no confidence, crossed the Bohemian frontier, and effected a junction
with Count Thurn. After his decisive victory near Leipzig,
Gustavus devoted the remainder of the autumn to subduing
Franconia. November, which brought news of the capture of
Prague, saw him on the march for the Rhineland. Thence-
forward the story of his triumphal progress seemed to the
exiles of the Hague too good to be true. Aschaffenburg and
Frankfurt on the Main opened their gates. Mainz, which sur-

rendered in Christmas week, became his headquarters. The King of Bohemia sent one of his Bohemian refugee advisers with a message of congratulation to the Protestant hero of Europe. The result was a warm invitation for the King of Bohemia to proceed to Mainz without delay.

The New Year of 1632 was full of happy events for the King and Queen of Bohemia. On January 2nd Elizabeth gave birth to a son. She had entered upon her "second dozen" of offspring. Frederick still longed to call a son after his lost heir, but Elizabeth suggested that this one must be the godchild of their new champion.[1] Prince Gustavus Adolphus was a very lovely but very fragile infant. Frederick settled the date of his departure as soon as his wife was safely delivered, and gladly wound up his affairs at the Hague. He made an inventory of his remaining treasures and pawned his plate. On January 12th he took a formal farewell of the States General, thanked them for their long hospitality and commended his wife and children to their care. He did not fail to mention that he hoped, in a few months, to send for his family and give the States a substantial proof of his gratitude. The Prince of Orange made the volunteer king a gift of 20,000 francs for his personal use. The States contributed 50,000 francs towards his military expenses. Frederick drew a like sum from the Lixheim money invested in the Bank of Holland at Amsterdam. On January 13th he attended his child's christening. By the 16th he had done everything except write to Charles I and say good-bye to his wife.

The King of England was behaving most disappointingly. It was true that he had allowed the gallant Marquis of Hamilton to enlist six thousand English and one thousand Scots to assist the King of Sweden, and he had agreed to finance the force; but he had insisted that his name must be kept out of the business, since he was still treating with the Emperor and trusting

[1] S.P. 81. 38.7.

to the promises of the King of Spain. Elizabeth wrote personally to thank her "good cosen" Hamilton for his "worthie actions". "I think myself infinitlie beholden to you and ame sorrie that I have no meanes than by this paper to give you the thankes you deserve for it. The King hath desired me to say the same for him, which he would doe himself but that he cannot write English." [1] She also wrote to her brother, telling him frankly that the Palatinate would never be restored by treaty, and that if he thought so he was living in a fool's paradise. "If this opportunity be neglected wee may be in despair of ever recovering anything. . . . If you now do nothing but treat, I beseech you give me leave to say that the world will wonder at it." This letter irritated Charles exceedingly. He had sent Sir Henry Vane to see the King of Sweden, and Gustavus had promptly asked for English assistance to the tune of twenty thousand foot and five thousand horse, to be kept in the field for four years. Sir Thomas Roe, who had originally been chosen for the mission, said resentfully that after all available information had been "fished out of him" he had been set aside because Vane was thought a better peace-maker. The King of Sweden, who had flatteringly assured Sir Thomas that "by his most secret counsels and conferences with him, he was excited and animated to this just and honourable war", was disappointed to receive the pacificatory Vane as English Ambassador, and took an instant dislike to him.[2] "What!" exclaimed Gustavus, "a brother of the King of Great Britain protected by the States, and must he come to me in his doublet and hose! Let him come, howsoever, and I will do my best to restore him to his patrimony." [3]

The Queen of Sweden was with her husband at Mainz. Elizabeth longed to accompany Frederick. But she realized that he could not postpone his departure until she was fit for

[1] Hamilton MS., p. 10. Hist. MS. Commission.
[2] *Court and Times of Charles I*, ii. 114.   [3] *Ibid.*, ii. 160.

midwinter travelling through devastated country.[1] He comforted her by the promise that this was to be his last long
journey without her. Very soon he would be sending for her
and the children. They were to be happy again at Heidelberg,
as they had been in the golden days. The moment came for
the Winter King to set out on his last journey. In the courtyard
below the house in which the exiles had spent nearly eleven
years, a string of carriages waited. Words of command were
sounding in the Kneuterdijk. The Voorhout was crowded by
sightseers. The States were providing an escort of two thousand
five hundred cavaliers to accompany the King of Bohemia out
of the town. The king's luggage was embarked—the coffers
containing his clothes, a portfolio of maps, a pewter camp service, his little writing-desk which he would use as often as
possible, the portraits of Madame the Queen and Madame the
Electress Dowager Palatine. The first stages of his journey
were familiar to his wife. He was going to call at Leyden to
say good-bye to the children; he would sleep at Rhenen. The
faithful Christopher Dohna was going with him and another,
younger man, in whom the Queen of Bohemia had come to
repose a particular trust. Quite recently she had discovered
what she had been looking for ever since the death of
Colonel Schomberg. She would have felt much more uneasy
about this separation had not Lord Craven been going with the
king. Lord Craven was the kind of young man that she understood and appreciated. At the age of twelve he had inherited
a prodigious new fortune. His father had been a Lord Mayor of
London. But, at the age of nineteen, William Craven had deserted Trinity College, Oxford, for the wars of the Low
Countries. He had served with distinction under both Maurice
and Frederick Henry of Nassau. He was now a commander in
the army raised by the Marquis Hamilton for the relief of the
Palatinate. To cynical observers, the open-handed and singularly

[1] *Court and Times of Charles I,* ii. 160.

unsophisticated bachelor peer, of small stature, who incomprehensibly preferred the hardships of the camp to the pleasures of the court, was chiefly remarkable for his money-bags. But Elizabeth of Bohemia knew that William Craven had also a heart of gold. He was devoted to children, and always had a pocketful of little gifts for her nursery.[1] She had made him god-father to her last-born. By an odd chance, Lord Craven was the owner of Combe Abbey. Lucy Bedford had sold it to his father.

XI

The Winter King's procession struggled south-east through unseasonably warm, but very wet, weather. The roads were in an appalling condition. At more than one ford the seat of the carriage in which the king travelled was flooded. An equipage carrying some of his gentlemen overturned. His chilled and wearied Majesty wrote that the little lackey had brought him his wife's dear letter at ten o'clock last Wednesday night, just as he was going to sleep. He longed to be assured that she was perfectly well again.[2] He was using such a bad pen that he was almost out of patience.

He reached Hanau on horseback, and there had to wait for two days until his train could come up. Every wheeled vehicle accompanying him was firmly stuck in the mire of Upper Hesse. Frederick of Bohemia and Gustavus Adolphus of Sweden first set eyes on one another at Höchst, near Frankfort on Main, at seven o'clock on the morning of February 11th, 1632.

The Scandinavian hero-king's appearance at this date has been vividly described by a contemporary. "Tall and well proportioned, there was a majesty in his aspect that at once inspired awe and affection. His complexion was fair, his cheeks

---

[1] *Memoirs of Sophie Electress of Hanover*, p. 26.   [2] Aretin, vii. 190.

tinged with ruddy colour, his hair and beard of a yellow tint, his forehead broad, his nose aquiline, his eyes of a brilliant blue, sparkling with energy and intelligence. His self-possession never forsook him; never did he lose his vigilance, his quick penetration, his promptitude and decision." [1] Gustavus, who had been heard to remark that "the feast answered better than the rack to extract secrets", proceeded to entertain his guest with all possible honour. The presence of the King of Bohemia in his camp was essential to his schemes for the reconquest of the Palatinate. At their first meal together he addressed Frederick repeatedly as "*mon frère*", and called the Landgrave of Hesse Darmstadt sharply to order for neglecting to give his Bohemian Majesty his correct title. But even had he been ignorant of his guest's unfortunate history, a single glance at the faded and sagging figure before him would have told Gustavus Adolphus that no reasonable man would unreservedly entrust the command of either an army or reconquered territory to this pathetically ingratiating neurasthenic.

XII

The waiting queen at the Wassenaer Hof heard with delight of the "wonderful welcome" given to her husband by his brother-monarch and his hereditary subjects. As his battered coach jolted the exhausted but expectant Frederick towards the headquarters of his hale saviour, the inhabitants of Hanau had come out in driving rain, two Dutch miles, to cry "*Vive le Roi de Bohème!*" As the kings advanced into the Palatinate, the scenes of enthusiasm redoubled. Three fortresses only of Frederick's patrimony were still in enemy hands. At the capture of Kreuznach, Lord Craven, although wounded, was the first to mount the breach. The Protestant hero of Europe clapped the stupendously wealthy young English volunteer on

[1] Gualdo-Priorato.

the shoulder—"I perceive, sir, you are willing to give a younger brother a chance of coming to your title and estates!"

Spring came to the Hague, and Elizabeth wrote cheerfully to "honest Harry" Vane, asking for information. "I see by the king's letters that the King of Sweden does not desire he should make levies, saying it will spoil his army." Gustavus had decided that the taking of Heidelberg and Frankenthal must be deferred. Tilly was on the move again in Franconia. Gustavus recrossed the Rhine to rout him. Frederick, advised by Vane to keep in touch with the King of Sweden, followed him to Munich, where he had the satisfaction of feasting on a May evening in the palace of Maximilian of Bavaria. The ladies of many German princelings were present, but Frederick wrote to Elizabeth that he had not seen a true beauty yet on his travels. His brother's wife, whose acquaintance he now made, appeared to him to be good-natured, though definitely plain. He waxed far more poetic over the charms of Bavarian scenery. At the château of Freising, deer cropped the grass close to windows from which could be seen a distant view of Munich and the snow-capped Tyrolean mountains. "I could wish", wrote Frederick, "that your daughter might become a marvellous beauty, and that I could procure a splendid marriage for her." [1] An English miniaturist had arrived at the Hague, and Elizabeth had commissioned him to paint her husband, herself and all their offspring, so that the King of Bohemia could carry with him on his campaigns an easily portable family picture-gallery. The likenesses of his eldest son and daughter by Mr Alexander Cooper, reached Frederick in camp near Nürnberg. [2] [3]

The Princess Elizabeth Palatine was now about to enter her fifteenth year, and marriageable. Her figure was as yet rather heavy, and she would never be a true beauty, for she had in-

[1] Bromley, pp. 34–41.   [2] Ibid., pp. 47–8.
[3] This set of miniatures is reproduced opposite p. 26 of vol. i. of G. C. Williamson's History of Portrait Miniatures.

herited her sire's melancholy cast of countenance and over-large nose. But his gentle scholar daughter, who was a little mother to her many younger brothers and sisters, was particularly dear to Frederick. The Princess Elizabeth, who had been left behind at Heidelberg when her parents set off on their Bohemian adventure, had been most carefully educated by her pious grandmother and spinster aunt. The Electress Dowager had suffered terribly as the result of her son's imprudence. She had lost her dower palaces and her income, and been obliged to spend twelve years as guest of her Brandenburg son-in-law, retiring from one to another of his residences as enemies approached. At Krossen on the Polish frontier, at Brandenburg, and at Berlin, she had gathered under her wing the three children shed by Elizabeth and Frederick on their headlong progress across Europe. Louisa Juliana, a far more agreeable character in adversity than prosperity, never allowed a word of criticism of her son or daughter-in-law to cross her lips, and when the exiles, settled at the Hague, sent for Charles Louis, Maurice, and finally Elizabeth, she patiently relinquished charges whose accomplishments did her great credit. A page of Charles Louis's handwriting was a beautiful sight and far superior to that of his elder brother.[1]

Charles Louis, like many a German princeling, kept an autograph book, in which he invited celebrated persons to inscribe their names, and a sentiment. Their armorial bearings, brilliantly painted, faced their signatures.[2] Charles Louis's "Album Amicorum", or "Stammbuch", was a proud possession for a young gentleman. Some of its pages were marbled, others were of vellum. One vellum sheet was entirely covered by a lush green landscape in which a hooded child led a little dog past a ruin. A smear of scarlet paint marred the sheet on which his mother's signature appeared. Poor Christian of Brunswick

---

[1] See his letter to Charles I on the birth of Charles II. "Recieve" is the only mistake in this production. S.P. 81. 36.34.

[2] See his mother's coat of arms, reproduced facing p. 144.

had written "*Tant pour Dieu et ma très chère Reine*". Charles
Louis had collected the Kings and Queens of England and
Bohemia, and the Princess of Orange, and Christopher Dohna,
and old Baron Rupa, and old Count Schlick, and many a
visiting English peer.[1]

The Princess Elizabeth had been solemnly warned that the
dear parents who had summoned her to their court had suffered
many sorrows, great trials. It would be her duty to annoy
them as little as possible by unnecessary childishness. The result
was that, when she was ushered into an apartment containing
a large fair lady with a quizzical expression, a nervous drooping
gentleman and many other relations whom she could not
identify, the demeanour of the little princess was so closely
modelled on that of her widowed grandmother, that one of
the company burst into loud laughter. "*Voilà!*" cried the
Prince of Orange, pinching her ear. "Another Louise Julienne,
as demure as the prototype!"[2] An attempt had been made to
accommodate the eldest daughter of the King and Queen of
Bohemia in a manner suitable to her rank. She lived under the
roof of an English peeress resident at the Hague. Lady Vere,
who had five daughters of her own, was the wife of Lord Vere
of Tilbury, a military commander who knew the Palatinate all
too well. The princess sat for her portrait to local artists. Two
famous painters of Utrecht depicted her in classical costume
as the principal lady in a hunting group. The effort of Cornelius van Poelenburg[3] was designed to show the artistic King
of England how all his "little pensioners" were progressing.
This "great picture", much heralded by letters from Frederick,[4]

---

[1] The Album Amicorum of Charles Louis is to be seen at the British
Museum, King's MS. 436. It is described on p. 302, vol. 62 of *Archaeologia*
by M. Rosenheim, who suggests that it was begun by Frederick Henry and
continued by Charles Louis. This seems probable, as the earliest signatures
in it are dated when Charles Louis was scarcely five years old.

[2] Blaze de Bury, p. 86.   [3] Now at Hampton Court.

[4] Harl. MS. 7352.88.B.

can only have convinced Charles I that his sister had indeed a great number of children, all of whom appeared to be cold and hungry. In the year preceding Frederick's departure from the Hague, Gerard van Honthorst attempted the same subject much more conscientiously. But he was luckier than his predecessor, in that he was only required to represent the four eldest children of the King and Queen of Bohemia. His hunting group showed Princess Elizabeth, as Diana, receiving the gift of a dead hare from Charles Louis. Rupert stood behind his sister in an explanatory attitude, and Maurice restrained one of the four well-bred greyhounds in attendance. The Queen of Bohemia was a lavish, but not a discriminating, patroness of the arts. When she visited the studio of another Utrecht master, Abraham Bloemaert, the picture bought by her was the portrait of a dog bearing a touching resemblance to her favourite hound Babbler. Utrecht lay almost half-way between the Hague and Rhenen, and was the place at which she invariably spent a night on her journeys to and from her country house. Gradually she ceased to employ Michel of Delft. "Gerard of the Night", a pupil of Bloemaert, who had returned to his native town from Rome in 1622, with a great reputation for depicting candlelight, moonlight and torchlight effects, suited her much better for several reasons. He was twenty-three years younger than Michel, and costume had recently undergone a revolutionary change. The fashions of Europe were now being set in London, where a daughter of France was Queen Consort. In 1628 Gerard paid a visit to the English court, and was commissioned by their Majesties, by Lord Arundel, the Duke of Buckingham, Lady Bedford and many other connoisseurs. He was a vigorous-looking, slightly coarse-featured man, with a flourishing black moustache, a merry eye and a head of waving dark curls. After his English tour he painted the Queen of Bohemia again and again in the style of *toilette* sponsored by her elegant young sister-in-law. Costly simplicity was now

Y

the mode. In her early thirties the penurious Elizabeth found herself condemned to annihilate her complete wardrobe. The Queen of Bohemia gallantly submitted to having her darkening fair hair arranged in a classical knot behind and a row of ringlets on the brow. To display a bushel of jewellery was no longer good taste, and she had been proud of her jewellery. Skirts and neckwear had ceased to be distended by wires, and whaleboned bodices and pot hats had vanished. It is not remarkable that when she found her husband writing from the neighbourhood of Frankfort, Elizabeth forwarded a shopping list. Frederick replied that Frankfort Fair was not what it had been, and he feared he would find difficulty in getting the stuffs she wanted.[1] Sir Harry Vane, however, accepted orders with alacrity.

The King of Bohemia complained from Frankfort of pain and deafness in his left ear. He gloomily hoped that the trouble was not to become permanent. The King of Sweden continued to show him personal courtesy, but since the taking of Heidelberg and Frankenthal was indefinitely postponed, his position as a volunteer with no command was increasingly unsatisfactory. The Emperor had recalled Wallenstein, who had subdued Bohemia with alarming rapidity. For a month Gustavus attempted to provoke the great Imperialist general to action outside Nürnberg. Frederick wrote to his wife that if a battle took place, it would resemble one in the days of chivalry, for the many noble ladies present would be able to watch the prowess of their champions from the battlements.[2] They all assured him repeatedly that they were longing to see the Queen of Bohemia, but for his part he disapproved of their presence here, and would not dream of sending for his wife until a decisive victory had been obtained.[3] The Imperialist camp remained mysteriously inactive. Sarcasms at the expense of his ally, Maximilian of Bavaria, seemed to be the chief occu-

[1] Bromley, p. 32.   [2] *Ibid.*, p. 47.   [3] *Ibid.*, p. 32.

pation of Wallenstein at the moment. The stars had told him that the King of Sweden's good fortune must endure until November.

When Gustavus Adolphus broke camp and marched for Swabia, in an attempt "to draw the fox", he offered no objection to the King of Bohemia's request to be allowed to visit the Palatinate. Letters containing a characteristic mixture of hope and despair began to reach Elizabeth. The devastated Palatinate in autumn weather was a heartbreaking spectacle. At Oppenheim Frederick found the house in which they had stayed on their honeymoon, a tragic ruin. Half the pretty old town had been burnt. The view from his lodgings at Alzei was of a house without a single door or window. However, once he was restored, the work of restoring his possessions could be taken in hand speedily. He went out hare-hunting, and as usual on such occasions, much wished for his wife by his side. He was amazed to see how little the Spaniards had done in the way of fortifying the country which they had captured. Since Frankenthal was only four leagues distant, and he did not wish to be the victim of a flying raid, he had decided to move to Mainz. "The Rheingrave and the King's people have offered me apartments in the castle. It will be pleasanter than this place and I shall get your letters more regularly."

Elizabeth was not without her own troubles as the months of separation from her husband dragged by. Plessen, the elderly nobleman in charge of the children's establishment at Leyden, died suddenly, and she was faced with the responsibility of appointing new tutors and governors. She had to write tactfully to Sir Harry Vane, who had contrived to annoy her husband and infuriate Gustavus Adolphus. While she was at Rhenen for a few weeks, Charles Louis developed smallpox. She was relieved when a letter from Mainz told her that her husband had suspended the wearisome travelling which seemed

[1] Bromley, pp. 28–30.

to be degenerating into a mere nervous habit. But he expressed himself "verie wearie of laying still and doing nothing".[1]

As Frederick had expected, he heard more news at Mainz. Wallenstein had taken Leipzig, and the King of Sweden was hastening to encounter him at last in the open field. By the first week of November it was obvious that the trial of strength long hoped for by Gustavus was imminent. "God grant", wrote Frederick, "that his accustomed success awaits him." This prayer was not granted. On the foggy morning of November 6th the troops of Gustavus Adolphus closed in battle with those of Wallenstein on the border of the great plain which opens east of the Saale upon Lützen, Markranstädt and Leipzig. Late that evening Wallenstein ordered his trumpeters to sound the retreat. The Swede had beaten him. But the naked body of Gustavus Adolphus lay, riddled with wounds, on the field of his victory.

The news of the death of the King of Sweden, in the flower of his age and at the height of his fame, staggered Protestant Europe. It found Elizabeth feeling extraordinarily ill. She believed that she was sickening of the same disease which had carried off her brother twenty years ago at this season.[2] She roused herself to write instantly to England, adjuring Charles I to support her husband, who would now have to assume the vacant supreme command. To add to her trials, she had no word from Frederick—"the King of Bohemia failing to write, or his letters not finding their way hether this last week". On November 27th her anxiety was allayed. Frederick wrote from Mainz that he was making a good recovery from an attack of fever, and was coming to fetch her to Germany, now that the decisive victory for which they had waited so long had been granted, though at terrible cost.

[1] Hamilton MS. 192.
[2] Conrart MS. 575.29. Bibl. de l'Arsenal.

Two days after she had heard from her husband that the end of their separation was in sight Elizabeth was not much surprised by the entrance of a familiar official whom she had not summoned. Dr Christian Rumph, who bore in his hand a long medical report written in Latin, begged for her attention. The kindly and formal old German had something to tell her.

The report of Dr Peter Spina, chief physician to the Landgrave of Hesse Darmstadt, informed Dr Christian Rumph that on Saturday, November 16th, he had been summoned from Darmstadt to attend the King of Bohemia. He had found his Majesty delirious. He had learnt from his Majesty's attendants that his Majesty had recently returned from a visit to his cousin, the Duke of Zweibrücken, in whose dominions the plague was raging. They further deposed that yesterday their master had announced himself free of fever, had laughed at the mention of plague, and said that as soon as a painful swelling in his neck burst, he would be perfectly well. Indeed, he had seemed so well that his secretary had obeyed instructions to leave for Frankfort last night. Dr Spina had administered sudorifics, and three tumours had developed on the patient's body. To Dr Spina's surprise, the patient had slept well and on the following day attended to his correspondence, and even issued some orders referring to urgent military operations. The inevitable end had come very peacefully at seven o'clock on the morning of Tuesday, November 19th, 1632. His Majesty, who had been conscious at the last, had sent messages to his children, urging them to constancy in the Protestant faith and obedience to their mother. He had expressed himself confident that the States General, the Prince of Orange and the King of England would care for his widow, who would lose in him merely one to whom she had ever been the dearest object in existence. The Queen of Bohemia's own account of her reception of the news of widowhood exists :

"Though Dr Rumph tolde it me verie discreetlie, it was the first time that ever I was frighted." [1]

[1] S.P. 81. 39.189 & 221; S.P. 16. 236.44; S.P. 84. 145.155–6e. Van Sypesten (*Het Hof van Boheme*, p. 32), and A. W. de Vink (*Die Haghe Jaarboek* 1921–22, p. 142) relate, without giving their authority, that the news of her widowhood reached Elizabeth at a moment when she was sitting for her portrait by Mierevelt. No portrait of Elizabeth by Mierevelt later in date than 1629 is forthcoming, but it is of course possible that a picture with such tragic associations was abandoned.

CHAPTER VI

"THOSE UNFORTUNAT CHILDREN"

I

THE Queen of Bohemia's devotion to her husband was so well known that the news of his death reached England with melo-dramatic additions. In the streets of London citizens learnt without surprise that the Lady Elizabeth had been unable to survive her mate. For over a week even the inhabitants of Whitehall believed this sequel probable. Mr William Boswell, British envoy at the Hague, sent word that those closest about the queen much doubted whether she would long be able to bear her grief. "Certainly", wrote Sir John Meautys, a companion of her old Combe days, "no woman should take the death of a husband more to heart than this queen doth." [1] Charles I forwarded to his sister a letter displaying exquisite feeling. He simply begged her to come home. Sir Francis Nethersole, the bearer, was provided with passports for every possible route by which a favourable wind might carry him fastest to the widow. Queen Henrietta Maria, who sadly knew herself to be most unpopular in her beloved husband's country, bravely resigned herself to the prospect of welcoming a Queen of Hearts to England. The English court assumed deep mourning, and the premier peer, Lord Arundel, was ordered to proceed to the Hague at the head of an embassy of condolence numbering a hundred and twenty persons.

But in a shuttered bed-chamber, zealously hung with black serge by lachrymose attendants, the Queen of Bohemia, who

[1] Cornwallis, p. 252.

had been "frighted" for the first time in her life, lay glassy-eyed and motionless in a trance-like stupor, "petrified with grief". Her total inability to answer her brother's kind invitation caused him serious inconvenience. At Whitehall the suite of apartments "where she lay when she was a maid" were swept and garnished. Eltham Palace was refurnished as a country nursery for her many children. A fleet received orders "for the transportation of the Queen of Bohemia". The inappropriately named *Victory*, selected to bear homeward the Winter Queen, was provided with rich new cabin hangings, a standing bed for her Majesty and four pallets for her ladies in waiting. The King's barge was detailed to attend at Gravesend: finally, lodgings in the Kentish village on her route to London were bespoken.[1] Five months after her loss, Elizabeth gave Sir Thomas Roe an accurate account of her sufferings, "because it may be you might have heard some extravagant lies". The truth was that on hearing the totally unexpected news so gently broken by Dr Rumph, she lay "as colde as ice, and coulde neither crie, nor speake, nor eate, nor drinke, nor sleepe for three days". For a further five days she was obliged to keep her bed, "not being able to doe otherwise".[2] At the end of that time she arose, having "passed through fire and water, sighs and tears . . . not without some marks of her agony",[3] and assuming widow's costume, prepared to receive official condolences. "The first that came in to her relief was the excellent Prince of Orange, no worse a comforter of ladies than conqueror of his enemies. The next were the States, firm and open in their affections." On December 14th she approached her correspondence.

MY DEAREST ONLY BROTHER, wrote the widow,

I know not how I can sufficiently express my most humble thanks for your two most affectionate letters. They

[1] S.P. 81. 55.261.   [2] *Ibid.*, 16. 236.44.   [3] *Ibid.*, addenda 448.

found me the most wretched creature that ever lived in the world. And this I shall ever be, having lost the best friend I ever had, in whom was all my delight, having fixed my affections so entirely upon him that I should long to be where he is were it not his children would be left utterly destitute.

To Sir Thomas Roe she enlarged upon her loss—

"which I shall greave for as long as I live. Though I make a good shew in companie, yett can I never have anie more contentment in this world. For God knows I had none but I tooke in his companie, and he did the same in mine. For since he went from hence he never failed writing to me twice a weeke, and ever wished either me with him or he with me . . ."

The long-hoped-for invitation to England had come, but she could not possibly accept it. Home to the widow of the Prince Palatine was Heidelberg, not London. Elizabeth, who had so stoutly resisted efforts to make her "all Dutch", took solemn counsel with the elderly Countess Solms and other sympathetic Palatine ladies as to the exact etiquette to be observed by the widow of a German prince. To her brother, she explained with dignity, "I entreat you to pardon me that I cannot at present obey your command and my own wishes— the custom in Germany being not to stir out of the house for some time after such a misfortune. Since I was married into this country, I should wish to observe its customs carefully." Nor could she hold out hopes of being able to visit England after her first period of deep mourning had elapsed. For the sake of her children she must at all costs stay where she was. She had realized that her retirement to her native country would be interpreted by all Europe as withdrawal from a losing fight. "I must prefer the welfare of my poor children to my own satisfaction. The last request that their father made me, before his departure, was to do all that I could for them, which I wish to do, as far as lies in my power, loving them

better because they are his, than because they are my own." [1]
She believed that henceforward her career was to be that of
the mother of the Elector Palatine. But it was as the mother
of another son that the widowed Queen of Bohemia was
destined to be remembered. She buckled to her business of
fighting for Charles Louis. No friendly European power must
be left unsolicited. Formal phrases began to flow from her
pen :

"It has pleased Almighty God to call from this scene of woe
my ever and most entirely beloved consort, an event of which
I desire to transmit to you the account, not doubting of your
full and generous participation in my sorrow. . . . It is for a
widow, for her orphans that I now implore your protection . . ."[2][3]

[1] Conrart MS. Bibl. de l'Arsenal, 575.29. Re-translated into English
from a French copy.   [2] *Mercure Français*, p. 1632.
[3] The body of the unfortunate Winter King continued upon melancholy
travels after his death, and mystery surrounds its ultimate fate. It lay
embalmed, in Mainz, for months, while Elizabeth conferred with Charles I
as to its safe and honourable disposal. It was then temporarily interred in
her dower-town of Frankenthal. In 1635, when Frankenthal was threatened
by enemy troops, the Duke of Simmern warned Elizabeth to protect his
brother's corpse from possible insult, and on July 6th of that year Sir H.
Vane informed Lord Conway (S.P. 16. 293.46) : "the Duke of Deuxponts
and council, with the dead body of the King of Bohemia, are come to Metz,
in France. From thence they go to Sedan." The mausoleum of the Dukes of
Bouillon, at Sedan, had been chosen as the next sanctuary of the coffin, and
Johann von Rusdorf was detailed to take sole charge of it for the remainder
of its journey. This grave responsibility he refused to assume without
written authority. He left the coffin in Metz. Dr. J. G. Weiss, at present
engaged upon a biography of Frederick, is of the opinion that "Rusdorf
must have been able to give Elizabeth a satisfactory explanation concerning
the fate of the body, as her confidence in him remained undiminished".
Recent enquiries made in the Ardennes, by the present author, have ascertained that Sedan does not lay claim to be the burial place of the King of
Bohemia. On October 12th, 1930, when seven coffins, the contents of the
mausoleum of the sovereign princes of Sedan and Bouillon, were solemnly
translated from the disused church in the Rue des Francs-Bourgeois, Sedan,
to the new church in the Place d'Alsace Lorraine, orations were delivered by
many local dignitaries and the chaplain to her Majesty the Queen of the
Netherlands. The coffin of Prince Philip, son of Frederick and Elizabeth, had

II

Gerard van Honthorst began to ply his facile brush inde-
fatigably on behalf of the anguished Queen of Bohemia. He
painted her again and again, both surrounded by her lovely
children in defensive attitudes, and all alone, against a background of thunder-clouds, but always arrayed in romantic
mourning robes of white satin, shrouded by a voluminous
black veil secured to her head by a small crown. In the year
of Frederick's departure, Gerard had embarked upon an enormous allegorical group of optimistic sentiment. The King of
Bohemia, garbed as a Roman general, was shown leading his
consort and family, garlanded with flowers, through classic
groves towards the Temple of Peace. Thirteen pregnancies, and
almost as many years of town life and Dutch fare, had taken
their toll of Elizabeth's celebrated fair beauty. Her figure was
no longer that of the Diana of the Rhine. Her last portraits as
a wife show her as a large, lustreless, pallid lady, with a fixed
smile. At Rhenen, in the autumn before her husband's death,
her attendants doubted whether the king's favourite English
hunter, Carnarvon, which her Majesty was eager to exercise,
would prove a suitable mount for her.[1] But many tears, much
hunting and a succession of attacks of ague worked another
pathetic change in the appearance of the Queen of Bohemia.

been identified and was re-interred with appropriate comment. "An eighth
coffin is missing." Diligent search had failed to discover that of the King
of Bohemia. "His body was faithfully brought by his Chancellor, Rusdorf,
as far as Metz. The insecurity of the roads caused Rusdorf to stop there, and
there its trace is lost. On the request of a friendly nation, anxious to honour
its last national sovereign, we have sought for it in vain." (Translation
solennelle des cercueils des princes de Sedan. Syndicat d'initiatives de
l'Arrondissement de Sedan 1930.) Dr Weiss is of the opinion that since
the Duke of Simmern took refuge in Metz for over a year after quitting
Frankenthal, he may have arranged during that time for the safe and
secret burial of his brother's coffin in that town.

[1] S.P. 16. 223.44.

By the time that her court artist attempted his second enormous family group, her aspect was again so decorative and dignified as to leave no doubt as to her identity in the mind of a stranger. Henceforward, except that her features and figure became increasingly gaunt and her hair darkened, she altered little in looks to the day of her death.

Her Nassau aunts and mother-in-law, as soon as they became widows, had adopted for ever the full uniform of the dowager, which included a highly cumbrous wired hood and peaked cap, with dependent veils, and a rigid stay bodice, buttoning to the chin and wrists. After her first period of deep mourning had expired, Elizabeth never again wore a costume most unfitted for a lady of early middle age who intended to lead an active life. Her presence-chamber was hung with black velvet, and on certain anniversaries she remained invisible, praying and fasting,[1] but her ordinary dress was a perfectly plain black or pure white gown of silk, satin, or wool with a *berthe* and cuffs of point lace. Her only jewels were a necklace of large pea-shaped pearls and pendant pearl ear-rings. On festal occasions she sometimes wore further pearls, draped on her bodice, twisted in her hair and fastening her sleeves. Elizabeth's "bare neck" was much disapproved by severe critics. Seven years after her bereavement a deputation of Dutch ministers waited upon her chaplain, to beg him to preach against the fashion. Mr Samson Jonson, however, replied that he was "not sent to tell Her Majesty how to dress herself".[2]

Making an idol of her grief was foreign to Elizabeth's temperament, nor would her duty allow her to do so. Her tall, handsome sons needed her supervision. When Lord Arundel's fleet prepared to sail for England at the conclusion of his mourning embassy, Colonel Sir Charles Morgan was surprised by the arrival of two determined schoolboys who announced that they had come to see his Excellency aboard. When Sir

[1] Evelyn, i. 22.   [2] S.P. 84. 155.255.

Charles attempted "to persuade them from it" he was informed that "he had nothing to do with them". "The Queen of Bohemia's two eldest sons", who had "a great desire" to lie all night in an English man of war, applied themselves successfully to Sir Charles's superior officer.[1] Prince Rupert had rowed the boat that brought them thither, and as soon as he stepped aboard the *Victory* Prince Charles Louis had "sweetely and discreetely" observed that now he was "in a part of his unckles dominions".[2]

A deputation of English Puritans presented themselves at the Hague in the New Year of 1635. To their scandalization, as they approached the house of the widow, they perceived it brilliantly lighted; the thud of music sounded, and presently the air was rent by "devilish hallooings". The Princes Palatine had staged a masque of hunters to entertain their mother and her court. "Dressing up" in her past finery was a popular sport with Elizabeth's nursery, and the favourite game of the young Palatines was pretending that they were staying at an inn *en route* for Heidelberg.

Gerard's companion picture to the approach of the exiled royal family to the Temple of Peace represented the approach of the widow and orphans towards the portals of paradise, occupied by composedly tragic figures of the late king and late crown prince. He enthroned Elizabeth in a triumphal chariot drawn by lions, controlled by her last-born child. The silver-fair haired Prince Gustavus Adolphus had already begun to terrify his mother by fits of epilepsy.[3] The queen's youngest daughter, the future ancestress of the Hanoverian line, a substantial child of five, was depicted upheld by unconvincing wings, about to bestow a laurel wreath on her mother's head. The pensive eldest daughter of the family was also provided with laurel wreaths, and witty Princess Louise Hollandine, aged thirteen and a half, with a flowering branch. The gentle Princess

---

[1] *Court and Times of Charles I*, ii. 226.   [2] Hervey, p. 325.
[3] He died, aged 9.

Henrietta Maria, god-child of the Queen of England, and the only blonde daughter of Elizabeth's family, was grouped at her mother's feet. The waif-like figures of the princes Edward and Philip, already painfully and obviously supernumerary, were inconspicuously accommodated in the left-hand bottom corner of the picture. Behind the queen rode her chief protector, Charles Louis, wearing his electoral robes, attended on either hand by his soldier brothers, Rupert and Maurice.

Elizabeth, like Volumnia, had sent her idolized heir to the wars when he was yet tender-bodied, and she did not desire to lose an hour of his company. She had not opposed his "hasting to the feelde", with the Prince of Orange, in his sixteenth year. "His minde and his bodie is so fitt to goe as I have given him leave. . . . I think he cannot to soone learne to be a soldier in this active time." [1] When, however, she heard of a scheme to marry him to an archduchess, many years his senior and "of no comely person", she was observed to go white. She confessed that she had ever loved him best, even when he was but a younger son.[2]

Gerard's second vast family group marked the end of a chapter in Elizabeth's history.[3] Charles Louis was about to leave home on his first long journey. He was going to London, on a surprise visit, to plead his own cause with the King of England. At last a child of the Lady Elizabeth was to see her native land. "I do often", wrote her secretary to Sir Thomas Roe, "look upon her with wonder, when I see how inflexible she is to the blows of time. . . . Though all goes backward in Germany, yet she looks forward to another country. I hope God hath filled her quiver so full of shafts rather to gall her enemies than pierce her heart. . . . She purposeth to shoot them abroad . . ." Once more the Queen of Bohemia was to take

[1] S.P. 16. 236.44.   [2] S.P. 16. 525.47.
[3] Both these paintings are now at Herrenhausen.

part in agonizing scenes of farewell. But now the hero of them
was a son, not a husband.

The widow's first three years of toil on behalf of what she
described as "those unfortunat children that my deare housband
left me" [1] had not been attended by any marked success. The
situation of Charles I had been decidedly eased by the deaths of
the King and Crown Prince of Bohemia. Nobody was now
asserting fantastic claims to the crown of that country. But the
King of England was still all for recovering as much as possible
of the Palatinate by peaceful means, and his sister was for the
sword and *"tout ou rien"*.[2] Frankenthal and Heidelberg had
fallen to Swedish arms, but the ineffective Duke of Simmern
presided most unwillingly as Administrator for his nephew,
and even the Protestant electors were not unanimous in
recognizing the succession of Charles Louis to his father's
hereditary territories. When the Swedes evacuated the fortresses
they had won, since neither money nor troops were forthcoming from England, French garrisons succeeded to them.
Well-meaning Sir Francis Nethersole went to London, animated
by "too hot zeale", and succeeded in making bad much worse.
Amongst other indiscretions, he forwarded to the Secretary of
State an extract from an urgent letter written by the Queen of
Bohemia's secretary, which he garnished with a postscript in
his own hand, declaring that James I had lost the Palatinate once
by a treaty and Charles I seemed determined to achieve this
result for a second time. Hearing that he was likely to be
arrested, Sir Francis then took shelter in the Dutch Embassy,
whence he sent his mistress a furious screed, informing her
that she had better look elsewhere than to her native land for
charity. Charles, much enraged, committed him to the
Tower. His effects were seized, and the Queen of Bohemia
heard with dismay that her brother's Privy Councillors had
regaled themselves with a reading of all her correspondence

---

[1] Hamilton MS. 32.   [2] S.P. 16. 318.10.

with her secretary. She said with dignity that had she realized that her brother wished to know what private instructions she had given Sir Francis Nethersole, she would have been very willing to oblige him. "I do not desire to hide the least thought of my heart from my dear brother." She would not trouble the Council at present to read any more letters from her. They must have seen enough of her handwriting.[1] She found their treatment of "poor Nethersole" very strange. "Being my servant they might have used him more gently. I am sure", added the widow of a German prince, "they would not have done it to any other foreign princess's servant."[2] Sir John Dineley, an excellent official, who had long been a tutor at the Prinsenhof, had served her as secretary during Nethersole's absence. Unfortunately he became involved in Nethersole's disgrace. The Queen of Bohemia was requested by her brother to transact her business with him in future by means of the British Ambassador at the Hague. Sir William Boswell, said Elizabeth, was "a true honest man, yet he is a servant". At the end of four months Nethersole was released, on the condition that the Queen of Bohemia never again employed a gentleman who did not appear to be in his right mind. A distinct coolness followed between the King of England and his sister, and Charles became nervous that an affronted lady might turn to France for aid. French troops had recaptured Heidelberg. His fears were groundless. Elizabeth had a violent aversion from the French. Most of them were Papists, besides "the deere late King", had never liked them. His opinion of the nation had been uncompromising. "*Les François sont ordinairement fort salles.*"[3] "I", explained Elizabeth, "fear the physician more than the disease. For though the French have succoured Heidelberg, yett I cannot trust them as long as they call not my brother-in-law Administrator, nor my son Elector."[4]

[1] Hamilton MS. 36. [2] Add. MS. 4163.182.
[3] Bromley, 65. [4] Add. MS. 4163.182.

The most important of Swedes, Chancellor Axel Oxenstierna, arrived at the Hague in April, 1635. The Queen of
Bohemia was "not able to stand upon her legs". She was
recovering from an attack of ague, which had included twenty-
three fits of alternate shivering and high fever.[1] But she must
not lose the chance of meeting a man who had complete control
of all the country won by his great master. Three years had
passed since she had written "I have a sonne and another hath a
daughter". The clever child-Queen of Sweden would now be
an even more resplendent match for Charles Louis.[2] The
Queen of Bohemia had herself arrayed to entertain a visitor,
and the great guest was introduced to her bed-chamber. No
Scandinavian ever proclaimed his nationality more clearly in
appearance than Axel Oxenstierna, for the hair and beard of
this sapient man were white as snow, his countenance was of an
innocent rosiness, and his eyes as sharp as the frosts of the north.
Three hours after he had been admitted to the invalid, the
queen's ladies still heard cheerful conversation in the French
tongue proceeding from the sickroom. The· benevolent
Chancellor, who knew what men mattered in what countries
nowadays, gave an anxious Protestant mother the benefit of
his advice. All the polite letters and little dogs sent to the
Queen-Mother of France had been wasted. Marie de Medicis
had been ousted by a man whom she had raised to power, a
crafty priest with a silent tread and a dry cough—Armand du
Plessis, Cardinal de Richelieu. The French Cardinal and the
Swedish Chancellor were on the best of terms. Richelieu
flatteringly described Oxenstierna as "an inexhaustible source
of well-matured counsels". At present the Cardinal needed
Swedish troops as much as the Chancellor needed French
money.

A priest was becoming important in England too. The old
Archbishop of Canterbury had died, aged seventy-one.

[1] Cornwallis, p. 275.   [2] S.P. 81. 38.245.

z

George Abbot, whose father had been a tradesman in a county town, left the Queen of Bohemia two hundred pounds in his will. The legacy was kindly meant, but already, four years ago, her Majesty had owed her butcher exactly twice that sum, and the "Milkboore" £140 18s. and the Fruiterer £470 4s.[1] The new Archbishop of Canterbury, who was also of humble birth, was said to have great influence with his king. Sir Thomas Roe suggested to Elizabeth to address herself to William Laud. She said dryly that she was glad to hear someone commend the new Archbishop. "There are few that do it." She had been willing to enter into correspondence with him since he was archbishop, "but you know I do not love to begin. He hath indeed sent me sometimes a cold compliment and I have answered it in the same kind." However, acting on Sir Thomas's advice, she had thrown out a feeler—made her secretary write to apply for relief for some poor Palatine preachers. The Archbishop's reply told the Queen of Bohemia that he had prevailed upon his Majesty to start a fund in aid of distressed Palatine clergy. Elizabeth thereupon proceeded to enter into direct and intimate correspondence with William Laud.

"*It is all one to me*," she wrote emphatically of her son's restoration, "*by what ways he bee restored, so he be so fullie and honourablie. But indeed I doe not think he will be restored fullie, otherwise than by armes, 16 yeares experience makes me belieeve it.*"[2]

"Under favour, good Madam," replied the prelate, "not so. For it cannot be all one to Christendom nor to yourself, to have him restored, be it never so honourably, by arms as by a treaty . . . I am a priest, and as such I can never think it all one to recover by effusion of Christian blood, and without it, provided that without blood, right may be had."[3]

"I confess as a woman and a Christian," affirmed the queen,

[1] S.P. 16. 94.17–18.   [2] *Ibid.*, 325.18.   [3] *Ibid.*, 327.79.

"I shoulde rather desire it by peace. But I have lived so long among soldiers and wars as *it makes one to me as easie as the other, and as familiar and especiallie* when I remember never to have read in the Chronicles of my ancestors that anie King of England got anie good by treaties but commonlie lost by them, and on the contrarie by wars made always good peaces. *It makes me doubt the same fortune runns in a bloud and that the King my Brother will have the same lucke.* I know your profession forbids you to like this scribbling of mine, yet I am confident you *cannot condemne me* for it, having hitherto seene little cause to have a contrary opinion by my experience in this our great business. All I feare is that you will think I have too warring a minde for my sex. But the necessitie of my fortune has made it." [1]

During the first days of October, 1635, the Queen of Bohemia informed Archbishop Laud and the Marquis of Hamilton that since her son was now of age, he wished his first independent action to be a visit of gratitude to his uncle the King of England. The Prince Elector was setting sail forthwith. She had not seen fit to advise the British Ambassador at the Hague. [2]

III

Charles Louis [3] at eighteen seemed to his proud mother indeed a prince to win English hearts. He had been born a small and weakly "black babie", but now in build, colouring and features, he was unmistakably the Lady Elizabeth's child. This resemblance was destined to pass disappointingly unremarked in England, for in manners and expression the young

[1] S.P. 16. 329.49.
[2] Hamilton MS. 193.
[3] The mother of Charles Louis called him simply Charles, and his letters to her are so signed. Since this biography must contain continual references to his uncle, Charles I, and his cousin, Charles II, he is given throughout the two Christian names, which were always used by him for a formal signature.

Prince Palatine nothing recalled his mother. He carried his
inches stiffly, his grey eyes had a wary look, his fair hair
waved from a brow that was broad but not frank, his fine
mouth in repose had a disapproving line.[1] The Prince Palatine
was, in fact, already at eighteen an extremely careful young
man. He had inherited something of the brain of James I,
but neither of the qualities which had redeemed that monarch
in the opinion of his subjects—passionate devotion to field
sports and decidedly ludicrous geniality.

The Queen of Bohemia wrote to Sir Harry Vane, begging
him to give her fledgling his best advice, and protect him as far
as possible from the results of inexperience. The prince was,
explained his innocent parent, particularly young and raw.
"I fear damnablie how he will do with your ladies, for he is a
verie ill courtier; therefore I pray, desire them not to laugh too
much at him, but be mercifull to him." [2]

Letters bearing the magic addresses of Whitehall and Theobalds began to arrive at the Hague. The Prince Palatine,
like his father before him, found life as chief guest at the King
of England's court a moving experience. He was not particularly enthusiastic about what he described as "a perpetual
hunting and changing of lodgings". Much to her surprise, his
mother learnt from several sources that he was considered
quite a squire of dames.

Three months after Charles Louis landed at Gravesend,
another "penniless Palatine" arrived there. The second surviving son of the Queen of Bohemia had given that lady no
peace until she had allowed him to follow in his brother's footsteps. Prince Rupert had always been a remarkable child.
His first recorded utterance had startled and entranced his
mother's exiled Bohemian suite. "Praise the Lord!" quoth the

[1] The bust of Charles Louis, aged nineteen, by François Dusart, probably
made for Thomas Earl of Arundel, now in the collection of the Duke of
Norfolk, represents him as very handsome.
[2] S.P. 16. 300.1.

infant born in Prague, using the Czech tongue. At thirteen
he had insisted on being allowed to accompany the Prince of
Orange to the wars, and had won golden opinions for "manly
carriage" on active service. At sixteen he had outgrown the
angelic loveliness of his nursery days, and was decidedly at the
awkward age. His spirits were ebullient. Elizabeth forwarded
her second uninvited son to her brother's court with apologies
and considerable nervousness. "I hope for bloud's sake he will
be welcome. . . . I believe he will not trouble the ladies much
with courting them. . . . He is still a little giddie, though not
as much as he has bene. I pray tell him when he doth ill, for
he is good-natured enough." [1] Rupert's worst fault, explained his parent, was that he was apt to act before he
thought.

Charles Louis beheld his brother with no benevolent feelings. The disinherited Elector Palatine was considering an
interesting discovery which would have gone to the head
of a less cautious princeling. In spite of his careful deportment,
he could not deceive himself that he was popular in his uncle's
immediate circle. But in a much wider circle, of growing
importance, he was thoroughly appreciated. To the Puritans
of England "the hopeful issue of the Lady Elizabeth" were
infinitely more desirable than any member of their king's
family.

Disturbing news of Rupert's prowess in her native country
soon reached his mother. In vain Sir Thomas Roe assured her
Majesty that his Majesty took great pleasure in her younger
son's "unrestfulness". "For he is never idle, and in his sport
serious." She was hearing simultaneously from Charles Louis
that he saw little of Rupert, who was continually in the
company of the Papist queen and her satellites. Charles Louis
feared that his brother, who was "very shy" when asked his
plans, was making some undesirable acquaintances. Presently

[1] S.P. 16. 313.11.

Sir Thomas Roe got a letter from the Hague which sent him hurrying, despite his gout, to ask the private opinion of an authoritative City acquaintance. The streets of London were ringing with ballads in praise of the Lady Elizabeth's second son, who was going to Madagascar, "a great island, eight hundred miles long in the East Indies", to establish an English colony of which he was to be governor. His prospects were dazzling. "He that is lord of Madagascar may in good time become Emperor of all India." The King, who sympathized warmly with his nephew's laudable desire to carve a career for himself, had sent to ask the advice and assistance of the East India Company.

Sir Thomas Roe's merchant friend said thoughtfully that although Prince Rupert's design was gallant, it was not one on which he would venture a second son. The City of London was well aware of the East India Company's attitude. The Company, being heavily in debt, regretted that they could not assist an enterprise they wished well and would not obstruct. Well-informed Londoners had heard that "my Lady Elizabeth" had set her face against the scheme. She had said that she would have "none of her sons to be knights-Errant".[1] The Queen of Bohemia had indeed written to Sir Thomas Roe that "Rupert's Romance of Madagascar" sounded to her "like one of Don Quixotte's conquests, where he promist his trustie squire to make him king of an island". She had denounced the scheme as "neither feasable, safe, nor honourable", and bidden her son dismiss it from his mind. If he was looking for conquests there was "worke enough to be had for him in Europe". Besides, argued her Majesty with strong common sense, "if Madagascar were a place either worth the taking or possible to be kept, the Portugals by this time woulde have had it, having so long possessed the coast of Afrik neare to it". Having delivered herself of these sentiments, she waited with trepida-

[1] Howell, p. 257.

tion for some response from the would-be governor. "What he will answere God knows." [1]

Rupert's eventual answer was dutiful. He reluctantly consented to abandon Madagascar. In the following summer he got his long-dreaded summons "home" to the Hague. Before his last morning's hunting with his uncle, the prince, who had nothing English in his appearance, alarmed his companions by announcing a hope that he might break his neck to-day "so he might leave his bones in England". He was in this mood when he presented himself before his parent, who immediately subjected him to a religious inquisition. Prince Rupert's replies were so unsatisfactory that the Queen of Bohemia declared that, had her son stayed ten days longer in England, he would have returned to her a Papist. When this remark reached the ears of the Queen of England, she said regretfully that, had she known her nephew's conversion was so near, she must have contrived to detain him a little longer.

The Queen of Bohemia had to derive what comfort she could from the knowledge that all Protestant Europe was commending her eldest daughter for refusing a crown sooner than change her religion. A match for the Princess Elizabeth Palatine with Prince Wladislaus of Poland had been mooted as long ago as the autumn of 1631. The princess's mother had then thought it a thing "very unlikely to be ever effected". But Wladislaus, on succeeding his father, had approached Charles I. He was, it appeared, desperately attracted by the prospect of a bride so talented, virtuous and beautiful as the King of England's niece. He hoped that when the marriage had taken place the King of England would assist him to gain the throne of Sweden from which his father had been deposed in 1599. The Queen of Bohemia was horrified at the proposal that she should lend herself to any scheme injurious to the infant orphan of Gustavus Adolphus. "I cannot find it in my

[1] S.P. 16. 317.12 & 352.41.

heart to consent that his child should be disinherited to whom we have had all so much obligation." She was nettled when Charles informed the States General of an offer of marriage for her daughter which had not yet been made in due form. When his envoy arrived at the Hague to announce that articles ensuring the princess the free exercise of her own religion had been drawn up, she waxed possessively indignant. She told Mr Francis Gordon that no one should conclude a match for any of her children without her knowledge, be it "never so reasonable", she would break it. The fact was that she did not for a moment believe that this marriage would take place. Throughout the tedious negotiations,[1] she professed the utmost indifference to their result. She knew that at present her daughters were unmarketable, and she painfully resented the fact. "For myself, if it be found good for my son's affairs, and good conditions for religion, I shall be content with it. Else I assure you I shall not desire it, my son being more dear to me than all my daughters." Charles Louis wrote from London that he did not see why Wladislaus should not be in earnest. He appeared to be giving way to Charles I upon every point. At Whitehall courtiers were applying for posts in the new Queen of Poland's household. At the Prince of Orange's court the Princess Elizabeth was observed to blush "very remarkably" when the Polish Ambassador saluted her. Her nose was too long, but her soulful eyes and profuse ringlets of darkest sepia were lovely, and at seventeen she had a perfect complexion. She complained pathetically to her brother that her mother treated her with coldness. At the last possible moment the Diet of Poland insisted that their king should demand that the Princess Elizabeth became a Catholic. Wladislaus refused to sign conditions which he knew would meet with instant rejection. Eventually the ambassadors set forth, empowered to make the unwelcome request verbally.

[1] S.P. 81. 46.120.

The inevitable result followed, and next year Wladislaus gloomily approached a faded daughter of Ferdinand II. Charles I wrote to his sister in lofty disdain. "He is unworthy of either of our thoughts, except it be to make him smart for his base dealing with us." Wladislaus, who was in his forty-third year and a widower, was not prepared to make sweeping changes in his domestic habits on the arrival of this bride. Before she left Vienna, the Archduchess Cécilie received an intimation that she must be prepared to tolerate in her court not one, but two, ladies who had previous claims on her bridegroom's affections. The Queen of Bohemia commented, "I like his plain dealing well", and added philosophically that although "this rarest article" would not have appeared in any marriage treaty negotiated by her, probably the result would have been the same.[1] Wladislaus IV, who was, as she admitted a brave and intelligent man, eventually died childless. Whether the Princess Elizabeth regretted him or not, she never had the slightest chance of accepting him. But eighteen years later, she was not averse from mentioning to sympathetic audiences that for the sake of her religion she had refused a husband and a crown.

IV

"It seemeth to me a dream . . . and too happy", said Charles Louis when his English uncle at last agreed to lend him a fleet.[2] Lord Craven offered ten thousand pounds and his own services. Her two eldest sons came in high spirits to take farewell of the Queen of Bohemia at her summer palace before setting out for the wars. They had collected "a jolly considerable army"[3] for the invasion of the Lower Palatinate. On October 17th, 1638, their determined but far from cohesive force, which included desperadoes of many nations, encountered troops commanded by the Austrian General

[1] S.P. 16. 373.27.   [2] Bromley, p. 96.   [3] Howell, p. 256.

Hatzfeld, at Vlotho on the banks of the Weser. Over a fortnight later Elizabeth still knew little more than that her young adventurers, after distinguishing themselves by marked personal courage, had been soundly beaten. Lord Craven's fate was certain. He was a severely wounded prisoner. "I am sorry", said Elizabeth. She feared that he would not be released speedily. Charles Louis was said to have been dragged from the stricken field by protesting attendants. "My comfort", said his mother, "is though he had the worse, yet he has lost no honour." Rupert was wounded and missing. The Queen of Bohemia exclaimed passionately that she wished him rather dead than in his enemies' hands.[1] "The ill news", as she justly described it, reached her at a time when she was suffering physical disability. Six weeks before, she had been bled in the right arm to allay fever, but the operation had brought her no relief. "The uglie Surgeon did binde my arme so hard as it swelled and grew black and putt me to much paine."[2] This "scurvie mischance" prevented her from employing her active pen for three weeks. By November 1st she was on the road to recovery. "That Tunn of Beer sent a 1000 cuirassers against my sonne, else the enemie durst not have fought with him.[3] . . . Him I love most is safe."[4] The Tunn of Beer was George, Duke of Brunswick Lüneburg. "Him she loved best" charging from the lost field in his coach, accompanied by the English General, King, was very nearly drowned in the Weser. Fortunately a willow grew aslant the scene of Charles Louis's immersion. He reached Minden wet through and on foot.[5] History had repeated itself. Amongst the Prince Elector's lost baggage was the Garter sent to him by the King of England. His brother, all his mother's letters to him, and his cash-box, were also missing. Elizabeth regretted that "in my passion" she had wished Rupert dead rather than a prisoner. "I pray God

---

[1] S.P. 81. 45.227.   [2] Ibid., 169.   [3] Ibid., 220.
[4] Ibid., 227.   [5] Howell, 265.

I have not more cause to wish it before he be gotten out."
Rupert had managed to send her an heroic message by a
servant of Lord Craven, assuring her that neither good nor ill
usage should make him change either his religion or his
party. "I know", said Elizabeth, "that his disposition is good,
and he never did disobey me at anie time, though to others
he was stubborn and willfull." But she knew also that Rupert
was no bird for a cage, and she dreaded the effect of close
confinement on his resolution. "I am borne to so much
affliction that I cannot be confident." Lord Craven had applied
in vain to be allowed to share the young prince's prison.
Elizabeth planned a scheme for Rupert's escape. She feared
that it sounded hopelessly romantic, "yett such things have been
done". Since the cypher in which she corresponded with her
family was now known in Vienna, she was obliged to ask the
British Ambassador at the Hague to put the details of her plot
into another code for transmission to England.[1] Months
passed, bringing no worse tidings of Prince Rupert than that he
had been removed to the distant castle of Linz on the banks of
the Danube, but Elizabeth could not get into touch with him.
A letter to General Hatzfeld, asking for permission for a
messenger from his widowed mother to visit the captive,
received no answer.

Sir Thomas Roe, dragging agonizing gout about Europe
as Ambassador Extraordinary to peace conferences, made a
private tryst with Charles Louis at Glückstadt. There the King
of Denmark received his young relative with great kindness,
and to Charles Louis's relief, did not press him to drink more
than he could carry.[2] But old Christian IV regretted that at
present he could not engage himself in a campaign. Within
seven months the deaths of Duke Bernard of Weimar and
William, Landgrave of Hesse Cassel, left two large armies of
valuable troops without leaders. Charles Louis made over to

[1] S.P. 81. 45.227.   [2] Bromley, p. 103.

London, where Charles I sang to the same tune as Christian IV.
He sympathized with his nephew's desire to be active, but was
unable to assist him at the moment. There was "a show of war
in Scotland". Archbishop Laud's new prayer book seemed
likely to start a religious conflict within the British Isles.
Officers of the Weimar army were sending Charles Louis
tempting invitations to assume their command. He decided
to take a circuitous route through France and Switzerland to
Germany. His father had once travelled *incognito* through
Paris to the Palatinate without experiencing any trouble. The
Prince Elector sailed without a passport, but found himself
greeted by a salvo at Boulogne, and assigned all the honours
due to a reigning potentate. Elizabeth heard with satisfaction
of the winning courtesies extended to her young hero by
France—now ally of England, Sweden, Holland and the
Protestant princes of Germany. She had recently despatched
three of her younger sons to complete their education in Paris.
Their father, whose manners had been charming, except
during his melancholic bouts, had learnt his elegant French at the
court of his uncle, the Duke of Bouillon. Elizabeth's third
surviving son, Maurice, was demonstrably in need of a little
French polish. At fifteen he had grown to an absurd height,
overtopping Charles Louis. At seventeen, having assisted the
Prince of Orange to capture Breda, he had expected to be
allowed a command in the army for the invasion of the
Palatinate. Elizabeth had declared in the hour of his birth that
this child must prove a soldier, but she thought now that he
must first learn to resemble a Christian gentleman. Although
the Voorhout was a fashionable neighbourhood, it was badly
lit at night, and cup-shotten gallants delighted in breaking the
windows and unscrewing the door-knockers of its sumptuous
mansions. Complaints that Prince Maurice, in rowdy company,
had been scaring respectable citizens and their wives, after
nightfall, in the streets of the Hague, reached his mother. He

took part in a duel, which ended fatally for one assailant.[1] The prince who had been born at Cüstrin was the "shadow" of the prince born at Prague a year earlier. The fourth surviving son, Edward, a more tractable character, had exactly the same type of over-pronounced good looks. Prince Philip, at eleven, was merely a tawny-haired, remarkably scraggy schoolboy, with a deceptively ingenuous air. The Queen of Bohemia forwarded this trio of young hopefuls to the politest nation in the world, without much fear that their religious convictions would suffer damage.

Charles Louis paid his brothers a visit on his way through Paris, and found them well. He then left the French capital *incognito*, and posted south. Elizabeth, on her annual early autumn holiday at peaceful Rhenen, found, as usual, no news worth writing "but the death of hares, and which horse ran best, which, though I say it that should not say it, was mine". Her "worthie cousen" the Marquis of Hamilton, had sent her a welcome gift of geldings. "I like them all verie well, especiallie the bay and the fleabitten. . . . I have given the least gray to my second girll, Louyse, because she loves riding and hunting as well as I." [2] The Princess Louise Hollandine was now seventeen. Her nose, had it not belonged to a princess, must have been termed impertinent, but she managed to make people think her a beauty, for her auburn hair and eager expression were highly attractive. In colouring she resembled her little brother Philip, but in gait and carriage she was very like Rupert. Louise and Rupert, who had many tastes in common, were the artists of the family. Gerard van Honthorst found the princess a most promising pupil.

The Queen of Bohemia cut short her hunting holiday, so as to be at the Hague when the first news from Charles Louis could arrive. She took her grown-up daughters with her for a two days' visit to Amsterdam, after leaving Rhenen. The

[1] Van Sypesteyn, p. 38.   [2] Hamilton MSS., p. 193.

little trip was a great success. The queen wrote to "honest fatt Thom Roe" that the generous merchants of Amsterdam had made her a present of porcelain and given the princesses oriental cabinets.[1]

No letter from Charles Louis awaited Elizabeth at the Hague, but presently incredible rumours explained his silence. They reached the Prince of Orange by means of his Ambassador in Paris.[2] The Prince Elector had been arrested at Moulins by order of Cardinal Richelieu. He was being removed to the fortress of Vincennes. No one was allowed to speak to him, except in the presence of a guard, and he was commanded to conduct all his conversation in French. The three younger princes in Paris had also been arrested. Several days passed before Elizabeth knew that these tidings of "devilish usage" were indeed true. A gentleman sent by the Elector arrived at the Wassenaer Hof. Sympathizers described the Queen of Bohemia as "another Niobe", but she showed no signs of being petrified by the tidings of her children's fate. The royal lioness, robbed of her cubs, raged alarmingly. "That ulcerous priest" and his confederates "the fickle Monsieurs" should rue the day when they had caged the Prince Elector. The stout Prince and Princess of Orange listened with genuine concern to their gaunt, disordered guest's passionate declaration that her late husband had travelled through France *incognito* with perfect safety, even when that country was at peace with Austria. She loudly proclaimed that the affront offered to her son was the chief cause of her dismay. She had no fear that he would suffer personal injury.[3] Amalia of Solms, not very tactfully, told her old mistress that the French agent at the Hague said that the reason for France's desire to prevent the Prince Elector from leading the Weimar army was that he was

---

[1] S.P. 81. 48.96. The sand with which the Queen of Bohemia dusted this hastily written letter still clings to its blots.

[2] S.P. 81. 4.137.   [3] *Ibid.,* 48.164.

considered too much attached to England. The Queen of
Bohemia returned home to write feverish letters to the Kings
of England [1] and Denmark, the Archbishop of Canterbury,
the Regents of Sweden and the principal officers of the late
Duke Bernard's army, adjuring them all to do their best to
expedite her son's release.[2]

Charles Louis was detained in France for seven months. He
did not suffer inordinately in what he described as his
"dungeon". At lonely Linz Rupert was beguiling monotony
by the study of drawing in perspective, and taming a hare
which he had discovered on one of his escorted promenades in
the castle grounds. "Twelve musketeers and two halberds
attended the Prince in all his motions." So did a white poodle
puppy, "Boy", whom Lord Arundel had sent to the prince
from Vienna. The prince had outgrown his bed and his
clothes. He had steadfastly refused to change his religion, or
ask pardon for bearing arms against the Emperor, or accept
a command against the French and Swedes. His mother had
reluctantly abandoned her "romance-like" plot for his escape.
She had heard with mixed feelings that, after a friendly visit
from the pious Archduke Leopold, brother of the Emperor,
Rupert had been allowed more liberty. He had given his word
to abstain from attempts to escape.[3] But at the end of two and
a half years Rupert was being more strictly guarded than ever.
His brother Maurice was with a Swedish army whose advance
was causing the Emperor anxiety.

Maurice was the first of the family to return to his mother
from Paris. He reached the Hague early in 1640. Charles Louis
wrote in mournful but noble vein from Vincennes in February.
He thought that the States General and Swedish Ambassadors
displayed less sense of the injury done to him than desire to
engage his uncle of England to a disadvantageous treaty while
he was held as hostage. His confinement was depriving him of

[1] S.P. 81. 48.131.   [2] *Ibid.*, 84. 154.101.   [3] *Ibid.*, 81. 48.164.

health and strength, but he would not be persuaded to agree to anything unworthy of her Majesty's most humble and devoted son and servant. He dared say no more, since this letter might never reach her.[1] By Eastertide he was writing more cheerfully. He had been to St Germain to witness Louis XIII, and his niece "Mademoiselle", perform the traditional ceremony of washing the feet of a band of carefully selected indigents, and serving them with a meal. "Mademoiselle performed very prettily, but not without the disaster of letting two dishes of pease fall upon her gown." The King had recognized the Elector Palatine, and been most affable.[2] Elizabeth said thàt she doubted her son had "signed something". On April 16th Edward and Philip left Paris. Their elder brother was being allowed more freedom, on the condition that he made no attempt to lead the Weimar army. Elizabeth considered that her son had promised "more than he should have done, but that necessity hath no law". She complained that the spring came very slowly at Rhenen this year. Charles Louis acquainted her in July "with the news of my entire liberty", but did not return to her until August. Louis XIII had suggested that he would do well to stay awhile in Paris, and he was "not very unwilling" since, until he had some hopeful news from Charles I, he could do little anywhere.[3]

An Imperial Diet was to be held at Ratisbon in July. Elizabeth confessed to Sir Thomas Roe, who had just toiled home from Hamburg, that she had begged her brother to send him abroad once more, "to treat for us. . . . I hope you will not be against another such employment, though I did desire it without your knowledge.[4] . . . I pray God send you health for it." The old Emperor had died, and Ferdinand III, aged thirty-six, was reported to be less fanatical than his father, and anxious for peace. Unfortunately his election had never been recog-

[1] Bromley, p. 106.   [2] Ibid., p. 107.
[3] Ibid., pp. 107-19.   [4] S.P. 16. 354.43.

nized by Charles I, since the disinherited Elector Palatine
had not been allowed to vote. Sir Thomas Roe set out for
Ratisbon empowered to address Ferdinand III by his Imperial
title, with an attendant explanation that he did so in confidence
that justice was about to be done to his master's nephew. Over
quarter of a century had passed since the handsome Englishman
who had been an admired esquire of the body to Gloriana had
attired himself in the full and ornate court costume of his
country for an audience with the Mogul Emperor of Hindustan, at far Ajmir. The English Ambassador who mounted
heavily into his coach to make on from Ratisbon to Vienna
in the hard winter of 1641–2 was an enormous figure soberly
clad in long robes of dark velvet and fur. His countenance
resembled that of an elderly bloodhound. He had fulfilled
the ambition of his type, and bought "a cell for his old age"—
a remote and inconvenient English country house, whence he
need adventure no further than to try the waters of Bath for
his gout. A most weary old servant whipped up his spirits
to make a last effort on behalf of the beloved mistress. The
Queen of Bohemia had particularly begged him to press the
release of Prince Rupert. "I have", announced the new
Emperor after giving audience to Sir Thomas Roe, "met with
many gallant persons of many nations, but I scarce ever met an
AMBASSADOR till now." [1] Ferdinand added that had his
Excellency been a lady, and a beauty, he feared that the charm
of his conversation must have proved too much for the virtue
of his Imperial Majesty. [2]

Eighteen months after the Winter Queen's "honest Thom"
had set out on his last pilgrimage in her service, Sir William
Boswell, at the Hague, was startled to find himself hailed in the
darkness of a December night by an enormously tall young
man, springing from a post-waggon outside the Binnenhof.
Prince Rupert "in perfect health, but lean and weary", had

[1] De Wicquefort, p. 165.   [2] Sydney papers, II. 541 n.

AA

come home at last. He surprised his mother about to sit down to supper.[1] The prince, whose captivity had lasted three years, had been released on the conditions that he paid homage to the Emperor and refrained in future from taking up arms against him. Rupert had accomplished the first condition characteristically. In a lower Austrian glade, Ferdinand III had found his hand enthusiastically saluted by an unknown huntsman who had despatched a boar of exceptional ferocity under the Imperial nose. Prince Rupert had been loath to agree to the Emperor's second condition, but more than a hint had reached him that martial employment in his mother's native country was alas! too likely awaiting him.

V

On the morning of March 11th, 1642, a carriage bearing the Queen of Bohemia and her two youngest daughters drove rapidly out of the Hague in the direction of the Prince of Orange's new country palace at Honsholredijk. To the princesses, the sight of two hundred and eighty-eight torches on poles being erected along familiar streets through which they were to re-pass this evening, in a procession, was an exciting novelty. Their mother, attired in a severely simple black gown and splendid pearls, was nerving herself to meet for the first time the Papist Queen Consort of England. She had made the acquaintance of Henrietta Maria's mother four years ago. Marie de Medicis, driven out of France by Richelieu, had paused at the Hague before arriving uninvited in England. She had given mortal offence at the Prince of Orange's court by kissing none but the Queen of Bohemia. "Queen Mother", as Elizabeth invariably called her, had proved a terrifying old dame with a towering coiffure of metallic gold curls and sharp features, strongly marked by rage and chagrin. She had stayed in London until her son-in-law's

[1] S.P. 16. 486.53.

subjects began to break her windows. Elizabeth attributed most of her brother's present troubles to the baleful influence of his wife and "Queen Mother", and that his troubles were growing acute she was gloomily convinced. Once again Europe had been amazed by the poverty of the match made by a King of England for his eldest daughter. The Princess Mary, aged ten, had been given last May to the Prince of Orange's fifteen-year-old heir. Elizabeth herself had considered that her brother's second daughter would have been a sufficiently resplendent match for the son of Amalia of Solms. Charles Louis, although on the spot, had absolutely refused to attend the wedding ceremony at Whitehall. His uncle should have kept the Prince of Orange dangling. The Princess Mary should have been reserved for the Elector Palatine. But the large and cheerful Prince of Orange had objected that the younger English princess was said to be sickly. He had insisted on the eldest daughter and got his way. Now his second bold request, that she should be sent to reside at his court, had met with tame compliance.

Frederick Henry of Nassau, who could never quite forget that his consort was not of royal birth, had been thrown into a fever of excitement when he was abruptly informed that the Queen of England and the Princess Mary were at Dover awaiting a favourable wind. Admiral van Tromp, with a squadron of fifteen ships, was ordered to sea; the civic authorities of Rotterdam and Dordrecht were ordered to stage street pageants. The Princess of Orange would be unable to accompany her guests on their triumphal entry into the Hague. She was expecting a child. The Queen of Bohemia was invited to play hostess. For several days Elizabeth was vexed by contradictory rumours. Her sister-in-law was still at Dover. Suddenly her sister-in-law had reached Helle-voetsluis and steadfastly refused to put out to sea again. The young bridegroom, accompanied by the Princes Rupert and

Maurice Palatine, had left the Hague to escort his bride and mother-in-law by water to Rotterdam. The royal ladies had crossed the island of Voorn to Brill, and had been met by the Prince of Orange. At last a frantic message begged the Queen of Bohemia to speed to Honsholredijk, where a banquet was toward.

The wife and sister of the King of England were unlikely to become friends. They possessed only two notable tastes in common—love of Charles I and love of animals. Unfortunately the French-born queen regarded her adored husband's widowed sister as a persistent claimant upon his patience and resources, and Elizabeth thought Henrietta Maria a disastrous mate for her "dear and onelie brother". Moreover, the Queen of England's favourite pet was an elderly lady called Mitte, who slept on her Majesty's bed, while the Queen of Bohemia's notion of a dog was a well-trained greyhound, typified by her Babbler or Apollon.

Towards evening the inhabitants of the Hague cheered the entry into their transformed capital of a remarkable coach-load. In a lumbering vehicle, upholstered in crimson velvet, the principal seats were occupied by two queens. The extreme graciousness with which her stately Majesty of Bohemia conversed with the tiny, black-ringleted, gesticulating French lady by her side, was noted with edification. Opposite them sat the bride and bridegroom. Prince William, a promising, frank-faced lad, was said to be already devoted to his little English wife. In the "boots" of the carriage were accommodated four more personages—the Prince of Orange, Prince Rupert and two Princesses Palatine. Princess Henrietta Maria was god-daughter and namesake of the visiting queen. Sharp little Princess Sophie had been brought because she was near in age to her English cousin. Only two members of this party were enjoying feelings of unalloyed happiness. Frederick Henry of Nassau did not as yet know that the bargain which he had struck was not as brilliant as it appeared. He was unaware that his principal guest bore amongst her luggage a considerable portion of the crown jewels of England, which she proposed to pawn or sell in his principality. Henrietta Maria's vivacity concealed tragic facts. Her progress to Dover had resembled a flight. Charles had taken with him all the equipage for the chase, so as to disarm his subjects' suspicions, but the truth was that as soon as he had seen his wife safely out of his country, he had turned north, to Hull, to obtain possession of all the military stores collected for his Scottish campaign. The queen, whose ill luck at sea was proverbial, had lost important property on this passage. One of her baggage-ships had foundered entering port. It had contained all the plate for her chapel and all the gala attires of her ladies in waiting. The eagle eye of the Queen of Bohemia had instantly noted, in her sister-in-law's train, the infuriating sight of four priests. Her youngest daughter, who had inherited many of her qualities, had also been observing things which could not be made the subject of conversation. Twelve-year-old Princess Sophie had discovered that the Queen of England was by no means as lovely as the brush of Vandyk represented. Her court painter had disguised the facts that her Majesty's shoulders were not quite even and her teeth projected. Sophie's benevolent feelings towards her new aunt had increased when that lady had drawn the attention of all present to the striking likeness between her own daughter, the heroine of this occasion, and the most insignificant member of the Queen of Bohemia's family. Thereupon some of the strange English milords attendant had remarked to one another in audible asides that the Princess Sophie Palatine bade fair to outshine all her sisters.[1]

[1] *Memoirs of Sophie, Electress of Hanover*, pp. 12–14.

VI

Henrietta Maria, who had hoped to rejoin her husband within a few weeks, stayed in Holland nearly a year, but no close friendship with her sister-in-law resulted. The Jews of Amsterdam became the possessors of many famous pieces of jewellery which Elizabeth had last seen decorating the persons of her parents. Boats loaded with arms for the destruction of Englishmen began to pass quietly out of the mouth of the Maas towards English ports. English ships, commanded by officers appointed by Parliament, beat up and down the North Sea and the Channel, ordered to intercept communications between their king and queen. Nevertheless, many of Elizabeth's countrymen managed to slip across to the Hague. Only such as were personal friends paid their respects to the Queen of Bohemia, and even they would disclose nothing of their business. Elizabeth said loftily, "I am not curious to ask, what I see is not willingly to be told". "I hear all and say nothing".[1] Henrietta Maria, half crazy with toothache and over-entertainment, was writing passionately to her husband that if he took no steps to protect his children's interests, she would immure herself in a nunnery. The Queen of Bohemia, who had feared that she had too warring a mind for her sex, listened in silent despair while her French-born sister-in-law railed "abominably" at Parliament. "I find by all the Queen's and her people's discourses that they do not desire any agreement between his majesty and the parliament, but that all shall be done by force."

On the cloudy evening of August 22nd, 1642, Charles I raised the Royal Standard at Nottingham. With him under his insecurely erected banner stood his two eldest sons and the Princes Rupert and Maurice Palatine. Henrietta Maria had warned her husband, in italics, that the nephew to whom he

[1] S.P. 16. 490.63.

was entrusting the command of his cavalry was "very *young* and *self-willed*". The clouds of war descended upon England, and the Hague became a breeding-ground of rumour. The earliest accounts of the first important engagement of the campaign declared that both the Palatine princes had been slain, and the King and Prince of Wales were prisoners. Henrietta Maria's opinion of Rupert was endorsed by later reports of the indecisive battle of Edgehill. Rupert's Horse, after routing the Parliamentarian cavalry, imprudently pursued them nearly two miles beyond the field. By the time that the dashing young general returned to the scene of his victory the royalist foot had broken, and his troops were in too great disorder to retrieve the fortunes of the day. The army against which Elizabeth's sons were arrayed was commanded by one of her oldest friends. Robert Devereux, Earl of Essex, had at last his opportunity of opposing the system of royal privilege. Its abuse had robbed him of his youth and blighted him for life.

Civil War in her native country was a calamity for the Queen of Bohemia. One distressing consequence was immediately apparent. Her monthly allowance from England ceased. At the suggestion of Sir Thomas Roe, she addressed to the Speaker of the House of Commons a letter which, while it referred in affectionate terms to her brother and Rupert, was calculated to conciliate Parliament. She also wrote to the House of Lords and to Essex. At the request of the Commons, she dismissed her chaplain, Dr. Jonson, a protégé of the unfortunate Laud. But the sums eventually forwarded to her, after repeated applications, bore no relation to her official grant.

Her first New Year since the outbreak of the Great Rebellion was remarkably miserable. While she was prostrated by pleurisy she received the dying blessing of her mother-in-law. Her eldest and her youngest daughters were seriously ill during the following spring. In June she lost her best English adviser. When the Queen of Bohemia heard from Sir Thomas Roe that he was preparing to quit a world in which he was useless, she wrote eagerly contradicting that statement. She wanted him to come over to the Continent and consult a Polish doctor, or at least try the waters of a celebrated French spa. Sir Thomas Roe's last letter assured her that if he had another life to wear out, he would deem it too poor a sacrifice to be offered in her cause. The Queen of Bohemia's only comfort as the second anniversary of the raising of the Standard approached was in the growing fame of her second son.

Prince Rupert, who had desired to leave his bones in England, had been created Earl of Holderness and Duke of Cumberland. The mere sight of the young victor of Chalgrove field in their midst put spirit into his uncle's troops. He was enormously popular in the camp, but not much liked by the nobles and officials of Charles I's Oxford court. To impressionable Puritans, the exotic apparition of an unusually tall and lean black-a-vised foreign prince, wrapped in a scarlet cloak, attended always by a fawning white dog and sometimes also by a gibbering monkey in a green coat, seemed iniquity personified. "Prince Robber," "the Diabolical Cavalier", "the Bloody Prince", had an uncanny habit of appearing where he was least expected. Some of his scared opponents declared that his "Divell Dogge" and "little Whore of Babylon" were familiar spirits who possessed the power of making themselves invisible, and brought their prince of darkness secret tidings as to the movements of godly troops. His mother was amused by Rupert's nicknames, and herself came to call him "Robert le Diable".[1] On July 2nd, 1644, Rupert, whom his followers had begun to acclaim as invincible, suffered a ghastly reverse. Colonel Oliver Cromwell's "New Model" troopers, mostly young yeomen farmers of splendid physique and strong

[1] Hist. MS. Comm. 2nd Report, Appendix, p. 171.

character, were at last ripe for action. Rupert himself narrowly escaped capture; amongst the four thousand Royalist dead left on Marston Moor lay the little white body of "Boy". The dog, who had been the only companion of the prisoner of Linz, had broken his lead and dashed on to the darkening field in search of his master.

Rupert's reputation was not destroyed by his first serious reverse in his uncle's service. Charles I proceeded to appoint him Commander-in-Chief. But the tide had already turned against the Cavaliers. Within thirteen months of Marston Moor came the crushing defeat of Naseby. The Queen of Bohemia never relished the thought that her son's military successes involved the slaughter of thousands of her countrymen. "I know there bee some of my good friends that putt it out that [I] counselled both him and Maurice to go to the King". This, Elizabeth bluntly declared, was "verie false". As for Maurice, she had done her best to get him employment elsewhere. "But I neither coulde nor woulde hinder them from goinge, seeing the King and Queen desiered them."[1] Upon the whole, her eldest son's conduct was causing her the more disquiet. Charles Louis had withdrawn quietly from his uncle's vicinity as soon as hostilities became imminent. He spent his time flitting between his mother's court at the Hague and Essex House, London, whence he assured his uncle's enemies that neither he nor his mother were responsible for the actions of Rupert and Maurice. Elizabeth confessed that she "did not much approve the fashion" in which Charles Louis had left her brother. "I thought his honnour somewhat ingaged in it. . . . I thought it not much to his honnour to leave him at that time. . . I fear, he getts but little reputation as he lyves now heere, in these active times." But since the most cautious prince in Europe hinted at considerations beyond his mother's intelligence, the Queen of Bohemia, who never

[1] S.P. 81. 53.228.

abandoned the belief that her favourite son had inherited her sire's brain, resigned herself to the rôle of dowager. "He is now of age to governe himselfe and choose better counsells than mine are and so I leave him to them, not meaning to medle with them." [1]

Rupert's surrender of Bristol, in September 1645, resulted in a quarrel with his uncle, who deprived him of his commission and asked him to leave England. Rupert refused to be condemned unheard, and posted north to Newark, demanding a court martial. He was declared "not guilty of any lack of courage", but his discretion was questioned. He was not reconciled to Charles I until December, and even then remained without a command. In the same month his mother received worse news of another son. Edward was perhaps the handsomest of the dashing Princes Palatine. At one and twenty he was unmistakably a brother of Rupert and Maurice —an upstanding, olive-skinned, haughty young patrician, with the blackest of flashing eyes and curling locks. But, unlike his martial brothers, he possessed polished manners. His mother observed with satisfaction that she had not sent "Ned" to France in vain. Unfortunately Ned stalked Paris unemployed. When the Queen of Bohemia heard that her fourth son's conversion had been effected by a Catholic bride she announced that she wished she was dead. She blamed herself for not having sent him to England to fight for her brother. Charles Louis, from London, said, unhelpfully, that he doubted whether sending Edward to his uncle would have been a way to confirm him in the right faith. So many of Charles I's friends were either Papists or without any religion whatsoever. The head of the family approved his mother's recall of her youngest son from the company of the pervert, and asked her to expedite the dismissal of a Catholic gentleman attendant. Prince Philip's project for raising troops

[1] S.P. 81. 53.228.

for Venetian service must be encouraged. Charles Louis further asked that before parting from Philip his parent should bestow upon him, in addition to a mother's blessing, the threat of a mother's curse should he ever change his religion. Edward's defection had put his eldest brother in a very awkward position. Charles Louis's letters on the subject, composed rather in hopes than fears of their inspection by Parliamentary authorities, offered cold comfort to Elizabeth. He would prefer not to voice his opinion as to the reason why she continued to await her promised pension. He gloomily prophesied that henceforward Edward would be less obedient to his mother than to the Church of Rome, a community which he had undoubtedly joined from interested motives.[1]

But Charles Louis was wrong. Prince Edward Palatine succeeded in becoming an excellent son of his adopted Church, while remaining an affectionate child to a militant Protestant. His prospects of domestic happiness did not sound promising to an idealist parent. Mademoiselle Anne de Gonzague, second daughter of Charles de Gonzague, Duke of Nevers, Montferrat and Mantua, was eight years her bridegroom's senior. She was celebrated in Parisian society for her beauty, wit and great possessions. Her *liaison* with Henry, Duke of Guise— an affair from which the Duke had emerged very shabbily—had caused far less scandal in her circle than her secret sudden marriage to a penniless exile. Her elder sister and co-heiress had recently achieved a royal match. Louise Marie de Gonzague had become the consort of the widower King of Poland. Anne, however, was genuinely infatuated with her ardent, inexperienced young convert. Henceforward her only important intrigues were political. She was known at the French court as "la Princesse Palatine", and under that name, and some pseudonyms, plays a conspicuous part in contemporary French memoirs and fiction. Edward, for his part, settled down

[1] Bromley, pp. 127–30.

gratefully to improved circumstances, and never appeared to find his career as *le mari de madame* oppressive. He rolled in his splendid coach to every fashionable festivity; he served France in arms with credit. When he was thirty-six his aunt, Henrietta Maria, gladly availed herself of the escort of so presentable a relative of her own faith for a visit to England. Edward had a strong sense of family ties. In 1651 he achieved some fleeting notoriety by offering a public insult to Cromwell's representatives as they proceeded through the streets of the Hague to an audience with the States General. Although Elizabeth was obliged to ask him to apologize to her hosts, she was not displeased by his action. Ned, she said, had only called the pretended ambassadors by their true names. Three times during the first seven years of Edward's marriage, an express from Paris dutifully informed the Queen of Bohemia that she had a beautiful little grand-daughter. Elizabeth found herself totally unable to sustain righteous indignation against her handsomest son, who never applied to her for money. The persistent amiability of Edward and his wife wore her down. Before too long the couple penetrated to the Hague. Princess Edward Palatine tactfully patronized the Queen of Bohemia's favourite artist. Companion portraits of her Catholic son and daughter-in-law appeared on the walls of the Queen of Bohemia's palace. The likeness of Edward, in full armour and a scarlet cloak, offered its own explanation as to his reinstatement in his mother's lacerated heart. That of his wife equally told its own story. "La Princesse Palatine", in a modish masquing costume, appeared as no more than a conventionally pretty woman with refined features lit by an unalarming degree of intelligence.[1]

[1] These pictures are now at Hampstead Marshall. They formed part of the gallery of family portraits left by the Queen of Bohemia.

VII

Prince Philip Palatine was the unluckiest of the Queen of Bohemia's unfortunate children. Six months after his brother's apostasy he performed an action which caused even more scandal. The memoirs of Elizabeth's youngest daughter affirm that at this date slander was very prevalent at the Hague. Contemporary accounts of the murder of M. de l'Epinay certainly bear out this statement.

Lieutenant Colonel Jacques de l'Epinay, Sieur de Vaux, was a young French exile of insinuating manners. The widowed queen, who had reached the age of fifty, saw nothing amiss in him, and shut her ears to rumours that his reputation was unwholesome. She did not usually like Frenchmen, but she was prepared to make an exception in the case of this witty young dog. Her children did not share her opinion of their new acquaintance. Charles Louis, on one of his visits to her court, was umbraged by the sight of his mother walking in the Lange Voorhout attended by a cavalier who was wearing his hat. Oblivious that rain was falling and that the queen might have desired her companion to remain covered on that account, Charles Louis knocked off the headgear of a notorious lady-killer. Prince Philip, aged nearly nineteen, asked M. de l'Epinay to discontinue haunting the Wassenaer Hof. The frequency and length of the French gallant's visits were causing people to ask which royal lady there was the attraction. M. de l'Epinay maddeningly replied that he would cease calling upon the queen when she asked him to desist. The Hague heard of a duel in the Bosch between the French colonel and the young Palatine, frustrated by the arrival of the watch. Between ten and eleven on the night of June 20th, 1646, Prince Philip was returning to his mother's palace along the Vijverberg with a single attendant, when he came into collision with M. de l'Epinay and three French satellites. A street brawl worthy of the houses of Montagu and Capulet ensued, in the course of which witty Mercutio, personified by M. de l'Epinay, exercised his active tongue at the expense of the penniless Palatines. Unfortunately the youngest son of the Queen of Bohemia was indeed a fiery Tybalt. Next evening as he drove through the Place d'Armes, he caught sight of his assailant of last night, complacently returning from a dinner-party at the French Embassy. The French gallant had time to draw his sword before the young Palatine sprang upon him, and he succeeded in inflicting a slight wound. Prince Philip, who had not paused to reflect that his only weapon was a hunting-knife, used that with such effect that he severed his enemy's jugular vein.[1] Fiery Tybalt proceeded to pluck his weapon from the lifeless body of his foe, fling it far from him and, mounting back into his coach, give the order for headlong flight to the Spanish Netherlands frontier.

Naturally so good a story was soon supplied with all it needed to bring it to perfection—the addition of a love interest. The mortal insult which the young Palatine had wiped out in blood had been directed against the ladies of his house. The unconventional artist princess Louise was so universally appointed the heroine of this romance that, when a French lady of high rank visited the Hague a few months later, she observed the second daughter of the Queen of Bohemia with particular interest. Madame de Longueville's spiteful comment was that nobody who had seen the Princess Louise would envy her countryman his martyrdom. Elizabeth was reported "bowed weeping from her high sphere, bewailing the misfortune of having such a son". This rings true. That her unemployable supernumerary sons should drift into courses unworthy of their high birth and pretensions had always been her nightmare. The curriculum of the Prinsenhof,

[1] Contemporary accounts differ as to whether de l'Epinay was unarmed.

remarkable for its rigid insistence on tedious etiquette, had been designed to combat exactly these dangers. The great business of keeping up appearances at all costs had received a mortal blow from Prince Philip as surely as M. de l'Epinay. She had, moreover, a strong personal reason for grief. The most scurrilous rumours consequent on her son's action declared that the taunt which had provoked Prince Philip to murder had been a boast of the French Don Juan that he had enjoyed the favours not only of the Princess Louise, but also of her widowed mother.

No word of Elizabeth on this dark affair has survived. There is evidence that she expressed violent disapproval of her son's behaviour,[1] but stories that she forbade him her presence for ever, that she accused her eldest daughter of having instigated a premeditated crime, and that her unkindness drove the Princess Elizabeth from home for ever, are disproved by after events. Princess Elizabeth did leave the Hague in the autumn after the tragedy, but she returned, and to the day of her mother's death was in constant correspondence with her. The Queen of Bohemia had no occasion to deny her son admittance to her palace. On July 4th, when a Proclamation of the States General summoned him and his suite to trial at the Hague, he was already at Hamburg. In spite of repeated summonses he never appeared to answer the Dutch legal authorities, but in 1648 he accepted an invitation of the Princess of Orange to meet her brothers at a banquet. Evidently the French Embassy had ceased to press for explanations of the violent death of a dissipated political exile, and the States General had decided to let ill alone. The following letter from Charles Louis, singularly involved in style and disagreeable in tone, is printed in full, as it is one of the few contemporary sources of information on this family tragedy.

[1] Bromley, pp. 133-4.

To the Queen.

MADAM,

My brother Rupert sending this bearer to your Majesty about his business, I cannot omit to accompany him with my humble request in favour of the suit he hath to you in my brother's behalf; which, since he can more fully represent it to your Majesty, and that I have by the last post acquainted you with it, I will not be farther troublesome therein. Only Madam, give me leave to beg your pardon in my brother Philip's behalf, which I should have done sooner, if I could have thought that he needed it. The consideration of his youth, of the affront he received, of the blemish had lain upon him all his life-time if he had not resented it; but much more that of his blood, and of his nearness to you, and to him to whose ashes you have ever professed more love and value than to anything upon earth, cannot but be sufficient to efface any ill impressions which the unworthy representation of the fact, by those who joy in the divisions of our family, may have made in your mind against him. But I hope I am deceived in what I hear of this, and that this precaution of mine will seem but impertinent, and will more justly deserve forgiving than my brother's action; since I will still be confident, that the good of your children, the honour of your family, and your own, will prevail with you against any other consideration; and thus I rest

Your Majesty's most humble and obedient son and servant

CHARLES.

July 10th, 1646.[1]

The remainder of Prince Philip's brief career was not distinguished. He duly went over to England, where his eldest brother had received Parliament's consent that he should attempt to raise troops for Venetian service. The result was

[1] Bromley, pp. 133-4.

disappointing, and he was not happy in his first employers, who, he wrote to his brother Rupert, were "unworthy pantaloons".[1][2] He passed on to offer his inexperienced sword to Spain, to France. He degenerated into exactly what Elizabeth had sworn that none of her sons should become, a soldier of fortune. Few flashes of light illuminate his wanderings, in which he was attended by a faithful English squire, a tall young man of the name of Craven. On the night of February 16th, 1650, the casualty list, after a Spanish attack on an obscure fortress of the Ardennes, contained the name of a young cavalry officer, Prince John Philip Frederick Palatine, aged 23. When this news reached the Princess Elizabeth Palatine at Krossen on the Silesian border, she was unable to sleep for several nights. "The image of my dear brother Philip was continually before my eyes."[3] The youngest daughter of the Queen of Bohemia, whose memoirs contain lively descriptions of many members of her family only once mentions the name of the brother nearest to her in age. But she took a portrait of him with her to her new home when she married. This likeness of Prince Philip, painted by Honthorst before the nine days' wonder of the de l'Epinay murder, shows a pale, thin-faced youth with light eyes and lank, tawny hair. His features are sharp, his expression is pathetic but not pleasant.[4]

[1] Scott, p. 212.

[2] Several subsequent letters of Prince Philip addressed to his eldest brother and to William Curtius, his late father's secretary, survive, but they contain no interesting details. Hauck, *Briefe der Kinder, etc.*, pp. 36–8, 42, 44.

[3] Godfrey, pp. 239–40.

[4] Contemporary accounts of the murder of M. de l'Epinay by Prince Philip Palatine differ in detail. See *Theatrum Europaeum*, v. 880; *Théâtre du Monde*, p. 1646; Heinsius, iii. 709; Van Sypesteyn, pp. 39–41. Söltl, in his Life of Elizabeth Stuart, published 1840 (pp. 402–3), and Varnhagen in his Life of Sophia Charlotte of Prussia, published 1872 (pp. 247–8), repeat without criticism or explanation the scandal that de l'Epinay had been the lover of the widowed queen.

VIII

Twenty-two years after the travel-worn procession of the Winter Queen had swept past the walls of Münster, hurrying towards safety and exile, ambassadors of many nations began to converge upon the ancient cathedral city. The Thirty Years War was drawing towards its close. Two towns of Westphalia had been adjudged neutral territory and chosen as the scenes of peace negotiations. At Osnabrück, Count John Oxenstierna, eldest son of the famous Chancellor, never showed himself except in semi-royal state. The King of Denmark's representatives, instructed by their deep-drinking master to spare no expense, launched into spectacular entertainments. The French plenipotentiaries arrived at Münster ten months after the official date fixed for the opening of the great peace conference, and their pompous entry into the town lasted an hour. No nation wished to appear exhausted by the sacrifices of the all-destructive struggle, or the first to sue for a cessation of hostilities. For another four years the picturesque arcaded streets of Münster and the winding lanes of Osnabrück echoed to the babble of many tongues. Oxenstierna brought forward the Swedish propositions in Latin. The King of Spain's principal envoy, a gorgeous grandee, wrangled interminably with the United Provinces, each of which was individually and stolidly represented. To add to the confusion, the Swedes at Osnabrück and the French at Münster quarrelled amongst themselves. That affairs progressed as fast as they did was largely due to the Emperor's chief representative. Count Maximilian von Trautsmansdorff had inherited some of the theories of the murdered Wallenstein; he was determined to carry his task to a successful issue and was celebrated for his tact and personal charm.

At length, on October 27th, 1648, the Peace of Westphalia was signed at Münster, in the presence of plenipotentiaries of every Christian power. The Kings of England and Poland were included in the treaty as allies of the Empire and Sweden; the Grand Duke of Muscovy as the ally of Sweden only. The setting was worthy of the historic occasion. The eminent men of all nations, whose portraits were destined to decorate the walls of the Friedensaal, moved against a stately background of well-waxed panelling. Through windows filled with stained-glass coats of arms, the autumn morning light cast patches of warring colour upon many a sombre gown of velvet and cloth, and the scarlet silks of a cardinal who was a future Pope.

The settlement, as far as the Palatinate was concerned, was not the "all or nothing" demanded by the Queen of Bohemia in her younger days. The proud title of First Elector of the Empire, of which her husband had been deprived, was not restored to her son. That, together with the whole of the Upper Palatinate, remained the property of Maximilian of Bavaria. The Bergstrasse went to the Elector of Mainz, Germersheim to Hesse. An eighth electorate, ranking least in dignity, was specially created for the benefit of the young ruler of the Lower Palatinate. A subsidiary clause of the treaty declared that in case of failure in Maximilian's line, the Electoral title and Palatine territory enjoyed by him should return to the family of Charles Louis. Moreover, the diminished inheritance awaiting the peaceful arrival of its long-exiled owner was no longer the paradise remembered by the Queen of Bohemia. Thirty years of march and countermarch, siege, relief, invasion, occupation and devastation by friend and foe alike, had altered the face of the "Garden of Germany". In districts of the Rhineland famed for their vineyards and cattle, the bodies of peasants who had dropped by the roadside chewing grass to assuage the pangs of starvation, lay rotting unburied. Between famine, disease, emigration and death by fire and sword, the population of the Lower Palatinate was now reckoned at one tenth of its pre-war figure. Home, however, was once more to be Heidelberg, though a Heidelberg horribly mutilated, and for the attractive sisters of a reigning prince, however poor, there would be matrimonial prospects. Many more months were to pass before the Helen of Germany realized that personally she was rather a loser than a gainer by the treaty signed at Münster. Meanwhile her attention was painfully obsessed by the march of events in her native country. At a time when she had good reason for the first time in years to feel hopeful, fresh calamity was about to overtake her.

Rejoicings at the Hague in honour of the great peace were still in progress when the news arrived that Charles I had been brought under guard to his capital to be tried for his life by his own subjects. All signs of festivity in the house of the Queen of Bohemia were instantly extinguished, and on January 19th, 1649, a London publication, "The Army's Moderate Intelligencer", reported that the Lady Elizabeth was making arrangements to sail for home. Her brother's trial began the next day. "Her affection", said he in one of his last letters, "truly speaks her my sister." Needless to say, the authorities, who had already decided on the abolition of the monarchy in England, had no intention of allowing a popular royal lady to land there at this critical moment. Elizabeth got her first accounts of her brother's sufferings from public prints and flying rumours.

The King of England had been hurried from Westminster Hall while struggling to speak in his defence. English soldiers had broken off shouting "Justice!" and "Execution!" to puff tobacco-smoke in his face. Two days later, Lord Northumberland, the husband of the Lady Elizabeth's old playmate Frances Devereux, brought a little prince and princess by coach from Syon House to St James's to receive a father's last blessing. The Elector Palatine's offer to wait upon his Majesty was firmly declined by the condemned man. At one-thirty on the bitterly cold afternoon of January 30th, the King of England walked out through one of the windows of the Banqueting House of Whitehall on to a scaffold draped in black. There two muscular men, dressed in coarse, tightly fitting woollen clothes and masks awaited him. The groan which went up from the London crowd a few minutes later was echoed throughout Europe. The Queen of Bohemia, who had abstained from identifying herself with her brother's policy while he was alive, became fiercely and openly royalist from that moment. She cut off for ever all communications with her Parliamentarian friends, and her language regarding them was violent. She refused to recognize the existence of the Commonwealth, and when, as a result, her English pension was cancelled, she fought what she described as the decision of a "mock Parliament" with the assistance of the States General. Her household received an intimation that any person holding intercourse with the so-called English Ambassadors at the Hague would be thrown down her stairs and kicked out of doors. As to the identity of "his pretious highness" [1] the Lord Protector, she was never in any doubt. He was the Beast described in the Book of Revelation. "I wish him the like end and speedilie." [2] Five years after the tragedy at Whitehall the Queen of Bohemia's steward wrote to her eldest son that he had not dared to suggest that she should apply personally "to Cromwell, in the behalfe of her creditors . . . being most certaine shee would never consent to it, but onely fly into a passion against those who should advise her to it". [3] In 1658 the Queen of Bohemia's pew in the English church at the Hague stood "naked and voyd, she having taken away the hangings and cushions". The clergyman now officiating at the church where she had so long worshipped did not pray for the King of England. [4] The anniversary of

[1] Evelyn, v. 262. [2] *Ibid.*, 214. [3] Cottrell MS. [4] Thurloe, vii. 257.

the martyrdom of King Charles was kept as a day of perpetual mourning in her court, and she wore continually upon her finger a ring bearing the initials C. R. The lock of hair which it contained was of a greying tint. The brother whom she remembered as a diffident stammering boy of thirteen had been brilliantly golden-haired.

When Charles Louis made a decidedly ignominious re-appearance at the Hague in the April after the tragedy, his mother enclosed him with her, in her bedchamber, for an interview so unpleasant that he recalled it with resentment five years later.[1] This interview was momentous. It marked the beginning of the end of Charles Louis's happy relations with his mother. Elizabeth enquired her favourite son's "intentions" with nothing of her usual "mildness and complaisance". She proceeded to dictate his conduct. He must pay his court to the new King of England, and refrain from visiting the Parliamentary agent to the States General. Charles Louis, who had left London requesting his friends there to continue his pension, suggested that his cousin might not wish to see him. But the very ugly French-looking youth of nineteen who was now Charles II had particularly easy manners, and a family party at Rhenen, engineered by Elizabeth, passed off without a hitch. Charles Louis then departed to take up the only career open to him, that of the Restorer of the Rhenish Palatinate. He was thirty-one and at last in a position

---

[1] Bromley, p. 178. Amongst the exploits of Charles Louis in England had been siring the first grandson of the Queen of Bohemia. The Elector Palatine had reached his thirties without being able to make a suitable marriage. His father had been a proud and loving parent at seventeen. Elizabeth had the boy, who was known as "Freiherrn von Selz" and "Ludwig von Rotenschild", to stay at the Wassenaer Hof early in 1660, and sympathized with her son when the boy died suddenly, a few months later, in Paris, where he had been sent to be educated under the roof of Prince Edward Palatine. Charles Louis was passionately devoted to his son by an unnamed English lady. In one of his letters (Wendland, 88) he hints that both parents were of exalted rank. Elizabeth was well aware of the existence of another—German—mistress of her son, "Limbourg". *Ibid.*, p. 181.

to take a wife. He meant to marry suitably and raise a family. His conduct during his uncle's trial had not been much worse than that of his grandfather during the trial of Mary, Queen of Scots,[1] but he had the chagrin of knowing that he had sacrificed his reputation in vain. The most calculating prince in Europe had lamentably failed to foresee the possibilities of General Cromwell. At Cleves, a letter from his mother, upbraiding him for neglecting to condole with the widow of King Charles the Martyr, enlivened the journey of the Elector Palatine towards his devastated principality.[2]

IX

A few weeks before Elizabeth realized with disillusionment that her favourite son was no hero, a true hero visited her court.

The old house which had been her home for upwards of quarter of a century now proclaimed her increasing poverty. It had been built upon insecure foundations of peaty soil. Great cracks were beginning to appear in its walls; many of its beams showed signs of dry rot.[3] At some date during February 1649, a Scottish gentleman of slight and active figure, with a quiet brow, penetrative grey eyes and a stately carriage, crossed the threshold of the Wassenaer Hof and passed through its tapestry-hung hall and outer chambers, dimly lit by small windows filled with brilliant coats of arms, towards the presence of his murdered master's beloved sister. James Graham, Marquis of Montrose, who had fainted on hearing of the execution of Charles I, had come to the Hague to offer his services and advice to Charles II. He was well known to Elizabeth by reputation. Her soldier son Maurice had served with him. No evidence exists as to whether the poet-general

---

[1] Elizabeth took a lenient view of James I's conduct. "As for my father, he coulde punish none for my Grandmother's death, they being not in his hands, and dead before he came into England, Queene Elisabeth having disavoued the fact" (Wendland, pp. 173-4).

[2] Bromley, p. 150.   [3] de Vink, p. 147.

first saw the tarnished gilded leathers and fraying silk panels of the Queen of Bohemia's audience chambers by winter daylight or by candle-light. He left the Hague again in March, with the title of Lieutenant-General of Scotland, bound for Denmark and Sweden to raise money and troops. According to the memoirs of Elizabeth's youngest daughter, the hand of the artist princess Louise was demanded by him as a reward for victory. There is undoubted evidence that, short though their acquaintance was and shadowed throughout by tragedy, the Great Marquis and the Winter Queen understood one another instantly and perfectly. Ten letters from Elizabeth addressed to Montrose between June 1649 and January 1650 are forthcoming.[1] Their note is that of intimate friendship.

Montrose's great anxiety was lest the desperate young king should accept the invitation of Scottish Covenanting Commissioners to proceed to his northern kingdom. The Commissioners' terms included the imposition of the Covenant upon the monarch and the entire Scottish kingdom, and an engagement by Charles to dismiss Montrose and land in Scotland accompanied by not more than a hundred persons, none of whom had served his late father. The Commissioners arrived at the Hague in March, and waited upon the Queen of Bohemia. They solemnly besought a Scottish-born princess to use her influence with her nephew. They were convinced that the miseries of their nation were the result of the evil advice accepted by the late king. If Charles II would entrust himself to their direction, all should go well. The grim deputation sat to meat in the Queen of Bohemia's dining-room, but a courteous hostess made them no promises. When they had taken their leave, she wrote to "Jamie Grame" that she had erected his portrait in her cabinet "to fright away the

---

[1] Montrose MS. at Buchanan Castle. Hist. MSS. Commission, Appendix to Second report, p. 171.

bretheren". She had learnt by chance that the Prince of Orange was likely to press her nephew "extremely" to grant their requests, and so ruin himself. Fortunately the king was at the moment more attracted by the idea of a descent upon Ireland, where Rupert, in command of a squadron of seven loyal men-of-war, was blocking Kinsale harbour.

While she wrote thus cheerfully, the Queen of Bohemia was engaged in a heart-breaking business—the dispersal of her stable. She, with whom horses were a passion, had been brought to realize that she could no longer afford to go "riding a' hunting". From Rhenen, "a place very barren of news, especially of English affairs" which were kept "so in a cloud" that she could be certain of nothing, she requested the marquis to find employment for several old servants, one of whom was the nephew of her late Master of the Horse. She was spending her days, now that she had no hunters, taking exercise on foot and "renewing herself" in the art of shooting at the butts. She flattered herself that she was becoming no mean archer, and hoped one day to challenge her correspondent to a match. Lord Jermyn, Henrietta Maria's Majordomo, was coming to Holland—according to some accounts to make arrangements concerning the sale of more royal jewellery, according to others to concert with the Duke of Hamilton, Lord Lauderdale and the Commissioners "to cross wicked Jamie Grahame's proceedings. But this will lead to nothing, as the King is constant to his principles. . . . They say Rupert is at sea. . . . Many letters say all goes ill in Ireland." The Queen of Bohemia's last letter to the Marquis of Montrose dated January 16th, 1650, prayed God to send him safety in Scotland.

Montrose sailed for the Orkneys in mid-March, 1650, to take command of a small force which had been sent before him. On April 27th he was surprised and routed at Corbiesdale in Ross-shire. On May 21st "that detestable bloodie murtherer and excommunicated traitour James Gream" was hung, drawn and quartered in the Grassmarket of Edinburgh. Charles II, who had accepted the Commissioners' terms before he heard of Montrose's defeat, was greeted on his arrival in Scotland by the spectacle of dismembered limbs of his late Lieutenant-General decorating the high places of his dearly bought kingdom. During the next twelve months he had ample reason to regret his rejection of the advice offered by his idealistic aunt, who made a special expedition to Breda to plead with him not to listen to the enemies of Montrose.[1]

x

By the close of the year which witnessed the execution of Montrose, the Queen of Bohemia's most congenial daughter, "my second girll, Louyse", was the only one of her children left under her roof.

The second wedding in Elizabeth's family was far more pleasing to her than the first. The marriage of Charles Louis, which took place in February, 1650, promised admirably. The nineteen-year-old bride was said to be a blonde beauty, and was certainly well dowered. She was a rose of Hesse, the house in which Henry, Prince of Wales, had once dreamt of finding the ideal Protestant princess. Charlotte Elizabeth, sister of the Landgrave of Hesse Cassel, was already connected with her bridegroom's family. She was a great-grand-daughter of William the Silent. Her sister-in-law, Hedwig of Brandenburg, was a first cousin of Charles Louis. Within a few months of the wedding Elizabeth heard news from Heidelberg which had a familiar ring. The Electress Palatine persisted in hunting, although she was pregnant. His young mother became possessively devoted to the sickly little Charles, whom she nicknamed "Karellie". Charles Louis much preferred the healthy girl born in the following year. The pleasantest

[1] *Memoirs of Sophie, Electress of Hanover*, p. 23.

passages in his letters to his mother were those in which he dwelt with paternal pride on the charm and liveliness of his daughter Elizabeth Charlotte—"Liselotte".

As soon as he was settled in his capital, Charles Louis invited his eldest and youngest sisters, and his brother Edward, to visit him. All accepted, but the Princess Elizabeth, who was staying with the Dowager Electress of Brandenburg at Krossen, on the Silesian frontier, was detained there some months by what her brother described in letters to the Hague as "the Transylvanian business". This business was romantic. At last a solid offer of marriage had been made for a daughter of the Queen of Bohemia. It was for the beauty of the family, the Princess Henrietta, aged twenty-four. Charles Louis's reinstatement had come too late for his elder sisters. The Princess Elizabeth at thirty-two was rather stout and very serious. When she finally arrived at Heidelberg, her elegant Parisian brother Edward asked her sister Sophie, "What has become of her spirits? Whither has her entertaining conversation vanished?" [1] The spirits of the Princess Elizabeth, which had never been high, had recently received their quietus. Reserve had always been the key-note of her character. Apparently no member of her family realized any connection between the change in her and the death, in Sweden, of a French philosopher.

XI

M. René Descartes made his first appearance at the Queen of Bohemia's court during the winter of 1640. The famous philosopher had been resident in Holland since 1637, but there were reasons why he had not hitherto been presented to the Winter Queen. There was much in his history that must be obnoxious to her. He had been educated at the Jesuit college

[1] *Memoirs of Sophie, Electress of Hanover*, p. 42.

of La Flèche. As a young volunteer in the service of
Maximilian of Bavaria, he had assisted at the Battle of the
White Mountain, and watched the enemies of the Winter
King go into action to the cry of "Santa Maria!" The appearance of M. Descartes at forty-four, however, was not
reminiscent of his career in arms. The Queen of Bohemia
welcomed to her circle a man of letters who was obviously
of good family and in weak health. M. Descartes had sold his
seigneurie in Poitou, and was at the moment the owner of a
charming little property called Endegeest, near Leyden.
To make expeditions from the Hague, "disguised as bour-
goises", to visit the sage in his picturesque seclusion, was a
favourite pursuit of ladies of intellectual pretensions. At
Endegeest they enjoyed bachelor hospitality in perfection.
M. Descartes employed, in his moated château, a first-class
French cook and a devoted valet who was also a mathema-
tician. Naturally Princess Elizabeth joined a party bound for
idyllic Endegeest.

It is unlikely that the Queen of Bohemia made any diligent
efforts to comprehend the Cartesian philosophy, but she
offered no objection to her scholar daughter becoming a
disciple of the fashionable savant. It transpired that the
princess, whose learning had won her the lovely name of
"The Star of the North",[1] could not study in moderation.
The theories of M. Descartes seemed to promise her an explanation of her existence. She had always been of a ductile disposition, too ready, complained her mother, to be "governed
all by one person".[2] The person in that case had not been
the Queen of Bohemia. The Princess Elizabeth's violent
schoolgirl friendship with a lady of her mother's household
had come, after the manner of such affairs, to a disappointing

---

[1] Elizabeth was nicknamed by her sisters "La Grecque". In one letter to
her brother, dated April 17th, 1660, she refers to herself as "Else". *Briefe der
Kinder des Winterkönigs.*

[2] S.P. 16. 311.22.

end. Mrs Crofts had revealed herself as a shallow and unworthy character. On a visit to England, she had regaled the Papist queen's court with many humiliating disclosures as to life at the court of the starveling Palatines.[1] The Princess Elizabeth pined for a true and helpful friend. She pored over the philosophy of her new acquaintance until her long, sad nose, always her worst feature, grew red as fire. The Queen of Bohemia liked her daughters to wait upon her every evening. These formal visits, which were part of the eternal business of keeping up royal appearances, were a source of apprehension to the princesses. Her Majesty had an eagle eye for any oddity of costume or manner, and her much-praised sweetness of temper was not always remarkable in her dealings with her daughters. The four handsome, talented, shabby princesses could not understand why the mere sight of them, trooping in to kiss her hand and recount their day's adventures, sometimes seemed to madden their incurably youthful mother. Far from making attempts to find them husbands, she seemed rather inclined to stamp upon such tentative proposals as arose from time to time. They did not realize that the Queen of Bohemia knew all too well that no solid offers would result, and that she would only expose her daughters to humiliation by ardent match-making on their behalf. Her bitter resentment that she could not provide them with even a semblance of the fun and frivolity which had been lavished upon her in her teens, expressed itself in sharp criticism and impatient orders. "How", asked the Princess Elizabeth in despair, "am I to go to our mother with this nose?" "Do you", enquired Princess Louise, "wish us to wait until you have got another?" [2]

For a little over two years, while M. Descartes abode at Endegeest, the Princess Elizabeth experienced, if not happiness, at any rate an unusual existence, full of startling sunshine and

[1] Bromley, p. 88.   [2] *Memoirs of Sophie, Electress of Hanover*, p. 14.

terrifying shade. Her labours under the direction of her new
great friend were prodigious. The sage recommended female
scholars to study Geometry and Algebra. The Princess
Elizabeth applied herself to the exact sciences, and her astonished
master pronounced that in her alone were united those generally
separated talents for metaphysics and mathematics which were
characteristically co-operative in the Cartesian system. Presently
he announced to the most retiring of her sex his decision to
dedicate his *Meister-werk* to her. "I have never met anyone
who could so thoroughly understand all that is contained in
my writings."

The end of this happy relationship came suddenly. M.
Descartes, an inveterate wanderer, discovered that he had been
in the vicinity of Leyden long enough. He sold his property
and purchased another even more desirable, but not nearly so
close to the Hague. He re-visited France. Henceforward
he met his best pupil seldom. But the blow of separation
was softened by his promise to continue her instruction by
correspondence. The Princess Elizabeth, who fell ill soon after
her philosopher's departure, became the recipient of many
bracing letters. She employed her little sister Sophie to forward
her replies. There was nothing in them that might not have
met the eye of the Queen of Bohemia. Nothing in the nature
of a flirtation had ever taken place between the Sage of Endegeest and the Star of the North. M. Descartes would never
so far have forgotten himself as to address an amorous glance
or word to the penniless royal lady who had refused the King
of Poland. The Princess of Bohemia would never have dismayed and disgusted her famous and refined teacher by a display of low emotionalism. Nevertheless, for another seven
years the letter from M. Descartes occupied the first place in
the Princess Elizabeth's mind. Then came a trial more difficult
to bear. After long coquetting with the idea, M. Descartes
decided to accept the dazzling invitation of the young Queen

of Sweden to repair to her court. He was surprised that his
Princess and his Queen, who had philosophic tastes in common,
did not receive with enthusiasm his well-meant suggestion
that they must become great friends.

M. Descartes' splendid young queen killed him in twelve
weeks. The Princess Elizabeth received one letter from
Stockholm extolling the virtues and accomplishments of the
exuberant Christina, who could offer her philosopher so much
—a country estate, a title. . . . M. Descartes did not divulge
that Christina was inconsiderate enough to summon him to
give her instruction in bed before 6 A.M. in the depths of a
Swedish winter. On a dark day, early in 1650, the Princess
Elizabeth received a lachrymose epistle from a stranger in
Stockholm, telling her that her renowned friend had succumbed
to pneumonia after a short illness. She received this news at
Krossen, where she was busy with the preparations for her
sister Henrietta's betrothal. She drove this business to a
successful conclusion, more in the manner of a benevolent
maiden aunt than an elder sister, and then repaired to Heidelberg, where her changed looks shocked her family.

At the age of forty-two the Princess Elizabeth became a
Canoness of Herford, an ancient Westphalian convent which
had been Protestantized after the Reformation. At the age of
forty-nine she was enthroned as Abbess of this community.
When Princess Sophie heard of her sister's election, she wrote
to the Elector Palatine that for the first time in her life Elizabeth had succeeded in something. Sophie, much the successful
young matron, visited her eldest sister at intervals, and was
appalled by her situation—surrounded by companions of
gloomy piety and deprived of all amusements. The establishment of Herford did not become a centre of scholasticism or
attain any new celebrity under its erudite abbess. Elizabeth
died in her sixty-second year, after a long and agonizing illness
which she bore with the resignation which was always a leading

trait of her character. However it is told, the story of the
Queen of Bohemia's eldest daughter is pathetic.[1]

XII

The Dutch seventeenth-century kitchen, with its sun-
splashed tiled floors and glittering array of well-polished culinary
utensils, was an attractive place, as is attested by many contemporary paintings. While her brothers Rupert and Maurice
led cavalry charges and scoured the high seas in men-of-war,
and her sisters Elizabeth and Louise wrote page upon page to
M. René Descartes and filled innumerable canvases under the
tuition of Gerard van Honthorst, the Princess Henrietta
Palatine was happy in the kitchen. "Nennie", as her mother
called her, was the perfect little *Hausfrau*. "Her talents lay
in the direction of embroidery and preserve-making." Princess Sophie, who had the sweet-tooth natural to her age,
urged her prettiest sister on to fresh triumphs of confectionery.[2]
Princess Henrietta, who had inherited her mother's cloud of
fair curly hair and large grey-blue eyes, was distressingly
fragile. More than once her family thought that they had lost
her. She was universally beloved, for she was as sweet-
tempered as her appearance promised.

On an autumn day of 1650 a family council was held in a
Transylvanian castle bearing the name of Sarosnagypatak.
The widowed mother and elder brother of Prince Siegmund
Rakoczy of Siebenburgen had a choice of three brides to
present to him. The heiress of the Voivode of Moldau was a
near neighbour. A daughter of Count John of Nassau would

---

[1] In the National Portrait Gallery the likeness of a dark-haired young
princess, with haunting almond-shaped eyes and a drooping scarlet mouth
is superscribed—"Friend and correspondent of Descartes". The princess,
who desired to be buried without a funeral oration, "which is but flattery",
would undoubtedly have rejoiced to be so remembered.

[2] *Memoirs of Sophie, Electress of Hanover*, p. 16.

also bring a handsome dowry. The third sister of the Elector Palatine was the best match as far as birth was concerned. But the titular Queen of Bohemia was well known to be fantastically in debt, and her son was but newly established in devastated dominions. Prince Siegmund, a romantic young man of seven and twenty, chose the Cinderella amongst the candidates. George Mednyanski, an envoy newly returned from Heidelberg, had brought with him a portrait of the Princess Henrietta Palatine.

When the Princess Elizabeth heard that an offer had been made to her brother for Henrietta, she wrote to him that her only fear was lest their mother "out of crossness" would at the very last moment refuse her consent. But the Princess Elizabeth was wrong. When the Queen of Bohemia heard that a wealthy bachelor prince of unexceptionable character was making a firm offer for her domestic daughter she came forward with an instant and practical suggestion. Her wedding gift would be the coach to carry the girl to her new home. Charles Louis, who liked to pose as the "*Herr Vater*" of his attractive sisters, was the person to prove difficult. He knew that in south-eastern Europe princes were plentiful. Princess Elizabeth wrote to him that the Duke of Courland had assured her that Prince Siegmund's title was acknowledged by the Emperor. A visitor at Krossen, who had recently spent six weeks in an unpronounceable castle belonging to the suitor, reported that Prince Siegmund always kept two hundred men-at-arms and fifty gentlemen in attendance. His large household was invariably served on silver plate. Still Charles Louis was dissatisfied. He hinted that he had another marriage in view for his most marketable sister.

Henrietta, who was with Elizabeth on a visit to Krossen, survived smallpox without damage to her complexion "literally of lilies and roses",[1] but began to be prostrated by

---

[1] *Memoirs of Sophie, Electress of Hanover*, p. 16.

nervousness. Her kind hostess, the Dowager Electress of Brandenburg, did her best to reassure a bride-to-be who looked like fainting when she heard that a wooing ambassador had arrived. The Dowager Electress unhelpfully proceeded to quarrel with Charles Louis. The Rakoczys had very naturally approached her court with their proposals. Her own sister-in-law had been the wife of a Prince of Transylvania. The Rakoczys were no upstarts. The Bohemian village from which they took their name had been in their family since the thirteenth century. Another aunt, Catherine, spinster sister of the Winter King, "fulminated" against the selfishness of her nephew. For several weeks, while the roads were blocked by snow, negotiations were suspended. Princess Elizabeth said sternly that "Nennie" must not give way to foolish fancies. Once she was safely settled amongst good people, she would be happy. But the gentle "Nennie", learning that the head of her family disapproved of her actions, offered "with a torrent of tears", to send back the diamond watch and terrifyingly ardent love-letter from the unknown prince "beyond the woods". Personally she was accustomed to being poor, and would rather not be sent so far, although she was ready to sacrifice herself for the good of her family. Princess Elizabeth doggedly began to buy the trousseau. She sent to Holland for the laces, to Frankfort on the Main for the silver passementerie to adorn the wedding dress. These places offered the best bargains in such commodities. She informed Charles Louis that he would do well to furnish the necessary money and meddle no further with "the richest and most desirable match that could be found amongst the Protestants". Henrietta, who was not well enough to write herself, sent him a message. If she could be provided with just sufficient gowns to cause her new relations to respect her from the first, she would ask for no more. Charles Louis said that the match was not worth so long a pilgrimage, however, his sister would only have to undertake this journey once. Late in March 1651 the marriage articles were signed. The coach promised by the bride's mother materialized, accompanied by a grandiloquent epistle recalling the old alliance between the late King of Bohemia and Transylvania. Ten days before the wedding Princess Elizabeth enquired sarcastically whether her brother imagined that the bride's attendants had wings. No vehicles for their transport had arrived from Heidelberg, and as yet no cash. On May 17th Princess Siegmund, seated in the splendid vehicle somehow conjured into existence by her penniless mother, set off in tears towards her unknown and distant husband. Her wedding by proxy had taken place three days earlier. Her trousseau was pathetically meagre. Princess Elizabeth's list of "barest necessities" included but six night-gowns, twelve chemises, two dozen pocket handkerchiefs in a bag, a few cravats, and five gowns, one of which was the wedding dress. . . .

Princess Elizabeth repaired exhaustedly to Heidelberg, and there, after a due interval, ecstatic letters from the Queen of Bohemia's married daughter gladdened her eyes. Prince Siegmund was "very stately". He drove always with six horses. If he had a single fault it was that he was too kind, too generous. A little sister could not thank the Elector Palatine enough for her happy marriage. All the new relations were caressing her. Yesterday she had put on for the first time the national costume of her new country. "I looked so pretty in it that my lord's mother could not express her pleasure, yet it is not at all a splendid dress—quite *bürgerlich*, resembling that worn by the peasants. This would not please your Highness, but all the ladies wear it. . . . The men are very fine and mostly very well-mannered. . . . I wish my lord could be so happy as to be known to your Highness. Forgive me that I keep you so long with my chatter. . . ."

Princess Henrietta's chatter did not vex her brother long.

One more illiterate epistle assured him of her continued bliss. She apologized for writing briefly. She had been suffering from fever for three days, and felt so tired that she could scarcely stand. A postscript of later date explained that she had been abed again.

Within five months of her daughter's marriage, letters with black seals from Transylvania startled the Queen of Bohemia. Visits with her mother-in-law to the celebrated spas of Tasnyad and Semiyod had not produced the hoped-for improvement in the health of fragile Princess Siegmund. To her husband's despair she had died suddenly and peacefully on a September morning.

The Queen of Bohemia cherished tender memories of the flower of her flock. Years later she explained her extraordinary indulgence of Charles Louis's little daughter with the words, "her shape and humour make me think of my poor Henriette".[1] [2]

XIII

When the Queen of Bohemia's third surviving son was two and twenty and indeed a handsome young officer, his harassed uncle Charles I wrote to him from Oxford—

NEPHEW MAURICE,

Though Mars be now most in vogue, yet Hymen may be sometimes remembered. The matter is this. Your Mother and I have been somewhat engaged concerning a Marriage between your Brother Rupert and Mademoiselle de Rohan, and now her friends press your Brother to a positive answer which I find him resolved to give negatively. Therefor I have thought

---

[1] Wendland, p. 132.

[2] Hauck, *Briefe der Kinder des Winterkönigs*, pp. 63–5; Wendland, *Die Heirath der Princessin Henriette, etc.*, pp. 240–78; Westner, *Die Heirath Henriette, etc.*; Godfrey, *Sister of Prince Rupert*, pp. 225–44. Prince Siegmund wrote, a month after his bride's death, "I hold my life for nothing worth". He survived her but five months.

fit to know if you will not, by your engagement, take your Brother handsomely off.[1]

But Prince Maurice was no more prepared than his brother to go a-wooing the French Protestant heiress, who, to her friends' dismay, had fallen in love with the reputation of Prince Rupert, the cavalier.

While their sisters read philosophy and painted portraits and made preserves, and their mother wrote to Lord Craven that it was certain truth that next week she would have neither bread, meat nor candles in her house, "having no money, nor credit for any", the Princes Rupert and Maurice were continually at sea. Two sons of the princess of Great Britain at whose wedding festivities "The Tempest" had been performed, saw the very isles of which mariners had spoken in the hearing of William Shakespeare. Prince Rupert had got a new commission—Lord High Admiral of his Majesty's Fleet. The brother who was his "shadow" was his Vice-Admiral. Their ships were "all extremely unfurnished both of men and provisions". At Rotterdam, in the winter of 1648–9 the ordnance of the *Antelope*, "a stately ship", had been sold "to victual and rig up the rest. . . . The Queen of Bohemia pawned her jewels, or it had not been done." [2]

The fleet with which they set out for the West Indies in the spring of 1651, numbered five sail—the *Constant Reformation*, the *Swallow*, the *Loyal Subject* and the *Honest Seaman*. Their business, these dark days, was taking prizes at sea—any English ship that refused to salute his Majesty's Lord High Admiral, and, since Spain had allied herself with the Commonwealth, any Spaniard. His Roundhead enemies, in an England no longer merrie, deemed "Prince Robber" happy. Admiral Blake described him outright as "that pyrate". The hawk-faced princes dined to sound of black rushing waters and creaking timbers. They paced blinding decks, watching

[1] Harl. MS. 6988.149.   [2] Warburton, iii. 273, 286.

haggard men, with their sweating brows tied up in pied handkerchiefs, toiling at the oars, dreaming of a cloud on the horizon that might prove an island rich in negroes and elephants and rose-emeralds and strong liquors. "Misfortunes being no novelty to us, we plough the sea for a subsistence, poverty and despair being our companions, and revenge our guide." They had their successes. "Two proper ships, the *John Adventure* and the *Hopeful Adventure*, both bound from London for St Lucar", were taken by Rupert *en route* for Portugal, after defending themselves stoutly. "The *Marmaduke of London*, bound for Archangel in Muscovy," surrendered to Maurice after a running fight off the Barbary shore. The Queen of Bohemia heard with satisfaction that the King of Portugal, "a young man of great hope and courage", learning that an English fleet, commanded by a Prince of the Blood, was hovering off his coasts, had invited Rupert to his court and been "extreme kind and civil".[1] But most of her news of her sailor sons came from Public Prints.[2] They sold their captured goods in "the Island of Madeira under the command of the Portugal". Their cavalier Highnesses were received in the Bay of Funchal by the governor and officers of the fort, and taken to see the sights of an island remarkable for cascades of flowers, the eternal patter of mules' hooves, mist on the mountains, and vines springing from soil the colour of tan in the riding-school. The Queen of Bohemia received a packet "from Rupert from the Madera Isle . . . I doe not know now where he is. I woulde he were neerer. . . ."[3]

The abiding fear of the princes was separation. For several days after being parted from Rupert by storm off the coast of Tunis, Maurice, at Toulon, refused to leave his cabin "until it pleased Heaven to remove all obstacles of sorrow by the happy tidings of his brother's safety". They were detained in the

[1] Cary's *Memorials*, 2. 164.   [2] S.P. 28.1.54.   [3] Wendland, p. 20.

luscious Azores five months, by officers and men who were not minded to make on to the Barbadoes, and during that time were driven out to sea by a tempest in which the Admiral lost his flagship, and very nearly his life. "Prince Maurice, bearing under his stern, and being sadly sensible of his brother's ruin, was not apprehensive of his own, but commanded his master to lay him aboard, resolving to save his brother or perish with him. But the officers, in mutinous words, refused to obey him in such a case, and not without reason. . . . The Princes endeavoured to speak to one another, but the hideous noise of the winds and seas overnoised their voices. . . ." [1]

Exactly a year later, the final separation they had long dreaded took place. Within twelve leagues of the Virgin Isles they ran into what "they call in these parts a hierecane . . . the sails blew quite away. . . . We lay at the mercy of God." The weather, that midnight of September 14th, 1652, was "so thick we could not discern our ship's length before us." The Admiral's crew guessed afterwards that they had driven betwixt a high rock ominously named the Sombrero, and "an island called Anguilita where never ships were known to sail before". On the third day the hurricane abated, but Rupert's ship alone arrived at the uninhabited isle of St. Anne in the Virgins.

"In this fatal wreck, besides a great many brave gentlemen and others, the sea, to glut itself, swallowed Prince Maurice, whose fame the mouth of detraction cannot blast, his very enemies bewailing his loss. Many had more power, few more merit: he was snatched from us in obscurity." [2] In the opinion of most contemporaries Prince Maurice was far inferior to Prince Rupert as a commander. "He understood very little more of the war than to fight very stoutly where there was occasion."

The Queen of Bohemia, after the manner of mothers,

---

[1] Warburton, iii. 334.   [2] *Ibid.*, iii. 382.

refused to believe that a son reported "missing" would not some day return to her. Maurice, born amongst the snows of her flight from Prague, the child whom she had dedicated to be a fighter, had never disappointed her. A year after his disappearance she wrote hopefully to Lord Craven that the Duchess of Courland had heard from the Electress that "her husband's people in the Indies" reported that Maurice was safely arrived in "the Lomnema island", but his ship was "pitiably torn and without a mast". She had sent to ask the Duchess for more particulars.

The Winter Queen waited in vain for the sounds of a travel-worn chariot arriving in her courtyard and the dashing entry of an incredibly bronzed son. A year later the sort of news which was worse than none reached her. On June 19th, 1654, a Hague letter-writer reported, "Here is news of Prince Maurice, who was thought and believed to be drowned and perished, that he is a slave at Africa. For being constrained, at that time that he parted from Prince Rupert, to run as far as Hispaniola in the West Indies, he was coming back thence towards Spain in a barque laden with a great quantity of silver, and was taken by a pirate of Algiers. The Queen, his mother, hath spoken to the Ambassador of France, to the end he may write in his behalf to the Great Turk, for it is pre-supposed this State dare not speak for him for fear of offending the Protector." [1] Elizabeth did more. She ordered Rupert to set off instantly for Constantinople to expedite his brother's release. Charles Louis, with whom Rupert was staying at Heidelberg, replied cautiously that his brother thought "if the news be true", he would do better to begin enquiries at Marseilles.[2] "I send all about to knowe the certaintie of it", wrote Elizabeth.[3] Three months later she was grateful to Henrietta Maria for efforts to get tidings from Leghorn.[4] Presently another

[1] Thurloe, ii. 238.   [2] Bromley, p. 167.
[3] Wendland, p. 42.   [4] *Ibid.*, p. 43.

tantalizing rumour declared that a mysterious prisoner in a fortress named "The More at Porto Rico" was none other than the missing Vice-Admiral.

No letter or anecdote relates when the Queen of Bohemia gave up hope, and exchanged the horrible vision of the nameless captive of the Black Fort, or the Turkish galley-slave, for that of "full fathom five", and the shrill laughter of the mermaidens of the Atlantic stilled in wonder to behold so handsome a mortal princeling sleep so soundly.[1]

XIV

Charles Louis's suitable marriage was a failure. His sister Sophie discovered this within a few hours of her arrival in his domains. The new Electress Palatine was certainly handsome— "very tall with an admirable complexion and most beautiful bust". Unluckily, haunted by the besetting fear of the silver-blonde that she may appear insipid, she had dyed her eyebrows an unconvincing black. The newly married couple came to meet Sophie at Mannheim. "The Elector, with his hearty manner, seemed delighted to see me." The Electress was haughtily immobile, until Sophie, with the best intentions, praised the coach in which they were jolting towards Heidelberg. Her sister-in-law's stormy countenance warned her that she had touched upon a sore subject. She afterwards learnt that the Electress was disgusted with this equipage, since she considered that her married sister possessed one more expensive. Next morning, on their return from church together, the Electress deigned to speak at some length. Relieved to find a confidante of suitable rank, she embarked upon a melodramatic autobiography. She had been forced by

[1] In the year after his mother's death, Prince Rupert, Lord High Admiral of England, sent out a ship to search for tidings of the brother he had lost eleven years before.

her mother to accept "a jealous old man", when she might have had her enamoured cousin, Duke Frederick of Würtemberg Neustadt, the attractive Dukes George and Ernest Augustus of Brunswick Lüneburg, Philip, Palsgrave of Sulzbach, "and several counts". The youngest daughter of the Queen of Bohemia had reached her twentieth year without ever having heard a lady complain in company of her wedded lord. For a moment she wished herself back at the Hague, "where such behaviour was considered a crime". But the resilient Sophie, who was a psychologist, contented herself with remarking in interested accents to the walls of her maiden chamber that her clever brother had married a fool.[1]

Charles Louis was for some time enchanted by his young wife's perversity. But his temper had never been sweet, and he had begun to suffer from rheumatism.[2] His learned sister nicknamed him after Timon of Athens, the misanthrope.[3] Appalling stories of the scenes at his court reached the Hague. The Electress Palatine had thrown a dish at her husband during dinner, whereupon he had boxed her ears. After seven years of domestic strife, Charles Louis's wife left his court for ever. He had, not surprisingly, begun to seek consolation amongst her damsels in waiting. Early in 1658 he announced, in the presence of a notary, his repudiation of his Electress. He found a clergyman complaisant enough to unite him in morganatic marriage to a humbler partner. But his actions were not unquestionable, even from the legal point of view, for his first wife had refused to consent to a divorce. She continued to refuse, even after the death of her rival, twenty years later. Luise von Degenfeld, daughter of an old Suabian family, was no light of love. She had attracted the attention of Charles

---

[1] *Memoirs of Sophie, Electress of Hanover*, pp. 35–9.
[2] Charles Louis's pain in his right shoulder is a leading topic in his letters to his mother.
[3] Bromley, p. 254.

Louis by her scholarly tastes and maidenly modesty. He revived for her the old Palatine title of Raugrafin, and she bore him fourteen children. His sister Sophie, who had heard the story from both sides, and his only daughter by his first marriage, treated these children with generosity, but when one of them presumed to remark that she was supposed to bear a striking likeness to her grandmother, the Queen of Bohemia, she encountered a devastating snubbing.[1]

The Queen of Bohemia was entirely taken aback when she discovered that her son was unhappy in his marriage. She approached the subject tremulously. "I am verie sorie to hear of the trouble you have in your house. I wish you had more contentment." She turned to classical romances for pseudonyms when writing of so delicate a matter.[2] Charles Louis was "Tiribaze", his spouse "Eurydice", she herself "Candace". At first her sympathy was with her son. She remembered that "the dear late King" had always prayed to be delivered from the House of Hesse.

Long after the situation was obviously hopeless, poor "Candace" continued to offer old-fashioned counsels of mutual toleration. The pupil of Combe Abbey harboured no doubt as to the rights and wrongs of this affair. Her son's marriage to Charlotte Elizabeth of Hesse Cassel was a life-sentence, and Luise von Degenfeld was "that wench". "If everie bodie coulde quitt their housbands and wives for their ill humours, there wolde be no smale disorder in the worlde. It is against

[1] "Good gracious, dear Amelisse! You must not continue to flatter yourself that in youth you resembled our grandmother, the Queen. I remember her as well as if it were to-day. Not only had she quite a different countenance, but you have sandy hair, a broad face and a high colour. The Queen of Bohemia had black hair, a long oval face and a high nose. In a word she was of a totally different type. The Elector Palatine, further, bore a great likeness to his mother." Menzel, p. 43.

[2] This was always her habit when discussing intimate family concerns. "Berenice" was her name for Sophie and "Roxane" for the Princess Dowager of Orange.

both God's law and man's law, for though you be a soverain, yett God is above you." She always hoped ingenuously that a long silence meant that things were going better, or at any rate, "reasonable well". Again and again a sickening letter from Heidelberg disillusioned her and spoilt her day.

Charles Louis declared that in his second match he was only following the example of his ancestor, John of Gaunt. His children by Degenfeld would be legitimate and might inherit his titles and honours as John's had done. But the pupil of Combe knew her English history better than that. "You are deceived in naming John of Gaunt. . . . You had better name William the Conqueror." The only disgrace in the career of John of Gaunt, "a verie brave worthie prince" had been his association with Catherine "Swingfosh", "a low woman". "We shoulde seek to follow our ancestours vertues and not their vices." Gradually the queen's sympathy veered towards the errant but aggrieved Electress who, she considered, would have needed to be "a verie patient Grizell". She reminded her son of other couples who, although cross-mated, managed to make a show in the eyes of the world for the sake of their children. "Rashness" in leaving an unfaithful spouse was the worst sin of which the Electress could be accused. "Wherefore I conjure you—take her again, at least to live well with her outwardlie, if you cannot forgive, which I hope you will in time. . . . I will not dispute with you the case, though I ame not of your minde, having too well read the Scriptures to be of it, besides having heard and read few examples of people in your condition having done as you doe, so openlie to avouch sinne. I pray take not this plaine dealing ill, for God is my witness, I have no other end in it but your good and honnour. But if you doe resolve to be parted from your wife, I pray think how you will doe about Sophie, for she cannot with anie honnour stay with you." The Queen of Bohemia thought upon the whole that her maiden daughter had better retire from Heidelberg with the Electress. She warned her son that no woman of credit would accept the office of governess to his children while his "open keeping" continued. Charles Louis replied furiously that he had known all women were selfish, but he was surprised to hear that the dames of Holland were so "squeamish". He feared that he was less patient than two favoured members of his mother's circle whom he quoted by name as notorious cuckolds.

The Queen of Bohemia continued to bleat pathetically. She pitied her daughter-in-law. "All persons in misfortune shoulde pittie one another." After her first meeting with Charles Louis's little daughter, she mingled with her praises the suggestion that her son must feel gratitude to the high-born bride who had given him such lovely offspring. Charles Louis never paid the slightest attention to his mother's counsels or reproaches, but four years after his wife's departure, he made a startling admission: "As for the accidents fallen out in my domestic affairs, it is likely they had not happened if your Majesty had been present." [1]

XV

On Wednesday, December 19th, 1657, a cover was laid in vain in the hall hung with tarnished gilt leather where the Queen of Bohemia was accustomed to dine at noon. The failure of the artist-princess Louise to appear for the mid-day meal did not at first cause alarm. She had vaguely mentioned some scheme of visiting acquaintances at Scheveningen. The results of enquiries made in the household as to her expedition, however, were disquieting. No carriage was missing from the stables, no attendants were absent. Neither halberdier, footman,

[1] Wendland, pp. 33, 39, 65, 69, 77, 82, 92, 110, 154, 157, 165, 169; Bromley, p. 236.

page, lady-in-waiting nor *fille de chambre* had seen anything of the princess since last night. She had apparently left
the house in darkness, on foot, alone and without money.
Her bed-chamber was searched, and a note addressed to her
mother was found. The gist of this entirely formal document
was that when the princess arrived at a destination which she
was not yet at liberty to disclose, she hoped to inform her
Majesty of her reasons for taking the veil in a Catholic
nunnery.[1]

The household of the Winter Queen knew no more peace
that winter's day. A French gentleman, M. le Bocage, who
had brought a letter for the princess last night, was summoned
for interrogation. The French Ambassador's coach drew up
in the courtyard of the Wassenaer Hof. M. de Thou was able
to plead with perfect conviction that the news which he heard
from her Majesty was indeed news to him. It was true that
since his box at the comedy was next to that of her Majesty,
he had frequently conversed with her daughter. But her
Royal Highness had never given him the least hint of her
conversion to his faith. M. de Mérode, President of the
Assembly of the States General, was more helpful. By three
o'clock that afternoon, despatches were being forwarded to
the Governors of Hellevoetsluis, Bar le Duc and Bergen op
Zoom, desiring them to arrest the Princess Louise Hollandine
Palatine "with all civility and respect" and bring her back to
the queen, her mother.

A further search of Louise's apartments discovered two more
letters, which afforded valuable clues as to her whereabouts.
They were written by the Princess of Zollern.[2] This lady,
although a Catholic, was a close friend of the Queen of
Bohemia, with whom she had been in the habit of making

---

[1] Wendland, p. 101.
[2] Marie, daughter and heiress of Count Henry of Bergen op Zoom, and
wife of Eitel Friedrich, Prince of Hohenzollern.

local pleasure expeditions. One of the letters suggested that Louise should ask the queen's leave to visit her brother Edward at Antwerp; the second contained the scheme which Louise had adopted. Before daylight that morning she had silently quitted the house in which she had been born thirty-six years before, and taken her solitary way to Delfshaven. There, the priest of a M. La Roque, captain of the Guard to William II, Prince of Orange, had escorted her aboard a ship bound for Bergen op Zoom. Her destination was Paris, via the English Carmelite convent at Antwerp.

The Queen of Bohemia never saw her most congenial daughter again. On a March day of the following year, a family party—King Charles II, his sister the Princess of Orange, and his brother, the Duke of York—alighted solemnly at "Louyse's monastery", empowered by her mother to chide her for leaving home "so unhandsomelie", and for her change of religion. Louise expressed herself "very sorry" that she had displeased her mother, but "very well satisfied with her change". Elizabeth said that she was most grateful to her nephews and niece for visiting a relation who did not deserve such an honour, at a moment when their support was essential. The Princess Louise's reputation had been impugned as a result of her pusillanimous flight. The scandalmongers of Paris and the Hague were hearing with amusement that an elderly spinster daughter of the Queen of Hearts had been obliged to seek convent shade to be delivered of an illegitimate child. Elizabeth, although infuriated by her daughter's conduct, never doubted her integrity. She wrote to Louise, adjuring her to deny the "base lye" current. She laid before the States General all her own correspondence with her ex-friend, the Princess of Zollern, and they proceeded to deprive that lady of the privileges which she enjoyed, as her father's heiress, of naming the magistracy of Bergen op Zoom. Louise had been the god-daughter of the States, and they felt righteous indignation against the person who had perverted her. The Princess of Zollern, who had begun by writing piously to the Queen of Bohemia, found her letters answered violently and the doors of the Wassenaer Hof closed to her. Prince Edward, from Paris, accused his mother of having infuriated a Catholic who had acted with the best intentions, but Elizabeth was able to assure him that long before she had uttered a single reproach, five people had heard from the lips and even from the pen of the Princess of Zollern the "piquante calumnies" now prevalent. She said with reason that if the Princess of Zollern had been content to plume herself upon having effected a conversion and not descended to "a scandalous lye" to justify herself, "all Papists would have taken her part". As things were, she had no friends, save those "her purse keeps to her". "She is detested by Protestant and Papist."

The Queen of Bohemia wrote to her eldest son, imploring him, as head of the family, to write "sharplie" to the calumniator, demanding that she should either prove or deny her story. When this letter was *en route*, the stricken parent repented of it. She would prefer that Charles Louis should simply insist that the Princess of Zollern retracted her story. To ask her to prove it might seem to suggest that the Elector doubted his sister's purity. Charles Louis answered cautiously, warning his mother of the undesirable results of publicity. Elizabeth said that if the Princess of Zollern spoke the truth, "you need not fear her or any body else". As for the possibility of the lady disclosing any secrets of a disgraceful nature regarding the family of the Queen of Bohemia, her Majesty defied her or any soul to find such a thing. The unhappy queen reported sordid details. M. le Roque was generally mentioned as Louise's lover. "If you saw the gentleman you woulde soone juge he is no Adonis, for he is leane like a skellet, and hath but one eye that is good, a redd face, and goes verie weake upon his pasternes. But he lacks no witt." The attendants of

Louise had voluntarily deposed before a notary that their mistress, at the date of her flight, had been "verie free from being with childe". The Princess of Orange had told the queen that she had seen Louise in her convent three months after the flight, attired in a simple gown, without cloak or coat, "as lanke as she was heere".

The Bishop of Antwerp assured Prince Edward that his sister had been maligned, and Louise, having parted in wrath from the Princess of Zollern, made on to Paris, where she received a rapturous welcome from Henrietta Maria. The Queen-Mother of England wrote to the Queen of Bohemia that she would care for the convert as for her own daughter. She implored forgiveness for Louise. Elizabeth excused herself "as civily as possible" from granting the desired forgiveness, and begged the Catholic queen to consider how she would feel if her daughter deserted her without warning to embrace Protestantism. Eventually, however, the Queen of Bohemia decided to "forgive and forget". But she told her daughter that she only did so at the request of royalty—the King and the Queen-Mother of England.

Louise passed on from Henrietta Maria's foundation of Chaillot to the convent of Maubuisson, near Pontoise, whence in September 1660 she informed her mother that she had exchanged the white veil for the black. She became Abbess of this community, and lived a blameless existence to the age of eighty-eight. Unlike her Protestant sister, she made an extremely cheerful Abbess. "She said she had always liked a country life, and fancied she lived like a country girl." She continued, until after her eightieth year, to execute oil-paintings of considerable merit.

Alone of the surviving children of the Queen of Bohemia, she received no mention in her mother's will. Elizabeth's final word to Charles Louis on the subject of the "unhappie wench" was a vain request that he should attack the Princess of Zollern for her "base accusation, which I ame confident is false, by all that I can imagine or know".[1]

XVI

The youngest daughter of the Queen of Bohemia decided early that her chances of success in life rested with herself alone. Fortunately the Princess Sophie had character as well as talent. When she was not quite eleven, her elder sisters allotted to her a very small part in the tragedy of "Medea", which they were preparing to act, in French, for the entertainment of their mother. Sophie made herself word-perfect in the complete play before the night of the performance at Rhenen.[2] She was a plain child, and sensitive as to her appearance. To her relief, although she never became as strikingly handsome as her sisters, she grew up pretty. "I had light brown naturally curly hair, a gay and easy manner, a good though not very tall figure, and the bearing of a princess." [3]

Her *métier* was obviously marriage, but in the important business of finding a husband she had no hopes of assistance from her mother. From her earliest days she had heard talk of suitors for her elder sisters which had never resulted in a wedding. Before she could remember, a match for the Princess Elizabeth with the King of Poland had broken down on the question of religion. The same fate had befallen an offer from the Catholic Duke of Neuburg. When the young Protestant champion, Bernard of Saxe Weimar, had visited the Hague, there had been rumours that he was to receive the hand of the eldest Princess Palatine, but he had been slain in battle

[1] Wendland, pp. 84–5, 87–8, 95, 111–12, 118; Bromley, pp. 286–9; Thurloe, vi. 690, 719, 732, 738, 782, 793; Harl. MS. 4525.626.635 and 4526.68–70; Craven MS.; *Mercurius Politicus*, Dec. 24th and 31st, 1657; *Gazettes de France*, 1658, 34, 58, 106; Van Sypesteyn, pp. 54–5.

[2] *Memoirs of Sophie, Electress of Hanover*, p. 12.

[3] *Ibid.*, p. 17.

within fifteen months. Count Waldemar of Denmark had been frozen out of the Wassenaer Hof by the Winter Queen, who knew that his family did not approve of his courting a penniless bride. That closed the list of the Princess Elizabeth's suitors.

Princess Louise had come within measurable distance of matrimony but once. Her tall, handsome first cousin, Frederick William of Brandenburg, had been attracted by her when she was fifteen and faithful to her memory for four years. The Queen of Bohemia had not discouraged a wooing which seemed likely to promise her daughter happiness.[1] But Frederick William had been "dashed" by opposition from his relatives, and when he returned to the Hague it was to marry a Princess Louise who had a dowry, a child of Amalia of Solms. The Queen of Bohemia took all her daughters to witness their cousin's wedding.

Sophie, aged nineteen, accepted with alacrity her brother's invitation to visit his court at Heidelberg. "I will never", said her mother, "keep anie that has a mind to leave me".[2] Elizabeth was annoyed that Sophie should be leaving the Hague at this juncture. The Queen of Bohemia, in spite of the disastrous state of his fortunes, still nourished hopes that Charles II might make her youngest daughter Queen of England some day. The cousins were almost of an age. When Sophie unromantically pleaded a corn as an excuse for avoiding a walk with the King of England, her mother was exasperated with her. But on their last promenade together—down the shady alleys outside the Wassenaer Hof—the desperate-looking young exiled king had told Sophie that he admired her even more than Mrs Barlow. Sophie was "highly offended", and not without reason. Mrs Barlow was the name by which a ruined Royalist lady, Lucy Walter, passed at the Hague. She had recently borne the extraordinarily gauche and black-a-vised Charles a fair son. When Sophie learnt that his exiled

[1] S.P. 16. 484.51.　　　　[2] Wendland, p. 9.

Majesty's sudden and frequent visits to the Wassenaer Hof were attributed by some of his attendants to a desire to raise a loan from Lord Craven, her disillusionment was complete. Amalia of Solms was welcome to secure him for one of her daughters. Amalia was said to have told the Presbyterian leaders of the king's suite that the Princess Sophie Palatine was not a good Presbyterian, and Sophie had certainly noticed that when the Scots Commissioners were present her cousin avoided her. She wrote him down a weakish youth, and did not regret sacrificing her chances of marrying him. Her reason told her that they had never been good.[1]

To discover within an hour of her arrival at her new home that her host was on bad terms with his wife was a chilling disappointment, but Sophie stayed on resolutely at Heidelberg, exercising all her tact. She had been right in thinking that the Elector Palatine would receive offers of marriage for the favourite sister residing under his roof. A tentative approach made on behalf of the Portuguese Duke of Aveiro was not much considered, but the first suitor to appear in person was brilliant indeed. The Emperor's son, Ferdinand, King of the Romans, was a resplendent *parti*, and what was more to the point, he fell in love with the Princess Sophie at first sight. There were obvious difficulties to be surmounted, since he was of course an arch-Catholic. Death carried off the ardent Ferdinand, and to Sophie's dismay, her mirror told her that an attack of smallpox, although it had not spoilt her countenance, had definitely banished her youthful bloom. However another prince was presenting himself. Adolphus John of Sweden was a nephew of Gustavus Adolphus and a Lutheran. His offer in form for the Princess Sophie was promptly accepted by her brother. Her mother wrote to ask whether the King of Sweden had given his consent, and whether the prince, who was a widower, had any children.[2]

[1] *Memoirs of Sophie, Electress of Hanover*, pp. 22–5.   [2] Wendland, p. 48.

A trousseau was ordered in Paris. When the affair had gone thus far, it transpired that the King of Sweden, an ally of Cromwell, was opposed to his brother making this match. Sophie professed relief. It would have required a virtuous effort to overcome her aversion from Adolphus John. "He had a disagreeable face, with a long pointed chin like a shoe-horn." He was said to have beaten his first wife.[1] But she realized that the history of her matrimonial projects had begun to bear a ghastly resemblance to those of her elder spinster sisters. When Duke George William of Brunswick Lüneberg "spoke the great word", requesting "my permission to ask the Elector for my hand, I failed to act like the heroine of a romance, for I unhesitatingly said 'Yes'." The Brunswick Lüneberg brothers enjoyed great prestige at the court of the Elector Palatine. They were good company, accomplished and travelled. George William "a mighty Nimrod", was also a connoisseur of the new wine, champagne. Ernest Augustus played the guitar exquisitely.[2] Indeed Sophie had broken off a correspondence with him on this subject some seasons past, since she did not wish her name to be linked with that of a charming detrimental.[3] Her contract of marriage with George William was duly signed, and the brothers departed to winter, according to their elegant custom, in Italy. The engagement was not announced, since the Swedish match was not as yet formally abandoned, but Sophie began to prepare for residence at Hanover. Her *fiancé's* love-letters became cold and infrequent. He failed to return to Heidelberg to claim her. "The Elector was very uneasy, but pride kept me up." Presently Charles Louis had a perfect excuse for flying into one of his worst tempers. George William, whose tastes were expensive and not domestic, had only contemplated matrimony at the desire of his Estates, who had promised him an increase of revenue on his marriage. "Plunged in the dissipations

---

[1] *Memoirs of Sophie, Electress of Hanover,* p. 52.
[2] *Ibid.,* p. 50.   [3] *Ibid.,* p. 47.

of Venice", he had decided that he could not give up his liberty. He apologetically proposed an arrangement which he hoped might be agreeable to all parties. His youngest and favourite brother, Ernest Augustus, should take over all his property, including his *fiancée*. George William merely asked, in return, for a handsome pension.

Charles Louis considered his sister insulted, and the third son of the house of Brunswick Lüneberg, as naturally, protested that his interests were not being considered. The substitute bridegroom fell dangerously ill, and negotiations languished. Sophie feigned to lend "a willing ear" to the proposals of Ranuccio II, Duke of Parma, who uncompromisingly demanded a Catholic bride. But the Princess Sophie Palatine, in her twenty-eighth year, was not minded to risk further delays. When her brother wrote to her from Frankenthal, telling her that Ernest Augustus appeared definitely willing, she replied frankly that a good establishment was all that she cared for, and that if this was secured to her by the younger brother, the exchange would be to her a matter of indifference.[1] Charles Louis wrote unenthusiastically to his mother. "In the present condition of our Familie we must be satisfied to take hold of what we can." Elizabeth, although nettled that neither her advice nor consent had been required, answered benevolently. She had "a great esteem" for Ernest Augustus. "I doe not at all dislike the match." She only hoped that her son would remember the old English proverb, "Merry's the wooing that's not long a-doing". She wished Sophie happy.[2]

Ernest Augustus recovered and prepared to do his duty. George William executed an extraordinary deed entitled an anti-contract of marriage, which Sophie carefully copied into her memoirs. On October 17th, 1658, she was escorted to the chapel of Heidelberg castle by her brother. Charles Louis gave her a dowry and trousseau as handsome as he could afford,

[1] *Memoirs of Sophie, Electress of Hanover*, p. 47. [2] Wendland, pp. 94-5.

and wrote to warn his mother that on account of the stunning expenses of her youngest daughter's wedding, she must expect very little from him at present. Sophie went to the altar, as a princess should, in a gown of white silver brocade, with a train of enormous length borne by many noble virgins. She wore her hair flowing on her shoulders under a diamond circlet, and made a radiant bride. She was absolutely determined to make a good wife and mother. Her husband was her own age, good-looking, robust and reasonably intelligent. She had liked him even when he had no prospects. Now, of the three brothers who stood between him and succession to all his father's principalities, the eldest, seven years married, was childless, the second had renounced matrimony, and the third had leanings towards Roman Catholicism.

Sophie's troubles, however, were not over when her wedding-bells rang. George William proceeded to live with the newly married couple at Hanover, and now that she was safely his favourite brother's wife, he discovered that the Princess Sophie Palatine was the most engaging princess in Europe. His admiration became obvious, and Sophie's husband displayed pangs of rage, jealousy and suspicion. For the fourth time a frightful family scandal seemed likely to assail the Queen of Bohemia. But the Queen of Bohemia, from the Hague, wrote calmly to her eldest son, "You may chance heere of some love, and rumors of love, but do not beleeve it, for there is no shew towards it. . . . I looke for your sister heere about Wednesday".[1] Sophie, with consummate tact and not without humour, had refused to accompany her agitated husband and brother-in-law to Italy. She hoped that she had the best of reasons for wishing to spend this winter very quietly with her widowed mother. But she was far from guessing that the child that she was to bear next spring was a future King of England.[2]

[1] Wendland, p. 120.
[2] *Memoirs of Sophie, Electress of Hanover*, pp. 54–78, 84–92.

CHAPTER VII

THE MOTHER OF PRINCE RUPERT

I

THE Queen of Bohemia's passionate love for her eldest surviving son did not die quickly or easily. "Though he has not much obliged me, yet that shall not make me hate him, or wish him ill." Occasionally in their correspondence Charles Louis would afford her a tantalizing glimpse of the delightful relationship that should have existed between a handsome, clever, grown-up prince and his adoring widowed mother. Charles Louis could be amusing.

"I am much puzzled whom to send into England. Most of our counts and noblemen hereabouts are either stupid or fools, and of no breeding, and care for nothing but good drink. There is a young Baron of Limbourg . . . I believe not unknown to your Majesty, who hath been in France and Italy . . . notwithstanding his travelling, somewhat bashful. . . . The Count of Laine desires to be excused, because he is not master enough of the French tongue, and to send a German statue thither will not be worth the charges. . . . I believe your Majesty will have the Princess of Zollern's Marquis of Bady here very often. He is a very gaudy old gentleman and pretends much friendship to us, but I doubt he is somewhat double, at least is reported so. . . . If Mademoiselle Marie gets my cousin of Simmern she will get a precious piece. God bless it! they say he loves no company but pages and footmen. . . . I have given orders to send down your Majesty's wines, as soon as I can make these dull Dutch engines move." [1]

Too often, however, Charles Louis's letters to his mother were chilling in tone and even unpleasant.

When her favourite son quitted her at Rhenen on an April day of 1650, Elizabeth little thought that she had looked upon his face for the last time. For the next eleven years she quarrelled incessantly with him on paper. From the moment that the Peace of Münster was signed, she looked hopefully to the Elector Palatine for financial relief. Some of her demands upon him were impossible. Charles Louis, who was himself living in a house in Heidelberg town until some portions of the ruined castle could be made fit for his occupation, had no prospect of allowing her the jointure promised to her by his late father. It was all very well for Lord Craven, who was a romantic, to squander a fortune in the service of the Winter Queen, but the Elector Palatine had other duties. He knew that his mother was a deplorable manager. She herself thought it a subject for mirth that her fatally indulged servants fought "like gladiators".[2] "I know your ways", the King of Bohemia had written tenderly to his partner, "you never can refuse anybody anything." [3] Her Majesty's chaplain spoke of her "gracious and facile disposition often to her own prejudice".[4] Her generosity was famous, but her son had not much opinion of royal generosity performed at other people's expense. Charles Louis quailed at the thought of his incorrigible parent running up a fresh array of debts amongst his subjects. He had their welfare much at heart. He had dreams of making Heidelberg once more a centre of culture and refinement. He doled out to his mother "pitifull small" instalments of money and produce from her dower lands, upon which she commented sarcastically. He invited her to come and live under his roof, where he

[1] Bromley, pp. 117, 209, 215, 301, 213; Wendland, p. 35.
[2] Thurloe, i. 674.   [3] Bromley, p. 59.   [4] S.P. 16. 441.47.

could keep a sharp eye upon her. But to live with a young married couple, as an apologetic dependant, by no means suited Elizabeth's ideas. She refused to come to Heidelberg, and demanded to be established in one of her dower palaces of which she had pleasant memories. Charles Louis replied with truth but scant patience that the residences she mentioned were uninhabitable. Their restoration would employ years and a fortune.

Elizabeth, after much complaint, agreed to come to Heidelberg in her own time. The Winter Queen declared that she could not face a journey in bad weather. "I will not stir this winter, let him be as tyrannical as he will be to me. . . . I believe he means to starve me out of this place as they do blocked towns. I know he may do it and has already begun pretty well; but he will have as little comfort as honour by it, for if I am forced by ill usage to go I shall be very ill company there. . . . I know my son would have me to be rid of all my jewels, because he thinks he doth not deserve so well of me that he should share in them after my death. But that will do him no good, for I can leave to my children what he owes me, which will trouble him more than my jewels are worth." At length she really seemed resigned to her fate, and stipulated for two sitting-rooms as close as possible to her bedroom.[1] Charles Louis wrote warningly of the disadvantages of the apartments in the Otto Heinrich wing being put in order for her,[2] and of the low state of education and manners amongst those who would be her future companions.[3] But after all he was not forced to play the unwilling host. When the Queen of

---

[1] Wendland, p. 34.

[2] Princess Elizabeth also wrote, begging her mother's *maître d'hôtel* to hurry to Heidelberg to "drive on the worke" of repairing the lodgings assigned to the queen. "My brother's businesse doe not give him leisure to atende it. His officers are as you know them to be." Both "fine glasse" and "dry boards" were lacking. Cottrell MS.

[3] Bromley, p. 178.

Bohemia's Dutch creditors heard that she was preparing to leave Holland, they raised such a howl that she was obliged to postpone her journey indefinitely and apply to the States General for aid. "It is with extreme sorrow, my Lords, that after so much assistance and relief, we do find ourselves obliged to make this demand of you." [1] The States, as ever, were generous, although their policy no longer favoured ruined Stuarts. Elizabeth wrote to her son in genuine and incoherent distress:

"I send this by the post to let you know that the States have given me for my kitchen, one thousand guilders a month, till I shall be able to go from hence, which God knows how and when that will be, for my debts. Wherefore I earnestly entreat you to do so much for me as to augment that money which you give me, and then I shall make a shift to live a little something reasonable. And you did always promise me that as your country bettered you would increase my means, till you were able to give me my jointure. I do not ask you much. If you would add but what you did hint, you would do me a great kindness by it, and make me see you have still an affection for me, and put me in a confidence of it. Since you cannot pay me all that is my due, that will shew to the world you desire it if you could. I pray do this for me. You will much comfort me by it, who am in so ill a condition as it takes all my contentment from me. I am making my house as little as I can, that I may subsist by the little I have till I shall be able to come to you. . . . As you love me, I do conjure you to give an answer." [2]

But Charles Louis's answers to his mother's begging letters were never such as to encourage her in belief in his filial love. Six years later, when her Dutch creditors, having almost given up hope, were more willing to let her depart, she wrote again in

[1] Thurloe, ii. 677.   [2] Bromley, p. 203.

the same strain—"I desire not to ruin you. . . . I cannot give my servants their wages. . . . I am forced to sell that little remnant of plate I have . . . it being neither in honour nor conscience to thrust poore people out of doores to starve in recompense of their oulde services. . . . When I wrote to you of some things of that nature I never received answer." The pitifully bad housekeeper even offered to send to her careful son a note of all the sums of money which she had received from him during the past twelve years. "I hope your Majesty will also examine what my expences and receipts were, in that time", replied Charles Louis nastily. "I very well remember that your Majesty seldom wrote to me but upon money matters since I was in Germany. As for taking your Majesty's debts upon me, which were made upon another score, I believe it cannot justly be claimed." [1]

Soon after reading these words, the queen came to a great decision. She abandoned the picture of the dignified Dowager, residing in genteel poverty in her son's capital, for that of the King of England's aunt, Prince Rupert's mother, happy and honoured in her native land. The Restoration had taken place. The date was January, 1661. For some time past she had promoted the astonished Rupert to the vacant first place in her affections. "As for Rupert, you need not trouble yourself. We understand each other verie well." [2]

Rupert's career since he had lost Maurice had been characteristic. He had gone to Paris and offered his services to Charles II, who had promptly appointed him Master of the Horse. But an otiose existence in a court of exiles, tormented by rivalries and jealousies, had not suited the soldier prince, and after a tedious illness and a narrow escape from drowning in the Seine, he had betaken himself to Heidelberg. Marriage was

---

[1] Bromley, pp. 159–61, 176–9, 203–4, 230–8; Craven MS. printed in Everett Green, pp. 379–80; Wendland, pp. 44, 57.

[2] Wendland, p. 8.

at last in his mind, but by ill luck the damsel whom he liked
best in his brother's court was Luise von Degenfeld, whom
Charles Louis had already privately selected as his second wife.
The brothers quarrelled irrevocably, and Rupert passed on to
Vienna. His movements were eagerly watched by Cromwell's
spies, who reported that "the Black Prince" was engaged in the
Pomeranian-Hungarian wars, that he was in the Imperial
service, and had led the troops which captured the Swedish
entrenchments at Warnemünde. He certainly offered his sword
to the Duke of Modena.

For six years his mother did not see him. But she showered
affectionate letters upon him—"I pray God bless you, whatever
you resolve to doe". Between his many journeys Rupert
resided very quietly and economically with his friend the
Elector of Mainz. He devoted himself to studying philosophy,
science and art, particularly the art of engraving in mezzotint.
His "sparkish" days were past.

II

The same tragedy which deprived the Queen of Bohemia of
her last hopes of her pension from England drove to her court
a horde of royalist refugees. For about eighteen months
after the execution of Charles I, she managed, with the aid of
Lord Craven, to stave off the day of reckoning, but in the
winter of 1652, Sir Charles Cottrell, late Master of the Ceremonies to the Martyr King, set off for Heidelberg armed with
a formidable sheaf of documents. Their inscriptions displayed
that his task also was formidable—"Queen of Bohemia's
Commission concerning Her demand of Her Joynture upon
Her Son, the Elector Palatine"; "Queen of Bohemia's Instructions how to treat with Her son"; "Instructions for Sir Charles
Cottrell to talk upon with the Elector Palatine"; "State of the

Produce of the Queen of Bohemia's Joynture lands, in the Palatinate, drawn up in Latin and sign'd by her Husband on the word of a Prince, June ye 29th, 1613". [1]

After the unfortunate envoy reached his destination, a fresh flood of instructions reached him. The originals of some of the Queen of Bohemia's letters to Sir Charles Cottrell are written in very pale ink on paper which shows signs of having been singed. Elizabeth wisely employed invisible ink for such confidences as the following:

"I easilie beleeve my sonne woulde be glade to have me at Heidelberg, but I cannot resolve upon it, his humour and mine being so divers. When he was heere I coulde not perswade him to aniething, and now much less. For he is so jealous, I mean, as he will never doe what I shoulde desire of him. . . . As for my daughter,[2] she is an hipocrit to the Root . . . trust her no further than you see cause. . . . Trust not Sophie with aniething, for she will tell all to carry on her Brother."

Sir Charles Cottrell had, in an ill hour for him, undertaken to cleanse an Augean stable. He had accepted the post of Steward to his late master's sister. For four and a half years he struggled manfully with a condition of affairs much aggravated since it had broken the health and spirits of Colonel Schomberg. At the end of that period, like the Colonel before him, he offered his resignation. But he was luckier than his predecessor. He passed on to serve another member of his old master's family—Henry, Duke of Gloucester. "My little gentleman", wrote the Queen of Bohemia of her youngest English nephew, "loves not to heare of a Governour." [3] Sir Charles received the title of Adviser to his fourteen-year-old Royal Highness.

A short study of one of the documents possessed by the

[1] Cottrell MS.
[2] This refers to the Princess Elizabeth, then resident at Heidelberg.
[3] Wendland, p. 61.

Queen of Bohemia's Steward gives an illuminating glimpse of the difficulties with which he had to contend in what he justly described as his "uneasy imployment". Fortunately for biographers of his mistress, he preserved it carefully. It was already thirteen years old when it was put into his hands, and was, even so, but a revised edition of an earlier set of "Orders of the House, which the deceased King of most happy memory, caused to be published sometyme before he made his last journey into Germany". These Orders demonstrated that "the Queen, our most gratious Lady and Mistresse" might well complain of "disorders crept into this her Court, in that the most part of the servants and domesticks of both sexes, take the liberty to live therein according to theyr fancy".

Twelve noon was her Majesty's dinner hour. As it drew near, the Wassenaer Hof presented a lively appearance. The courtyard became thronged with an array of uninvited feasters, whose entry the halberdier at the gate surveyed with good-humoured indifference. Nor was his fellow, who should have been standing outside the queen's dining-room "holding his partisan in his hand" to repel intruders, much more efficient. "Quarrelling, fighting, roaring, swearing and storming" offended the royal ears, as her Majesty partook dolefully of roasts "bloudy, or burnt on the outside" and other meats "served half sodden". Dirty plates and even food penetrated to her table. The cellar of a widowed lady was, of course, fair game and "great abuse" was described in this connection. Regular hours for the opening of the cellar doors had been imposed in vain. From the moment that they were opened, they were incessantly crowded by not only members of the household, but also total strangers "come to demand drinke as if it were a publike Taverne". The English beer in particular vanished as if by witchcraft. In the "Sylver Chamber" her Majesty's plate showed a tendency to "straggle abroad." Some of it was to be espied on the serving men's table, but much, together with innumerable "pyes, tartes, bunnes, sweet-meates, preserves and fruites", disappeared without explana-tion as miraculously as the best beer. Her Majesty's waiting men had fallen into the habit of sitting at ease around the fire in the cold season, while her half-frozen gentlemen and ladies were still dining. They further invited boon companions to "passe away the night" with them dicing and playing cards and utterly neglected to "lock up diligently the Cheese after every Meale, and keep it from the Cats and rats". The pages—"children descended from good and noble houses"—enjoyed an ideal existence. They were accustomed to "prate from one table to another" during meals, "thwart him who hath the direction of the said hall", bounce in and out of the room while their mistress ate, and even fall to fisticuffs.

Her Majesty supped at seven, but her nights were not peaceful. Her withdrawal was too often merely a signal for the halberdier on watch to make up a "great fyre", light his pipe of tobacco "and lett the fyre and Candells goe out before he awake". Other sounds kept the widow restless—"It hath often hapned . . . that the Laundresses and the Gentlewomen's Chambermayds goe up and down in ye night about theyr businesses, with Candells without Lanthorns, and coals in turf potts upon pannes, exposing the house and all therin to great danger."

Rule seventeen of the "Order for the Waiting Men in the Ladye's and Gentlemen's Hall" was the shortest item in the startling documents preserved by the Queen of Bohemia's Steward: "Lastly they shall suffer no Catt in the sayd dyning roome".[1]

III

In March, 1651, William, Lord Craven, was declared "an offender against the Commonwealth of England". From the

[1] Cottrell MS.

Hague he protested in vain that he had never borne arms against Parliament. The fact that he had supplied Charles II with £50,000 was notorious. His Berkshire estates, noble and lovely as their names—Hampstead Marshall, Benham, Ashdown—were sequestered. Dire tales reached the Wassenaer Hof of his "eternally generous" lordship's "goodly woods felling by the rebels". The Queen of Bohemia began to know what real poverty meant. She had already parted with much of her jewellery. "Our family misfortunes", wrote her youngest daughter, "had no power to depress my spirits, though we were at times obliged to make richer feasts than Cleopatra, and, often had nothing to devour but diamonds and pearls." [1] The queen, who was obliged to give, in exchange for butcher's meat and firing, pearls and diamonds hallowed by association, did so sadly. One by one the great pieces, so often depicted in her portraits, went into pawn, never to be redeemed. She wrote repeatedly to Charles Louis, begging him to save the table-diamond which had belonged to Henry, Prince of Wales, and the necklace of diamond knots and bows which had once decorated the throat of the Virgin Queen. Of these two family relics she was more attached to that which had been the gift of her dear dead brother. "Queene Elizabeth's chaine" vanished. In an agonizing moment her namesake had rashly given, as surety towards its redemption, an even dearer treasure—the gorgeous ring placed on her finger by the Elector Palatine on St Valentine's Day, 1613. " My wedding ring . . . Diamonds are much fallen . . . I shall be wiser another time." [2]

The Queen of Bohemia became too poor to leave the Hague when the weather became oppressive. Humbler folk might hasten to farm or seaside. "I must stay heere, having no monie." Her deserted country palace began to decay. The *concierge* appointed by Charles Louis proved a drunkard—"the

---

[1] *Memoirs of Sophie, Electress of Hanover*, p. 27.
[2] Wendland, pp. 49, 97, 120.

veriest beast in the world and knave".[1] The Princess of
Orange, who stopped at Rhenen for a night in November
1655, on her road from Cologne to the Hague, told her aunt
that "she had a minde to crie, to see the house so spoiled".
Elizabeth entreated her son to let or sell the place, before it
became worthless, although, as she pointed out, the right to
do so was really hers. "If I shoulde say for whome the king,
your father, has often said it was builte and furnished, you
would not beleeve me." She sent word to the *concierge* to
bring all furniture, and all pictures which were not framed
into the panelling above fireplaces, to the Wassenaer Hof. The
"uglie fellow", after delivering them, made off before they
could be unpacked and inspected. The queen found that even
the gold and silver lace from her bedhangings had been stolen.[2]
She, whose fine body-linen of cambric and gossamer lace had
been specially washed in sweet waters in London, scarcely
dared send a garment to be laundered lest it should drop to
pieces. The loss of a skilful *fille de chambre* "Bohemish Doll",
left her in despair. "I have not a smock but is all broken. . . ."
"Never a coat to my back", was her plaint as the winter of
1655 approached.[3]

During her last decade at the Hague, the scene in which she
moved remained almost unchanged, but the *dramatis personae*
altered considerably. The Queen lost her cousin, Sophie of
Nassau Dietz, and her sister-in-law, the Dowager Electress of
Brandenburg. "Such frends are but scarce in this worlde." [4]
Princes and Princesses of Orange embellished their capital
with new palaces, while the Wassenaer Hof became "so foul"
that the Queen of Bohemia longed for a spring cleaning. But
she could not raise the money for the journey elsewhere.[5]
Meanwhile gentlemen and ladies of her English nephew's
train, who were yet to cut a figure in the England of the

[1] Wendland, p. 67.   [2] *Ibid.*, pp. 8, 29, 62, 67.
[3] *Ibid.*, pp. 56–7.   [4] *Ibid.*, p. 142.   [5] *Ibid.*, p. 64.

Restoration, haunted her court. Many marriages resulted.[1] Many persons whose names were not to descend to history became even more familiar. There was the butcher's wife, who travelled to Heidelberg to present her bill to Charles Louis,[2] and the keeper of a tavern—"The Woman of the Spanish Armes"—who presented herself furiously and frequently in her Majesty's outer chambers. "Shee of 'The Golden Head', the Baker, poulterer and chaundler have also appeared", announced her Majesty's unhappy *maître d'hôtel*.[3] After Sir Charles Cottrell's departure, the Queen summoned "Matts, the cook", to her presence. Together the *chef* and her Majesty planned skilful schemes of retrenchment. Matts began promisingly, but an attempt "to put the gentlemen to board wages" was a failure.[4] No record is forthcoming as to the characteristics of "Benedict" in charge of the silver, "Old John of the Silver Chamber", "Adolphe, wayter in the Common Hall",[5] or the Amsterdam jeweller with whom the Winter Queen had many long and painful interviews.

Quite the oddest of the characters who were ever present was the Countess of Löwenstein. This title shrouded the identity of witty Bess Dudley, who had come from England with the Queen. The high-spirited English lady-in-waiting and the unwilling German nobleman, who had been herded

---

[1] A typical example of this is provided by the Andros family. Joshua, born 1615, was killed in the Thirty Years War. His brother, Sir Amias, Marshal of the Ceremonies to Charles I, served with Prince Maurice in the Civil War and married the sister of Sir Robert Stone, Captain of a troop of cavalry in the Prince of Orange's army, and Cup-bearer to the Queen of Bohemia. Sir Edmund, son of Amias, at the age of 24, accompanied Elizabeth to England as gentleman in ordinary and was in attendance at her death. Commander G. Stevens-Guille, R.N., descendant of the Andros family possesses many manuscripts and portraits testifying to the close connection of the exiled court at Breda with the Wassenaer Hof.

[2] Wendland, p. 79.   [3] Cottrell MS.
[4] Wendland, p. 70.   [5] Cottrell MS.

to the altar by their ideally mated master and mistress,[1] had not made good companions. When the Countess of Löwenstein heard a rumour of her husband's death, she remarked to the British Ambassador at the Hague that if the news proved untrue, a few tears would not be shed amiss. As a widow she became steadily odder every year. Her habit of "scrubbing herself" . . . "like Mother Eve", in the Rhine, at Rhenen, only amused her mistress,[2] but Charles Louis was enraged when he heard that his sister Elizabeth, aged eighteen, had been cuffed by the countess in full view of twenty people in the Princess of Orange's garden.[3] The Queen of Bohemia allowed the eccentric attendant who had been a childhood's friend to take extraordinary liberties. "The Countess would needs have us drinke limonade, which she brought us, and as she was giving it to my neece, she threw it all upon my neece's muff." [4] "As for the Countess, I can tell you heavy news of her, for she is turned Quaker and preaches every day in a tub." [5] The Countess of Löwenstein made expeditions to Ultra-Remonstrant gatherings at Arnhem where, according to her mistress, she joined with her spiritual brethren in "eating pig and prophesying".[6]

A gentler widow, always at the Queen's side, was "the Lady Jane, relict of Sir George Sayer, Master of the Horse". She had been born a Baroness Rupa, child of the Great Chamberlain of Moravia. Elizabeth had tried in vain to place the adopted daughter of the late Sir Thomas Roe in the household of some other princess. Eventually, after dismissing a wealthy suitor who was "an ass verily", the little damsel had made a love match, and the Queen of Bohemia had found both bride and bridegroom employment at the Wassenaer Hof.

---

[1] This match is Elizabeth's only recorded failure. Her most successful effort was the mating of her husband's cousin, Charlotte de la Trémoïlle to the heir of Lord Derby.

[2] Cottrell MS.   [3] Bromley, p. 88.   [4] Cottrell MS.
[5] *Archaeologia*, 21. 476.   [6] 6 S.P. 16. 484.51.

Sir Charles Cottrell was particularly exasperated by her Majesty's faithful ladies, who made no secret of their belief that her household would be better under female control. They clung to their privilege of ordering coaches from the stables without his knowledge. There was a humiliating occasion when he sent for a chariot for Sir Edward Hyde, Secretary of State to her Majesty's nephew, and received answer that the stables were empty. Shortly afterwards, when he summoned an equipage to bear Lady Hyde home, he learnt that Mrs Broughton had taken out the last, to do a bit of shopping for her Majesty. Her Majesty could not be persuaded to support his authority. Her dear Margaret Broughton had served her for five years without wages, "like a spaniel".[1]

In a moment of deep dejection, induced by the contemplation of wan servants waiting their wages, the widow who had quarrelled with her eldest son wrote to him that her existence was utterly "melancholique".[2] But the truth was that, until Charles Louis's divorce, and the flight of Louise, bowed her spirits, the Winter Queen preserved a spring-tide gaiety. "My journey up-hill",[3] as she described it, was still full of interest to her. Her pen had always been that of a ready writer. As her years increased, few days passed when she did not employ her "gold standishe enamelled"[4] for a discursive letter to a favourite correspondent. Even the weather was not beneath her notice as a topic. "Uppon Monday last it hailed hailstones bigger than a man's fist."[5] "The days are growen so short as there is no more walking heere after supper." "The thaw has done great wrong in melting the snow, our gallants being hindered going in sleids." On the wet morning of the new French Ambassador's pompous reception by the States General, the Queen of Bohemia settled herself complacently at her desk to report, "They will all be like drowned rats."

---

[1] Wendland, pp. 43, 69.   [2] *Ibid.*, p. 49.   [3] Evelyn, v. 194.
[4] S.P. 81. 56.28.   [5] Hervey, p. 310.

On a similar day she herself set out undaunted to pay a birthday visit to her "best neece", "not by lande but by water, for it
rains as if it were madd".

The Hague now presented the depressing spectacle of two
highly unpopular widowed Princesses of Orange, united in
nothing but affection for the widowed Queen of Bohemia.
Amalia of Solms invited her old mistress to lay the foundation-
stone of a new palace, designed to celebrate the virtues and
exploits of Frederick Henry. "House in the Wood", when
completed and filled with rarities from the Indies and Cathay,
was a gorgeous novelty. But such invitations reached Elizabeth
seldom. "Beggars cannot be choosers" [1] was her wise decision,
and she entered with zest upon what entertainment offered.
What she called a "jaunt" had an irresistible attraction for her,
and she never missed a memorable sight. Even the news of
an explosion in a neighbouring town caused the Queen of
Bohemia to order her carriage. "I was at Delft to see the
wrack that was made by the blowing up of the powder. It is
a sad sight—whole streets quite razed, not one stone upon
another. It is not yet knowen how manie persons are lost.
There is scarce anie house in the toune but the tyles are off."
An alarming cascade of ink decorates her letter at this point.
The Queen, whose nerves were strong, explains that her
pet greyhound Apollon "with leaping into my lapp, has made
this blott".[2] Before that wealthy lady lost her favour, she made
several little expeditions as guest and companion of the
Princess of Zollern. A trip into the South Netherlands was
their most daring venture. "At the Play" in Antwerp, the
Queen of Bohemia at last saw the daughter of Gustavus
Adolphus. She had long ceased to regret that Charles Louis
had not obtained the hand of Christina, whose eccentricities
were now a by-word in Europe. Her first comment on the
ex-Queen of Sweden was guarded. "She is extravagant in

[1] S.P. 16. 352.41.   [2] Evelyn, v. 204.

her fashion and aparell, but she has a good well favoured face and a milde countenance. One of the players that knew me tolde her who I was, but she made no shew of it. I went next day to Bruxelles, where I saw the Arch-duc at mass, and . . . his pictures and lodgins . . . stayed but Sunday, and returned to Antwerp upon Munday." Hearing that Christina now professed a desire to meet her, Elizabeth "made the more hast away . . . because I had no minde to speak with her, since I heard how unhandsomelie she had spoken of the King my deare Brother, and of the King my deare Nepheu, and indeed of all our nation". To her "deare nepheu's" secretary she confided further that the amorous Christina's presence in his domains was said to be causing the Archduke some nervousness, "for she persecutes him verie close with her companie, for you know he is a verie modest man. I have written to the King some particulars of it, which are verie rare ones".[1]

Her martyred brother's children occupied a foremost place in the queen's thoughts. Of the four known to her, she considered "young Gloucester" her "sweetest" nephew, but her godson, James, Duke of York, was her favourite."Tint",[2] as she called him, resembled her family in appearance, and his moodiness was powerless to depress the relict of the King of Bohemia. With her eldest nephew she had little in common, save a sense of humour. There was much in the career of the youthful Charles II that was unacceptable to her. But the Queen of Bohemia permitted no criticism of the King of England; Charles, too, made allowances, and their relationship was cordial. Most of their correspondence dealt with festivities and the humorous side of servant troubles. A fancy-dress ball gave the queen an ideal subject for a letter to Cologne. "Your sister was very well dressed, like an Amazone, the princess Tarente like a shepherdess, Mademoiselle d'Orange, a nimph. . . . Mrs Hare was a Sutler's wife. But I wished all the night

[1] Evelyn, v. 206, 213.   [2] This nickname is nowhere explained.

your majestie had seene Vanderdonc. There never was seene the like. He was a Gipsie. Nan Hide was his wife. He had pantalons close to him, in red and yellow striped, with russet sleeves. He looked just like Jock-a-Lent." [1]

Christmas and Kermesse were the gay seasons at the Hague. During the Kermesse, when the Voorhout was lined by booths, the Queen of Bohemia's palace was continually thronged by merrymakers. "The masks kept coming in till five in the morning." The winter of 1655 was distinguished by a ballet, arranged by her to entertain her niece. "Our Dutch ministers sayde nothing against it in the pulpet, but a little french preacher, Carre, said in his sermon, we had committed as great a sinne as that of Sodom and Gomorra, which sett all the church a-laughing." [2] "We have gotten a new diversion of little plays after supper. . . . I hope the godlie will preach against it also."

Charles's replies to his "dearest Aunt" were in the same vein.

"My sister and I goe on Sunday, in the afternoone, towards Frankeforde, and as much incognito as your Majesty went to Antwerp, for it is so great a secret that not above halfe the towne of Collen knows of it.[3] . . . I am just now beginning this letter in my sister's chamber, where there is such a noise that I never hope to end it. . . . I shall only tell your Majesty that we are now thinking how to pass our time, in which we find two difficulties, the one for want of the fiddlers, the other for somebody both to teach and assist at the dancing. . . . I have got my sister to send for Silvius, as one that is able to perform both; for the fiddle-de-dees, my Lord Taafe does promise to be their convoy, and in the meantime we must content ourselves with those that makes no difference between a hymn and a coranto. I have now received my sister's picture, that my dear cousin the Princess Louisa was pleased to draw, and do desire

---

[1] Lambeth MS. 645.76.　　[2] Ibid., 82.　　[3] Cottrell MS.

your Majesty thank her for me, for 'tis a most excellent picture." [1]

Charles's elegant signature assured his aunt that he would "yield to none in being your Majestie's most affectionate nephew".[2]

"La bonne Duchesse Sophie", now that she was a comparatively wealthy married woman, sent to her royal mother, who dared not send her linen to the laundress, little luxuries— full-length kid gloves and scent. The queen was disappointed that she could not muster the fare to meet her daughter for a holiday at Utrecht, but in June 1659, she struggled to Brussels "incognito, to see the King, not having seen him these nine yeares". She spent a delightful week, rambling "up and doune with my nephves and other good companie". She was careful to explain to her son that, as she lodged and fed under the roof of the Palatinate agent, she incurred no expense.[3]

IV

The career of Mary, the Queen of Bohemia's "best neece", had been somewhat unfortunate from the moment she had landed in Holland. Frederick Henry, Prince of Orange, regardless of his wife's feelings, had announced that his son's ten-year-old bride must be addressed as the Princess Royal. He himself set the example of remaining bareheaded in her presence. The Dutch were disgusted by this homage to "greatness of birth", and Amalia of Solms conceived an undying jealousy of her little daughter-in-law. Henrietta Maria retained no warm feelings for a child reft from her untimely to match with an arch-Protestant who could not offer her a crown. Mary was much her father's daughter. She was a regular Stuart child, with fine features, narrow brows, auburn

---

[1] Thurloe, ii. 488.   [2] Cottrell MS.   [3] Wendland, p. 108.

curls and a delicate air. Her character was not strong, but she could be amazingly obstinate. From the first she leant heavily upon her robust aunt. The Queen of Bohemia's own daughters resented their parent's maternal attentions to their cousin, who, in spite of the possession of a handsome young husband, ample means and presently hopes of a family, never ceased to complain. At the age of fifteen Mary suffered a severe miscarriage. Her husband had just succeeded to a troubled heritage. The last years of Frederick Henry had been embittered by conflicts with the States General and with his heir, who, nevertheless, proceeded to persist in the policy which had dimmed the popularity of the captor of s'-Hertogenbosch and Maastricht. The day when Oldenbarnevelt should be avenged was approaching.

Elizabeth was delighted when, after a lapse of five years, her niece again became pregnant. At four o'clock on the afternoon of November 4th, 1650, the Queen of Bohemia broke off a letter to her son with the words, "Whether it bee labour or not I know but I must goe to her".[1] A message had arrived that her niece felt unwell. Five hours later Mary, Princess of Orange, gave birth to a posthumous son. Her husband had died of smallpox eight days previously. Although he had not been a model of faithfulness, she was inconsolable, and her situation was certainly wretched. William II had just failed in a violent attempt to raise the authority of the Stadholderate at the expense of the provincial liberties. The States, in consequence, refused the infant Prince William succession to his father's dignities. Mary's claim to be his guardian was disputed by her inimical mother-in-law and the Elector of Brandenburg. Her aunt rejoiced with her when the States eventually decreed that she should be "absolute tutoress" of her child, while his grandmother and uncle by marriage officiated as joint inspectors of his property, but further trials

[1] Wendland, p. 13.

awaited the young widow. The days when Princes of Orange could invite exiled royal Stuarts to reside indefinitely in their territories were past. The States, whose sympathies had always been with the English republicans, entered into formal alliance with Cromwell, and Mary was forbidden to receive her brothers in Holland. She had never been liked by the Dutch, whose language she had refused to learn. Protracted visits to her relations at Spa, Aix-la-Chapelle, Cologne, Brussels and Paris failed to effect a permanent improvement in her health or spirits. By the time that she was four and twenty she displayed every sign of drifting into semi-invalidism. Her aunt at first suffered great anxiety lest Mary's fears of consumption might be grounded on fact.[1] Hysterical messages repeatedly summoned the Queen of Bohemia in inclement weather to a sick-chamber where the patient's worst complaint appeared to her sympathetic but sharp-sighted visitor to be lack of occupation. Mary, who did not care for riding or walking, was commanded by her tonic aunt to take violent exercise in a form unusual amongst royal princesses. Charles II's secretary learnt from the lady whom he termed "the best of Queens", "My deere Neece begins, God be thanked, to mend in her lookes and health since she saws billets every morning. . . . If she will exercise enough she will be soone well. After I had my first child I was just so. . . . I tell her of it, but she is deadlie lasie." [2]

Mary's nervous distaste for public appearances led her to perform unavoidable duties at the last possible moment and without due preparation. Elizabeth deplored her niece's unceremonious behaviour, and did her best to set her an example. When the new French Ambassador, M. de Chanut, asked for an audience of the Queen of Bohemia, her Majesty took pains to appear with due *éclat*. She issued invitations for a large Saturday evening reception at the Wassenaer Hof, a

[1] Wendland, 72.   [2] *Archaeologia*, 37. 239.

form of entertainment at which no square meal need be offered and the calls made upon shabby and infirm furniture would not be exacting. Her largest expenditure would be upon the wax candles, whose ends were so carefully hoarded by her *Maître d'Hôtel*. Charles Louis had demanded his share of his late father's State hangings, and Elizabeth had forwarded all the gilt leather wall-covering from her dining-room and the red leather from her "great cabinett". However, she had skilfully packed her denuded walls with pictures, hung so close together that the most inquisitive visitor might not detect her loss.[1] When the great night of her entertainment came, she observed with satisfaction, and much in the spirit of her godmother Elizabeth Tudor, that her chief guest "had a verie handsome prospect, as he came to me, of at least eight or nine verie handsome young gentlemen", and seven blooming young ladies, daughters of eminent English royalist or Dutch families. "The ladies took it a little ill that my neece did not send for them when he had audience of her." All whom the Queen of Bohemia had invited to lend her court a dazzling appearance had accepted "verie civilly, and desired me to tell my neece that at any audience herafter, if she would let them know of it, they would not fail to wait upon her". Elizabeth heard with regret that Mary had received the Ambassador supported by none but her usual attendants. "Not so much as my Lady Brainford, who was not sent for, so that she did not goe. . . . But", adds the queen "she was with me."

The little Prince of Orange was, like many only sons of neurotic widowed mothers, preternaturally quiet and self-contained, "a verie extraordinarie childe. . . ." He had "not the witt of a childe, but of a man".[2] "My little Nephue was at the super and sett verie still all the time", recorded the Queen of Bohemia in a cheerful letter to the secretary of Charles II,

[1] Wendland, p. 68.   [2] *Ibid.*, p. 200.

describing "how I have beene debauched this last weeke in sitting up late to see dancing".[1] This weakly boy of four, on whom many hopes were pinned, had recently been involved in a carriage accident. The Queen of Bohemia had arrived "upon the bridge at the Princess of Orange's house" to discover that "God be thanked there was no hurt, onelie the coache broken. I tooke him into my coache and brought him home".[2]

When the prince was nine, his benevolent great-aunt supplied him for a season with a lively playmate, aged seven. Duchess Sophie had brought to the Hague the child of a broken home—Elizabeth Charlotte, only daughter of Charles Louis by his first marriage. To the amusement of all her world, the Queen of Bohemia, who had never evinced much delight in the antics of her own offspring, was transformed at the age of sixty-three into the willing slave of an imperious grand-daughter. "Liselotte", or "Lisette" reminded her Majesty of the beauty of her family, her short-lived Henriette. In character the daughter of the Elector Palatine, who afterwards rightly described herself as "tough", was very like her successful aunt Sophie. "The Queen", wrote Sophie to Charles Louis, "talks no more of sporting dogs or monkeys, but only of Liselotte, for whom she has taken a violent fancy. . . . I have never seen a mother more besotted of a child." Her doting grandparent not only allowed Liselotte to sit by her side, her Majesty actually fetched a chair herself for her small companion. She superintended at length the toilette of the "prettie talking childe", who, she proudly declared, "is not like the House of Hesse. She is like ours".[3]

The Queen of Bohemia led a round-eyed and impressionable little girl, with bobbing fair ringlets and rosy cheeks, beneath many portraits of a dark, melancholy-looking gentleman,

[1] Evelyn, v. 214.   [2] *Ibid.*, 195.
[3] Bodemann, pp. 20, 21.

and told his grand-daughter the sad but stirring story of the Winter King. Liselotte ardently begged for a picture of the hero to hang above her own bed. After its arrival at Hanover, Duchess Sophie wrote to the Hague that Liselotte had talked for eight days of the letter of thanks which she was writing to the queen-grandmother. "Without doubt it will be something remarkable." Liselotte received the present of a puppy, and the promise of another gift when she spoke French better. She began to pick up English. The Queen sent to Heidelberg portraits of "my favorits together"—the likenesses of Liselotte and "Celadon, the pretiest beagle that ever was seene."[1]

The dancing master attended daily at the Wassenaer Hof. Happy dreams floated through the brain of a royal grandmother as she watched a princess, who loved dancing, dance with vigour "the sarabande with castagnettes". Europe was not rich in Protestant princes of a suitable age and rank to make Liselotte happy. The Queen of Bohemia decided that she hoped she saw the future Queen of Denmark. Her letters to Charles Louis became unconsciously comic. "I ame taken with her. . . . You know I care not much for children. . . . You may beleeve me when I commend a childe." The impressions made by the Queen of Bohemia's grand-daughter on several withered ladies-in-waiting, and on the small Prince of Orange, were solemnly described. The prince was highly attracted by a lady who could not abide him. There was a sad scene one bedtime, when Duchess Sophie remarked in English that Liselotte's brother had the better face. "She understood, and manie a teare was shed." But the Queen of Bohemia saved the situation by announcing firmly that in her opinion the face of Liselotte was the more agreeable.

Sophie wrote that the Queen was spoiling Liselotte, and the Queen wrote that although Sophie was inclined to spoil Liselotte, and the Hague was "madd about her", the child

[1] Duchess Sophie confided to her brother that personally she was nervous of being "eaten up" by the many dogs kept by her mother.

was miraculously unspoilt.[1] "Poor Sophie", as her mother now called her, had entered her thirtieth year in October, 1659. She had been married thirteen months. It was essential to her happiness that she should be fruitful. Sophie cautiously took to her bed when her expert parent told her that her symptoms were unmistakable.

To the satisfaction of Liselotte, her grandmother chose her as companion for a call at the court of the Princess of Orange. Sixty years later, Liselotte remembered clearly every detail of this exciting adventure. "Before I departed, my aunt said to me, 'Lisette, take care not to do as you usually do, and wander off so that you cannot be found. Follow the Queen closely, so that she will not need to wait for you.' I said, 'Oh, aunt, you will see that I have behaved very nicely'". When the oddly assorted royal relatives arrived at their destination, Liselotte was instantly fascinated by the appearance of a prominent court lady, whose complexion denoted indigestion. She had never seen her hostess, but her host was well known to her. The most important child at the Hague had already been summoned several times to the Wassenaer Hof to play with the Queen of Bohemia's grand-daughter. "Please", said Liselotte to small Prince William, "tell me who is the lady with such a fiery nose?" "That", replied the correct princeling with evident enjoyment, "is the Princess Royal, my mother." Horror and chagrin struck Liselotte dumb, until an attractive maid of honour called Anne Hyde suggested to Prince William that he should invite his little friend to play in his mother's bedchamber. Determined not to err further, Liselotte only consented to retire out of earshot on the condition that the good-humoured English *mademoiselle* would remember to call her when the Queen of Bohemia was ready to leave. She soon recovered her spirits, playing "all sorts of games" with Prince William. Unluckily, when her summons came, they were

[1] Wendland, pp. 122, 125, 126, 132, 138, 200.

delightfully engaged, rolling together in their best clothes, upon a Turkey carpet. "I took one leap and rushed into the drawing-room, but the Queen was already in the ante-chamber. However I was not scared." After giving the skirt of her hostess a good tug, to attract her attention, Liselotte performed "a very pretty curtsey". She then proceeded to imitate pompously "step by step" the stately farewell progress of the Queen of Hearts towards her waiting equipage. She could not understand why beholders appeared entertained.

When the royal ladies reached the Wassenaer Hof again, they repaired immediately to Duchess Sophie. Seating herself on her daughter's couch, the Queen of Bohemia gave way at last to peals of laughter. "Lisette has had a fine outing!" Her Majesty then related all the exploits of her companion, but, to Liselotte's relief, her aunt, whom she feared much more than her grandmother, "laughed even more than the queen. She called me to her and said, 'Well done, Lisette, you have revenged us on that haughty princess'." [1][2]

v

The Queen of Bohemia, whose admirers declared that she might justly lay claim to her godmother's impress, "Semper Eadem", was beginning at last to show some unmistakable signs of age. Duchess Sophie noticed that her mother was inclined to doze after meals. Liselotte afterwards recounted

[1] Stevenson, ii. 256-7.

[2] The after-career of the favourite grandchild of Elizabeth of Bohemia was sad. Liselotte was early bartered by her callous father to France. She became the unloved wife of the decadent widower, Duke of Orleans, and mother of the notorious Regent Orleans. She resembled her grandmother in her passionate love of pet animals and hunting, and her quarrels with her son. Throughout a long life at the artificial French court she remained obstinately German and remarkable for her integrity and freedom of speech. In 1689 Heidelberg Castle, the beloved home of her infancy, was plundered and irreparably ruined by French troops sent into the Palatinate by Louis XIV to assert the hereditary claim of his unwilling sister-in-law.

[3] Bodemann, p. 366.

memories of a dowager mild as milk. "They tell a story that my grandmother, the Queen of Bohemia, inspired by ambition, never gave her husband a moment's peace until he was declared King. There is not a single word of truth in that. The Queen used to think of nothing but seeing comedies and ballets and reading romances." The grandchild forgot that the Queen's first experience of a playwright had been a spell-binder—William Shakespeare. During her last decade at the Hague, the Winter Queen, eternally scribbling in a palace insufficiently warmed and lighted, complained often of hard weather. She was "deadlie colde". "I have such an extreme colde, my nose and eyes running like a fountaine, as I cannot say aniething to you. . . . I pray tell Sir Charles Cottrell I have the colde so extremelie as I cannot write to him till Thursday." [1] Her instructions to Sir Charles became increasingly rambling. He must remember to buy a collar for one pet dog and go to visit another "and inquire what Broughton's maide has done with the little bitche and let me heare all the news . . ." [2] The cold, and the noise made by the young people of Holland rushing down the snow-clad avenue beneath her windows in their sledges tinkling with bells, distracted her so that she could not complete a description of a Twelfth Night party. [3] But she retained many of her old tastes and a marvellous memory for the past. She, who could no longer afford diamonds, remembered exactly which towns of Germany supplied the best semi-precious stones. The "prettie braseletts of black agatt" which she needed would be best bought at Zweibrücken. [4] She was as pleased as a girl when her son sent her from Heidelberg a trifling turquoise ornament. She much admired its modern setting, and now that it was quite the fashion for widows to have apartments decorated in colours, she would certainly wear the lucky blue stone. [5]

[1] *Archaeologia*, 37. 238.   [2] Cottrell MS.   [3] Evelyn v. 217.
[4] Cottrell MS.; Craven MS.   [5] Wendland, p. 12

FF

With February 1660, the visit of the Queen of Bohemia's married daughter and pet grandchild drew towards its close, but a distraction raised her spirits. Before dawn on the last night of that month, her nephew Charles left Brussels hurriedly for Breda. A message from General Monk had urged him to quit Spanish territory, lest, in the event of a Restoration, he should be detained by a nation at war with England. In reply Charles forwarded the famous Declaration of Breda. Elizabeth wrote imploring her son to advance her a little ready money. She could no longer obtain any garments on credit, and expected to "see great companie here verie shortlie". She was not wrong. On May 4th the Princess of Orange triumphantly informed the States General that her brother had been officially requested by Parliament to return to England, whereupon the States of Holland besought his Majesty, by special embassy, "that he would grace that province with his royal presence" *en route* for his kingdom. The unbelievable had happened. The Queen of Bohemia was to witness a Restoration. Henrietta Maria, in her French convent, spoke tearfully of "a miracle", but Elizabeth's motto to the last had been "One day I hope it will change". At first she dared not hope too greatly. "Monk is come into London with two regiments of horse and three of foot. What he will doe none knows." Affairs in England at the end of February 1660, appeared to her to be in "as great a disorder as ever".

On good St Davy's Day she wrote with growing confidence of "the change that is come in England". By March 8th she was unable to settle to her writing-desk. Congratulatory visitors kept on pouring in to tell her news that was "better and better".[1] For eight stormy spring days, from May 15th–23rd, the Queen of Bohemia was the chief lady in a series of festivities at the Hague "which could not have been more splendid if all the Monarchs of Europe had met there". She

[1] Wendland, pp. 133, 136, 142.

was waiting on the steps of the palace assigned to Charles when he arrived. The Mauritshuis, built by Prince John Maurice of Nassau, Governor of Brazil, was one of the noblest additions to the largest village in Europe effected during her residence in Holland. It was to a gallery of this sumptuous house, rich in heavily carved balustrading and Dutch oil-paintings, that the king summoned his relatives next day to feast their eyes on the sight of gold sent to him from England, lying a-glitter in a portmanteau.[1] On the first evening of revelry Elizabeth retired early, with Mary, who had slept badly the night before. But no inhabitant of the Hague was destined to sleep well on the night of the King of England's arrival. Cannon fired so violently until a late hour that fears were expressed lest the walls of the antique Buitenhof should collapse. Henceforward the English royal family dined in public daily, the seat on the king's right hand being invariably reserved for the Queen of Bohemia. "He useth me more like a Mother than an Aunt."[2] Charles, "the civilest person that can be", at once mentioned his desire to see Prince Rupert in his kingdom.[3] To add to the gaiety of the occasion, the widowed queen, who detested trappings of woe, brightened her usual attire by the addition of a white undergown, a white *berthe* and full-length white kid gloves.[4] A band played throughout meals, and many a health was drunk by a company with "teares of joye in their eyes". In the streets outside, crowds waited day and night, bonfires blazed and bells pealed. The Hague was crowded by English visitors, all eager to see His Majesty, his aunt, sister and brothers, the Prince of Orange's palaces, the "House in the Wood", the Great Church in the market-place and the little one at Lausdune, celebrated for its monument to a lady who produced three hundred and sixty-

---

[1] Pepys, i. 54.   [2] Wendland, pp. 145–7.   [3] *Ibid.*, p. 148.
[4] According to a painting by Janssen in the Royal collection, Windsor Castle, representing a **ball** given during this week.

five infants. English gallants bought themselves new suits of
fine Holland stuffs, and drove around in coaches, singing
cheerfully, accompanied by ladies wearing many patches.
Amongst those who pressed to kiss the hand of the Queen
of Bohemia was the Secretary to the Navy Board. Mr
Pepys found her Majesty "very debonair", but was amazed
by the simplicity of her attire.[1] After dining, his Majesty
spent alternate evenings with his sister and his aunt. Both
accompanied him to a spectacular fête offered by the Spanish
Ambassador.

At length the wind was reported favourable for a passage to
England, and throughout the night of May 22nd the town
was as busy as on a market day. Long before dawn, upwards
of fifty thousand people had stationed themselves along the
dykes leading to Scheveningen. Luggage began to rumble
down from the Mauritshuis before 8 A.M. next morning, and
presently the Queen of Bohemia's coach formed one of a long
procession of vehicles, moving slowly towards dancing waters.
The firing of cannon and musketry on the shore, to which the
warships at anchor responded, produced so dense a smoke
that for some time the brightest and youngest eyes could
discern nothing of the English fleet which had come to fetch
Charles II home. A luxurious barge had been provided by
the States to bear the royalties out to the *Royal Charles*,
but the crowds were so great that the family party got separated.
His Majesty's aunt reported jubilantly: "The King and I went
alone, in one long boat that belonged to the ship. As soone
as they had him in" the jolly English tars cried out "Wee have
him! Wee have him! God bless King Charles!" The Queen
of Bohemia dined in state as chief guest of the swarthy,
laughing king. All of his subjects, whom he presented to her
on this happy exciting day, sang the same song. They hoped
soon to see her Majesty in London. The king's last words

[1] Pepys, i. 59.

were a reminder that she should tell Rupert to hasten to him.[1]
The admiral's ship was already under weigh "with a fresh
gale and most happy weather", when the Queen of Bohemia
supported the weeping Princess of Orange into a boat bound
for the Dutch shore.

Mary was to visit her brother as soon as possible. She made
no secret of her intention of settling in her native land. When,
however, the day came, four months later, for her to set sail,
she did so in deep gloom. She had been seized at the last
moment by an apprehension that some mischance might
befall her only child during her absence. She consigned the
strange, clever little boy, with many tears, to the care of the
aunt who had been a mother to her. No sooner had she
stepped on board Lord Sandwich's ship than she learnt news
which prostrated her. Her youngest brother, Henry, had died
of smallpox at Whitehall four days previously. The Queen
of Bohemia mourned her "sweetest nepheu" sincerely. She
had loved him as much as if he had been "my owne childe",
His premature death was "a great loss to our House." [2]

After her "best neece's" departure, Elizabeth complained
of finding the Hague a desert. Lord Craven, too, had gone to
England, where, in concert with Sir Charles Cottrell, he was
doing his best to represent to Parliament the distressful situation of the Queen of Bohemia. In September, 1660, ten
thousand pounds a head were voted to all English princesses
of the blood royal. In the following December a further ten
thousand was added to the grant made to the Queen of Bohemia, as a token of the high esteem in which she was held by
Parliament. She was still in correspondence with Charles
Louis on the subject of her settlement in his principality, but
already by November the thought of paying at least a visit to
England was firing her imagination. She waited eagerly for the
London news retailed by Lord Craven. Her correspondent

[1] Wendland, pp. 148–9.   [2] *Ibid.*, p. 175.

did not lack for matter. The news of the Duke of
York's secret marriage to Anne Hyde, daughter of the Chancellor and ex-maid of honour to the Princess of Orange,
startled Europe in October, 1660. The Queen of Bohemia
wrote loftily to her eldest son, assuring him that he might
disbelieve the story. That Anne was expecting a child was a
fact. Old Dr. Rumph had been consulted as long ago as May
by a distracted maid of honour who had come to him with a
tale of fish-poisoning, asking for violent remedies. The Queen
of Bohemia's physician had proceeded to bleed her, but suddenly perceiving her condition, had forborne, prescribed the
mildest of medicines and held his peace. If the wretched girl
had been a wife, argued the Queen, why should she have been
so desirous to end a pregnancy? [1] Presently it appeared that
the "base marriage" had taken place, but none too soon, and
Henrietta Maria left Paris for London, announcing that she
was going to break a match which had been cemented within
eight weeks of the wedding ceremony by the birth of a son.
Elizabeth's comments on her sister-in-law's actions always
bore signs of strong effort to behave with Christian forbear-
ance towards an impossible character. Even when she had
heard of Henrietta's attempts to coerce the stripling Duke of
Gloucester into a change of religion, she had permitted herself
no more than the reflection that she "would not have believed
that the queen would have proceeded thus".[2] She did not
now follow Henrietta's example. As soon as she discovered
that Charles II had acknowledged Anne Hyde as his brother's
wife, she followed suit with all possible dignity. "My godson's
marriage afflicts all his kindred and doth himself no small
wrong." Henceforward from her bland references to "the
Duchess of York" no stranger could have detected that she
bitterly resented the intrusion of a maid of honour whom she
had once liked, into her family.[3]

[1] Wendland, pp. 181–5.　　[2] Evelyn, ii. 152.　　[3] Wendland, pp. 187, 212.

Prince Rupert wrote to his mother that he had been very kindly entertained by the Lord Mayor of London. Henrietta Maria had promised to suggest to her son that he should ask his aunt to visit him, but had not yet done so. Lord Craven told the same story. To be French was fashionable in London now, and the Queen-Mother was all French. She was much more liked than the Princess of Orange. She was continually surrounded by such a crowd of courtiers that Lord Craven could not even approach her. Elizabeth, who had heard that Henrietta was furiously jealous, waited tactfully. "Patience", wrote the single-hearted Lord Craven, "is a spestiall vertue in this age. The King has dun nothing for me but putts me off with good words."

The Princess of Orange had done little to win popularity since her arrival in England. She had actually been outside Whitehall but once in eight weeks—for a trip to Hampton Court—and, what was more incredible, had only once dined in public even within the precincts of the palace. She stayed in her own suite of apartments and considered her symptoms. The smoke of the city of London gave her, she decided, an oppression on the chest. By Christmas week she had developed an illness to which physicians could give a name. On December 20th she was declared to be suffering from smallpox, but on the following day she was reported so much better that hopes were entertained that her indisposition might, after all, be no more than measles. The Duke of Gloucester's death had been attributed by many busybodies to the failure of his physicians to bleed him sufficiently. The Princess of Orange was bled repeatedly.

On a short last day of 1660 a coach from the Wassenaer Hof thundered along the familiar road to Leyden, where the young Prince of Orange was pursuing his studies. Tears streamed down the face of the Queen of Bohemia as she took into her arms an orphan great-nephew. Mary, who had so often ailed without reason, had died with dramatic promptitude on Christmas Eve. Observers noticed with surprise that her undemonstrative little son appeared to feel his loss "more acutely than might have been expected from a child of his age". The Queen of Bohemia was "so sad, I feare I write nonsense".[1]

VI

"I beleeve", wrote the Queen of Bohemia to her eldest son, on Monday, May 6th, 1661, "that you will be surprised to find by this that I ame going for England. I goe from hence Thursday next. The States give me ships. . . . I cannot tell you how long I shall stay there." She added that she had "resolved on the idea" before a recent visit from Rupert, but so suddenly that she had been unable to apprise Sophie, who was even now *en route* for Holland. Her reason for acting hastily was that her creditors had begged her to go to London while Parliament was still sitting. She had therefore decided not to wait for an escort from England, but "now that the Coronation is well passed with great gallantrie" to avail herself without further delay of the warm invitation given to her by her nephew on board the *Royal Charles*.[2]

The invitation had been warm, but it had never been repeated. In her less buoyant moments, now that she had committed herself, Elizabeth realized that the habits of forty years had a deadening effect, and that she might do worse than stay where she was. With the money which had already arrived from England she had managed to settle some debts and recover some jewellery. In December even Lord Craven had admitted that "all things were going very crosse" in London, and that he was glad that her Majesty was not there. But the thought of England had been irresistible, and she believed that she knew her nephew. Presented with a *fait accompli*, the most

<hr>

[1] Wendland, p. 189.   [2] *Ibid.*, p. 203.

civil being in Europe would be incapable of acting " un-
handsomely". Only laziness withheld him from sending for
his dear aunt.

Her final decision had been hasty for several reasons. As
soon as the daughters got wind of her plan, they had overwhelmed her with well-meant attentions. "The hipocrit to
the Root" had written in her usual depressing manner that
she would naturally wish to pay her humble respects before
her royal parent embarked upon a journey which would no
doubt conduce to her satisfaction. The Princess Elizabeth
would be ready to set out for the Hague at a day's warning.
No more would be necessary, since she proposed to take with
her nothing but a change of linen and her night clothes.
Duchess Sophie also wrote typically. She intended to accompany her mother to London, and wrote cheerfully that the duke
and she need bring in their train no more than eight lacqueys
and six pages. The only drawback was that she suspected
that she was with child again.

On Wednesday, May 8th, the Queen of Bohemia made her
will. She was in her usual health, but common sense told her
that any lady in her sixty-sixth year about to undertake a sea-
passage would do well to face facts. After announcing that
the Elector Palatine was her heir, she deliberately proceeded
to bestow elsewhere everything of value of which she might
die possessed. Rupert was to have all her rings, plate, furniture and ready money. To her spinster eldest daughter, who
was deplorably poor, her Majesty left her valuable emerald
ear-rings. Duchess Sophie was allotted something which she
would recognize—the fashionable short necklace of large
pearls which had been the Queen of Bohemia's invariable wear
since her widow-hood. Her Majesty's Catholic son was also
handsomely remembered. Prince Edward was to be sent the
great table diamond which would be found somewhat feebly
attached by a ribbon to a bracelet. Nothing else of outstanding

value remained in the queen's little gold enamelled box in fashion of a trunk. The remains of her small store might be classed as trinkets—bracelets of jet, coral, cornelian and small brilliants, the "bisars stones" sent to her from Constantinople by poor "Thom Roe" and "a little bracelet of diamonde set in gold with C. H." (for Christian of Halberstadt) "under ye Locket".[1] The last will and testament of the Queen of Bohemia was duly witnessed by Sophie's brother-in-law, George William of Brunswick Lüneberg, the Margrave of Brandenburg's resident at the Hague, and two Dutch gentlemen, one of whom bore the name of Wassenaer. All parties appeared personally before the Hague Notary Public, Martin Beechman, on May 9th.[2]

Her Majesty's last days in the dilapidated house which had been her home for forty years were spent in the exhausting business of receiving farewell visits. Her departure eventually took place twenty-four hours later than she had expected, and not unattended by confusion. All inhabitants of the Wassenaer Hof experienced relief when the French Ambassador's coach drew up in its courtyard. M. de Thou was enchanted to oblige her Majesty with the loan of an equipage to bear her on the first stage of her journey.

The queen's cabinet did not look unfamiliar on that early May day. Her larger furniture and pictures had not yet been disturbed. Since she was to be Lord Craven's guest on her arrival in her native land, she would not require immediately anything save her personal effects. While she was at her writing-desk, a messenger who could not be denied entrance, even on this morning of flying footsteps and high resolve, was admitted to her. The captain of a little English frigate was the bearer of a letter from the King of England.

The small train of attendants who left the Voorhout in the wake of the Queen of Bohemia presented a perfect chronicle

[1] Wendland, p. 214; S.P. 81. 56.28.   [2] Camden Society, vol. 83, p. 109.

of her career. Scotland, Warwickshire, the Palatinate, Prague and the Hague were all represented. In the coach with the Queen and M. de Thou sat a Bohemian countess and three attached Dutch gentlewomen. At Delft the royal traveller was ecstatically greeted by a beaming matron and an excited small girl. Sophie, although she was now certain that she was with child again, had managed to bring Liselotte to see the dear grandmother-queen, who had so often with a sinking heart waved farewell to a ship bound for England, at last herself the heroine of an adventure.

The family party set sail in the small vessel which was to bear them to Hellevoetsluis, where the three warships provided by the States General lay at anchor. As Dutch shipping and towers and fruit-stalls began to move slowly past the windows of her cabin, the Queen of Bohemia settled to her pen again. She had already once to-day addressed herself to Prince Rupert. The letter which she headed "Between Delft and Delf-shaven" was one of the most emotional ever indited by her. She had every reason for agitation. The messenger who had caught her just before she left the Wassenaer Hof had brought her a nerve-shattering epistle. The King of England begged his aunt to defer her journey. He had hoped that Lord Arlington and Prince Rupert had made clear to her that she should not come into England until he thought fit. Her Majesty had thereupon deferred her journey while she wrote two more letters. To her nephew she had explained that since she had taken pompous farewell of all authorities and friends at the Hague, she could not, without causing grave scandal, abandon her plans at the last moment. She offered piteously to make her stay as short as he might direct. To her nephew's Chancellor, whom she entreated to stand her friend, she said simply that she had thought his Majesty would be glad to see her as soon as the coronation was over. She had quite understood that her presence at that ceremony would have involved him in undesirable expense. To her son, now that she was defiantly and irrevocably bound for the unknown, she wrote: "I go with a resolution to suffer all things constantly. I thank God He has given me courage. I shall not do as poor Neece,[1] but will resolve upon all misfortunes. I love you ever, my dear Rupert. . . ."[2]

VII

As the Dutch coast-line faded from the Queen of Bohemia's view that evening to the sound of a mighty rushing wind, the French Ambassador at the Hague reported at length to Paris. M. de Thou's opinion of the King of England's aunt was high.

"She told me very frankly that she would not oppose the interests of France; that she was rejoiced that your Majesty was sending an ambassador in ordinary to reside in that court. She talks of returning again to the Hague, but I doubt whether the king her nephew will permit her to do so, for assuredly she cannot but be very useful to him, being a good creature, of a temper very civil and always equal, one who has never disobliged anybody and who is thus capable, in her own person, of securing affection for the whole royal family, and one who, although a sexagenarian in age, preserves full vigour of body and mind. Although she is in debt here, more than 200,000 crowns, to a number of poor creditors and trades people who have furnished her subsistence during the disgraces of her house, nevertheless from the friendship they had for her person they let her go without a murmur, and without any other assurance of their payment than the high opinion they have of her goodness and generosity, and that as soon as she shall have means to give them satisfaction, she will not, although absent and distant, fail to do it."[3]

[1] This refers to the unhelpful behaviour of the deceased Princess of Orange during her stay in England.
[2] Bromley, pp. 188–9.   [3] Harl. MS. 4530, i. 972.

VIII

The princess, whose exit from England had been attended
by unprecedented crowds and pageantry, slipped home, after
nearly half a century's absence, under cover of dark, so that the
poverty of her welcome might pass unnoticed.[1] One of the
most inveterate sightseers and gossips in the capital was abroad
on the night that she came up river from Gravesend. Mr
Pepys spent the evening enjoyably at a tavern opposite the
Exchange, listening to a skilful fellow who could both play
the bagpipes and give realistic bird imitations.[2] Nobody
recorded meeting a string of coaches bearing the Craven arms,
bowling up the elm avenue towards the entrance gate of
Drury House, Drury Lane.[3]

"I love to live in quiet"[4] had for some time been the vain
plea of the Winter Queen. In his London house Lord Craven
was able to provide her with the peace commanded by the
possessor of ample means. Turkey carpets without a single hole
in them stilled the footsteps of attentive servitors who displayed
no signs of being potential gladiators. Magnificent and docile
furniture and punctual and appetizing meals were suddenly
the daily lot of a lady long unaccustomed to such things.
Drury House had a spacious and picturesque garden.

The weather that greeted the exile was thoroughly English.
On the first Tuesday and Wednesday after her arrival, hail-
storms of exceptional ferocity swept the streets of London.[5]

---

[1] Add. MS. 10116.342.   [2] Pepys, i. 164.

[3] Drury House, built by Sir William Drury (d. 1579) and enlarged by
Lord Craven, who re-named it Craven House, was a large red-brick
mansion. An engraving of it is reproduced on page 174 of Besant's "London
in the Time of the Stuarts". By the end of the eighteenth century it had
become much dilapidated, and part of it was a tavern. The antiquary
Thomas Pennant noted that "in searching after Craven House, I knew it
instantly by the sign—that of the Queen of Bohemia's head". A fresco,
representing Lord Craven on horseback, long decorated its courtyard.
The house was demolished early in the nineteenth century.

[4] Wendland, 186.   [5] Pepys, i. 65.

The court was in mourning for the Duke of Cambridge—
the infant son borne to James, Duke of York by Anne Hyde.
Nevertheless, the fact that no effort was made to entertain
his Majesty's aunt caused comment in court circles. A story
that she had come contrary to his will persisted and was offered
as explanation of the fact that no apartments in Whitehall or
Denmark House had been allotted to her. Londoners prophesied
that the stay of the Queen of Bohemia in their midst would
not be prolonged.[1] Elizabeth, however, had made up her mind
within a month of her return to settle in London. Charles,
as she had expected, was incapable of asking her to withdraw
from his capital. But he did not offer her a home. She could
not impose upon Lord Craven's generosity indefinitely. The
worst of housekeepers cheerfully faced the prospect of becoming
once more the mistress of a large house belonging to someone
else. In June she came to an agreement to take a lease of a
palatial London residence at present occupied by Dutch
Ambassadors. She planned to move into Exeter House, Strand,
in August.[2] Her first choice had been Leicester House, Leicester
Fields, but its owner had not displayed enthusiasm at the
prospect of being the landlord of royalty. Old servants begging
to be received again into her Majesty's employment began
to present themselves at Lord Craven's gates. Old servants,
left behind in Holland, received with surprise and delight
wages and tidings forwarded by her Majesty's own gracious
hand. "Your Majesty is a woman of her word." Her loving
servants rejoiced to learn that her Majesty's visit was most
acceptable to his Majesty, and that she was extremely satisfied
with her entertainment in England. Her old servants had told
this to everybody they met, since a lying report had declared
quite otherwise. Charles Louis, too, had heard quite otherwise

---

[1] Add. MS. 10116.350.
[2] Exeter House, Strand, stood on the site of the present Burleigh Street,
and was built by Thomas Cecil, first Earl of Exeter.

and needed reassurance. As the summer progressed, the Queen of Bohemia's letters to Heidelberg took on the tone of a condescending society favourite. The names of attentive English peers and peeresses shone in her correspondence like a Milky Way. Far from being lonely, she was continually surrounded by the best "good companie" obtainable in England. "Everie week I march to one place or other with the King." [1] The Duke of Ormonde had feasted his Majesty's aunt at his Kensington country house. She had accepted an invitation to visit Lady Herbert, who had taken a house for the summer at Hampton Court. The Duchess of Richmond and Lady Sunderland, by an odd coincidence, had both developed smallpox on the same day—the one in London, the other at Rufford. Finally, the King was going to take his aunt to a theatrical entertainment—"Davenant's 'Opera', as he calls it".[2]

July 2nd was the date chosen by Charles II to bear the Queen of Bohemia to witness the second part of "The Siege of Rhodes" by Sir William D'Avenant.[3] The theatre was packed when the hour appointed for the raising of the curtain arrived, but the curtain could not be raised, for the expected royalties had not yet made their appearance. During a long and weary wait the audience grew restive, and presently some flooring in the upper part of the house collapsed, discharging volumes of dust upon periwigged gallants and patched and ringleted ladies in low-necked gowns of blush satins. At last a welcome sound of cheers rent the air outside the playhouse, and a nonchalant king entered, gallantly squiring an upright lady, well stricken in years, fair of complexion, with prominent features and blue-grey eyes of truly royal penetration.

[1] Wendland, p. 206.   [2] *Ibid.*, pp. 203, 212.
[3] Either at Salisbury Court or the Cockpit. D'Avenant's company was not established in the new Opera House, Lincoln's Inn Fields, until the following spring.

Only the most elderly Londoners warmed to the name of the Lady Elizabeth, daughter of the last king but one. Their best hope of explaining her importance to their descendants was to represent her as the mother of Prince Rupert. England had passed through a chastening storm since she had married abroad. The performance, which began as soon as the royalties were seated, was considered by Mr Pepys "very fine and magnificent".[1] Apparently nothing in the air of either Charles or Elizabeth told beholders that their unpunctuality was due to distressing family circumstances.

In view of her move to Exeter House, Elizabeth had instructed an agent at the Hague to pack and send over to London all her remaining furniture and effects from the Wassenaer Hof and Rhenen. A few minutes before Charles had arrived this evening, she had learnt from one "Michel" that all her goods had been arrested by order of the Elector Palatine. The King of England's coach waited outside Drury House, and the would-be spectators of "The Siege of Rhodes" waited at the theatre, while the Winter Queen, pathetically decked in gala attire, poured out to her royal nephew her tale of woe and insult. Charles, with his usual tact, refrained from expressing more than great surprise at her story, eventually got her off to the Opera and, remembering her obsolete taste for pageantry, left her comforted by an invitation to come to the House of Lords next week to see him arrayed in his royal robes and crown.[2] But if he thought that he had heard the last of the Elector Palatine's "staying" of the Queen of Bohemia's "stuffs", he was mistaken. Until a "Great Cold" laid her low in November, Elizabeth continued to revile her unnatural son. Charles Louis explained verbosely that he had merely intended to delay the cargo for a fortnight, in order that it might be inspected, lest any property which belonged to him, as his father's heir, might mistakenly have been

[1] Pepys, i. 176.   [2] Wendland, p. 206.

included in it. He denied having stirred up his mother's creditors. In less conciliatory vein he rebuked her for having complained of him publicly to the Ambassador of Brandenburg, warned her to beware of mischief-making servants, and expressed himself surprised to learn that the goods which she had needed so urgently had lain unloaded in the docks of London a fortnight after their arrival. He was also amazed to discover that the King of England had not the means to furnish a house for the Queen of Bohemia.[1]

The Dutch Ambassadors still lingered at Exeter House. Elizabeth was still the honoured guest in an opulent establishment. She answered haughtily: "If I had as much means to buy hangins as my Lord Craven has, I shoulde not have been so rigorous as to take what is my right. But his house will not be troubled with them, I think." She added that people would be surprised if they saw the furniture of which her son had attempted to deprive her. His drunken castellan at Rhenen had allowed all that came from there to get into such a condition that she was having to send the whole collection to the upholsterer. Neither stools, chairs nor canopies were fit for human use. She did not know of which servants her son bade her beware. She had so few. It was untrue that she had credited a tale that he had beaten his lawful wife or run at her with a naked sword. "You are apt to catsh at aniething against my nepheus." Her nephew the king was allowing her a thousand pounds a month, for life, and had promised her to use his utmost influence to obtain from his Parliament the arrears of the pension settled upon her at her marriage, twenty thousand pounds of which was already in course of payment.[2] Charles had done more. At her request he had written to ask Charles Louis whether a larger portion of her dower revenues could not be produced. The reply of Charles Louis, which opened silkily, "As for the queen my mother's

[1] Bromley, pp. 222-4.   [2] Wendland, pp. 208-11.

G G

affairs with me, which your Majesty is graciously pleased to mention . . ." was unsatisfactory.

Last year Elizabeth had told her son "under the rose" that she believed Charles II would not be in any hurry to marry.[1] His engagement to the Infanta Catherine, sister of the King of Portugal, had now been formally announced. Elizabeth hid her disappointment that the future Queen of England was a Catholic, told her son that the match would be good for trade, and wrote cordially to the unknown princess, who replied most promisingly that she would look upon the Queen of Bohemia as her mother in England. Since Henrietta Maria and her daughter had returned to France after a very brief experience of Whitehall, Elizabeth was the only lady of the blood royal in England. The Genoese Ambassador committed to paper his impressions of an audience with her this autumn:

"I made the last visit in the evening to the Queen of Bohemia, sister to the late king, and mother to the Prince Palatine . . . I went thither conducted by the master of the ceremonies, and found her in her cabinet, where she had assembled many ladies, to receive me with the greater decorum. She sent attendants to welcome me as I alighted from my coach, and at the head of the stairs I was met by Lord Craven, proprietor of the house where she lives and the principal director of her court. It is incredible the pleasure which her majesty showed at this my office, and the familiar courtesy with which she discoursed with me for a very long time upon the state of the most serene republic and other various matters, even inviting me to come sometimes to see her. This princess has learned from nature, and continued through the changes of her fortune, an incomparable goodness. . . Now she is re-stored to some authority, and thus is heightened the lustre of that affable manner with which she wonderfully conciliates the esteem and love of the court." [2]

[1] Wendland, p. 198.   [2] Everett Green, p. 409.

In October Duchess Sophie gave birth to another fine son. Sophie, fishing diligently for an invitation, thanked her mother for a perfect "packet" of letters of London news and wrote flatteringly that she feared her Majesty would find her "very homely" compared to the beautiful English ladies who came to Drury House every day. "There will doubtless be great magnificence in London when the lovely Infanta arrives." [1] Sophie's opinion of England had always been high. Elizabeth wrote to her Parisian son, Edward, asking him to send her patterns of gold and silver fringe, the second volume of *The Romance of Pharamond*, and reports of the latest fashions. She remembered the elegance of the *étui* cases once sent to her from the French capital by the Winter King. She would like also some little cases for scissors. Edward shopped obediently, and informed her that sable muffs were still being worn, but not so large as last season.[2] Her children were relieved to discover that the Queen of Bohemia appeared to have settled down perfectly happily to old age in her old home. Fifty-seven years later Liselotte remembered her grandmother as a most comfortable dowager. "Historians often tell lies. They tell a story about my grandfather, the King of Bohemia, to the effect that my grandmother, the Queen of Bohemia, inspired by ambition never gave her husband a moment's peace until he was declared King. There is not a single word of truth in that. The Queen used to think of nothing but seeing comedies and ballets and reading romances." [3]

Lord Craven was once more in possession of his noble Berkshire estates, but it does not appear from any letter of Elizabeth that she ever visited him in the country.

· By the close of the eighteenth century a story was current that, at some period during her widowhood in Holland, the Queen of Hearts had secretly bestowed her hand upon her benefactor. The wife of the sixth Earl Craven repeated the

[1] Bromley, pp. 262–5.   [2] *Ibid.*, 242–3.   [3] Stevenson, vol. 2, p. 168.

rumour in her memoirs.[1] Subsequently visitors to Hampstead Marshall and Ashdown, struck by the sight of gate-posts bearing a crown and coronet intertwined, and a painting of the Queen and Earl attended by Cupid, eagerly credited a romantic ending to the tale of a great friendship.[2] No contemporary document as yet forthcoming even hints at such a possibility, indeed the gossip at the court of Charles II was that Lord Craven might be rewarded by the hand of Elizabeth's eldest daughter, not yet an abbess and only seven years his junior.[3] Scandal was rife as to the relations of Henrietta Maria with her majordomo Lord Jermyn, and Anne of Austria with Cardinal Mazarin, but none touched the names of Elizabeth of Bohemia and William, Lord Craven, although her host was the queen's cavalier on many public occasions. When a French contemporary heard that the queen was at last going to remove her penurious household to Exeter House, he expressed his opinion that "*le pauvre Milor* Craven will be glad to be rid of her, so as not to be altogether eaten up".[4] There is ample evidence, however, that Elizabeth's memory was cherished to the last by her chivalrous host, who remained upon friendly terms with her children, and was appointed by Prince Rupert sole executor, and guardian of his natural daughter, Ruperta.[5]

Lord Craven survived Elizabeth of Bohemia by thirty-five years, loaded with honours and titles. During the Plague, with his accustomed courage, he refused to quit the capital, and with his accustomed generosity he gave some of his London property to be employed as plague houses and plague

---

[1] *Memoirs of the Margravine of Ansbach*, ii. 103.

[2] Miss Benger (ii. 432-3), without giving her authority, states that Sir Balthazar Gerbier was employed by Lord Craven to erect at Hampstead Marshall "a miniature Heidelberg" to be "consecrated to Elizabeth". Lysons (i. 286), quoting from the epitaph on Gerbier's tomb, points out that this building was only begun in 1662, and Elizabeth died in the February of that year. This house was burnt down before it was completed.

[3] Kennet, ii. 871.

[4] Harl. MS. 4530. ii. 245.   [5] Bromley, XXVI-XXIX.

pits.[1] He was equally active at the time of the Great Fire, and ever afterwards took particular interest in directing the suppression of fires in London streets. The little figure of the elderly earl, mounted on a favourite white horse, became so familiar to terror-stricken Londoners on such occasions, that they declared the sagacious steed was capable of carrying his helpful master unbidden to the scene of a conflagration. Lord Craven died unmarried at the age of eighty-eight. Hundreds of portraits of the Winter Queen, her family and her circle looked down from the walls of one of his country houses upon his declining years. The entire collection left by Elizabeth was brought by him to Combe, the home of her infancy. It included many oil paintings of the queen—as a fair child, as wife and mother, and as widow—several miniatures and one fine bust. Her poignant-eyed elder daughters, for whom she never found husbands, were represented again and again, in gowns of varying hues and designs, her luckless king and stirring sons in civil and military garb, her happily married daughters, smiling calmly. This historic collection remains intact,[2] and at Hampstead Marshall dozens of sporting trophies, the result of countless happy hunting expeditions made by the Diana of the Rhine, are still preserved.[3]

IX

On December 7th, 1661, her eldest son congratulated Elizabeth on her recovery from a "Great Cold".[4] She replied cheerfully on January 10th, 1662. Her nephew's physicians were in attendance upon her. One of them, Sir Alexander Fraizer, was well known to her. This talented Scot, from whom no secret of the English royal family was hidden, had

[1] The names of Craven Hill and Craven Road, W. 2, record one of these gifts.
[2] Collection of Cornelia, Countess of Craven.
[3] *Ibid.*   [4] Wendland, p. 212.

long been the companion of Charles II in exile. The doctors had "forced or persuaded" the Queen of Bohemia "to take phisick, to be quite ridd of my cold. It made me as sick as a dogg, but I think it did me good. Yet my owne physick did me most good, which was letting of blood, for now I am very well. It is so hott weather here as I have felt it colder in May."[1] London had experienced the green Yule which makes a fat kirkyard. On February 1st, Charles Louis voiced his hopes that "a faire Spring will rectifie, and a good air perfectly recover" her Majesty who should not have troubled to write with her own hand.[2] Before this letter arrived, the Winter Queen had made a winter flitting. Leicester House, Leicester Fields,[3] was after all to be hers. The Dutch Ambassadors had lingered maddeningly at Exeter House. Lord Leicester, taking pity on her, had agreed to let her have her first choice.

But the business of changing house, even in the mildest of Februaries, proved too much for a lady who had for many winters past struggled with a succession of colds in an insufficiently heated antique palace. Her long-standing bronchitis returned at once in aggravated form. Her heart was affected. Rupert had arrived from Vienna and was with her. On February 10th she suffered a haemorrhage from the lungs, and she sent her son to ask the King, the Duke of York and Chancellor Hyde to call upon her. She communicated "after the English rite". She had frequently declared that she had no ambition to live to a great age. To the concerned group who assembled around her bedside on February 11th, she calmly gave final instructions. She particularly begged Charles that the pension recently granted to her might be continued to her executors, so that the last of her old Hague creditors might be

[1] Hauck, *Briefe der Kinder des Winterkönigs*, p. 190.   [2] Wendland, p. 213.
[3] Leicester House stood on the north-east corner of the square now bearing its name, and its garden occupied the site of Lisle Street. It was a three-storied red-brick mansion, built 1632-6 and demolished in 1781.

paid. Charles's conscience smote him. In vain he told himself that his heroic aunt would never have mingled successfully with the lax, languishing belles and cynical gallants of his brilliant court. He had played the dutiful nephew, coming every week to take her out for little jaunts suitable to her age and tastes. She had appeared content in her circle of patrician dowagers with no pretensions to fashion or influence. Yet Charles was painfully struck by the spectacle of her coughing and panting in a strange, hired house, sparsely furnished with some incredible relics from the Heidelberg of forty years past. Her brain was perfectly clear and her spirits were obviously high. He pressed her to make one more move—this time to the comforts of Whitehall.

But the long-hoped-for invitation had come too late. Next night, shortly after midnight, as she sat propped upright in a chair, by the fireside of her hired home, the Winter Queen, who had only been "frighted" once in her life, became conscious of an extraordinary sensation.[1]

x

The news that the Queen of Bohemia had gone out like a candle, caused very little distress in her nephew's gay and subtle court. The most fashionable architects disparaged "the Gothick manner", and the Queen of Bohemia had been astonishingly Gothic. In Paris, Louis XIV refused to sign the letters of condolence prepared by his secretary for transmission to the mourning King of England and Duke of York. The King had been seen at Newmarket, the Duke out hunting. Letters expressing a less profound sympathy on the death of an aunt were drafted.[2] Le Roi Soleil had never met the

---

[1] *Theatrum Europaeum*, ix. 661; Estrades, i. 253. Bronchiectasis, resulting in dropsy and cardiac failure, was the eventual cause of the queen's death.
[2] Everett Green, p. 412.

Winter Queen. He did not understand that the deceased would have been horrified to think that her nephews had abstained from the pleasures of the stable because Elizabeth Stuart had completed her long "journey uphill".[1] In London, Lord Leicester, a nephew of Sir Philip Sidney, wrote to his brother-in-law, Lord Northumberland, with modish levity— "My royal tenant is departed. It seems the fates did not think it fit that I should have the honour, which indeed I never much desyr'd, to be the landlord of a Queene. It is a pity she did not live a few hours more, to dye upon her wedding daye, and that there is not as good a Poet to make her Epitaph as Dr. Donne, who wrote her Epithalamium on that day, unto Saint Valentine."[2] On February 17th, John Evelyn wrote in his diary: "This night was buried in Westminster Abbey, the Queene of Bohemia, after all her sorrows and afflictions . . ."[3]

The body of the queen, who had been denied that title even by her father and her brother, was preceded to the grave by a royal crown borne by Norroy and Clarencieux Kings at Arms, supported by Sir Richard Craven, her Master of the Horse, and Lord Craven. Prince Rupert was chief mourner. Neither the King of England nor the Duke of York took part in the long and stately procession that moved by torchlight up the Thames towards "the church of Westminster", where, by her Majesty's express injunction, her body was to be interred "amongst those of her ancestors, and close to that of her late elder brother, Prince Henry".[4] While the burial service was being spoken in Henry VII's chapel, there raged outside "such a storm of hail, thunder and lightning, as never was seen the like in any man's memorie . . ."[5] "as though heaven had

---

[1] Charles behaved with generosity to his aunt's stranded dependants. The Countess of Löwenstein, Lady Sayers and Mrs Broughton and many others all received pensions.

[2] *Sydney Papers*, ii. 273.   [3] Evelyn, ii. 188.

[4] Wills from Doctors' Commons. Camden Society, 83.109.

[5] Evelyn, ii. 188.

designed thereby to intimate that those troubles and calamities which that princess and the royal family had suffered, were now all blown over, and like her, to rest in repose".[1]

The calamities that could overtake the House of Stuart were far from being exhausted, but the royal lady laid to rest that night was indeed to prove the grandmother of Europe.[2]

[1] Benger, ii. 431.

[2] In 1938 every ruling sovereign of Europe, with the exception of the king of the Balkan State of Albania, traces descent from Elizabeth of Bohemia. Their majesties of Denmark, Great Britain, Greece, Jugo-Slavia, the Netherlands, Norway, Roumania and Sweden are descendants of her daughter, Sophie; the Kings of Belgium, Bulgaria and Italy, of her favourite grand-daughter, "Liselotte". Debrett, Coronation Edition, 1938.

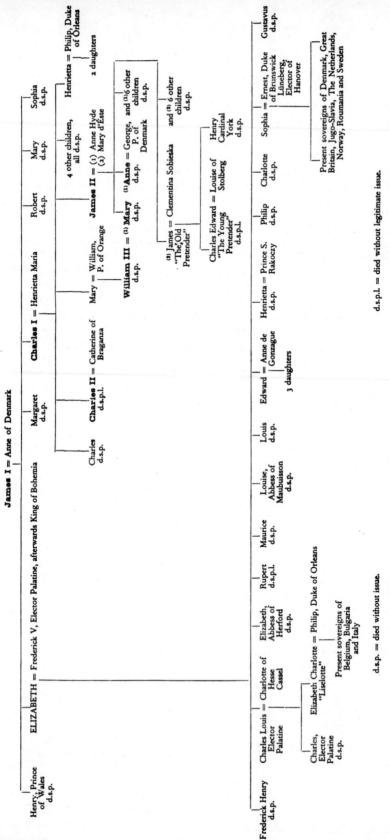

James I = Anne of Denmark

Henry, Prince of Wales d.s.p.

ELIZABETH = Frederick V, Elector Palatine, afterwards King of Bohemia

Charles I = Henrietta Maria

Margaret d.s.p.

Robert d.s.p.

Mary d.s.p.

Sophia d.s.p.

Henrietta = Philip, Duke of Orleans

2 daughters

Charles d.s.p.

Charles II = Catherine of Braganza
d.s.p.l.

4 other children, all d.s.p.

James II = (1) Anne Hyde
(2) Mary d'Este

Mary = William, P. of Orange

William III = (1) **Mary**
d.s.p.

(1)Anne = George, and **(1)6 other children**
P. of Denmark, d.s.p.

(2)James = Clementina Sobieska
"The Old Pretender"

and **(2) 6 other children**
d.s.p.

Charles Edward = Louise of Stolberg
"The Young Pretender"
d.s.p.l.

Henry Cardinal York d.s.p.

Frederick Henry d.s.p.

Charles Louis = Charlotte of Hesse Cassel
Elector Palatine

Elizabeth, Abbess of Herford d.s.p.

Rupert d.s.p.l.

Maurice d.s.p.

Louise, Abbess of Maubuisson d.s.p.

Edward = Anne de Gonzague

Henrietta = Prince S. Rakoczy
d.s.p.

Philip d.s.p.

Charlotte d.s.p.

Sophia = Ernest, Duke of Brunswick Lüneberg, Elector of Hanover

Gustavus d.s.p.

Charles, Elector Palatine d.s.p.

Elizabeth Charlotte = Philip, Duke of Orleans
"Liselotte"

Present sovereigns of Belgium, Bulgaria and Italy

3 daughters

Present sovereigns of Denmark, Great Britain, Jugo-Slavia, The Netherlands, Norway, Roumania and Sweden

d.s.p. = died without issue.

d.s.p.l. = died without legitimate issue.

The Act of Settlement, 1701, debarred from succession to the throne of Great Britain the descendants of the daughters of Henrietta, daughter of Charles I, and Edward, son of Elizabeth of Bohemia, on account of their being Roman Catholics.

INDEX

Boulogne, 348

Bowes, Robert of Aske, Treasurer of Berwick, 1, 2

"Boy", poodle dog, favourite of Prince Rupert, 351, 360, 361

Brandenburg, Eleanor of, *see* Sweden, Queen of

Brandenburg, Elizabeth Charlotte, Princess Palatine, Margravine of, married to George William of Brandenburg, 151; converts him to Calvinism, 232; takes charge of Prince Maurice, 243; entertains her nieces Elizabeth and Henrietta, 379; approves of Henrietta's marriage to a Rakoczy, 368; death of, 418

Brandenburg, Frederick William, Margrave of, "The Great Elector", in love with Princess Louise Palatine but marries her cousin, 403; guardian of William III, Prince of Orange, 426, 427

Brandenburg, George William, Margrave of, entertains Elizabeth on her honeymoon journey, 105, 106, 107; becomes her brother-in-law, 150 151; a fair-weather friend, 232, 233, 234, 239, 242, 243; is host to his mother-in-law, 319

Brandenburg, Joachim I, Margrave of, 234

Brandenburg, Louise of Nassau, daughter of Frederick Henry Prince of Orange, Electress of, 403

Braubach, 108

Brazil, 435

Breda, 243, 273, 277, 289, 304, 348, 434

Brederode, Baron of, entertains Elizabeth, 283

Brediman, Thomas, a soldier, utters seditious speeches, 294

Breitenfeld, battle of, 312

Breslau, Frederick at, 204; Elizabeth's luggage sent to, 222; Elizabeth at, 233, 234

Brill, the, 267, 284, 356

Bristol, surrendered by Prince Rupert, 362

Brno, Frederick visits, 201; Elizabeth receives gifts from, *ibid.*

Broughton, Margaret, lady-in-waiting to Elizabeth, serves Elizabeth "like a spaniel", 421; message about, from Elizabeth, 433; pensioned by Charles II, 456 n.

Brunswick Lüneberg, Christian Louis, eldest son of George, Duke of, 407

Brunswick Lüneberg, Ernest Augustus, fourth son of George, Duke of, husband of Princess Sophie Palatine, 394; plays the guitar exquisitely, 405; is loved by his bride, 407

Brunswick Lüneberg, George, Duke of, described by Elizabeth as "that Tunn of Beer", 346

Brunswick Lüneberg, George, Duke of, second son of above, 394; becomes engaged to Princess Sophie Palatine, 405; suggests that his brother shall take his place as bridegroom, 406; falls in love with Sophie, 407; witnesses Elizabeth's will, 442

Brunswick Lüneberg, John Frederick, third son of George, Duke of, 406, 407

Brunswick Wolfenbüttel, Christian, Duke of, Temporal bishop of Halberstadt, nicknamed "the mad Halberstadter", 264; takes up arms as Elizabeth's champion, 264, 271; letter of, to Elizabeth, 265; appearance and character of, 265, 281; portrait of, on horseback, 246; quarrels with the Margrave of

11